BCBA Independent Fieldwork

TrainABA Supervision Curriculum: Volume 2

Edited by:
Benjamin Theisen
Zachary Bird
Jason Zeigler

BCBA Independent Fieldwork
TrainABA Supervision Curriculum: Volume 2

Edited by Benjamin Theisen, Zachary Bird, & Jason Zeigler
Copyright©2015

ISBN13: 978-0-9856329-4-6
3 4 5 6 7 8 20 19 18 17 16

Bx Dynamic Press
SAN: 990-1396
5031 Fair Ave #424, N. Hollywood, CA 91601

BCBA Independent Fieldwork
TrainABA Supervision Curriculum: Volume 2

Edited by Benjamin Theisen, Zachary Bird, and Jason Zeigler

TABLE OF CONTENTS

About the Authors

Executive Editors

Ben Theisen founded TrainABA in January 2014 as an excuse to deliver supervision seminars. He is a BCBA and has worked in applied behavior analysis since 2006.

 Email: ben@trainaba.com

 Cell: 1+310-801-5450

Jason Zeigler is a BCBA currently working for the Walpole Public School District in Walpole, Massachusetts. He received his Master's of Education with a concentration in autism spectrum disorder and applied behavior analysis from Cambridge College in 2011. He has worked in a variety of settings serving students of various age ranges and cognitive abilities. Previously, Jason had worked as a head teacher at the Evergreen Center, an assistant clinical director at the May Institute, and as a BCBA in the Marlborough Public School district. This wide range of experiences has given him a well-rounded professional outlook with experience serving students with various disabilities as well as typically developed students with behavioral issues. His research interests include functional behavior assessment, behavioral skills training, sensory processing disorder, interventions for students with ADHD, sensory deficits, and anxiety, and effective training methodologies. Jason's current position has him consulting, assessing, and providing programming and behavioral support for a number of students ranging from preschool to high school. He enjoys research, training others in applied behavior analytic principles, assessment, and problem solving various maladaptive behavior concerns to create effective interventions for students on his case load.

My name is Zachary Bird. I'm a BCBA and a managing partner at TrainABA. You won't find my phone number here but I still share the same vision you hear when Ben speaks passionately about TrainABA.

I'm currently working on my PhD in Behavior Analysis at Simmons College. I used to live near Los Angeles, but Boston was as far away as my wife and I could get from Ben without leaving the country.

I work hard each day to learn ways to advance the field of behavior analysis. ABA is my greatest passion. Everyone who knows me, knows this about me. I've spent time in center-based programs, non-public schools, in-home programs, and worked as a consultant internationally. TrainABA is a company designed to provide tools for the behavior analytic community in general, whether it be in a university setting, an ABA center, or in-home ABA program.

I hope the work Ben and I have done over the last two years will result in a supervision system you appreciate and can use every day. If you don't like it, or you don't use a TrainABA product in your work or school every day, please bombard Ben's cell phone with discouraging text messages.

Additional Editors

Casey Clay is a BCBA-D. He earned his Ph.D. in the Disability Disciplines program at Utah State University and his Master of Science in Applied Behavior Analysis from Northeastern University. He has several years of clinical experience at the New England Center for Children and the Utah Behavior Support Clinic. His research interests include assessment and treatment of challenging behavior, social interaction and preference assessment methodologies, and training procedures in these areas. His work has been published in multiple peer-reviewed journals. He has also served as a guest reviewer for the Journal of Applied Behavior Analysis (JABA) and the Journal of Positive Behavior Interventions (JPBI).

Caleb Davis is a BCBA. Currently, he is a PhD student in the Behavior Analysis program at Simmons College. He received his Master of Science in Applied Behavior Analysis from Western New England University. During graduate school he received his BCBA supervision requirements while working at the New England Center for Children. His research interests include the assessment and treatment of severe problem behavior and errorless learning procedures. Caleb has presented his research at both national and regional conferences.

Additional Authors
Dalena Anzivino is a BCBA. She completed her undergraduate degree from York University, a post-graduate certificate program from George Brown College, and a Master's of Applied Disabilities Studies with a Specialization in ABA from Brock University, Canada. Her studies at Brock University led to a publication as a contributing author of a chapter in a handbook for ABA practitioners on genetic syndromes and ABA. Over the past ten years, she has worked with children and adolescents diagnosed with autism, providing direct service, clinical supervision for both home based and centre based Intensive Behavioural Intervention (IBI) programs, as well as facilitating training workshops for direct support staff and parents.

Candice Colón-Kwedor is a BCBA. She was first introduced to behavior analysis as an undergraduate at Virginia Tech. She then received her Master of Science in Applied Behavior Analysis from Northeastern University and fulfilled her graduate assistantship requirements and BCBA supervision requirements at the New England Center for Children. Her research interests include the treatment of automatically maintained behavior, verbal behavior and the assessment and treatment of severe challenging behavior. Her research has been published in the Journal of Applied Behavior Analysis (JABA) and has been presented at national and regional conferences. She has also served as a guest reviewer for The Analysis of Verbal behavior (TAVB) and Behavioral Interventions (BI). She is currently a doctoral candidate in the Behavior Analysis Ph.D. program at Western New England University and is a Senior Clinical Director at the May Institute's May Center for Autism and Developmental Disabilities in Randolph, Massachusetts.

Emma Martin graduated in 2007 from the University of Bath with a Bachelor's degree in Psychology. Her Bachelors included a placement year and as such she spent a year working at the Institute of Child Health in London with two research teams conducting research on autism. She worked as a Lead Teacher at the Jigsaw School in the UK, which is an Independent Day School for children with autism and severe learning difficulties. At that time, she also completed a Master's Degree in Education with a concentration in high-incidence disabilities with Nicholls State University. In 2011, she moved to Bermuda and began work as a Senior Verbal Behavior Therapist for Tomorrow's Voices, an Autism Early Intervention Centre. She became a Board Certified Behavior Analyst in 2012.

Angela Pao-Johnson is a BCBA and has been in the field since 2004. She was first introduced to applied behavioral analysis while interning at UC San Diego's Autism Center for Excellence. Since then, she has worked with a wide range of individuals ages 1 to 70 across a multitude of settings, which include home, schools, clinics and adult group homes. She has created protocols for several agencies, designed and implemented social skills classes, overseen the training of over 100 behavioral interventionists and led a series of behaviorally based trainings for teachers across Los Angeles School District. She currently resides in Los Angeles with her loving husband, Mike and their daughter Imogen.

Pamela Shea is currently the clinical supervisor of Behaviour Services at Ottawa Children's Treatment Centre. She completed her Masters in Applied Disabilities (Brock University), a Graduate Certificate in Behavior Analysis (University of North Texas), Behavioural Science Technology (St. Lawrence College), an Honours Degree in Psychology (Queen's University), and is a BCBA. She has over 25 years of experience in the field of ABA, has worked as a clinical supervisor, a behaviour consultant, senior therapist, a BCBA supervisor and has taught at two colleges. She has worked in community based behaviour services and the provincial IBI within multidisciplinary teams, in residential, vocational, home, day care and school environments. She is a member of OCTC's Ethics Advisory Committee and has spearheaded the development of a Functional Analysis Ethical Review Committee for medium and high severity functional analyses and is a member of the Christian Horizons Ethical Review Committee.

Carolyn E. Stephens has worked in the field of autism and applied behavior analysis for over 30 years. Her academic training includes intervention in early childhood, learning disabilities, and moderate and severe intellectual disabilities. She has completed single subject research related to joint attention in children with autism. As an assistant professor in special education she taught and supervised undergraduate and graduate students in special education at the university level. She is currently working as a behavior analyst to design and implement individual behavior support plans for children and adults. To address the gap between needs and behavior training within public agency systems, she has designed and presented a year-long workshop to introduce applied behavior analysis concepts and skills to supervisors in an eight-county area serving adults with developmental disabilities.

Sarah Teske grew up in a small, historic town in New Hampshire. She studied Psychology and English at the University of New Hampshire. She spent three years teaching at the New England Center for Children while she acquired a master's degree in applied behavior analysis through Northeastern University. Sarah went on to receive her certification as a BCBA and also obtained her special ed. teaching certification in the state of N.H. She has been working in the field of autism for 15 years and currently works for William J. White Educational and Behavioral Consulting Services Inc., consulting for schools in both Maine and New Hampshire. In her spare time Sarah likes to write children's books and garden. She has been collaborating with other professionals to enhance the field of ABA. She currently lives on the seacoast of Maine with her husband and two sons.

Kelly Workman, M.A., M.S., is a BCBA who started her career in ABA in 2007. Her work in ABA has focused on assessment and intervention programs for individuals with autism and other developmental disabilities across the lifespan in the home, school, workplace, and group home settings. Kelly has also provided supervision, training, and consultation for several years. Kelly has an avid interest in clinical behavior analysis and is currently completing a doctoral program in clinical psychology at the University of La Verne, with the goal of applying behavior analysis to chronic and severe mental health issues. She received extensive training in behavioral and cognitive-behavioral therapies including ACT, DBT, CBT, and CBASP, and incorporates principles of operant conditioning to facilitate behavior change when treating individuals with mental health concerns. Kelly is passionate about her clinical work and is receiving specialized training in working with populations who present with pervasive emotional dysregulation, life-threatening suicidal and non-suicidal self-harming behavior, and trauma-related concerns.

Acknowledgments

We would like to thank certain individuals whose professional activities influenced the development of this book in some way.

Brooke Mackenzie was contracted for administrative edits worked expeditiously.

Natasha Harris helped organize legal and administrative paperwork.

Rabeha Motiwala helped with early research in summer 2014.

Angie Bird provided feedback and great ideas throughout the editing process.

Stephanie Ortega evaluated the logic of the supervision system to help Ben and Zach develop a conceptually-systematic approach. Her razor-sharp analysis and creativity was a tremendous help.

Christie Caccioppo, Vivienne Nelson, and Sharon Noble provided insightful feedback in an early stage collaboration group in summer 2014.

Ellie Kazemi's own work in supervision curriculum is important to the ethical practice of evidence-based supervision and we encourage readers to explore her resources. Ben had the privilege to work with Dr. Kazemi at the Southern California Consortium for Behavior Analysis, which she founded. It helped Ben understand the role project management played in helping service providers collaborate.

Gary Geer provided much-needed coaching support for project management. When the editors were fully immersed in the messy writing process, Mr. Geer helped us step back, prioritize, and focus.

Eduard S. Alterson generously provided his economic genius and industry knowledge in summer 2014, helping Ben analyze the ABA supervision industry mathematically. Mr. Alterson's calculations helped create a financial forecast for completing the book.

John Youngbauer coined the name of "Associated Aardvarks for Autism," a fictitious behavioral service provider. Ben borrowed the name for the case study in the Supervisor book. Dr. Youngbauer's lifelong contributions to behavior analysis could fill volumes of books this size.

OBMNetwork is an excellent resource with annual subscriptions available for the price of one dinner. At the time of publishing the first edition of this book, there were 21,233 BACB certificants and only 236 members of the OBMNetwork – a mere 1.11%.

Paula Braga-Kenyon provided support throughout entire book writing/editing process whether she was aware of it or not.

Olga Shapovalova provided insight and support with initial stages and various parts of editing. She inspires us with her work in multiple languages while we struggle to work in just one.

Carl Cheney contributed to our solid resource list on a few of the more difficult to find topics.

Gregory Hanley provided and continues to provide his vision for our field and a simple call-to-action to behavior analysts everywhere: "Read JABA."

Michael Ballard contributed ideas, inspiration and support.

Bill Ahearn advocated and continues to advocate for taking a big-picture perspective on our field and promoting systems to increase the quality of training in our field.

Foreward

Imagine my surprise when I returned to applied behavior analysis from a 3-year sabbatical in 2013. How different could things be? It was night and day. In less than a presidential term, the BACB® had doubled its membership, supervision had guidelines, and universities had ABA master's degrees online. My MBA no longer met the degree requirements. ABA students were talking about SAFMEDs. What the heck were SAFMEDs?

That was around the time I leaned back in an old squeaky chair at a school startup outside Los Angeles, manding to Zach Bird, my new colleague, from across the hall. "Zach," I said, waiting for him to unpeel his eyes from the computer screen. Zach's desk contained a red pen, no papers, and a week's worth of vegetarian meal replacement bars, some of which were opened. "Yeah?" he responded. He blinked a few times to let me know he was ready. I put my hands behind my head and stretched my heels onto the Craigslist desk. "What's a SAFMED?"

Zach looked at me like I had two heads. Then, he gave me a full explanation. Zach was different than any BCBA® I had met. He had just left New England Center for Children, where new BCBAs provided direct care, and arrived in Southern California, where every BCBA® was made an automatic manager. Here, exam pass rates were around 40% at popular schools and negative reinforcement was occasionally defined as taking away a preferred item to decrease behavior. Our differences were what brought us together.

Zach was hands-down the biggest behavior analysis geek I had ever met. Yet there was something lovable about the way he answered my questions that made me keep asking. As I write these words, I can hear his voice in my mind saying, "Reinforcement, Ben."

What was so reinforcing about talking ABA with Zach? We talked philosophy, private events, things Skinner said, and, of course, anything by Patrick Friman. I introduced Zach to some of my non-ABA friends and they thought he was the most interesting person they had ever met. He was bright, enthusiastic, and incredibly humble.

Zach and I cared deeply about the same thing – the future of ABA. My approach was through business and marketing, hoping to see a world where ABA organizations ran like clockwork and other industries would want to know our secrets. Zach was into technology and research.

We agreed that behavior analysts would benefit globally if supervisors had resources at a molecular level. This book may not look like much but it took us a very long time to make, not to mention our countless webchats, whiteboard sessions, Elon Musk blogs, and epic plans to change the world. We envisioned a world where behavior analysts could focus on supervision instead of spending time figuring out how to supervise. This book was a step in the right direction.

Yet we walked those steps slowly. Months passed. We made slow progress. And then there was Jason. Mr. Jason Zeigler was a Boston-area BCBA and absolute powerhouse. We worked with Jason 10 months before meeting him face-to-face, filming Registered Behavior Technician training videos at our "studio" (my tiny 1-bedroom apartment in the North Hollywood Arts District of Los Angeles). Jason was charismatic, fun, and cool.

Gary Geer, my longtime mentor and partner in TrainABA, had a good joke about Jason. He said, "Did you see his Cooper book, Ben?" I said, "Yeah. Lots of underlining and margin notes, right?" Gary laughed. "He could use a black highlighter, if you know what I mean," Gary said, playfully. "Yeah, because he has the whole thing memorized so he doesn't need to see the words," I replied. "Exactly," Gary said. From that day forward, whenever I thought of Jason I imagined him blacking out the Cooper text after memorizing each section. I was grateful that Jason lended his talents to finishing this book. He is an outstanding resource and gifted presenter, full of passion and creativity.

At the time this book was finished, we had plans to launch a mobile app version that would forever change the field of ABA. Buying this book was like voting with your dollars. With this purchase, you voted for TrainABA's vision – *to save time*. It was a vote for Zach and me to keep being ambitious, humble social entrepreneurs trying to bring the world more ABA. We thank you for buying this book – even if you have no idea who we are – and we look forward to seeing you someday soon. Launching this book is the biggest thing we have ever done. Thank you for sharing the moment with us. We appreciate you so much.

Here's to a better field. We will keep working hard to save you time. I hope this book helps you find a few hours to do something you love.

Ben Theisen, *Editor*

SECTION ONE
Getting Started

Chapter 1
Introduction

Thank you for purchasing this book as part of the *Train-ABA Supervision Curriculum* system. It will save you dozens of hours – enough to plan a nice vacation for yourself or find extra time throughout the week to jump on Facebook, search Google, add Ben on Twitter, or catch up on Netflix.

The system was built in response to two things happening at the same time – like weather when warm air mixes with a cold front and creates a storm. The warm air was the developing industry of applied behavior analysis (ABA) professional services, marked by variability in university training and fieldwork that resulted in low Behavior Analyst Certification Board® (BACB®) exam pass rates. The cold front was the shock of Ben's 15-month old niece dying from Sudden Unexplained Death of a Child in 2012. At the wake, her father urged parents to, "read one more story" or "give one more piggy back ride." Time was precious.

Ben was deeply affected. In the months that followed, he ran supervision webinars and was struck by how many unpaid hours BCBAs completed at home. "We have to," some would say, "There's no time to do it at work." Supervisors described reading emails during family dinners and writing reports with a laptop from the bleachers at soccer practice. It made Ben sad to think of what his brother-in-law said at the wake. Time was precious. If his sister had worked through dinner the night before his niece died, they may have regretted it forever. Ben knew the industry would eventually correct itself but it could take decades before supervision was structured.

Ben pondered the warm and cold weather conditions, metaphorically, and used his economics training to calculate when and who would create standardized supervision curriculum. Private agency supervisors created makeshift solutions but stopped developing them once the systems met their minimum needs. Universities focused on their own practicum programs.

The *TrainABA Supervision Curriculum* system took two years of full time effort to develop. There were only 3,000 BACB®-exam candidates in 2013. Even if Ben sold books to 25% of them, he would have made less than minimum wage. It was a pet project that Ben took way too seriously. Zach joined in to help, probably because he felt sorry for Ben and also realized Ben would finish the project but did not know enough ABA literature to do it justice. They made slow progress until Jason Zeigler joined the party. That guy was a powerhouse. (Other contributors are mentioned in the About the Authors section.) The result was the overly sophisticated TrainABA system that you hold today. We hope it keeps you organized and saves you time while the ABA profession develops.

In the coming years, we will see a more perfect ABA world. It will be beautiful. We are privileged to have a front row seat to the development of our field. We are honored to take this journey with you.

Okay, enough storytelling. Thank you for purchasing the system. Here is what you bought:

TrainABA Supervision Curriculum includes the items below.
1. **TrainABA Supervision Curriculum: BCBA Reference Manual**
2. **TrainABA Supervision Curriculum: Independent Fieldwork** (this book)
3. **TrainABA Supervision Curriculum: RBT Credential**

The *TrainABA Supervision Curriculum* system helps you:
a. Grow your company's management team with less stress on the system
b. Get from start to finish with a page-by-page, week-by-week program (supervision contract → fieldwork → BACB® application)
c. Find systems to help you track supervision hours and signature forms to email to the BACB®
d. Use Individual and Group meeting agendas
e. Save dozens of hours by not reinventing the wheel
f. Check pre-assigned homework
g. Track ongoing progress on the 4th Edition Task List™ assessment
h. Prepare for BACB®-exam with test topics built into fieldwork
i. Organize essential supervision materials and meetings in one place, accessible by phone or computer

TrainABA is a BACB®-Approved Continuing Education (ACE) provider. We specialize in responding to supervision-related problems that are global in scope and too complex or time-consuming for other organizations and universities to solve.

The 4th Edition Task List™ face sheets are organized by "segments" (more about those later) to make it easier to complete and check homework assignments.

TrainABA Supervision Curriculum: Independent Fieldwork contains exercises for the supervisee to complete in a week-by-week progression that cover all 168 items on the 4th Edition Task List with the following:
1. Individual meeting agendas
2. Group meeting agendas
3. Ongoing homework assignments
4. 4th Edition Task List™ assessment

The hours are not tracked in the book as a safeguard in case the book was lost. Keep your signature forms on a storage cloud online and in a paper file for seven years.

SECTION TWO
Supervised Fieldwork Curriculum

Chapter 2
Assessment for the 4th Edition Task List

Assessment Procedure

In a perfect world, every supervisor would sit one-on-one with a single supervisee and measure each item on the 4th Edition Task List directly. The supervisor would prepare detailed curriculum and use Behavioral Skills Training for every skill. What world is that? None of the 300+ participants who took the 8 Hour Supervisor Training workshop with Ben, the editor of this book, reported such circumstances. They were busy. We built the following supervision assessment tool for <u>efficiency</u>.

For all Sections of 4th Edition Task List:
   a. **Assess task list tems at the end of each *segment*** (one segment = two weeks). A segment is a set of related task list items. Segments follow a scheduled program to insure that all items are covered adequately. Supervisees should aim to satisfy all three criteria at once because supervisors do not have time to keep revisiting individual items. (You will see the segment grouping in the following chapter.)
   b. **You may assess some task list items only once** depending on how busy you are. Each task list item has three boxes. We call these "1, 2, and 3." When a supervisee demonstrates that skill, the supervisor indicates completion by shading that box with a marker or initials, draws a symbol, etc.

Examples:

FAIL: A supervisor counted 168 task items in the 4th Edition Task List with 3 criteria to assess each. She thought, "How am I going to assess 504 times in one year? I have too many things to do as it is." She decided not use an assessment since it seemed chaotic to manage.

WIN: Working through the 25 segments provided, a supervisee tackled segments of about half a dozen task list items per 2-week supervision period. That supervisee went home each night and prepared for the assessment she knew would come at the end of the segment period. It worked. The supervisee was well-prepared and earned a full score of all three (3) boxes shaded for all but one task list items in that segment. She prepared for the supervisor to reassess the skill when testing the next segment items. She was glad to pass because the supervisor was busy and they may not have had a chance to reassess that item.

Notes:
1. Sections I and II were based on Behavioral Skills Training.
   a. Mark "1" or first box when supervisees gives you a satisfactory written (i.e., homework assigned in the supervisee book) and vocal description).
   b. Mark "2" or second box when supervisee performs the skill with prompts
   c. Mark "3" or third box when supervisee performs skill independently
2. Section III is designed to evaluate Foundational Knowledge
   a. Mark "1" or first box when supervisees defines an item in technical terms
   b. Mark "2" or second box when supervisee performs the skill with prompts
   c. Mark "3" or third box when supervisee performs skill independently

Supervisors mark on the 4th Edition Task List Assessments found in supervisees' books.

Using the BACB® Fourth Edition Task List™

The BACB® Fourth Edition Task List has 168 items in 3 sections. The BACB® began using the Fourth Edition Task List for exams effective January 1, 2015. The major change of the Fourth Edition Task List™ is the three section structure that was not used to organize previous Task Lists™.

Overview of Fourth Edition Task List™

Section	Title	Purpose
(1)	Basic Behavior Analytic Skills	Train basic skills to be used with most, but not all clients
(2)	Client-Centered Responsibilities	Train skills needed for working in applied settings
(3)	Foundational Knowledge	ABA concepts that should already be mastered

The BACB® Fourth Edition Task List™ with Subsections

Section

(1)	Basic Behavior Analytic Skills
(2)	Client-Centered Responsibilities
(3)	Foundational Knowledge

I	Basic Behavior Analytic Skills
A 1-14	Measurement
B 1-11	Experimental Design
C 1-3	Behavior-Change Considerations
D 1-21	Fundamental Elements of Behavior Change
E 1-13	Specific Behavior-Change Procedures
F 1-8	Behavior-Change Systems

II	Client-Centered Responsibilities
G 1-8	Identification of the Problem
H 1-5	Measurement
I 1-7	Assessment
J 1-15	Intervention
K 1-10	Implementation, Management, and Supervision

III	Foundational Knowledge Accompanying the BACB 4th Edition Task List
FK 1-9	Explain and Behave in Accordance with the Philosophical Assumptions of Behavior Analysis
FK 10-42	Define and Provide Example of
FK 43-46	Distinguish Between the Verbal Operants
FK 47-48	Measurement Concepts

Notes for Supervisors
(Supervisees: skip this section)

Start by *assessing* the candidate's skills and knowledge. We interviewed 300 BCBAs when creating this book and none of them reported a surplus of *time resources* for conducting a non-billable assessment of their candidates.

ABA supervisors face the *Supervisor's Plight* – presented with competing contingencies for reinforcement, the supervisor selects professional behavior during her or his limited discretionary work hours. Will the supervisor respond toward the immediate, often *positive* reinforcement available for program development that directly benefits clients or caseload? Or will she respond toward reinforcement available for *developing* the candidate (performance management plan, personal development plan, 4th Edition Task List™, written feedback, pulling relevant research to share with candidate, etc.)?

In our assessment of supervisory conditions, we spoke with people from 5 continents at 300 companies. We discovered that, in general, more positive reinforcement is available to the supervisor for responding toward contingencies in their direct caseload than for selecting behaviors that *develop* the professional candidate.

These problems are most common for within-agency supervision. These problems are not seen as often in practicum or third-party supervision. If you are not supervising within an agency, skip ahead until you see the S^D below:

S^D

(If you supervise within an agency, the following section is likely to contain reinforcement.)

Under such conditions, the candidate may or may not be the supervisor's direct report. You cannot supervise your boss and therefore you will only supervise a colleague at your level or below at your organization. If the candidate is your direct report, you will likely have a subset of supervision-related issues that are not directly related to working with clients.

Such issues are common and fall under the domain of performance management issues. Examples include lateness, coworker boundaries, accurate and on-time billing, communication, etc. Therefore, the supervisor may have two sets of issues for *developing* the candidate: items for the task list and BCBA exam; *developing* the candidate *as an employee*. These are two different ideas. There will be some overlap because performance management is one application of applied behavior analysis.

> ## What are your responsibilities as a supervisor?
>
> ## Are you developing the *BACB-exam candidate* or developing *a better employee*?

Regarding the above question, the answer is often *both*. Managers, especially non-clinical managers, operate on negative reinforcement contingencies and may expect non-clinical outcomes of your Supervised Experience. You may think your job, as supervisor, is to *develop* a strong clinician who can manage a caseload, develop goals from an assessment, and pass the BACB® exam. Your manager may see it differently. Managers may view the supervision process as a chance to "fix" everything that is wrong with the employee.

In practice, managers generally meet with people to give feedback and seldom maintain the 5:1 ratio of positive to corrective statements unless they are highly trained in management technique. Fortune 500 companies invest millions of dollars in training every month to make better managers. ABA companies are not big enough to do that. It is common, therefore, for managers in ABA companies to develop their own management styles not from formal training but based on previous consequences, self-monitoring, mentoring, collaboration with others, and what they have read.

As the clinical supervisor, your role is to prepare a candidate for the board exam. If you can help them develop as an employee using the same interventions identified on the Fourth Edition Task List™, that would be ideal. However, that is a performance management skill set which is different from the typical focus of a Supervised Experience for a BACB-exam candidate. Again, we return to two issues intertwined:

Are you developing the *BACB-certification candidate*, or developing *a better employee*?

We recommend 3 interventions to solve this problem at the company level.

1. Meet with your candidate's non-clinical manager – often a Human Resources Manager – and ask what outcomes they expect from the Supervised Experience.

   a. The meeting is your opportunity to clarify that there are two sets of responsibilities for the supervisor. Explain that these are intertwined but that you will be so busy on the BACB-items that you may not have much time left to develop a performance management plan.

2.   Use Performance Management plans as a company.

3.   Invest in developing administrative management skills.

The following notes may help the clinical supervisor, communicate effectively with administrative managers:

a.   Do not get swept up in employee development areas during supervised fieldwork. You have little time. Stick to the task list. When the manager says, "We should talk to the scheduler about this," or brings another manager into the discussion, intervene. Be assertive. Supervised Experience hours are not the time to conduct a 360 feedback assessment and/or create a performance management plan for the clinical employees. That may be nice, but you do not see such behaviors listed on the Fourth Edition Task List™ because that's not the focus of what you are supposed to be doing. Tell the manager that you called the meeting to establish boundaries and set outcomes. Suggest to focus on the 4th Edition Task List now. Focus on performance management plans and employee development once the candidate has passed the certification exam.

b.   The non-clinical manager may indirectly, if not tacitly, evaluate your performance on whether the candidate achieved their expectations after spending 1,500 hours under your supervision.

c.   The manager may say, "If I spent 75 hours with that employee, they wouldn't (insert problem behavior here)." That may be true because their 75 hours would focus on something else. Stick to the core requirements.

d.   If the manager wants to spend more time developing the employee, let them. Don't confuse their goals with your goals.

e.   If you run into difficulty communicating with the manager, recall that your goal is complete the Supervised Experience Hours and help a candidate who passes the board exam. If this person is up for promotion or having performance issues, they need more help that 5% of clinical hours supervised.

f.   Ask the manager if they would like to budget/pay for development of the candidate's employee behavior.

g.   The manager will likely not know exactly what her expectations are. This is normal in companies.

S^D

(This section is labeled as S^D because reinforcement may be available to any supervisors – practicum, 3rd party supervision, and within-agency.)

What reinforcement is available to you for *developing* your candidates' professional behavior?

Reflection:
Write down the behaviors you need to supervise candidates.
Write down the reinforcement available for supervisory behavior.

Common Factors

You've been tasked with completing the Supervised Experience because the company needs supervisors and you were given the assignment.

You are not paid extra or offered positive reinforcers for the outcomes of effective supervision – such as being offered a bonus or paid time-off for each supervisee who passes the exam.

Given that the *supervisor's plight* is ubiquitous under current contingencies of ABA organizations with waiting lists and a shortage of certified professionals, it is prudent for supervisors to acknowledge the potential risks of supervising without identifying the reinforcement contingencies which influence their supervisory behavior.

What helps practitioner be more involved supervisors is to contact more reinforcement for doing it. If you do not *enjoy* supervising candidates you are not contacting enough reinforcement for the behaviors in your supervision repertoire.

Our experience shows that reinforcement is available to supervisors who use our assessment – which can be completed in the normal course of allotted supervision hours. Such reinforcers include:

a.   Less time and response effort to manage Supervised Experience process

b.   Visual display of candidate progress

c.   Organized, clear steps in process

d.   Easy to switch supervisors or take time off without losing track of where supervisee is

e.   Supervisor does not have to *guess* how to focus each meeting or week

f.   Less response effort needed to assess subsequent candidate

What is different about the 3 Task List™ sections?

- Section (2) is directly relevant to applied settings.
- Candidates will use a subset – but probably not all – of Section (1) with their current caseload.
- Section (3) emphasizes theoretical understanding and conceptual foundations of the science of behavior analysis.

Section (3) is indirectly addressed by this procedure because the knowledge is better suited for explanation in university settings rather than in applied situations. Group supervision for independent fieldwork – the target audience for this protocol – is generally conducted by practitioners, not researchers.

Practicums and intensive practicums may be supervised by researchers who may exercise professional judgment when choosing to focus on Section (3) beyond the recommendations set forth in this protocol. Practitioners from strong research backgrounds may also wish to spend more time with Section (3) during supervision.

> **The Task List has 3 sections.**
> **Separate the third section. Two remain.**
>
> **Is this candidate supervising others?**
> **If yes, start at Section 2.**
> **If no, start at Section 3.**
> **One section remains.**

Plus/Delta (+/Δ) for Separating Section 3 of Task List

+

1. Supervisee exposed to Section (3) from a researcher (i.e., university coursework professor), not practitioner

2. Convenient for practitioner

3. Protects practitioner credibility

Δ

1. Research-oriented supervisees may expect supervisor to focus on theory

2. Gossip may follow

3. Candidate may not describe supervisor as credible if s/he is not current on Section (3)

*Conclusion: Teach Section (3) if you can do it well.
If not, recommend that supervisees work more extensively with BACB® Fourth Edition Task List™

BACB® 4th Edition Task List™
Assessment

Section I: Basic Behavior Analytic Skills

Measurement

	Give Written & Vocal Description	Perform with Prompts	Perform Independently
A-01 Measure frequency (i.e., count).			
A-02 Measure rate (i.e., count per unit time).			
A-03 Measure duration.			
A-04 Measure latency.			
A-05 Measure interresponse time (IRT).			
A-06 Measure percent of occurrence.			
A-07 Measure trials to criterion.			
A-08 Assess and interpret interobserver agreement.			
A-09 Evaluate the accuracy and reliability of measurement procedures.			
A-10 Design, plot, and interpret data using equal-interval graphs.			
A-11 Design, plot, and interpret data using a cumulative record to display data.			
A-12 Design and implement continuous measurement procedures (e.g., event recording).			
A-13 Design and implement discontinuous measurement procedures (e.g., partial & whole interval, momentary time sampling).			
A-14 Design and implement choice measures.			
Experimental Design			
B-01 Use the dimensions of applied behavior analysis (Baer, Wolf, & Risley, 1968) to evaluate whether interventions are behavior analytic in nature.			
B-02 Review and interpret articles from the behavior-analytic literature.			
B-03 Systematically arrange independent variables to demonstrate their effects on dependent variables.			
B-04 Use withdrawal/reversal designs.			
B-05 Use alternating treatments (i.e., multielement) designs.			
B-06 Use changing criterion designs.			
B-07 Use multiple baseline designs.			
B-08 Use multiple probe designs.			
B-09 Use combinations of design elements			
B-10 Conduct a component analysis to determine the effective components of an intervention package.			
B-11 Conduct a parametric analysis to determine the effective values of an independent variable.			

Behavior-Change Considerations

C-01 State and plan for the possible unwanted effects of reinforcement.			
C-02 State and plan for the possible unwanted effects of punishment.			
C-03 State and plan for the possible unwanted effects of extinction.			

Fundamental Elements of Behavior Change

D-01 Use positive and negative reinforcement.			
D-02 Use appropriate parameters and schedules of reinforcement.			
D-03 Use prompts and prompt fading.			
D-04 Use modeling and imitation training.			
D-05 Use shaping.			
D-06 Use chaining.			
D-07 Conduct task analyses.			
D-08 Use discrete-trial and free-operant arrangements.			
D-09 Use the verbal operants as a basis for language assessment.			
D-10 Use echoic training.			
D-11 Use mand training.			
D-12 Use tact training.			
D-13 Use intraverbal training.			
D-14 Use listener training.			
D-15 Identify punishers.			
D-16 Use positive and negative punishment.			
D-17 Use appropriate parameters and schedules of punishment.			
D-18 Use extinction.			
D-19 Use combinations of reinforcement with punishment and extinction.			
D-20 Use response-independent (time-based) schedules of reinforcement (i.e., non-contingent reinforcement).			
D-21 Use differential reinforcement (e.g., DRO, DRA, DRI, DRL, DRH).			

Specific Behavior-Change Procedures

E-01 Use interventions based on manipulation of antecedents, such as motivating operations and discriminative stimuli.			
E-02 Use discrimination training procedures.			
E-03 Use instructions and rules.			
E-04 Use contingency contracting (i.e., behavioral contracts).			
E-05 Use independent, interdependent, and dependent group contingencies.			
E-06 Use stimulus equivalence procedures.			

E-07 Plan for behavioral contrast effects.			
E-08 Use the matching law and recognize factors influencing choice.			
E-09 Arrange high-probability request sequences.			
E-10 Use the Premack principle.			
E-11 Use pairing procedures to establish new conditioned reinforcers and punishers.			
E-12 Use errorless learning procedures.			
E-13 Use matching-to-sample procedures.			
Behavior-Change Systems			
F-01 Use self-management strategies.			
F-02 Use token economies and other conditioned reinforcement systems.			
F-03 Use Direct Instruction.			
F-04 Use precision teaching.			
F-05 Use personalized systems of instruction (PSI).			
F-06 Use incidental teaching.			
F-07 Use functional communication training.			
F-08 Use augmentative communication systems.			
Section II: Client-Centered Responsibilities			
Identification of the Problem			
G-01 Review records and available data at the outset of the case.			
G-02 Consider biological/medical variables that may be affecting the client.			
G-03 Conduct a preliminary assessment of the client in order to identify the referral problem.			
G-04 Explain behavioral concepts using nontechnical language.			
G-05 Describe and explain behavior, including private events, in behavior-analytic (non-mentalistic) terms.			
G-06 Provide behavior-analytic services in collaboration with others who support and/or provide services to one's clients.			
G-07 Practice within one's limits of professional competence in applied behavior analysis, and obtain consultation, supervision, and training, or make referrals as necessary.			
G-08 Identify and make environmental changes that reduce the need for behavior analysis services.			
Measurement Rating			
H-01 Select a measurement system to obtain representative data given the dimensions of the behavior and the logistics of observing and recording.			
H-02 Select a schedule of observation and recording periods.			
H-03 Select a data display that effectively communicates relevant quantitative relations.			
H-04 Evaluate changes in level, trend, and variability.			
H-05 Evaluate temporal relations between observed variables (within &between sessions, time series).			

Assessment Rating			
I-01 Define behavior in observable and measurable terms.			
I-02 Define environmental variables in observable and measurable terms.			
I-03 Design and implement individualized behavioral assessment procedures.			
I-04 Design and implement the full range of functional assessment procedures.			
I-05 Organize, analyze, and interpret observed data.			
I-06 Make recommendations regarding behaviors that must be established, maintained, increased, or decreased.			
I-07 Design and conduct preference assessments to identify putative reinforcers.			
Intervention Rating			
J-01 State intervention goals in observable and measurable terms.			
J-02 Identify potential interventions based on assessment results and the best available scientific evidence.			
J-03 Select intervention strategies based on task analysis.			
J-04 Select intervention strategies based on client preferences.			
J-05 Select intervention strategies based on the client's current repertoires.			
J-06 Select intervention strategies based on supporting environments.			
J-07 Select intervention strategies based on environmental and resource constraints.			
J-08 Select intervention strategies based on the social validity of the intervention.			
J-09 Identify and address practical and ethical considerations when using experimental designs to demonstrate treatment effectiveness.			
J-10 When a behavior is to be decreased, select an acceptable alternative behavior to be established or increased.			
J-11 Program for stimulus and response generalization.			
J-12 Program for maintenance.			
J-13 Select behavioral cusps as goals for intervention when appropriate.			
J-14 Arrange instructional procedures to promote generative learning (i.e., derived relations).			
J-15 Base decision-making on data displayed in various formats.			

Implementation, Management, and Supervision Rating

K-01 Provide for ongoing documentation of behavioral services.			
K-02 Identify the contingencies governing the behavior of those responsible for carrying out behavior-change procedures and design interventions accordingly.			
K-03 Design and use competency-based training for persons who are responsible for carrying out behavioral assessment and behavior change procedures.			
K-04 Design and use effective performance monitoring and reinforcement systems.			
K-05 Design and use systems for monitoring procedural integrity.			
K-06 Provide supervision for behavior-change agents.			
K-07 Evaluate the effectiveness of the behavioral program.			
K-08 Establish support for behavior-analytic services from direct and indirect consumers.			
K-09 Secure the support of others to maintain the client's behavioral repertoires in their natural environments.			
K-10 Arrange for the orderly termination of services when they are no longer required.			

Section III: Explain and Behave in Accordance with the Philosophical Assumptions of Behavior Analysis

	Define in Technical Terms	Define in Non-technical Terms	Provide 3 Examples
FK-01 Lawfulness of behavior			
FK-02 Selectionism (phylogenic, ontogenic, cultural)			
FK-03 Determinism			
FK-04 Empiricism			
FK-05 Parsimony			
FK-06 Pragmatism			
FK-07 Environmental (as opposed to mentalistic) explanations of behavior			
FK-08 Distinguish between radical and methodological behaviorism.			
FK-09 Distinguish between the conceptual analysis of behavior, experimental analysis of behavior, applied behavior analysis, and behavioral service delivery.			

Define and Provide Examples

FK-10 behavior, response, response class			
FK-11 environment, stimulus, stimulus class			
FK-12 stimulus equivalence			
FK-13 reflexive relations (US-UR)			
FK-14 respondent conditioning (CS-CR)			
FK-15 operant conditioning			
FK-16 respondent-operant interactions			
FK-17 unconditioned reinforcement			
FK-18 conditioned reinforcement			
FK-19 unconditioned punishment			
FK-20 conditioned punishment			

FK-21 schedules of reinforcement and punishment			
FK-22 extinction			
FK-23 automatic reinforcement and punishment			
FK-24 stimulus control			
FK-25 multiple functions of a single stimulus			
FK-26 unconditioned motivating operations			
FK-27 conditioned motivating operations			
FK-28 transitive, reflexive, surrogate motivating operations			
FK-29 distinguish between the discriminative stimulus and the motivating operation			
FK-30 distinguish between motivating operation and reinforcement effects			
FK-31 behavioral contingencies			
FK-32 contiguity			
FK-33 functional relations			
FK-34 conditional discriminations			
FK-35 stimulus discrimination			
FK-36 response generalization			
FK-37 stimulus generalization			
FK-38 behavioral contrast			
FK-39 behavioral momentum			
FK-40 matching law			
FK-41 contingency-shaped behavior			
FK-42 rule-governed behavior			
Distinguish Between the Verbal Operants			
FK-43 Echoics			
FK-44 Mands			
FK-45 Tacts			
FK-46 Intraverbals			
Measurement Concepts			
FK-47 Identify the measurable dimensions of behavior (e.g., rate, duration, latency, interresponse time).			
FK-48 State the advantages and disadvantages of using continuous measurement procedures and discontinuous measurement procedures (e.g., partial- and whole-interval recording, momentary time sampling).			

Optional Pre-Test – Section 3 of the 4th Edition Task List™

To Supervis**ees**

The following page contains an assessment activity to be completed under your supervisor's direction. If your supervisor directs you to complete it, finish the activity within your first month of supervision hours. Later, you can refer back to this exercise as you study for the board exam. You will have an opportunity to write more detailed, updated responses to these task list items in the ongoing homework assignments completed in the 4th Edition Task List Exercises later. This is an opportunity to take a snapshot of your knowledge at the start of supervision, which you may view later to observe how much learning has occurred.

To Supervis**ors**

Would you like your supervisees to complete a pre-test of Section 3 of the 4th Edition Task List™? If so, direct the supervisees to complete the pre-test found on page 28 of their books *(BCBA Independent Fieldwork)*. It is identical to the assessment found on the following page of your book.

You may want to assign the pre-test if:

1. You met or began working with your supervisee only recently
2. You are unsure what your supervisee was taught in university coursework
3. Your supervisee's coursework comes from a university with a pass rate below what you consider trustworthy
4. You can find time to read the supervisee's responses
5. Completing the assessment is a good use of your supervisee's time

If you assign the pre-test, make it due by the end of the first month of supervision. You will review it by the end of the second month. If you choose to assign the pre-test, we recommend giving the supervisee one week notice to prepare. We recommend having the supervisee complete the assignment without additional books, phones, computers, or internet. It is possible for supervisees to look up information in segments of their books. However, the time restriction makes it difficult for the supervisee to look up answers for the whole exercise. A possible indicator of looking up answers may be that early answers were completed thoroughly and a large number of responses were left blank toward the later portion of the list.

Optional Pre-Test – Section (3) of 4th Edition Task List™

Use with BACB® Fourth Edition Task List™

Instructions: *Supervisee uses only pen/pencil and paper to complete this exercise. Write short answers (1 to 5 sentences) to explain each item listed below. All items are from Section (3) – Foundational Knowledge from the BACB® Fourth Edition Task List™.*

No internet or computer devices are allowed. The supervisee should be given at least one week of prior notice before taking this exam.

Time allowed: 48 *minutes* (Work quickly – you have ONE MINUTE per task list item.)

Answer each item in the following sections.

Written Assessment of Section III: Foundational Knowledge
Explain and Behave in Accordance with the Philosophical Assumptions of Behavior Analysis
FK-01 Lawfulness of behavior
FK-02 Selectionism (phylogenic, ontogenic, cultural)
FK-03 Determinism
FK-04 Empiricism
FK-05 Parsimony
FK-06 Pragmatism

Written Assessment of
Section III: Foundational Knowledge

FK-07 Environmental (as opposed to mentalistic) explanations of behavior

FK-08 Distinguish between radical and methodological behaviorism.

FK-09 Distinguish between the conceptual analysis of behavior, experimental analysis of behavior, applied behavior analysis, and behavioral service delivery.

Define and Provide Examples

FK-10 behavior, response, response class

FK-11 environment, stimulus, stimulus class

FK-12 stimulus equivalence

Written Assessment of
Section III: Foundational Knowledge

FK-13 reflexive relations (US-UR)

FK-14 respondent conditioning (CS-CR)

FK-15 operant conditioning

FK-16 respondent-operant interactions

FK-17 unconditioned reinforcement

FK-18 conditioned reinforcement

FK-19 unconditioned punishment

Written Assessment of
Section III: Foundational Knowledge

FK-20 conditioned punishment

FK-21 schedules of reinforcement and punishment

FK-22 extinction

FK-23 automatic reinforcement and punishment

FK-24 stimulus control

FK-25 multiple functions of a single stimulus

FK-26 unconditioned motivating operations

FK-27 conditioned motivating operations

Written Assessment of
Section III: Foundational Knowledge

FK-28 transitive, reflexive, surrogate motivating operations

FK-29 distinguish between the discriminative stimulus and the motivating operation

FK-30 distinguish between motivating operation and reinforcement effects

FK-31 behavioral contingencies

FK-32 contiguity

FK-33 functional relations

FK-34 conditional discriminations

FK-35 stimulus discrimination

Written Assessment of
Section III: Foundational Knowledge

FK-36 response generalization

FK-37 stimulus generalization

FK-38 behavioral contrast

FK-39 behavioral momentum

FK-40 matching law

FK-41 contingency-shaped behavior

FK-42 rule-governed behavior

Distinguish Between the Verbal Operants

FK-43 Echoics

Written Assessment of
Section III: Foundational Knowledge

FK-44 Mands

FK-45 Tacts

FK-46 Intraverbals

Measurement Concepts

FK-47 Identify the measurable dimensions of behavior (e.g., rate, duration, latency, interresponse time).

FK-48 State the advantages and disadvantages of using continuous measurement procedures and discontinuous measurement procedures (e.g., partial- and whole-interval recording, momentary time sampling).

Chapter 3
Segments

STOP

This is very important.

Have you met the current BACB® criteria to begin supervision?

Go to http://TrainABA.com/track right now to find out.

Experience Supervision Forms

There are two forms supervisors sign to verify ABA fieldwork for the BACB® exam application:

1. Experience Supervision Forms (Need to be filled out for each supervision period—group or individual. Most people have 25 or more of these forms at the end of fieldwork.)
2. Experience Verification Form (One page attestation stating all the hours that were completed with a supervisor. It is the form you send to the board when applying to take the exam. It is the last form your supervisor signs.)

Experience Supervision Forms are <u>only on our website</u> for safety in case book is lost.

http://trainaba.com/track

Procedure for All Supervision Meetings

There are two types of supervision meetings – individual and group. Some supervisors will have only one supervisee and may not need the group supervision agendas. Other supervisors will have multiple supervisees and hold group supervision meetings every two weeks.

Many supervisors will use a combination of individual and group meetings. For example, a group supervision meeting may have been cancelled and only individual supervision was provided for that period. Yet supervision returned to a combination of group and individual meetings the following two week period.

The TrainABA supervision system is designed to accommodate any combination of individual and group meetings. Our Group Meeting Agendas were modeled after university "labs" in well-established behavior analysis programs. Individual Agendas were modeled after what appeared to be the standard practice in our field.

We think it is best practice to combine both types of supervision into "segments," or *sets of related task list items*. Segments insure that someone who sits for the BACB® exam has covered each task list item during fieldwork.

Segments consist of an individual and group meeting agenda. Both share a set of related task list items.

If you only do one-on-one supervision during all or select supervisory periods, omit the Group Supervision Agenda for that period and focus on the same set of task list items for that segment during Individual Supervision. Homework is due at the last meeting of the segment.

Individual Supervision Meetings

Individual supervision meetings lead to individualized feedback, discussion, and skills training. Individual observation meeting content is circumstantial (i.e., observing a session) and not programmatic (i.e., group meeting). Use these forms along with whatever Group Supervision forms are appropriate. Individual meetings are your opportunities to build skills with your supervisor. Use your 4th Edition Task List™ at all of your individual supervision meetings.

For Supervis**ors**: Homework Guidelines

(Supervisees – skip this section)

TrainABA Supervision Curriculum automatically assigns two types of homework:

I. Programmatic Homework – The system already assigns your supervisee four homework assignments for each segment:

- **Boxes on every task list item in supervisee book**
- **Presentation** (2-5 minutes) of a task list item from that segment at group meeting
- **Practice SAFMEDs cards to fluency** using the TrainABA flashcards
- **Asssessment-related homework –** Any other necessary work needed for individual supervisee to pass the assessment for that segment (either you assign these extra learning activities or your supervisee may take her or his own initiative)

II. Circumstantial Homework – including additional assignments or learning activities for your supervisees individually or as a group:

- **Specific exercises you assign under the "Assessment" headings** found on every single task litem in Chapter 6 (Annotated 4th Edition Task List™) of this book. Your supervisees do NOT have the same information in their books. Share whatever Assessment ideas you think will help them achieve a perfect score when you assess them at the end of a segment.
- **Special homework assignments** that you may create or assign. Ideas are listed in the tables for "Weekly Behavior Analytic Lesson" and "Homework Ideas" at the end of this chapter.

When learning this system, supervisors often ask, "Should I assign the assessment as homework?" No. It is already assigned in the system. You will assess skills in task list items at the conclusion of each segment.

Assess using what you learned about Behavioral Skills Training (BST) in your 8-Hour Supervisor Training workshop. A refresher is located in chapter 3 of the *Reference Manual*. You will need to observe supervisee behavior. It sounds time consuming – and it could be – but you can assess some skills indirectly (e.g., interview, video recording) or directly (e.g., role play live or via webchat; direct observation with a client).

A company using TrainABA's system could allow a supervisee to upload videos of herself performing task list skills for a given segment (e.g., role play; at a session; sitting in front of camera explaining something). The supervisor would receive a notification and log in to see it. That supervisor could provide an assessment score or written feedback. If the video was good, the company could save it in their video library for developing other behavior analysis professionals such as RBTs or future BCBAs.

Weekly Behavior Analytic Lessons

We included this section to provide some ideas for Weekly Behavior Analytic Lessons. Such lessons are practical in nature and relate directly to applied settings. Some topics are based on practical knowledge from "old school" BCBA®s who took their BACB® exams on paper. Some of these concepts are concepts developed by 30 years or more experience in the field. Other ideas come from research in performance management.

You may choose to use different items based on what is happening with your supervisees with their current caseloads. By marking the "Interesting" column, you have the flexibility to choose items in addition to the convenience of knowing which items you would not like to teach.

Explanations of each item are found on the TrainABA website in video form. Rather than deliver a lengthy script for each item, supervisors can turn on the video and watch during the group supervision meeting. It will provide convenience to the supervisor and talking points to the group.

Weekly Behavior Analytic Lessons

	Lesson Name	Date	Notes
1	Practice giving feedback		
2	Role play declining client gifts		
3	Coaching and mentoring		
4	Behavioral Skills Training presentation		
5	Compliance Code – defining client		
6	Performance management		
7	Franklin-Covey to-do lists		
8	Buy-in from clients & staff		
9	Problem = Opportunity + crisis		
10	1 problem, 2 solutions		
11	Treehugger-ninja-robot		
12	Assessing the 4th edition task list		
13	Master Class – Invite one supervisee to present a problem with their best ideas to solve it based on reading. Supervisees must know and prepare in advance (i.e., materials/thinking about problem to present)		
14	Case Study – present a problem to group. Let them work through the thought process and steps involved in how to tackle it.		
15	Talk show mode (warning: advanced supervision activity) – Pick a person with a problem that hasn't been solved. Walk them through the steps of solving that problem (identify, prioritize, conceptualize, troubleshoot) and give them 3 "lifelines" to ask the audience for help when stuck. Offer prizes.		
16	Read JABA articles		
17	Ethical situations of the week/month that have come up at the company		
18	Exam preparation tools/tips		
19	Programming ideas for common client issues related to that group		
20	Ethics: When administrative tasks interfere with clinical integrity (admin billing due dates have clear consequences and get prioritized over program development, which does not have a due date or immediate consequence)		
21	Professional behavior (with colleagues, conferences, in front of parents, staff to staff		
22	Ethical gray-area Events (EGE) training protocol		
23	Train-the-Trainer: have supervision group design their own training (they help arrange it but you are the one in charge of having the final say and making sure it's done behavior analytically on correct topics.		

	Lesson Name	Date	Notes
24	Performance management 101: Just like they have goals/programming for client, have them make one goal for staff in the level of detail needed by a funding source to report on a client's behavior. Operationalize, measurable, socially-significant, and all elements of ABA should be present in their finished product		
25	Rehearse how to give feedback (the BACB Supervisor Training Curriculum Outline way)		
26	Language what's working/not working and asking what got in the way		
27	Use performance management strategies to assess staff performance and diagnose problems as environmental or individual		
28	Functions of behavior: Iwata counts 3, Skinner counts 4, Cipani counts 6. What's going on here?		
	ADD YOU OWN IDEAS BELOW		

Suggested General Assignments

	General Homework Assignment Examples	Date
1	Make their own supervision binder (3-ring, to add materials as they go)	
2	4th Edition Task List™ items	
3	Ethical Guidelines	
4	Textbook	
5	Case Study from supervisor's experience	
6	Peer review each other's work	
7	Attend a talk/conference	
8	Online videos/talks/lectures	
9	Assign them to find 2 JABA articles they think would be interesting to read. Reinforce *finding* articles.	
10	Graphing their own data (on cumulative record)	
11	Graphing their own data for time spent on task list items (acquisition rates)	
12	Make their own standard celeration chart for learning task list items on Section I	
13	Graph their own data for Section II task list items	
14	Graph their own health or self-care behavior	
15	Graph their own data for interresponse time for emails (separate clinical from admin)	
16	Graph their own data for duration of time spent writing reports, by client. The supervision process is long enough for them to write multiple reports on each client and you will see the overall improvement (minutes per report) and individual performance (minutes per client) if they end up spending MORE time, it is usually because they learned more during training and they wanted to be more thorough or redesign programming that was not working.	
	ADD YOUR OWN IDEAS BELOW	

Deliverables for Supervisors

Under BACB® fieldwork guidelines, supervisors must complete the following every two weeks:
1. Do the hours (as required by BACB®)
2. Sign the forms (http://trainaba.com/track)

In the *TrainABA Supervision Curriculum* system, supervisors do items above AND:
3. Fill out Scorecard checklist
    a. Located at start of each segment
    b. Scorecard verifies that you received all of your supervisee's deliverables for a segment
4. Run the Individual and/or Group Meetings by following the agendas
5. Assess
    a. Assess your supervisee's skills for task list items identified on the scorecard
    b. Mark assessment task list items in your supervisee's book (see page 12)
    c. Do NOT use your copy of this book to track the supervisee's assessment

Deliverables for Supervisees

Under BACB® fieldwork guidelines, supervisees must complete the following:
1. Obtain signed supervision forms until hours are complete (http://trainaba.com/track)
2. Pass the board exam

In the *TrainABA Supervision Curriculum* system, supervisees do items above AND:
3. Complete all items on the Scorecard checklist (found at start of each segment)
4. Attend Individual and/or Group Meeting
5. Complete Homework
    a. Homework is due at the end of each segment or 2-week period, whichever is first
    b. Supervisees always have a minimum of 3 assignments due per segment
    c. Write in boxes for each task list item in segment. (Most are definitions, examples, and questions for your supervisor.)
    d. Create a 2-5 minute presentation of a task list item at that the group meeting for that segment.
    e. Practice SAFMEDs to fluency using TrainABA flashcards.
    f. Your supervisor may provide additional work to help you score well on the assessment for items in that segment.

*If you complete everything, your supervisor will check all the boxes on your Scorecard for that segment.

Presentation Calendar

We recommend that each supervisee prepare a short presentation related to a task list item for each segment. We did not include a calendar in this book because most people already have a personal and business calendar through their phones or in a paper book.

Assign a presentation for least one task list item per two week period. Present on item "#3 – Homework Assignments," found in each group agenda (except the first one).

Presentational behavior is important. Best practices for behavior analysis presentations are not discussed in this book. TrainABA offers continuing education webinars and live workshops. CEUs are optional. If you have not yet experienced a workshop with Ben, check the upcoming schedule. Ben runs a lot of seminars. Contact him email/text him at ben@trainaba.com/ 310-801-5450 for more info.

Segment Checklist

Segment Number	Topic	Task List Items	Complete
1	Introduction to Applied Behavior Analysis	B 1; FK 7-11, 33	
2	Philosophical Assumptions of Behavior Analysis	FK 1-6	
3	Reinforcement I	D 1, 19, 21; FK 17-18, 21, 23	
4	Reinforcement II	E 04-05; C 1; K 4; D 2, 20	
5	Punishment	FK 19-20; D 15-17; C 2	
6	Conditioning	E 11; FK 13-16; 24, 35	
7	Types of Measurement	A 1-7; I 1	
8	Continuous versus Discontinuous Measurement	A 12-13; FK 47-48	
9	Motivating Operations/ Discriminative Stimuli	E 1; FK 26-30	
10	Skill Acquisition I	D 3, 5-8; E 2, 6, 12-13; FK 12, 34	
11	Skill Acquisition II	D 4, 14; F 3-7; J 10	
12	Research Design I	A 10-11; B 3, 10-11	
13	Research Design II	B 4-9	
14	Measurement: Applications and Considerations	H 1-5; I 2	
15	Treatment Integrity and Fidelity Measures	A 8, 9; I 5; K 5, 7	
16	Verbal Behavior	D 9-13; F 8; FK 43-46	
17	Interventions	C 3; J 1-3, 5, 6-8; FK 22	
18	Assessment	G 1, 3; I 3-4, 6; J 13	
19	Behavioral Contingencies	E 3; F 1; G 4; FK 25, 31-32, 41-42	
20	Laws and Principles	E 7-10; FK 38-40	
21	Maintaining Professional Standards/Ethics	B 2; D 18; G 2, 8; J 9, 15	
22	Assessing Preference	A 14; F 2; I 7; J 4	
23	Supervision I	K 1-3, 6, 10	
24	Supervision II	G 5-7; K 8-9	
25	Generalization	J 11-12, 14; FK 36-37	

Segment 1 – Scorecard
Introduction to Applied Behavior Analysis

(Supervisor checks boxes)

☐ Presentation (2-5 minutes)

B 1
☐ Assessment
☐ SAFMED learned to fluency
☐ Workbook boxes completed

FK 7
☐ Assessment
☐ SAFMED learned to fluency
☐ Workbook boxes completed

FK 8
☐ Assessment
☐ SAFMED learned to fluency
☐ Workbook boxes completed

FK 9
☐ Assessment
☐ SAFMED learned to fluency
☐ Workbook boxes completed

FK 10
☐ Assessment
☐ SAFMED learned to fluency
☐ Workbook boxes completed

FK 11
☐ Assessment
☐ SAFMED learned to fluency
☐ Workbook boxes completed

FK 33
☐ Assessment
☐ SAFMED learned to fluency
☐ Workbook boxes completed

Segment 1 – Individual Supervision Agenda

Supervisor: _____ **Supervisee:** _____

Meeting Date: _____ **Time of meeting – From:** _____ **To:** _____

This document covers supervisory period from ____/____/____ **to** ____/____/____

1. Pass-in/Review Homework:

   Did the Supervisee satisfactorily complete this homework assignment?   Yes / No

   - If not, what is needed to complete assignment? Describe below.

2. Task List items addressed (B 1; FK 7-11, 33)

3. Definitions/SAFMEDs learned

   ☐ Flashcard(s) created   Was supervisee fluent with definitions? Yes ☐ No ☐

4. Discussion topics or activities completed during this meeting:

Evaluation of Supervisee's Performance				
(Record: S- "Satisfactory"; NI- "Needs Improvement"; U- "Unsatisfactory"; or NA- "Not Applicable")				
Arrived on time for meeting		Gave examples as needed		
Completed Homework Assigned		Accepted supervisory feedback appropriately		
Referred to literature/readings		Answered all questions thoroughly		
Maintained professional communication during supervision meeting				
Overall evaluation of supervisee performance during this meeting *(Circle one—use code above)*			S	NI	U
If "NI" or "U", please list corrective steps needed to achieve a score of "S"				

5. Homework assigned for next meeting

6. Closing questions/feedback

Segment 1 – Group Supervision Meeting Agenda

- <u>Meeting Topic</u>: Introduction to Applied Behavior Analysis

- <u>Segment 1 Task List Items</u>:
o B-01: Use the dimensions of applied behavior analysis (Baer, Wolf, & Risley, 1968) to evaluate whether interventions are behavior analytic in nature
o FK-08: Distinguish between radical and methodological behaviorism
o FK-09: Distinguish among the conceptual analysis of behavior, experimental analysis of behavior, applied behavior analysis, and behavioral service delivery.

o FK-07: Environmental (as opposed to mentalistic) explanations of behavior).
o FK-10: Behavior, response, response class
o FK-11: Environment, stimulus, stimulus class.FK-33: Functional relations

1. Housekeeping
   - Take attendance for the meeting.
   - State the duration of today's meeting (90 minutes).
   - Distribute BACB® experience forms to supervisees.
   - *Provide an overview of how supervision works*
   - Provide an overview of materials needed for supervision.
2. Assign Practice Homework
   - Homework assignment #1 is to "Complete "bio" questions on TrainABA.com and email answers to supervisor
   - Homework assignment # 2 is to complete the "self-assessment on personal 4th edition task list" via TrainABA.com and submit this document to supervisor
   - Explain presentation requirement. Have supervisees sign up on presentation calendar.
     o Give them presentation topic list
   - Model positive feedback using anecdote
   - Model corrective feedback using anecdote
   - Identify potential teaching moments within the context of presentations and provide appropriate feedback as needed.
3. Task List Discussion
   - Read assessment procedure at start of Assessment chapter
4. Task List Lesson
   - Discuss task list item B-01: Use the dimensions of applied behavior analysis (Baer, Wolf, & Risley, 1968) to evaluate whether interventions are behavior analytic in nature.
   - Discuss task list item FK-08: Distinguish between radical and methodological behaviorism.
   - Discuss task litem item FK-09: Distinguish among the conceptual analysis of behavior, experimental analysis of behavior, applied behavior analysis, and behavioral service delivery.
   - Discuss task litem item FK-07: Environmental (as opposed to mentalistic) explanations of behavior).
   - Discuss task litem item FK-33: Functional relations.
   - Discuss task litem item FK-10: Behavior, response, response class.
   - Discuss task litem item FK-11: Environment, stimulus, stimulus class.
5. Homework Review
   - Discuss homework policies and expectations for completion of assignments.
6. Questions
   - Answer any questions related to the homework or topics discussed.
7. Closing Notes
   - Close the meeting by inviting supervisees to request topics to be covered in upcoming meetings.

B – 01 USE THE DIMENSIONS OF APPLIED BE-
HAVIOR ANALYSIS (BAER, WOLF, & RISLEY,
1968) TO EVALUATE WHETHER INTERVEN-
TIONS ARE BEHAVIOR ANALYTIC IN NA-
TURE.

Definitions:
"Baer, Wolf, and Risley (1968) recommended that applied behavior analysis should be *applied, behavioral, ana-*
lytic, technological, conceptually systematic, effective, and capa-
ble of appropriately *generalized outcomes….*" In 1987 Baer
and colleagues reported that the "seven self-conscious
guides to behavior analytic conduct" they had offered
20 years earlier "remain functional; they still connote
the current dimensions of the work usually called applied behavior analysis". (Baer, et al., cited in Cooper et
al. 2007, p. 16)

1. The applied dimension relates to choosing target behaviors to change that are socially significant.
2. The behavioral dimension refers to the target behavior being systematically chosen for intervention
   based on its significance and this behavior must be
   measurable. Baer et al. (1968) summarized this point
   by stating, "Since the behavior of an individual is
   composed of physical events, its scientific study requires their precise measure."
3. The analytic dimension refers to "… a functional relation between the manipulated events and a reliable
   change in some measureable dimension of the targeted behavior." (Cooper et al. 2007). Baer et al.
   (1968) stated that, "An experimenter has achieved an
   analysis of behavior when he can exercise control
   over it."
4. "A study in applied behavior analysis is technological
   when all of its operative procedures are identified
   and described with sufficient detail and clarity."
   (Cooper et al., 2007).
5. Conceptual systems refer to the application of behavior analytic principles to create behavior change.
   "The field of applied behavior analysis will probably
   advance best if the published descriptions of its procedures are not only precisely technological, but also
   strive for relevance to principle." (Baer et. al. 1968).
6. "An effective application of behavioral techniques
   must improve the behavior under investigation to a
   practical degree." (Cooper et al., 2007).
7. The final dimension of applied behavior analysis outlined by Baer et al. (1968) was generality. "A behavior
   change has generality if it lasts over time, appears in
   environments other than the one in which the intervention that initially produced it was implemented,
   and/or spreads to other behaviors not directly
   treated by the intervention." (Cooper et al., 2007).

Example:
- Tim was evaluating the effectiveness of an intervention to decrease inappropriate comments for a first
grade student on his case load. The data indicated
that the behavior had decreased across all settings including when the child was home, displaying generalization of the intervention. He also noticed that the
intervention was analytic because the data indicated
that on days there was a substitute who was not thoroughly trained on the intervention there was a significant increase in rates of inappropriate commenting.
Finally, Tim deemed the behavior of inappropriately
commenting to be socially significant because it im-
peded the student from effectively accessing the
classroom curriculum.

Non-Example:
- Ross was evaluating an intervention on decreasing
stereotypy in one of his students. He analyzed the data
and noticed that the rates had barely decreased from
baseline rates and the student was still not making effective progress in the classroom. The intervention to
decrease stereotypy only worked occasionally with preferred staff in the classroom setting, but rates of stereotypy had actually increased across other settings. Ross
decided that this intervention was not meeting the
standards to be considered behavior analytic so he decided to try another intervention.

Write another example:

Questions to ask your supervisor

E x of dimensions
of ABA

Notes:

Relevant Literature:

Cooper, J.O., Heron, T.E. & Heward W.L. (2007). *Applied Behavior Analysis* (2nd Ed.), Upper Saddle River, NJ. Pearson Prentice Hall.   16-18, 235, 247-252.

Baer, D.M., Wolf, M.M., & Risley, T.R. (1968). Some Current Dimensions of Applied Behavior Analysis. *Journal of Applied Behavior Analysis*, 1, 1, 91-97.

Baer, D.M., Wolf, M.M., & Risley, T.R. (1987). Some Still Current Dimensions of Applied Behavior Analysis. *Journal of Applied Behavior Analysis*, 20, 4, 313-327.

Stokes, T.F. & Baer, D.M. (1977). An Implicit Technology of Generalization. *Journal of Applied Behavior Analysis*, 10, 2, 349-367.

Wolf, M.M. (1978). Social Validity: The Case for Subjective Measurement or How Applied Behavior Analysis is finding its Heart. *Journal of Applied Behavior Analysis*, 11, 2, 203-214.

Related Lessons:

B-04: Use withdrawal/reversal designs

B-05: Use alternating treatments (i.e., multi-element) designs

B-06: Use changing criterion designs

B-07: Use multiple baseline designs

B-09: Conduct a component analysis to determine the effective components of an intervention package

B-11: Conduct a parametric analysis to determine the effective values of an independent variable.

H-04: Evaluate changes in level, trend, and variability.

I-01: Define behavior in observable and measureable terms.

FK-07 ENVIRONMENTAL (AS OPPOSED TO MENTALISTIC) EXPLANATIONS OF BEHAVIOR.

Definition (Mentalism)

(Cooper, Heron, Heward, 2007, p. 699).
☐ Flashcard created   ☐ Learned to fluency

An environmental explanation of behavior can be described by physical events in the phylogenetic or ontogenetic history of the organism that cause behavior to occur. A behavior analyst believes that all behavior is a result of these physical events and that there is no reason to believe that there are some causes of behavior outside of physical dimensions.

It can be difficult sometimes, as we learn behavior analysis, to describe behavior without the use of mentalistic explanations (e.g., the hit me because he's frustrated). This is because in non-behavior analytic cultures, where many behavior analysts spend most of their lives, behavior is described this way and there is reinforcement available from that verbal community to perpetuate mentalistic explanations of behavior. For instance, it is common for people to believe that we each are responsible for our own actions and that the choices we make are done so with "free-will". Johnston (2014) mentions that, "After a lifetime of explaining behavior in terms of such apparent freedom, it is understandably difficult to accept what appears to be a helpless or passive role…" (p.5)

Much of behavior in society is controlled by consequences. Johnston (2014) says "…we assign the responsibility for behavior not to the individual but to sources of control in the physical environment. From this perspective, holding individuals responsible for their behavior by specifying the consequences for certain actions remains an important

contingency because it helps manage those tendencies to act in one way or another" (p.11).

Examples:
- Larry was inattentive during group rug activities in the classroom. His teacher did not know how to get through to him and tried everything to get him to pay attention and access the curriculum. This teacher thought he might have attention deficit hyperactivity disorder and mentioned this to the parents. After this meeting, the team chairperson asked for the behavior analysts to help in getting Larry to attend and focus. They wanted to do this to see if some simple environmental accommodations may help increase attending before recommending any treatment based on potential ADHD symptoms. After several observations, the behavior analyst noticed that Larry was always sitting towards the back of the rug with other students who were very talkative and distracting. The behavior analyst recommended moving Larry to the front of the room next to the teacher for rug activities to see if those would help attending. After a week, Larry was focusing more, attentive during groups, and not distracted by the students in the back.

Write another example:

Questions to ask your supervisor:

mentalism vs.
environmental
events

Relevant Literature:

Cooper, J. O., Heron, T. E., & Heward, W. L. (2007). *Applied behavior analysis.* Upper Saddle River, NJ: Pearson Education.

Skinner, B. F. (1953). Emotion. In *Science and human behavior (pp.160-170).* New York: Macmillan.

Related Lessons:

B-01 Use the dimensions of applied behavior analysis (Baer, Wolf, & Risley, 1968) to evaluate whether interventions are behavior analytic in nature.

G-04 Explain behavioral concepts using nontechnical language.

G-05 Describe and explain behavior, including private events, in behavior-analytic (non-mentalistic) terms.

I-01 Define behavior in observable and measurable terms.

I-02 Define environmental variables in observable and measurable terms.

K-02 Identify the contingencies governing the behavior of those responsible for carrying out behavior-change procedures and design interventions accordingly.

FK-01 Lawfulness of behavior

FK-03 Determinism

FK-07 Environmental (as opposed to mentalistic) explanations of behavior

Notes:

FK-08 DISTINGUISH BETWEEN RADICAL AND METHODOLOGICAL BEHAVIORISM.

Definition (Radical behaviorism):

(Skinner, 1989).

☐ Flashcard created   ☐ Learned to fluency

Definition (Methodological behaviorism):

(Moore, 2008).

☐ Flashcard created   ☐ Learned to fluency

Examples:

- The distinction between radical and methodological behaviorism can be summed up by the views on private events. Private events, or events observable by only the individual engaging in the response, are not included in the analysis of behavior by a methodological behaviorist position. Radical behaviorists consider private events to be no different than any other behavior, therefore, allowing it to be understood within the same conceptual framework understood for overt behavior.

Write another example:

Questions to ask your supervisor:

Relevant Literature:

Baum, W. M. (2011). What is radical behaviorism? A review of Jay Moore's Conceptual Foundations of Radical Behaviorism. *Journal of the experimental analysis of behavior, 95*(1), 119-126.

Cooper, J. O., Heron, T. E., & Heward, W. L. (2007). *Applied behavior analysis.* Upper Saddle River, NJ: Pearson Education.

Moore, J. (2011). A review of Baum's review of Conceptual Foundations of Radical Behaviorism. *Journal of the experimental analysis of behavior, 95*(1), 127-140.

Moore, J. (2009). Why the radical behaviorist conception of private events is interesting, relevant, and important. *Behavior and Philosophy*, 21-37.

Moore, Jay (2008). *Conceptual Foundations of Radical Behaviorism.* Sloan Pub.

Skinner, B. F. (1989). *Recent issues in the analysis of behavior.* Prentice Hall. Chicago.

Related Lessons:

B-01 Use the dimensions of applied behavior analysis (Baer, Wolf, & Risley, 1968) to evaluate whether interventions are behavior analytic in nature.

G-04 Explain behavioral concepts using nontechnical language.

G-05 Describe and explain behavior, including private events, in behavior-analytic (non-mentalistic) terms.

FK-01 Lawfulness of behavior

FK-07 Environmental (as opposed to mentalistic) explanations of behavior

Notes:

FK-09 DISTINGUISH BETWEEN THE CONCEPTUAL ANALYSIS OF BEHAVIOR, APPLIED BEHAVIOR ANALYSIS, AND BEHAVIORAL SERVICE DELIVERY.

The conceptual analysis of behavior is a combination of philosophical, theoretical, and historical investigations behind the science of behavior. The modern philosophy of behavior analysis is specifically referred to as Radical Behaviorism and was coined by B.F. Skinner. Radical Behaviorism is rooted in the idea that the science of behavior is a natural science encompassed by behavioral events that happen due to the way the universe is arranged (determinism) and explained by other natural events (Baum, 1995) like the phenomenon of gravity. These behavioral events are analyzed in relation to the past and present environment (ontogenic and cultural contingencies) and evolutionary history (phylogenic contingencies). This approach sets itself apart from other behavioral philosophies (e.g., methodological behaviorism) by including overt behavior as an important variable but also acknowledging unobserved behavior (i.e., private events) (Skinner, 1953). Moreover, internal states, intervening variables and hypothetical constructs (mentalistic explanations) are not used to understand or analyze behavior (Baum, 2011). This philosophy sets the foundation for the other three domains described below.

The experimental analysis of behavior (EAB) is a natural science approach to the study of behavior. The methodology includes rate of response as a basic dependent variable, repeated or continuous measurement of clearly defined response classes, within subject comparisons, visual analysis of data and an emphasis on describing functional relations between behavior and controlling variables. EAB methodology was founded by B.F. Skinner and first publicly presented in his book *The Behavior of Organisms* (1938/1966) (Cooper, Heron, & Heward, 2007). EAB is often referred to as basic research.

Applied behavior analysis (ABA) is a science that develops its technology based on the principles of behavior and applies them systematically to produce socially significant behavior change. Furthermore, experimentation is used to identify the independent variables responsible for behavior change. Lastly, the adequacy of ABA work is determined by the seven characteristics (applied, behavioral, analytic, technological, conceptually systematic effective and generalizable) set forth by Baer, Wolf and Risley (1968) (Cooper, Heron, & Heward, 2007).

Behavioral service delivery consists of putting ABA principles that have been experimentally validated into practice. Behavioral service providers design,

implement an evaluate behavior change procedures applied to socially significant behavior (Cooper, Heron, & Heward, 2007). It is important that behavioral service providers apply a consistent framework in analyzing and explaining causation of the observed behavior that are consistent with the established science of behavioral. However, it is also important that they relay these concepts to non-behavioral service providers and families in everyday nontechnical terminology that is not verbal repertoires (Johnston, 2013).

The four above mentioned domains have been described above in order to understand the similarities and differences between each domain. This view emphasizes the fact that the four domains should be dependent on each other and mutually influenced by developments in each of the other domains (Cooper, Heron, & Heward 2007; Moore, & Cooper, 2003). Moore and Cooper (2003) argue that students of behavior analysis be offered a balanced approach by incorporating all four domains into their training experience.

Write another example:

(handwritten annotations:) conceptual analysis of behavior, applied behavior analysis

3 service delivery

Questions to ask your supervisor:

Relevant Literature:

Baer, D. M., Wolf, M. M., & Risley, T. R. (1968). Some current dimensions of applied behavior analysis. *Journal of applied behavior analysis, 1*(1), 91-97.

Baum, W. M. (1995). Radical behaviorism and the concept of agency. *Behaviorology, 3*, 93-106.

Baum, W. M. (2011). What is radical behaviorism? A review of Jay Moore's Conceptual Foundations of Radical Behaviorism. *Journal of the experimental analysis of behavior, 95*(1), 119-126.

Cooper, J. O., Heron, T. E., & Heward, W. L. (2007). *Applied behavior analysis (2nd ed.). Upper Saddle River, NJ: Pearson*

Johnston, J.V. (2013). *Radical Behaviorism for ABA Practitioners.* Publisher Sloan Publishing

Moore, J., & Cooper, J. O. (2003). Some proposed relations among the domains of behavior analysis. *The Behavior Analyst, 26*(1), 69.

Skinner, B. F. (1953). *Science and human behavior.* Simon and Schuster.

Related Lessons:

B-01 Use the dimensions of applied behavior analysis (Baer, Wolf, & Risley, 1968) to evaluate whether interventions are behavior analytic in nature.

G-04 Explain behavioral concepts using nontechnical language

G-05 Describe and explain behavior, including private events, in behavior-analytic (non-mentalistic) terms.

G-06 Provide behavior-analytic services in collaboration with others who support and/or provide services to one's clients.

FK-01 Lawfulness of behavior

FK-02 Selectionism (phylogenic, ontogenic, cultural)

FK-03 Determinism

FK-04 Empiricism

FK-05 Parsimony

FK-06 Pragmatism

FK-07 Environmental (as opposed to mentalistic) explanations of behavior

FK-08 Distinguish between radical and methodological behaviorism

Notes:

FK-10 BEHAVIOR, RESPONSE, RESPONSE CLASS.

Definition (Behavior):

(Cooper, Heron, & Heward, 2007).
☐ Flashcard created   ☐ Learned to fluency

Definition (Response):

(Cooper, Heron, & Heward, 2007).
☐ Flashcard created   ☐ Learned to fluency

Definition (Response class):

(Cooper, Heron, & Heward, 2007).
☐ Flashcard created   ☐ Learned to fluency

Example:
- Opening a door
- Behavior: Beezus stands up from her chair, heads towards a closed door, and pushes on it. The door is now open.
- Response: When encountering a closed door, Beezus extends an open palm and pushes on it. The door is now open.
- Response Class: Beezus encounters many doors during her day. Sometimes she opens them with an open palm and sometimes with a closed palm. Sometimes she opens them with her left hand and at other times with her right hand. No matter which way she chooses to open a door, the result is always the same.

Write another example:

Questions to ask your supervisor:

Relevant Literature:
Cooper J.O, Heron T.E, Heward W.L. (2007). *Applied behavior analysis* (2nd ed.) Upper Saddle River, NJ: Pearson

Johnston, J.M., & Pennypacker, H.S. (1993a). *Strategies and Tactics for Human Behavioral Research (2nd ed.).* Hillsdale, NJ: Erlbaum.

Michael, J. (2004). *Concepts and Principles of Behavior Analysis (*rev. ed.). Kalamazoo, MI: Society for the Advancement of Behavior Analysis.

Skinner, B.F. (1969). *Contingencies of Reinforcement: A Theoretical Analysis.* New York: Appleton-Century-Crofts.

Related Lessons:
FK-36 Response Generalization
G-05 Describe and explain behavior, including private events, in behavior-analytic (non-mentalistic) terms.
I-01 Define behavior in observable and measurable terms

Notes:

FK-11 ENVIRONMENT, STIMULUS, STIMULUS CLASS.

Definition (Environment):

(Cooper, Heron, & Heward, 2007).

☐ Flashcard created   ☐ Learned to fluency

Definition (Stimulus):

Stimulus class

(Catania, 2013).

☐ Flashcard created   ☐ Learned to fluency

Definition (Stimulus class):

(Cooper, Heron, & Heward, 2007).

☐ Flashcard created   ☐ Learned to fluency

Example:
- Willis is shopping at the local mall. The local mall would be an environment.
- Willis is walking through the food court. He smells some pizza cooking from one of the establishments and suddenly his stomach starts growling. He stops and gets some food. All of the things in the food court, including the smells, the changes in his stomach, and the food are stimuli.

- At the food court, Willis will buy items that will all function as reinforcers for eating behavior. In this case, the burger, the fries, and the cookie he bought are in the same stimulus class.

Write another example:

Questions to ask your supervisor:

Relevant Literature:

Catania, A. C. (2013). *Learning* (5th ed.). Croton-on-Hudson, NY: Sloan.

Cooper J.O, Heron T.E, Heward W.L. (2007). *Applied behavior analysis* (2nd ed.) Upper Saddle River, NJ: Pearson

Johnston, J.M., & Pennypacker, H.S. (1993a). *Strategies and Tactics for Human Behavioral Research (2nd ed.).* Hillsdale, NJ: Erlbaum.

Michael, J. (2004). *Concepts and Principles of Behavior Analysis* (rev. ed.). Kalamazoo, MI: Society for the Advancement of Behavior Analysis.

Related Lessons:

FK-11 environment, stimulus, stimulus class

Notes:

FK-33 FUNCTIONAL RELATIONS.

Definition (Functional relation):

(Johnston & Pennypacker, 2009).
☐ Flashcard created   ☐ Learned to fluency

Definition (Functional relation):

(Cooper, Heron, & Heward, 2007).
☐ Flashcard created   ☐ Learned to fluency

Definition (Functional relation):

(Skinner, 1953)
☐ Flashcard created   ☐ Learned to fluency

Example:
- Sonny has been engaging in some eloping behavior within a school building. He has been known to leave his classroom area and to run to other rooms within the building. His teachers have started delivering small pieces of candy for on-task behavior, as he works on his schoolwork. The teachers have started seeing an increase in on-task behavior and a decrease in elopement. A substitute teacher came into the classroom for a week but did not know about the on-task candy delivery the first couple of days. Sonny started eloping again. When the aides told the substitute teacher about the contingency for on-task behavior, the substitute started delivering the candy on the same schedule as the other teacher. Sonny again started sitting down, remaining on task, and elopement decreased. It can be said that there is likely a functional relation between the schedule of candy delivery and the elopement and/or on-task behavior.

- Three semi-busy 3-way intersections in the small town of Passamaquoddy has had a series of accidents over the past few years. These intersections have had yield signs up but there have been several accidents at each location. The town decides to replace the yield signs with 3 stop signs instead. They use a multiple baseline design across locations. After seeing that when, and only when, the new stop signs are implemented, accidents have decreased in that location. It can be said that there is a functional relation between the placement of the stop signs and the change in accidents reported there.

Non-Example:
-   A child with autism has been engaging in some eloping behavior within a school building. He has been known to leave his classroom area and to run to other rooms within the building. His teachers have explained to him that the other rooms are off limits but this has not had an impact on his behavior nor has simply ensuring that the doors are closed. His teacher decides to put up a green light on rooms that it is o.k. to enter. There has been no change in behavior from the previously recorded levels of entering the off-limits classrooms. It can be said that there is no functional relation between the presence of green light signs and the off-limits classroom entering behavior.

Write another example:

Questions to ask your supervisor:

Relevant Literature:

Cooper J.O., Heron T.E., Heward, W.L. (2007). *Applied behavior analysis* (2nd ed.) Upper Saddle River, NJ: Pearson.

Johnston, J. M., & Pennypacker, H. S. (2009). *Strategies and tactics of behavioral research*. Routledge.

Skinner, B. F. (1953). *Science and human behavior*. Simon and Schuster.

Related Lessons:
B-03 Systematically arrange independent variables to demonstrate their effects on dependent variables.
FK-33 functional relations
H-03 Select a data display that effectively communicates relevant quantitative relations.
H-05 Evaluate temporal relations between observed variables (within &between sessions, time series).
I-05 Organize, analyze, and interpret observed data

Notes:

Segment 2 – Scorecard
Philosophical Assumptions of Behavior Analysis

☐ Presentation (2-5 minutes)

FK 1
☐ Assessment
☐ SAFMED learned to fluency
☐ Workbook boxes completed

FK 2
☐ Assessment
☐ SAFMED learned to fluency
☐ Workbook boxes completed

FK 3
☐ Assessment
☐ SAFMED learned to fluency
☐ Workbook boxes completed

FK 4
☐ Assessment
☐ SAFMED learned to fluency
☐ Workbook boxes completed

FK 5
☐ Assessment
☐ SAFMED learned to fluency
☐ Workbook boxes completed

FK 6
☐ Assessment
☐ SAFMED learned to fluency
☐ Workbook boxes completed

Segment 2 – Individual Supervision Agenda

Supervisor: _____ **Supervisee:** _____

Meeting Date: _____ **Time of meeting – From:**_____ **To:**_____

This document covers supervisory period from ____/____/____ **to** ____/____/____

1. Pass-in/Review Homework:

    Did the Supervisee satisfactorily complete this homework assignment?   Yes / No

- If not, what is needed to complete assignment? Describe below.

2. Task List items addressed (FK 1-6)

3. Definitions/SAFMEDs learned

    ☐ Flashcard(s) created   Was supervisee fluent with definitions? Yes ☐ No ☐

4. Discussion topics or activities completed during this meeting:

Evaluation of Supervisee's Performance				
(Record: S- "Satisfactory"; NI- "Needs Improvement"; U- "Unsatisfactory"; or NA- "Not Applicable")				
Arrived on time for meeting		Gave examples as needed		
Completed Homework Assigned		Accepted supervisory feedback appropriately		
Referred to literature/readings		Answered all questions thoroughly		
Maintained professional communication during supervision meeting				
Overall evaluation of supervisee performance during this meeting *(Circle one—use code above)*				S NI U
If "NI" or "U", please list corrective steps needed to achieve a score of "S"				

5. Homework assigned for next meeting

6. Closing questions/feedback

Segment 2 – Group Supervision Meeting Agenda

- <u>Meeting Topic</u>: Philosophical Assumptions of Behavior Analysis

- <u>Task List Items Reviewed</u>:

  o FK-01: Lawfulness of behavior
  o FK-02: Selectionism (phylogenic, ontogenic, cultural)
  o FK-03: Determinism

  o FK-04: Empiricism
  o FK-05: Parsimony
  o FK-06: Pragmatism.

1. Housekeeping
   - Upon entry to meeting have supervisees hand in the previous week's homework assignment and discuss several "Housekeeping Items" related to supervision.
   - Take attendance for the meeting.
   - State the duration of today's meeting (90 minutes).
   - Distribute BACB® experience forms to supervisees.
2. Task List Lesson and Discussion
   - Discuss task list item FK-01: Lawfulness of behavior.
   - Discuss task list item FK-02: Selectionism (phylogenic, ontogenic, and cultural).
   - Discuss task litem item FK-03: Determinism.
   - Discuss task litem item FK-04: Empiricism.
   - Discuss task litem item FK-05: Parsimony.
   - Discuss task litem item FK-06: Pragmatism.
3. Homework Review
   - Review homework that was assigned at the previous supervision meeting.
4. Questions
   - Answer any questions related to the homework or topics discussed.
5. Closing Notes
   - *Assign Homework (task list boxes, presentation) from today's segment, due at next group meeting*
   - Close the meeting by inviting supervisees to request topics to be covered in upcoming meetings.

FK-01 LAWFULNESS OF BEHAVIOR.

Definition (Lawfulness of behavior):

(Malott, 2012).

☐ Flashcard created   ☐ Learned to fluency

Definition (Lawfulness of behavior:

(Skinner, 1953).

☐ Flashcard created   ☐ Learned to fluency

Examples:

Mary was yelling in class and her teacher became concerned. Since this was usually during group time, the teacher thought that she was yelling to get out of participating in the group. She asked the behavior analyst for the school district to come observe Mary in class and try to figure out what was going on. The behavior analyst observed several times and noticed that Mary only yelled during music based and song activities when it got loud in the group. He decided to allow Mary to functionally ask for noise reducing headphones or a break away from the group while they were singing or listening to music that was loud. After some training, Mary's yelling decreased significantly as she started using the headphones and functionally communicating during group.

Write another example:

Questions to ask your supervisor:

Relevant Literature:

Malott, R. (2012). *Issues in the Analysis of Behavior.* Behaviordelia.

Skinner, B. F. (1953). *Science and human behavior.* New York: Macmillan.

Related Lessons:

B-03 Systematically arrange independent variables to demonstrate their effects on dependent variables.

FK-02 Selectionism (phylogenic, ontogenic, cultural)

FK-03 Determinism

FK-04 Empiricism

FK-05 Parsimony

FK-06 Pragmatism

Notes:

Questions to ask your supervisor:

Notes:

FK 02 SELECTIONISM (PHYLOGENIC, ONTOGENIC, CULTURAL)

Definition (Selectionism):

(Skinner, 1981).

☐ Flashcard created   ☐ Learned to fluency

Definition (Selectionism):

(Cooper, Heron, & Heward, 2007).

☐ Flashcard created   ☐ Learned to fluency

Examples:

- In evolutionary history, our ancestors ate certain foods because it had an adaptive value as it helped ensure survival (natural selection of behavior; phylogenic selection). The food did not necessarily need to be a reinforcer but was necessary for survival. However, in modern times, we all have food preferences and may eat food that has no nutritional value or health benefits, indicating that specific foods are eaten because of their reinforcing value (ontogenic selection). This type of eating habit is not adaptive (e.g., think about overeating, binge eating, obesity and the subsequent health problems that can emerge from this type of eating behavior) but it is strengthened and maintained by operant conditioning, thus reflecting selection by consequences (Skinner, 1981).

- Cultural Selection: Pennypacker (1992) provides examples of how selection by consequences is observed in education, economics, and politics and social organization.

Write another example:

Questions to ask your supervisor:

Relevant Literature:

Cooper, J. O., Heron, T. E., & Heward, W. L. (2007). Measuring behavior. *Applied Behavior Analysis* (pp. 72-101). Upper Saddle River, NJ: Pearson Prentice Hall.

Pennypacker, H. S. (1992). Is behavior analysis undergoing selection by consequences? *American Psychologist, 47,* 1491-1498.

Skinner, B. F. (1981). Selection by consequences. *Science, 212,* 501-504.

Related Lessons:

FK-15 operant conditioning
FK-31 behavioral contingencies
FK-33 functional relations
FK-41 contingency-shaped behavior
FK-42 rule-governed behavior

Notes:

FK-03 DETERMINISM

Definition (Determinism):

(Cooper, Heron, & Heward, 2007).

☐ Flashcard created   ☐ Learned to fluency

Definition (Determinism):

(Fisher, Piazza, & Roane, 2011).

☐ Flashcard created   ☐ Learned to fluency

Footnotes:
- Please refer to FK-04 through FK-06 for a description of the other attitudes of science.

Examples:
- A window does not just randomly bang shut; it bangs shut because a gust of wind has blown it and this has exerted enough force upon the window to close it.
- A water pipe does not just spontaneously burst; it bursts because there is a fault somewhere in the system, which has caused a buildup of water in the pipes, resulting in so much pressure within the system that the pipe has burst.
- A client's self-injurious behavior does not just suddenly decrease after days of high rates of SIB. It decreases because the sensory-blocking procedure that's in place has begun to extinguish the behavior.

Notes:

Write another example:

Questions to ask your supervisor:

Relevant Literature:
Cooper, J. O., Heron, T. E., & Heward, W. L. (2007). *Applied Behavior Analysis*, 2nd ed. Upper Saddle River, New Jersey: Pearson Prentice Hall.
Delprato, D. J., & Midgley, B. D. (1992). Some fundamentals of B.F. Skinner's behaviorism. *American Psychologist, 48*, 1507-1520.
Fisher, W.W., Piazza, C. C., Roane, H. S. (2011). *Handbook of Applied Behavior Analysis*. The Guildford Press, New York London.

Related Lessons:
FK-01: Lawfulness of behavior
FK-04: Empiricism
FK-05: Parsimony
FK-06: Pragmatism

FK-04 EMPIRICISM

Definition (Determinism):

(Cooper, Heron, & Heward, 2007).
☐ Flashcard created   ☐ Learned to fluency

Definition (Determinism):

(Fisher, 2011).
☐ Flashcard created   ☐ Learned to fluency

Examples:
- Mr. Johnson, a BCBA, conducts a functional analysis to determine the function of Billy's aggressive behavior in class. He completes rating scales, interviews, and other indirect assessment procedures, but doesn't use these to guess the reinforcer for Billy's aggression. Mr. Johnson uses the indirect assessment procedures to inform his experiment. He designs a pairwise functional analysis and runs out several phases of direct observation until results are conclusive. He concludes that Billy's aggressive behavior is sensitive to attention as a maintaining variable. At the IEP meeting, Billy's parents applaud Mr. Johnson's empiricism for completing such a thorough assessment and analyzing all the possible factors before determining a function.

Non-Example:
- Mr. Riley is a district BCBA and has been asked to conduct a functional behavior assessment for Mary in regards to her aggressive behavior. Mr. Riley hypothesizes that Mary is engaging in aggressive behavior to get access to her dolls because all little girls like dolls. Based on his reasoning he has already decided that Mary's aggression is maintained by access to dolls. Since he already has a strong hypothesis for the function of aggression, Mr. Riley writes a report and creates a treatment for Mary.

Write another example:

Questions to ask your supervisor:

Relevant Literature:

Cooper, J.O., Heron, T.E. & Heward W.L. (2007). *Applied Behavior Analysis* (2nd Ed.), Upper Saddle River, NJ. Pearson Prentice Hall. 5, 22, 159.

Baer, D.M., Wolf, M.M., & Risley, T.R. (1968). Some Current Dimensions of Applied Behavior Analysis. *Journal of Applied Behavior Analysis*, 1, 1, 91-97.

Fisher, W.W., Piazza, C. C., Roane, H. S. (2011). *Handbook of Applied Behavior Analysis*. The Guildford Press, New York London.

Schmidt, F.L. (1992). What do data really mean? Research findings, meta-analysis, and cumulative knowledge in psychology. *American Psychologist*, 47, 10, 1173-1181.

Related Lessons:

B-01: Use the dimensions of applied behavior analysis (Baer, Wolf, & Risley, 1968) to evaluate whether interventions are behavior analytic in nature.

H-01: Select a measurement system to obtain representative data given the dimensions of the behavior and the logistics of observing and recording.

H-03: Select a data display that effectively communicates relevant quantitative relations.

I-01: Define behavior in observable and measurable terms.

I-03: Design and implement individualized behavioral assessment procedures.

I-05: Organize, analyze, and interpret observed data.

J-01: State intervention goals in observable and measurable terms.

J-15: Base decision making on data displayed in various formats.

K-07: Evaluate the effectiveness of the behavioral program.

FK-10: Behavior, response, response class.

Notes:

FK-05 PARSIMONY

Definition (Parsimony):

Write another example:

(Cooper, Heron, & Heward, 2007).

☐ Flashcard created   ☐ Learned to fluency

Questions to ask your supervisor:

Examples:

- A non-verbal client hits her head repeatedly for a period of days each month. Although the analyst considered multiple environmental antecedent and consequent factors that might influence the client's behavior, she first looked at the calendar to see if the client's head hitting each month corresponded to her monthly menstrual cycle. She found that head-hitting occurred the last days immediately before her period began and the first day of her period. The analyst asked a nurse to review the data and recommend a medical intervention before the analyst continued to assess the influence of external environmental factors.

- An analyst was asked to design strategies for staff when responding to a client's aggressive behavior after asking him to brush his teeth. He reviewed the data staff had recorded about self-care behaviors and saw that aggression was a relatively new behavior during teeth-brushing. He learned that the client became aggressive toward staff shortly after they began buying a discounted toothpaste instead of the client's usual brand. When the analyst offered the client a choice between the two brands, the client chose his old brand and aggression did not occur after asking him to brush his teeth.

Relevant Literature:

Cooper, J.O., Heron, T.E. & Heward W.L. (2007). *Applied Behavior Analysis* (2nd Ed.), Upper Saddle River, NJ. Pearson Prentice Hall. 113-122.

Etzel, B. C., & LeBlanc, J. M. (1979). The simplest treatment alternative: The law of parsimony applied to choosing appropriate instructional control and errorless-learning procedures for the difficult-to-teach child. *Journal of Autism and Developmental Disorders, 9*(4), 361-382.

Related Lessons:

FK-01: Lawfulness of behavior.

FK-02: Selectionism (phylogenic, ontogenic, cultural)

FK-03: Determinism

FK-04: Empiricism

FK-06: Pragmatism

Notes:

FK-06 PRAGMATISM

Definition (Pragmatism):

Questions to ask your supervisor:

(Cooper, Heron, & Heward, 2007).
☐ Flashcard created   ☐ Learned to fluency

Examples:
- Gloria was looking for a reinforcement program for her classroom because her students were not turning their homework in on time. She consulted with the district BCBA and was able to come up with an effective and simple class-wide reinforcement program that helped her students to turn their homework on time.

Non-Example:
- Richard was a first grade teacher and wanted to represent his student's data using a scatterplot graph. However, he did not have previous training in this area and was unable to accomplish this task. He felt that this method for graphical display was too difficult to figure out.

Write another example:

Relevant Literature:
Bailey, J.S. (2000). A futurist perspective for applied behavior analysis. In J. Austin & J.E. Carr (Eds.), Handbook of applied behavior analysis (pp. 473-488). Reno, NV: Context Press.
Cooper, J.O., Heron, T.E. & Heward W.L. (2007). Applied Behavior Analysis (2nd Ed.), Upper Saddle River, NJ. Pearson Prentice Hall. 19, 22.
Heward, W.L. (2005). Reasons applied behavior analysis is good for education and why those reasons have been insufficient. In W.L. Heward, T.E. Heron, N.A. Neef, S.M. Peterson, , D.M. Sainato, G. Cartledge, R. Gardner, III, L.D. Peterson, S.B. Hersh, & J.C. Dardig (Eds.), Focus on behavior analysis in education: Achievements, challenges, and opportunities (pp. 316-348). Upper Saddle River, NJ: Merrill/Prentice Hall.

Related Lessons:
B-01: Use the dimensions of applied behavior analysis (Baer, Wolf, & Risley, 1968) to evaluate whether interventions are behavior analytic in nature.
G-04: Explain behavioral concepts using nontechnical language.
G-06: Provide behavior analytic services in collaboration with others who support and/or provide services to one's clients.
K-08: Establish support for behavior-analytic services from direct and indirect consumers.
K-09: Secure the support of others to maintain the client's behavioral repertoires in their natural environments

Notes:

Segment 3 – Scorecard
Reinforcement I

☐ Presentation (2-5 minutes)

D 1
☐ Assessment
☐ SAFMED learned to fluency
☐ Workbook boxes completed

FK 18
☐ Assessment
☐ SAFMED learned to fluency
☐ Workbook boxes completed

D 19
☐ Assessment
☐ SAFMED learned to fluency
☐ Workbook boxes completed

FK 21
☐ Assessment
☐ SAFMED learned to fluency
☐ Workbook boxes completed

D 21
☐ Assessment
☐ SAFMED learned to fluency
☐ Workbook boxes completed

FK 23
☐ Assessment
☐ SAFMED learned to fluency
☐ Workbook boxes ompleted

FK 17
☐ Assessment
☐ SAFMED learned to fluency
☐ Workbook boxes completed

Segment 3 – Individual Supervision Agenda

Supervisor: _____ **Supervisee:** _____
Meeting Date: _____ **Time of meeting – From:** _____ **To:** _____
This document covers supervisory period from _____ / _____ / _____ **to** _____ / _____ / _____

1. Pass-in/Review Homework:
   Did the Supervisee satisfactorily complete this homework assignment?   Yes / No

   - If not, what is needed to complete assignment? Describe below.

2. Task List items addressed (D 1, 19, 21; FK 17-18, 21, 23)

3. Definitions/SAFMEDs learned
   ☐ Flashcard(s) created   Was supervisee fluent with definitions? Yes ☐ No ☐

4. Discussion topics or activities completed during this meeting:

Evaluation of Supervisee's Performance		
(Record: S- "Satisfactory"; NI- "Needs Improvement"; U- "Unsatisfactory"; or NA- "Not Applicable")		
Arrived on time for meeting	Gave examples as needed	
Completed Homework Assigned	Accepted supervisory feedback appropriately	
Referred to literature/readings	Answered all questions thoroughly	
Maintained professional communication during supervision meeting		
Overall evaluation of supervisee performance during this meeting *(Circle one—use code above)*	S NI U	
If "NI" or "U", please list corrective steps needed to achieve a score of "S"		

5. Homework assigned for next meeting

6. Closing questions/feedback

Segment 3 – Group Supervision Meeting Agenda

- <u>Meeting Topic</u>: Reinforcement I

- <u>Task List Items Reviewed</u>:
  - D-01: Use positive and negative reinforcement.
  - D-19: Use combination of reinforcement with punishment and extinction.
  - D-21: Use differential reinforcement (e.g., DRO, DRA, DRI, DRL, DRH).
  - FK-17: Unconditioned reinforcement.
  - FK-18: Conditioned reinforcement.
  - FK-21: Schedules of reinforcement and punishment.
  - FK-23: Automatic reinforcement and punishment.

1. Housekeeping

   - Upon entry to meeting have supervisees hand in the previous week's homework assignment and discuss several "Housekeeping Items" related to supervision.

   - Take attendance for the meeting.

   - State the duration of today's meeting (90 minutes).

   - Distribute BACB® experience forms to supervisees.

2. Task List Lesson and Discussion

   - Discuss task list item FK-17: Unconditioned reinforcement.

   - Discuss task list item FK-18: Conditioned reinforcement.

   - Discuss task list item FK-21: Schedules of reinforcement and punishment.

   - Discuss task list item FK-23: Automatic reinforcement and punishment.

   - Discuss task list item D-01: Use positive and negative reinforcement.

   - Discuss task list item D-19: Use combination of reinforcement with punishment and extinction.

   - Discuss task list item D-21: Use differential reinforcement (e.g., DRO, DRA, DRI, DRL, DRH).

3. Homework Review

   - Review homework that was assigned at the previous supervision meeting.

4. Questions

   - Answer any questions related to the homework or topics discussed.

5. Closing Notes

   - *Assign Homework (task list boxes, presentation) from today's segment, due at next group meeting*

   - Close the meeting by inviting supervisees to request topics to be covered in upcoming meetings.

D-01 USE POSITIVE AND NEGATIVE REINFORCEMENT.

Write another example:

Definition (Positive Reinforcement):

(Cooper, Heron, & Heward, 2007).

☐ Flashcard created   ☐ Learned to fluency

Definition (Negative Reinforcement):

(Cooper, Heron, & Heward, 2007).

☐ Flashcard created   ☐ Learned to fluency

Example (Positive Reinforcement):

A rat is in a cage, which has a food dispenser lever. To access food, the rat pushes the lever and food pellets are dispensed. In the future, after a few hours of food deprivation, the rat is more likely to push the lever to access food.

A mommy sings a verse from "The Wheels on the Bus" nursery rhyme to her baby. The baby giggles immediately following the nursery rhyme being sung. The mommy is more likely to sing this nursery rhyme to her baby in the future, because the baby's giggling serves as a reinforcer.

Example (Negative Reinforcement):

A child asks her friend to turn down the music, as it is too loud for her. The music is immediately turned down. The child is more likely to ask for music to be turned down in the future when it is too loud.

It is raining so you put up your umbrella and immediately reduce the amount that you are getting wet. You are more likely to put up your umbrella in the future when it is raining to avoid getting wet.

Questions to ask your supervisor:

Relevant Literature:

Hall, R. V., Lund, D. & Jackson, D. (1968). Effects of teacher attention on study behavior. *Journal of Applied Behavior Analysis, 1*, 1-12.

Hart, B. M., Reynolds, N. J., Baer, D. M., Brawley, E. R. & Harris, F. R. (1968). Effect of contingent and non-contingent social reinforcement on the cooperative play of a preschool child. *Journal of Applied Behavior Analysis, 1*, 73-76.

Michael, J. (1975). Positive and negative reinforcement, a distinction that is no longer necessary; or a better way to talk about bad things. *Behaviorism, 3* (1), 33-44.

Osborne, J. G. (1969). Free-time as a reinforcer in the management of classroom behavior. *Journal of Applied Behavior Analysis, 2*, 113-118.

Skinner, B. F. *The behavior of organisms.* New York: D. Appleton-Century, 1938.

Thomas, D. R., Becker, W. C., & Armstrong, M. (1968). Production and elimination of disruptive classroom behavior by systematically varying teacher's behavior. *Journal of Applied Behavior Analysis, 1*, 35-45.

Related Lessons:

C-01: State and plan for the possible unwanted side effects of reinforcement

D-02: Use appropriate parameters and schedules of reinforcement

D-16: Use positive and negative punishment

D-17: Use appropriate parameters and schedules of reinforcement

D-19: Use combinations of reinforcement with punishment and extinction

D-20: Use response-independent (time-based) schedules of reinforcement (i.e., noncontingent reinforcement)

D-21: Use differential reinforcement (e.g., DRO, DRA, DRI, DRL, DRH)

E-10: Use the Premack principle

E-11: Use pairing procedures to establish new conditioned reinforcers and punishers

F-02: Use token economies and other conditioned reinforcement systems

FK-14: Respondent conditioning (CS-CR)

FK-15: Operant conditioning

FK-17: Unconditioned reinforcement

FK-18: Conditioned reinforcement

FK-19: Unconditioned punishment

FK-20: Conditioned punishment

FK-21: Schedules of reinforcement and punishment

FK-23: Automatic reinforcement and punishment

Notes:

D-19 USE COMBINATIONS OF REINFORCEMENT WITH PUNISHMENT AND EXTINCTION.

Write another example:

Definition:
A guideline for using extinction effectively is the simultaneous use of reinforcement procedures. Extinction used alone may result in a temporary increase in the target behavior known as extinction burst (Cooper, Heron, & Heward, 2007). Teaching an alternative behavior may decrease the extinction burst effects and other possible side effects such as aggressive behavior (Lerman, Iwata, & Wallace, 1999). Similarly, several studies have found that differential reinforcement procedures are most effective when used in conjunction with extinction (e.g., Fisher, Piazza, Cataldo, Harrell, Jefferson, & Conner, 1993; Hagopian, Fisher, Sullivan, Acquisto, & LeBlanc, 1998; Piazza, Patel, Gulotta, Sevin, & Layer, 2002). Using extinction with differential reinforcement ensures that concurrent access to reinforcement for inappropriate behavior is not favored, thereby increasing the likelihood of allocation to the alternative behavior targeted for increase.

Likewise, punishment procedures are most effective when used in conjunction with reinforcement-based procedures (Millenson, 1967). The main rationale for use of reinforcement with punishment procedures is that punishment is considered an intrusive treatment procedure. In addition, punishment procedures do not teach the individual any appropriate skills. Teaching appropriate skills helps to solve these problems. Reinforcing an alternative behavior makes it more likely that punishment procedures can then be faded out as the appropriate behavior replaces the inappropriate behavior. A study conducted by Holz, Azrin and Ayllon (1963) even found that punishment was ineffective without the use of reinforcement contingencies. Several studies have illustrated the benefits of using reinforcement in conjunction with punishment procedures (e.g., Fisher et al., 1993; Hagopian et al., 1998; Thompson, Iwata, Conners, & Roscoe, 1999).

Example:
George created a new reinforcement program for one of his students, but it was not helping to decrease the behavior. George decided to implement a response cost procedure in conjunction with the reinforcement to strengthen the current reinforcer. His student could earn up to 10 minutes on the IPad at the end of the day for engaging in appropriate classroom behavior. For every target interfering behavior such as verbal protest or noncompliance, a minute was taken off of that reinforcement break duration. This helped to increase appropriate behavior and decrease inappropriate classroom behavior at school.

D-21 USE DIFFERENTIAL REINFORCEMENT (E.G., DRO, DRA, DRI, DRL, DRH).

Definition (Differential reinforcement):

(Cooper, Heron, & Heward, 2007).
☐ Flashcard created   ☐ Learned to fluency

Definition
(Differential reinforcement of other behavior/ DRO):

(Cooper, Heron, & Heward, 2007).
☐ Flashcard created   ☐ Learned to fluency

Definition
(Differential reinforcement of alternative behavior/ DRA):

(Cooper, Heron, & Heward, 2007).
☐ Flashcard created   ☐ Learned to fluency

Definition
(Differential reinforcement of incompatible behavior/ DRI):

(Cooper, Heron, & Heward, 2007).
☐ Flashcard created   ☐ Learned to fluency

Definition
(Differential reinforcement of high rates of behavior/ DRH):

(Cooper, Heron, & Heward, 2007).
☐ Flashcard created   ☐ Learned to fluency

Definition
(Differential reinforcement of low rates of behavior/ DRL):

(Cooper, Heron, & Heward, 2007).
☐ Flashcard created   ☐ Learned to fluency

Examples:
- DRO: Providing a toy following the absence of inappropriate vocalizations for 5 minutes which decreases inappropriate vocalizations.

- DRA: Providing a break for handing over a break card which increases the use of the break card in the future.

- DRI: Providing social attention for having hands in their own pant pockets which subsequently decreases scratching at caregivers hands.

- DRH: A student typically only completes one math worksheet per class period. Providing a break with a preferred item contingent on finishing three math worksheets, which increases the number of worksheets completed by a student. The student only gets the preferred item when they complete three worksheets.

- DRL: Providing attention when a student says "excuse me" 2 times every 10 minutes and not providing attention if the behavior occurs more frequently within that 10 minute period which maintains low rates of the behavior

Write another example:

[blank box]

Questions to ask your supervisor:

[blank box]

Hanley, G. P., Iwata, B. A., & Thompson, R. H. (2001). Reinforcement schedule thinning following treatment with functional communication training. *Journal of Applied Behavior Analysis, 34*(1), 17-38.

Kahng, S. W., Abt, K. A., & Schonbachler, H. E. (2001). Assessment and treatment of low-rate high-intensity problem behavior. *Journal of Applied Behavior Analysis, 34*(2), 225.

Lalli, J. S., Casey, S., & Kates, K. (1995). Reducing escape behavior and increasing task completion with functional communication training, extinction and response chaining. *Journal of Applied Behavior Analysis, 28*(3), 261-268.

Lindberg, J. S., Iwata, B. A., Kahng, S., & DeLeon, I. G. (1998). DRO contingencies: an analysis of variable-momentary schedules. *Journal of applied behavior analysis, 32*(2), 123-35.

Mazaleski, J. L. (1993). Analysis of the Reinforcement and Extinction Components in DRO Contingencies with Self-Injury. *Journal of Applied Behavior Analysis, 26*(2), 143-56.

Petscher, E. S., Rey, C., & Bailey, J. S. (2009). A review of empirical support for differential reinforcement of alternative behavior. *Research in Developmental Disabilities, 30*(3), 409-425.

Rehfeldt, R. A., & Chambers, M. R. (2003). Functional analysis and treatment of verbal perseverations displayed by an adult with autism. *Journal of Applied Behavior Analysis, 36*(2), 259-261.

Seys, D. M., & Duker, P. C. (1978). Improving residential care for the retarded by differential reinforcement of high rates of ward-staff behaviour. *Behavioural Analysis and Modification, 2*, 203-210.

Vollmer, T. R., & Iwata, B. A. (1992). Differential reinforcement as treatment for behavior disorders: Procedural and functional variations. *Research in Developmental Disabilities, 13*(4), 393-417.

Vollmer, T. R., Roane, H. S., Ringdahl, J. E., & Marcus, B. A. (1999). Evaluating treatment challenges with differential reinforcement of alternative behavior. *Journal of Applied Behavior Analysis, 32*(1), 9-23.

Relevant Literature:

Cooper, J. O., Heron, T. E., & Heward, W. L. (2007). *Applied behavior analysis (2nd ed.). Upper Saddle River, NJ: Pearson.*

Cowdery, G. E. (1990). Effects and Side Effects of DRO as Treatment for Self-Injurious Behavior. *Journal of Applied Behavior Analysis, 23*(4), 497-506.

Deitz, S. M. (1977). An analysis of programming DRL schedules in educational settings. *Behaviour Research and Therapy, 15*(1), 103-111.

Deitz, D. E., & Repp, A. C. (1983). Reducing Behavior through Reinforcement. *Exceptional Education Quarterly, 3*(4), 34-46.

Related Lessons:

C-01 State and plan for the possible unwanted effects of reinforcement.

D-02 Use appropriate parameters and schedules of reinforcement.

D-19 Use combinations of reinforcement with punishment and extinction.

F-07 Use functional communication training.

I-07 Design and conduct preference assessments to identify putative reinforcers.

J-02 Identify potential interventions based on assessment results and the best available scientific evidence.

Notes:

FK-17 UNCONDITIONED REINFORCEMENT.

Definition (Unconditioned reinforcer):

[ ]

(Cooper, Heron, & Heward, 2007).

☐ Flashcard created   ☐ Learned to fluency

Example:

- Food, water, oxygen, warmth, and sexual stimulation are some examples of unconditioned reinforcers.

- A teacher gives a child a pretzel after the child does a task. The child's engagement in the task increases in the future. This is an example of unconditioned reinforcement.

Write another example:

[ ]

Questions to ask your supervisor:

[ ]

Bijou, S.W., & Baer, D.M. (1965). *Child Development: Vol. 2. Universal Stage of infancy*. New York, NY. Appleton-Century-Crofts.

Cooper, J.O., Heron, T.E. & Heward W.L. (2007). *Applied Behavior Analysis* (2nd Ed.), Upper Saddle River, NJ. Pearson Prentice Hall. 38-40, 269-270, 295.

Gerwirtz, J. & Pelaez-Nogueras, M. (2000). Infant emotions under the positive-reinforcer control of caregiver attention and touch. In J.C. Leslie & D. Blackman (Eds.), *Issues in experimental and applied analyses of human behavior*. Reno, NV. Context Press. 271-291.

Malott, R.W., Tillema, M., & Glenn, S. (1978). *Behavior Analysis and Behavior Modification: An introduction*. Kalamazoo, MI. Behaviordelia. 9.

Pelaez-Nogueras, M., Gerwirtz, J.L., Field, T., Cigales, M., Malphurs, J., Clasky, S., & Sanchez, A. (1996). Infants' preference for touch simulation in face-to-face interactions. *Journal of Applied Developmental Psychology*, 17, 199-213.

Skinner, B.F. (1953). *Science and Human Behavior*. New York, NY. McMillan.

Related Lessons:

C-01: State and plan for unwanted effects of reinforcement.

D-01: Use positive and negative reinforcement.

D-02: Use appropriate parameters and schedules of reinforcement.

D-19: Use combinations of reinforcement with punishment and extinction.

FK-02: Selectionism (phylogenic, ontogenic, cultural)

FK-13: Reflexive relations (US-UR)

FK-16: Respondent-operant interactions

FK-19: Unconditioned punishment

FK-21: Schedules of reinforcement and punishment.

FK-26: Unconditioned motivating operations.

FK-30: Distinguish between motivating operations and reinforcement effects

Notes:

FK 18 CONDITIONED REINFORCEMENT.

Definition (Conditioned reinforcer):

[blank box]

(Cooper, Heron, & Heward, 2007).

☐ Flashcard created   ☐ Learned to fluency

Example:
- Money, tokens, stickers.

- A teacher says "good job" after a student returns their homework. The student continues to return their homework in the future. This is an example of conditioned reinforcement.

Write another example:

[blank box]

Questions to ask your supervisor:

[blank box]

Relevant Literature:

Alessi, G. (1992) Models of proximate and ultimate causation in psychology. *American Psychologist*, 48, 1359-1370.

Cooper, J.O., Heron, T.E. & Heward W.L. (2007). *Applied Behavior Analysis* (2nd Ed.), Upper Saddle River, NJ. Pearson Prentice Hall. 40-41, 269-270, 295.

Higgins, J.W., Williams, R.L., & McLaughlin, T.F. (2001). The effects of a token economy employing instructional consequences for a third grade student with learning disabilities: A data-based case study. *Education and Treatment of Children*, 24, 1, 99-106.

Michael, J. (2004) *Concepts and principles of behavior analysis* (rev. ed.). Kalamazoo, MI. Society for the Advancement of Behavior Analysis. 66.

Morse, W.H., & Kelleher, R.T. (1977). Determinants of reinforcement and punishment. In W.K. Honig & J.E.R. Staddon (Eds.), *Handbook of Operant Behavior*, Upper Saddle River, NJ. Prentice Hall. 176-177, 180.

Related Lessons:

C-01: State and plan for the unwanted effects of reinforcement.

D-01: Use positive and negative reinforcement.

D-02: Use appropriate parameters and schedules of reinforcement.

D-20: Use response-independent (time based) schedules of reinforcement (i.e., noncontingent reinforcement).

D-21: Use differential reinforcement (e.g., DRO, DRA, DRI, DRL, DRH)

F-02: Use token economies and other conditioned reinforcement systems

J-04: Select intervention strategies based on the client's preferences.

K-04: Design and use effective performance monitoring and reinforcement systems.

FK-02: Selectionism (phylogenic, ontogenic, cultural)

FK-14: Respondent conditioning (CS-CR)

FK-15: Operant conditioning

FK-16: Respondent-operant interactions.

FK-17: Unconditioned reinforcement

FK-21: Schedules of reinforcement and punishment

FK-26: Unconditioned motivating operations

FK-27: Conditioned motivating operations

FK-21 SCHEDULES OF REINFORCEMENT AND PUNISHMENT.

Questions to ask your supervisor:

Definition
(Schedules of reinforcement and punishment):

(Cooper, Heron, & Heward, 2007).
☐ Flashcard created   ☐ Learned to fluency

Examples:

Intermittent: A student may have to complete 5 correct math problems on a computer game before progressing to the next level (this is a FR-5 schedule of reinforcement).

Variable Ratio: A young girl may be called on when she raises her hand quietly in class on average once every 5 times. Sometimes, the teacher calls on her every 4 times she raises her hand. Other times the teacher calls on her every 6 times she raises her hand. The teacher provides attention on average every 5 times (this is a VR-5 schedule of reinforcement).

Fixed Interval: An alarm clock is set for 7:00 am every morning. If an individual presses snooze, it will allow the individual to sleep in again for 10 minutes. The individual cannot press snooze before the alarm rings (this is a FI-10 minute schedule of reinforcement).

Variable Interval: A person goes to a fast food restaurant. Sometimes he has to stand in line, while other times, he may order immediately upon entering. This interval varies each time he goes to the restaurant.

Write another example:

Relevant Literature:
Cooper, J. O., Heron, T. E., & Heward, W. L. (2007). Measuring behavior. *Applied Behavior Analysis*, Upper Saddle River, NJ: Pearson Prentice Hall.

Related Lessons:
D-02 Use appropriate parameters and schedules of reinforcement
D-17 Use appropriate parameters and schedules of punishment

Notes:

FK-23   AUTOMATIC   REINFORCEMENT AND PUNISHMENT.

Definition (Automatic reinforcement):

(Cooper, Heron, & Heward, 2007).
☐ Flashcard created   ☐ Learned to fluency

Definition (Automatic punishment):

(Cooper, Heron, & Heward, 2007).
☐ Flashcard created   ☐ Learned to fluency

Questions to ask your supervisor:

Example:

Automatic Reinforcement: Scratching an insect bite removes an itch; eating food when hungry removes hunger, humming may be auditory reinforcement; nonfunctional movements such as hand flapping may produce a sensation, which is automatically reinforcing; some self-injurious behavior may produce a sensation, which the individual may enjoy.

Automatic punishment: Albert bites his canker sore, causing a shocking pain. Albert is becomes cautious as he eats with his canker sore until the canker disappears. A dog gets a thorn in his paw. He experiences pain when he steps down on his foot. He begins to walk on three legs.

Relevant Literature:

Cooper, J. O., Heron, T. E., & Heward, W. L. (2007). *Applied Behavior Analysis* (2nd Ed.). Upper Saddle River, NJ. Pearson Prentice Hall.

Vollmer, T. R. (1994). The concept of automatic reinforcement: Implications for behavioral research in developmental disabilities. *Research in Developmental Disabilities, 15*(3), 187-207.

Related Lessons:

FK-17 unconditioned reinforcement
FK-19 unconditioned punishment
FK-22 extinction

Notes:

Write another example:

Segment 4 – Scorecard
Reinforcement II

☐ Presentation (2-5 minutes)

E 4
☐ Assessment
☐ SAFMED learned to fluency
☐ Workbook boxes completed

K 4
☐ Assessment
☐ SAFMED learned to fluency
☐ Workbook boxes completed

E 5
☐ Assessment
☐ SAFMED learned to fluency
☐ Workbook boxes completed

D 2
☐ Assessment
☐ SAFMED learned to fluency
☐ Workbook boxes completed

C 1
☐ Assessment
☐ SAFMED learned to fluency
☐ Workbook boxes completed

D 20
☐ Assessment
☐ SAFMED learned to fluency
☐ Workbook boxes completed

Segment 4 – Individual Supervision Agenda

Supervisor: _____ **Supervisee:** _____

Meeting Date: _____ **Time of meeting – From:**_____ **To:**_____

This document covers supervisory period from ____/____/____ to ____/____/____

1. Pass-in/Review Homework:

    Did the Supervisee satisfactorily complete this homework assignment?   Yes / No

- If not, what is needed to complete assignment? Describe below.

2. Task List items addressed (E 04-05; C 1; K 4; D 2, 20)

3. Definitions/SAFMEDs learned

    ☐ Flashcard(s) created   Was supervisee fluent with definitions? Yes ☐ No ☐

4. Discussion topics or activities completed during this meeting:

Evaluation of Supervisee's Performance (Record: S- "Satisfactory"; NI- "Needs Improvement"; U- "Unsatisfactory"; or NA- "Not Applicable")			
Arrived on time for meeting		Gave examples as needed	
Completed Homework Assigned		Accepted supervisory feedback appropriately	
Referred to literature/readings		Answered all questions thoroughly	
Maintained professional communication during supervision meeting			
Overall evaluation of supervisee performance during this meeting *(Circle one—use code above)*		S NI U	
If "NI" or "U", please list corrective steps needed to achieve a score of "S"			

5. Homework assigned for next meeting

6. Closing questions/feedback

Segment 4 – Group Supervision Meeting Agenda

- <u>Meeting Topic</u>: Reinforcement II

- <u>Task List Items Reviewed</u>:

o E-04: Use contingency contracting (i.e., behavioral contracts).
o C-01: State and plan for the possible unwanted effects of reinforcement.
o E-05: Use independent, interdependent, and dependent group contingencies.

o K-04: Design and use effective performance monitoring and reinforcement systems.
o D-02: Use appropriate parameters and schedules of reinforcement.
o D-20: Use response independent (time-based) schedules of reinforcement (i.e., noncontingent reinforcement).

1. Housekeeping
    - Upon entry to meeting have supervisees hand in the previous week's homework assignment and discuss several "Housekeeping Items" related to supervision.
    - Take attendance for the meeting.
    - State the duration of today's meeting (90 minutes).
    - Distribute BACB® experience forms to supervisees.

2. Task List Lesson and Discussion
    - Discuss task list item E-04: Use contingency contracting (i.e., behavioral contrast).
    - Discuss task list item C-01: State and plan for the possible unwanted effects of reinforcement.
    - Discuss task list item E-05: Use independent, interdependent, and dependent group contingencies.
    - Discuss task list item K-04: Design and use effective performance monitoring and reinforcement systems.
    - Discuss task list item D-02: Use appropriate parameters and schedules of reinforcement.
    - Discuss task list item D-20: Use response independent (time based) schedules of reinforcement (i.e., noncontingent reinforcement).

3. Homework Review
    - Review homework that was assigned at the previous supervision meeting.

4. Questions
    - Answer any questions related to the homework or topics discussed.

5. Closing Notes
    - *Assign Homework (task list boxes, presentation) from today's segment, due at next group meeting*
    - Close the meeting by inviting supervisees to request topics to be covered in upcoming meetings.

E-04 USE CONTINGENCY CONTRACTING.

Definition:

"A contingency contract, also called a behavioral contract, is a document that specifies a contingent relationship between the completion of a specified behavior and access to, or delivery of, a specified reward such as free time, a letter grade or access to a preferred activity" (Cooper, Heron & Heward, 2007).

Contingency contracts have several components:

- Outlines the task to be completed- includes an objective definition of the task, who must complete the task and when the task must be completed.
- Specifies the reward contingent on task completion- includes are description of the reward, who will deliver the reward, who will measure whether the task has been completed to criterion and when the reward will be received.
- Outlines how performance will be measured and what data will be taken.

Contingency contracts can be highly effective if used properly because the individual whose behavior is to be changed is involved in the process from the start. Studies have shown that contingency contracting "can be an important step toward self-management of behavior" (Miller & Kelley, 1994) because by helping to determine the parameters of the task and outlining what and when rewards should be given, reinforcer assessments have already been identified and the individual is already motivated to engage in the target behavior, which can greatly increase compliance. However, Cooper, Heron and Heward (2007) caution against using contingency contracts with all populations. There must be set criteria that the individual must already possess in order for contingency contracts to be effective. The target behavior must already be in the individual's repertoire and the individual must already be able to discriminate when and which environments are appropriate for the response to occur. Additionally, the individual's behavior must be able to "come under the control of the visual or oral statements of the contract" (Cooper, Heron, & Heward, 2007). The individual does not need to be proficient in reading so long as the contract is adapted using symbols, icons, photographs, etc. and the individual thoroughly understands the reinforcement contingency.

Example:

- Rich asked his mom for a new video game at the store. She told him if he did his homework every night without a fight for a month, that she would buy him the game. They went home and wrote up rules for this agreement and signed it together.

Notes:

Write another example:

Questions to ask your supervisor:

Relevant Literature:

Cooper, J. O., Heron, T. E., & Heward, W. L. (2007). *Applied behavior analysis* (2nd Ed.). Upper Saddle River, NJ: Prentice Hall.

Miller, D.L., & Kelley, M.L. (1994). The use of goal setting and contingency contracting for improving children's homework performance. *Journal of Applied Behavioral Analysis 27(10)*, 73-84.

Related Lessons:

K-02 Identify the contingencies governing the behavior of those responsible for carrying out behavior-change procedures and design the interventions accordingly
FK-42 Rule-governed behavior

E-05 USE INDEPENDENT, INTERDEPEND-
ENT, AND DEPENDENT GROUP CON-
TINGENCIES.

Definitions:

The three group contingencies as defined by Cooper,
Heron, & Heward (2007):

"An independent group contingency is an arrangement in which a contingency is presented to all members of a group, but reinforcement is delivered only to
those group members who meet the criterion outlined
in the contingency."

"An interdependent group contingency is one in which
all members of a group must meet the criterion of the
contingency (individually and as a group) before any
member earns the reward."

"Under a dependent group contingency the reward for
the whole group is dependent on the performance of
an individual student or small group."

These three contingencies use the principles of reinforcement to change the behavior of a group of individuals. They involve "a common consequence (usually, but not necessarily, a reward intended to function
as reinforcement) contingent on the behavior of one
member of the group, the behavior of part of the
group, or the behavior of everyone in the group."
(Cooper et al. 2007)

Example:
- Independent Group Contingency
Each student was given a math worksheet and received
a special sticker if they completed the work without engaging in disruptive behavior. Billy, Johnny, and Sam
finished their work quietly and earned stickers, but
Danny was disruptive and only finished half his worksheet so he did not earn a sticker.

- Interdependent Group Contingency
Each student in Mrs. Kelly's class had to complete their
math worksheets before they were allowed to go outside for recess. The students who finished first were allowed to help any of the struggling students. Sam was
the last one working and Roger came over to help him
complete his work. Once Sam was finished the whole
class earned recess time.

- Dependent Group Contingency
At the end of football practice, Mr. Bill told the team
that they could stop running wind sprints if Roger
caught a long pass from the coach. Roger caught that
pass and the team cheered as they went to shower and
practice ended.

Write another example:

Questions to ask your supervisor:

Relevant Literature:

Cooper, J.O., Heron, T.E. & Heward W.L. (2007). *Applied Behavior Analysis* (2nd Ed.), Upper Saddle River, NJ. Pearson Prentice Hall. 567-573.

Kamps, D., Howard, W., Heitzman-Powell, L., Laylin, J.,
Szoke, C., Petrillo, T., & Culey, A. (2011). Class-Wide
Function-Related Intervention Teams: Effects of
Group Contingency Programs in Urban Classrooms.
Journal of Positive Behavior Interventions, 13, 154-167.

Litow, L. & Pumroy, D. K. (1975). A brief review of classroom group-oriented contingencies. *Journal of Applied
Behavior Analysis*, 8(3), 341-347.

Nevin, A., Johnson, D., & Johnson, R. (1982). Effects
of group and individual contingencies on academic
performance and social relations of special needs students. *Journal of School Psychology*. 116, 1, 41-59.

Theodore, L.., Bray, M., Kehle, T., & Jenson, W. (2001). Randomization of Group Contingencies and Reinforcers
to Reduce Classroom Disruptive Behavior. *Journal of
School Psychology*. 39, 3, 267-277.

Related Lessons:

C-01: State and plan for the unwanted effects of reinforce-
ment.
D-01: Use positive and negative reinforcement.
D-02: Use appropriate parameters and schedules of reinforce-
ment.
D-19: Use combinations of reinforcement with punishment
and extinction.
D-21: Use differential reinforcement (e.g., DRO, DRA, DRI,
DRL, DRH)
E-04: Use contingency contracting
F-02: Use token economies and other conditioned reinforce-
ment systems

Notes:

C – 01 STATE AND PLAN FOR THE POSSIBLE UN-
WANTED EFFECTS OF REINFORCEMENT.

Definition (Positive Reinforcement):

(Cooper, Heron, Heward, 2007).
☐ Flashcard created   ☐ Learned to fluency

Reinforcement has been long been defined as a crucial element to behavioral change. However, there are considerations that behavioral analysts should explore before implementing reinforcement strategies.

Considerations for the use of positive reinforcement:
- May suppress the desired response
- May not be feasible for an individual that has little or no learning history with that reinforcement contingency.
- Increases the frequency of the target behavior, thereby reducing the frequency in other responses that may also be desirable
- May evoke aggression in others, especially in conditions which there are limited quantities of the reinforcer.
- May also evoke aggression when group contingencies are used.
- Removal of positive reinforcer has been correlated with lower than baseline levels of responding (Balsam & Bondy, 1983).

Definition (Negative Reinforcement):

(Cooper, Heron, Heward, 2007).
☐ Flashcard created   ☐ Learned to fluency

Considerations for the use of negative reinforcement:
- Can result in more challenging behavior due to the continuation of aversive stimulation if target behavior is not displayed
- Research shows that even for escape-maintained behavior, positive reinforcement contingencies may compete with negative reinforcement contingencies, therefore, decreasing escape-maintained behavior (Lerman, Volkert & Trosclair, 2007).
- Negative reinforcement contingencies may reinforce minimal requirements needed to avoid/escape aversive stimulus; does not focus on quality of target response (Balsam & Bondy, 1983).
- Requires continuous aversive stimulation and aversive stimulation often elicits aggressive responses.

These unwanted effects of reinforcement can be curbed taking baseline levels of the target behavior before setting criteria for reinforcement, implementing preference assessments routinely, ensuring reinforcement schedule and reinforcers chosen are as natural to the individual's environment as possible to promote generalization, systematic thinning of the reinforcement schedule, and having concurrent schedules of reinforcement for positive and negative reinforcement when negative reinforcement is utilized.

Example:
- The availability of the reinforcer elicits behavior that may compete with the target response (Balsam & Bondy, 1983).

- An individual that is being taught to swallow solid food may not progress with a program solely using positive reinforcement due to low baseline levels of swallowing solid foods (Riordan, Iwata, Wohl & Finney, 1984).
- While teaching a student to raise their hand and wait until they are called on in class, the student no longer garners others' attention by calling their name (Balsam & Bondy, 1983).
- Aggression may be directed at individuals that are also competing for same reinforce
- performing teammates
- Removal of positive reinforcer has been correlated with lower than baseline levels of responding (Balsam & Bondy, 1983).
- A child that engages in aggression to escape tasks may be more likely complete tasks without aggression if access to an iPad was given contingent on work completion. This may be more effective than reducing aggression by providing breaks contingent on appropriate asking.

Write another example:

Questions to ask your supervisor:

Relevant Literature:

Balsam, P.D., & Bondy, A.S. (1983). The negative side effects of reward. *Journal of Applied Behavioral Analysis, 16(3),* 283-296.

Cooper, J. O., Heron, T. E., & Heward, W. L. (2007). *Applied behavior analysis* (2nd ed.). Upper Saddle River, NJ: Prentice Hall.

Flora, S.R. (2004). *The power of reinforcement.* Albany: State University of New York Press.

Lerman, D.C., Volkert, V.M., & Trosclair, N. (2007). Further examination of factors that influence preference for positive versus negative reinforcement. *Journal of Applied Behavioral Analysis, 40(1),* 25-44.

Riordan M.M., Iwata B.A., Wohl M.K., Finney J.W. (1984). Behavioral treatment of food refusal and selectivity in developmentally disabled children. *Journal of Applied Behavioral Analysis. 17(3),* 327-341.

Related Lessons:
D-01 Use positive and negative reinforcement.
D-02 Use appropriate parameters and schedules of reinforcement.
D-21 Use differential reinforcement (e.g. DRO, DRA, DRI, DRL, DRH).
E-11 Use pairing procedures to establish new conditioned reinforcers and punishers.
I-07 Design and conduct preference assessments to identify putative reinforcers.
J-04 Select intervention strategies based on client preferences.
J-05 Select intervention strategies based on client's current repertoires.
J-06 Select intervention strategies based on supporting environments.
J-07 Select intervention strategies based on environmental and resource constraints.
J-11 Program for stimulus and response generalization.

Notes:

K-04 DESIGN AND USE EFFECTIVE PERFORMANCE MONITORING AND REINFORCEMENT SYSTEMS.

Rationale
Staff performance in the application of behavioral strategies is critical to the success of the behavior intervention plan. Developing a system to monitor staff performance and motivate staff performance is just as important as developing an effective intervention plan.

Staff performance models
Richman, Riordan, Reiss, Pyles, and Bailey (1988) found that self-monitoring and supervision feedback increased staff performance.

Arco (2008) found that defining the process before training, providing on-the job supervisory feedback, and having staff provide self-generated outcome feedback before and after training was effective at increasing and maintaining the performance in behavioral treatment programs.

Codding, Feinberg, Dunn, and Pace (2004) found that treatment integrity increased following a one hour performance feedback session every other week. Social validity ratings provided favorable feedback for the frequent supervisions.

Iwata, Bailey, Brown, Foshee, and Alpern (1976) found that performance-based lottery improved the performance of institutional staff.

Questions to ask your supervisor:

Relevant Literature:
Arco, L. (2008). Feedback for improving staff training and performance in behavioral treatment programs. *Behavioral Interventions, 23*(1), 39-64.

Codding, R. S., Feinberg, A. B., Dunn, E. K., & Pace, G. M. (2005). Effects of immediate performance feedback on implementation of behavior support plans. *Journal of Applied Behavior Analysis, 38*(2), 205-219.

Iwata, B. A., Bailey, J. S., Brown, K. M., Foshee, T. J., & Alpern, M. (1976). A performance-based lottery to improve residential care and training by institutional staff. *Journal of Applied Behavior Analysis, 9*(4), 417-431.

Elements of providing effective performance based monitoring and reinforcement systems
- Provide clear instructions and objectives in observable measurable terms
- Develop treatment integrity checklist
- Train the supervisor to provide supervision and frequent on the job feedback (both corrective and positive)
- Train staff to collect a self-monitoring system for their performance
- Train the supervisor to provide social or tangible reinforcement based on performance of the staff
- Teach the supervisor to graph and monitor staff performance while looking for trend lines

Write another example:

Richman, G. S., Riordan, M. R., Reiss, M. L., Pyles, D. A., & Bailey, J. S. (1988). The effects of self-monitoring and supervisor feedback on staff performance in a residential setting. *Journal of Applied Behavior Analysis, 21*(4), 401-409.

Related Lessons:
D-01 Use positive reinforcement
F-01 Use self-management strategies
F-02 Use token economies and other conditioned reinforcement systems
F-03 Use direct instruction
H-03 Select a schedule of observation and recording periods
H-04 Select a data display that effectively communicates relevant qualitative relations
H-04 Evaluate changes in level, trend and variability
I-01 Define behavior in observable measurable terms
K-03 Design and use competency-based training for persons who are responsible for carrying out behavioral assessment and behavior-change procedures
K-05 Design and use systems for monitoring procedural integrity

Notes:

D-02 USE APPROPRIATE PARAMETERS AND SCHEDULES OF REINFORCEMENT.

Definition (Schedule of reinforcement):

(Cooper, Heron, & Heward, 2007).   ☐ Flashcard created   ☐ Learned to fluency

While there are several variations of schedules of reinforcement, the two most basic concepts involve continuous schedules of reinforcement (CRF) and intermittent schedules of reinforcement (INT). A CRF is useful when teaching a new response because reinforcement is provided for each occurrence of the target behavior, therefore strengthening the desired response. Conversely, an INT is in place when selected occurrences of the behavior are reinforced. INT are necessary for thinning schedules of reinforcement and transitioning to naturally occurring reinforcement contingencies.

INT may be defined as having a fixed ratio schedule, variable ratio schedule, fixed interval schedule, or variable interval schedule. When learning basic schedules of reinforcement, it is not only important to understand how the schedules are defined, but also understand the effects of each type of INT. Ferster and Skinner (1957) and Cooper et al. (2007) thoroughly discuss these concepts and it is strongly encouraged that supervisors and supervisees read this material.

Examples:

	Fixed Ratio (FR)	Variable Ratio (VR)	Fixed Interval (FI)	Variable Interval (VI)
Definition	A fixed number of target responses must be completed to produce a reinforcer.	A variable number of target responses must be completed to produce a reinforcer.	Reinforcement is provided for the first target response following a fixed duration of time.	Reinforcement is provided for the first target response following the end of variable durations of time.
Example	FR 7 means that every seventh target response produces a reinforcer.	VR 15 means that on average, every fifteenth target response produces a reinforcer.	FI 5 means that first target response following the end of a five minute period produces a reinforcer.	VI 12 means that the first target response following the end of an average duration of 12 minutes produces a reinforcer.
Schedule Effects	Produces a typical pattern of responding and high rates of responses. Post reinforcement pause occurs.	Produces a consistent, steady response rate, usually without a post reinforcement pause.	Produces a post reinforcement pause during the initial part of the interval. Rate of responding accelerates toward the end of the interval but overall, slow to moderate rates of responding are observed.	Produces a constant, stable, yet low to moderate response rate.

Write another example:

Questions to ask your supervisor:

Relevant Literature:

Cooper, J. O., Heron, T. E., & Heward, W. L. (2007). Schedules of reinforcement. *Applied Behavior Analysis* (pp. 304-323). Upper Saddle River, NJ: Pearson Prentice Hall.

Ferster, C. B., & Skinner, B. F. (1957). *Schedules of reinforcement.* New York, NY : Appleton-Century-Crofts.

Related Lessons:

D-19 Use combinations of reinforcement with punishment and extinction
D-20 Use response-independent (time-based) schedules of reinforcement (i.e., non-contingent reinforcement)
D-21 Use differential reinforcement (e.g., DRO, DRA, DRI, DRL, DRH)
FK-21 Schedules of reinforcement and punishment
FK-40 Matching law
FK-41 Contingency maintained behavior

Notes:

D-20 USE RESPONSE INDEPENDENT (TIME-BASED) SCHEDULES OF REINFORCEMENT (I.E., NONCONTINGENT REINFORCEMENT).

Definition:
"Noncontingent reinforcement (NCR) is the presentation of a potential reinforcer on a fixed-time (FT) or variable time (VT) schedule independent of the occurrence of the target behavior. The response-independent presentation of the potential reinforcer eliminates the contingent relation between the target behavior and the stimulus presentation while allowing any effects of the stimulus presentation alone to be detected." (Cooper, Heron & Heward, 2007).

Noncontingent reinforcement is sometimes used in applied research in an experimental design called the NCR reversal technique. This design involves a baseline phase, an NCR phase where a potential reinforcer is delivered on a fixed or variable time schedule independent of the target behavior, and then a phase where the reinforcer is delivered contingent on a set behavioral criteria. These phases are then repeated as necessary to indicate experimental control over the dependent variable. The NCR and baseline conditions function as a comparative measure to validate the independent variable in these studies.

In certain instances, differential reinforcement procedures may limit access to reinforcement if appropriate behavior occurs at low rates. One benefit of an NCR is that it gives consistent access to reinforcement.

Examples:
A DRO program was trialed for 3 weeks to decrease Jimmy's verbal protesting during group activities. Based on data collected, the DRO program was deemed ineffective for decreasing Jimmy's verbal protesting. Mr. Jones took data and found that Jimmy could quietly engage in group activities for 3 minutes before starting to protest. Mr. Jones decided to implement a 2 minute NCR program in which he would give Jimmy a sticker every 2 minutes regardless of the presence of interfering behaviors.

Non- Example:
Mr. Jack was concerned with Barry's aggressive behavior during group activities. He decided to give him a sticker for every 2 minutes that he did not engage in aggressive behavior.

Write another example:

Relevant Literature:
Cautela, J. R. (1984). General level of reinforcement. *Journal of Behavior Therapy and Experimental Psychiatry*, 15, 109-114.
Cooper, J.O., Heron, T.E. & Heward W.L. (2007). *Applied Behavior Analysis* (2nd Ed.), Upper Saddle River, NJ. Pearson Prentice Hall.
Hagopian, L. P., Fisher, W. W., & Legacy, S. M. (1994). Schedule effects of noncontingent reinforcement on attention-maintained destructive behavior in identical quadruplets. *Journal of Applied Behavior Analysis*, 27, 317-325.
Ingvarsson, E.T., Kahng, S., Hausman, N.L. (2008). Some effects of noncontingent positive reinforcement on multiply controlled Problem behavior and compliance in a demand context. *Journal of Applied Behavior Analysis*. 41, 3, 435-440.
Wilder, D. A., Normand, M., & Atwell, J. (2005). Noncontingent reinforcement as treatment for food refusal and associated self-injury. *Journal of Applied Behavior Analysis*, 38, 549-553.

Related Lessons:
B-04: Use withdrawal/reversal designs.
C-01: State and plan for the unwanted effects of reinforcement.
D-02: Use appropriate parameters and schedules of reinforcement.
D-21: Use differential reinforcement (e.g., DRO, DRA, DRI, DRL, DRH)
J-02: Identify potential interventions based on assessment results and the best available scientific evidence.

Notes:

Segment 5 – Scorecard
Punishment

☐ Presentation (2-5 minutes)

FK 19
☐ Assessment
☐ SAFMED learned to fluency
☐ Workbook boxes completed

D 16
☐ Assessment
☐ SAFMED learned to fluency
☐ Workbook boxes completed

FK 20
☐ Assessment
☐ SAFMED learned to fluency
☐ Workbook boxes completed

D 17
☐ Assessment
☐ SAFMED learned to fluency
☐ Workbook boxes completed

D 15
☐ Assessment
☐ SAFMED learned to fluency
☐ Workbook boxes completed

C 2
☐ Assessment
☐ SAFMED learned to fluency
☐ Workbook boxes completed

Segment 5 – Individual Supervision Agenda

Supervisor: _____ **Supervisee:** _____

Meeting Date: _____ **Time of meeting – From:** _____ **To:** _____

This document covers supervisory period from ____/____/____ to ____/____/____

1. Pass-in/Review Homework:

    Did the Supervisee satisfactorily complete this homework assignment?   Yes / No

- If not, what is needed to complete assignment? Describe below.

2. Task List items addressed (FK 19-20; D 15-17; C 2)

3. Definitions/SAFMEDs learned

    ☐ Flashcard(s) created   Was supervisee fluent with definitions? Yes ☐ No ☐

4. Discussion topics or activities completed during this meeting:

Evaluation of Supervisee's Performance			
(Record: S- "Satisfactory"; NI- "Needs Improvement"; U- "Unsatisfactory"; or NA- "Not Applicable")			
Arrived on time for meeting		Gave examples as needed	
Completed Homework Assigned		Accepted supervisory feedback appropriately	
Referred to literature/readings		Answered all questions thoroughly	
Maintained professional communication during supervision meeting			
Overall evaluation of supervisee performance during this meeting (Circle one—use code above)		S | NI | U	
If "NI" or "U", please list corrective steps needed to achieve a score of "S"			

5. Homework assigned for next meeting

6. Closing questions/feedback

Segment 5 – Group Supervision Meeting Agenda

- <u>Meeting Topic</u>: Punishment

- <u>Task List Items Reviewed</u>:

  - FK-19: Unconditioned punishment.
  - FK-20: Conditioned punishment.
  - D-15: Use positive and negative punishment.
  - D-16: Identify and use punishers.
  - D-17: Use appropriate parameters and schedules of punishment.
  - C-02: State and plan for the possible unwanted effects of punishment.

1. Housekeeping
    - Upon entry to meeting have supervisees hand in the previous week's homework assignment and discuss several "Housekeeping Items" related to supervision.
    - Take attendance for the meeting.
    - State the duration of today's meeting (90 minutes).
    - Distribute BACB® experience forms to supervisees.
2. Task List Lesson and Discussion
    - Discuss task list item FK-19: Unconditioned punishment.
    - Discuss task list item FK-20: Conditioned punishment.
    - Discuss task list item D-15: Use positive and negative punishment.
    - Discuss task list item D-16: Identify and use punishers
    - Discuss task list item D-17: Use appropriate parameters and schedules of punishment.
    - Discuss task list item C-02: State and plan for the possible unwanted effects of punishment.
3. Homework Review
    - Review homework that was assigned at the previous supervision meeting.
4. Questions
    - Answer any questions related to the homework or topics discussed.
5. Closing Notes
    - *Assign Homework (task list boxes, presentation) from today's segment, due at next group meeting*
    - Close the meeting by inviting supervisees to request topics to be covered in upcoming meetings.

E-11 USE PAIRING PROCEDURES TO ESTABLISH NEW CONDITIONED REINFORCERS AND PUNISHERS.

"Stimulus events or conditions that are present or that occur just before or simultaneous with the occurrence of other reinforcers (or punishers) may acquire the ability to reinforce (or punish) behavior when they later occur on their own as consequences. Called conditioned reinforcers or conditioned punishers, these stimulus changes function as reinforcers and punishers only because of their prior pairing with other reinforcers or punishers" (Cooper et al., 2007, p. 40).

Definition:

Conditioned reinforcer – "...a previously neutral stimulus change that has acquired the capability to function as a reinforcer through stimulus-stimulus pairing with one or more unconditioned or conditioned reinforcers" (Cooper et al., 2007, p. 269).

Some common conditioned reinforcers include social praise, tokens, and money because they are often paired with other reinforcers.

Conditioned reinforcers become stronger the more they are paired with other known reinforcers. For instance, paper money will likely not function as a reinforcer until he/she buy toys, candy, and other things that he enjoys with it. The more the child uses money to buy items that are appetitive, the more the paper money becomes a conditioned reinforcer.

The more items the conditioned reinforcer can "buy", the less sensitive to motivating operations they become. This is called generalized conditioned reinforcement. The more reinforcers that have been paired with the stimulus, the more generalized the conditioned reinforcer is.

Examples:

- Common conditioned reinforcers include social praise, tokens, and money because they are often paired with other reinforcers.

Write another example:

Questions to ask your supervisor:

Relevant Literature:

Cooper, J.O., Heron, T.E. & Heward W.L. (2007). *Applied Behavior Analysis* (2nd Ed.), Upper Saddle River, NJ. Pearson Prentice Hall. 40-41, 269-270.

Williams, B.A. & Fantino, E. (1978). Effects on choice of reinforcement delay and conditioned reinforcement. *Journal of Experimental Analysis of Behavior*, 29, 1, 77-86.

Engelmann, S. (1975). *Your child can succeed.* New York, NY: Simon and Schuster. (pp. 98-100).

Morse, W.H. & Kelleher, R.T. (1977). Determinants of reinforcement and punishment. In W.K. Honig & J.E.R. Staddon (Eds.), *Handbook of operant behavior* (pp. 174-200). Upper Saddle River, NJ: Prentice Hall.

Related Lessons:

C-01: State and plan for the possible unwanted effects of reinforcement.
D-01: Use positive and negative reinforcement.
D-02: Use appropriate parameters and schedules of reinforcement.
E-02: Use discrimination training procedures.
F-02: Use token economies and other conditioned reinforcement systems.
I-07: Design and conduct preference assessments to identify putative reinforcers.
J-04: Select intervention strategies based on client preferences.
J-11: Program for stimulus and response generalization.
FK-14: Respondent conditioning (CS-CR)
FK-16: Respondent-operant interactions
FK-18: Conditioned reinforcement
FK-21: Schedules of reinforcement and punishment
FK-27: Conditioned motivating operations
FK-34: Conditional discriminations

Notes:

FK-19 UNCONDITIONED PUNISHMENT.

Definition (Unconditioned punisher):

Relevant Literature:
Cooper, J. O., Heron, T. E., & Heward, W. L. (2007). *Applied Behavior Analysis* (2nd Ed.).Pearson Prentice Hall.
Herman, R. L., & Azrin, N. H. (1964). Punishment by noise in an alternative response situation. *Journal of the Experimental Analysis of Behavior, 7*(2), 185-188.

(Cooper, Heron, & Heward, 2007).
☐ Flashcard created   ☐ Learned to fluency

Example:
- Bright lights, loud sounds, extreme temperatures, certain tastes (sour, bitter), physical restraint, loss of bodily support, extreme muscular efforts.

Write another example:

Related Lessons:
D-17 Use appropriate parameters and schedules of punishment
D-16 Use positive and negative Punishment
D-19 Use combinations of reinforcement with punishment and extinction
E-11 Use pairing procedures to establish new conditioned reinforcers and punishers
G-07 Practice within one's limits of professional competence in applied behavior analysis, and obtain consultation, supervision, and training, or make referrals as necessary
J-10 When a behavior is to be decreased, select an acceptable alternative behavior to be established or increased
FK 20 Conditioned punishment

Notes:

Questions to ask your supervisor:

FK-20 CONDITIONED PUNISHMENT.

Definition (Conditioned punisher):

(Cooper, Heron, & Heward, 2007).
☐ Flashcard created   ☐ Learned to fluency

Definition (Conditioned punishment):

(Hake & Azrin, 1965).
☐ Flashcard created   ☐ Learned to fluency

Examples:

Similar to classical conditioning, a tone (neutral stimulus) is repeatedly paired with an electric shock (unconditioned punisher) whenever a dog barks, in time the tone (conditioned punisher) suppresses the bark in the absence of the electric shock.

A child engages in aggression. A parent responds to aggression by taking away their child's favorite video game contingent on every instance of aggression. The parent begins to pair removal of the video games with a reprimand. The reprimand may function as a conditioned punisher if aggression continues to decrease following the presentation of a reprimand without taking away the video games. This process illustrates conditioned punishment.

Write another example:

Questions to ask your supervisor:

Relevant Literature:

Bailey, J., & Burch, M. (2011). *Ethics in Behavior Analysis* (2nd ed). New York, NY: Routledge.

Cooper, J. O., Heron, T. E., & Heward, W. L. (2007). Measuring behavior. *Applied Behavior Analysis* (pp. 72-101). Upper Saddle River, NJ: Pearson Prentice Hall.

Hake, D. F., & Azrin, N. H. (1965). Conditioned punishment. *Journal of the Experimental Analysis of Behavior, 8,* 279-293.

Iwata, B. A. (1988). The development and adoption of controversial default technologies. *The Behavior Analyst, 11,* 149-157.

Related Lessons:

C-02 State and plan for the possible unwanted effects of punishment.

D-15 Identify punishers.

D-16 Use positive and negative punishment.

D-17 Use appropriate parameters and schedules of punishment.

D-18 Use extinction.

D-19 Use combinations of reinforcement with punishment and extinction.

FK-14 respondent conditioning (CS-CR)

FK-17 unconditioned reinforcement

FK-18 conditioned reinforcement

FK-19 unconditioned punishment

FK-21 schedules of reinforcement and punishment

Notes:

D-15 IDENTIFY PUNISHERS.

Definition:

"A stimulus change that decreases the future frequency of behavior that immediately precedes it (Cooper, Heron, & Heward, 2007)".

Punishers can be categorized as unconditioned or conditioned. Unconditioned punishers, or unlearned punishers, are stimuli whose presentation functions as punishment without previous pairing with any other punishers. Such punishers consist of stimulation such as pain, intense odors, visual stimulation, taste, sound, or extreme temperatures (Cooper, Heron, & Heward, 2007). Conditioned punishers, or learned punishers, are stimuli whose presentation has previously been paired with an unconditioned punisher or a previously conditioned punisher (Cooper, Heron, & Heward, 2007). The process of punishment is a naturally occurring phenomenon that causes behavior change. However, punishment procedures can also be an effective means for decreasing challenging behavior that is life threatening or resistant to other forms of intervention in an ethical manner. Iwata (1988) recommends that behavior analysts view the use of punishers as a default technology to be used when other interventions have failed.

Regarding the selection of a punisher to use in an intervention, it is important to note that punishers are idiosyncratic. A punisher for one person maybe a reinforcer for someone else, and perhaps a neutral stimulus to another. For this reason, a punisher assessment can assist in identifying stimuli that will likely function as punishers by measuring avoidance and escape behavior following the presentation with each stimulus (Fisher et al., 1994). Once potential punishers have been identified there are some factors to consider when choosing a stimulus to use in the treatment of challenging behavior. Research has indicated that the magnitude, or amount of the punisher, should be delivered at the optimum level at the outset of the intervention (Azrin & Holz, 1966; Thompson et al., 1999). Furthermore, in keeping with ethical considerations the selection of the least intrusive punisher(s) is recommended. Typically intrusiveness is outlined by hierarchically arranging interventions according to the degree to which the intervention limits individual freedom, intrudes into the child's life, or produces discomfort, pain, or distress (Luiselli, 2008). Pairing procedures may be beneficial in assisting with the identification of less intrusive punishers by establishing less intrusive conditioned punishers (Vorndran & Lerman, 2006). Lastly, it should be noted that Lerman and Vorndran (2002) highlighted the need for further basic and applied research on punishment due to a need for identifying strategies to enhance the effectiveness of least intrusive punishment procedures.

Example:

If a person eats yogurt and immediately gags or vomits, yogurt may become a conditioned aversive and thereby a conditioned punisher by decreasing the behavior of eating yogurt and possibly other food with a similar consistency to yogurt.

Write another example:

Questions to ask your supervisor:

Relevant Literature:

Azrin, N. H., & Holz, W. C. (1966). Punishment. *Operant behavior: Areas of research and application*, 380-447.

Behavior Analyst Certification Board (BACB) Behavior Analyst Certification Board professional and ethical compliance code for behavior analysts. 2014.   Retrieved   from http://www.bacb.com/Download-files/BACB_Compliance_Code.pdf.

Cooper, J. O., Heron, T. E., & Heward, W. L. (2007). *Applied Behavior Analysis* (2nd ed.). *Upper Saddle River, NJ: Pearson.*

Fisher, W. W., Piazza, C. C., Bowman, L. G., Kurtz, P. F., Sherer, M. R., & Lachman, S. R. (1994). A preliminary evaluation of empirically derived consequences for the treatment of pica. *Journal of Applied Behavior Analysis, 27*(3), 447-457.

Iwata, B. A. (1988). The development and adoption of controversial default technologies. *The Behavior Analyst, 11*(2), 149.

Lerman, D. C., & Vorndran, C. M. (2002). On the status of knowledge for using punishment: Implications for treating behavior disorders. *Journal of Applied Behavior Analysis, 35*(4), 431-464.

Luiselli, J. K. (Ed.). (2008). *Effective practices for children with autism: Educational and behavior support interventions that work.* Oxford University Press.

Thompson, R. H., Iwata, B. A., Conners, J., & Roscoe, E. M. (1999). Effects of reinforcement for alternative behavior during punishment of self-injury. *Journal of Applied Behavior Analysis, 32*(3), 317.

Vorndran, C. M., & Lerman, D. C. (2006). Establishing and maintaining treatment effects with less intrusive consequences via a pairing procedure. *Journal of applied behavior analysis, 39*(1), 35-48.

Related Lessons:

D-16 Use positive and negative punishment.

D-17 Use appropriate parameters and schedules of punishment.

J-02 Identify potential interventions based on assessment results and the best available scientific evidence.

J-10 When a behavior is to be decreased, select an acceptable alternative behavior to be established or increased.

FK-19 unconditioned punishment

FK-20 conditioned punishment

FK-21 schedules of reinforcement and punishment

FK-23 automatic reinforcement and punishment

Notes:

D-16 USE POSITIVE AND NEGATIVE PUNISH-MENT.

Definitions

Punishment: "Occurs when stimulus change immediately follows a response and decreases the future frequency of that type of behavior in similar conditions." (Cooper Heron, & Heward, 2007)

Positive Punishment: "A behavior is followed immediately by the presentation of a stimulus that decreases the future frequency of the behavior." (Cooper Heron, & Heward, 2007)*

Negative Punishment: "A…behavior is followed immediately by the removal of a stimulus (or a decrease in the intensity of the stimulus), that decreases the future frequency of similar responses under similar conditions." (Cooper Heron, & Heward, 2007).

Footnotes

- Alternatively Fox (1982) described positive and negative punishment as Type I punishment (contingent stimulation) and Type II punishment (contingent withdrawal of a stimulus).
- An emphasis on the ethical considerations of using punishment should be introduced when punishment is first discussed.

Example:

- Albert is learning to drive. Albert drives fast and speeds along the highway. His mother provides a firm reprimand directly following the speeding. Albert no longer speeds when his mother is in the car.

Relevant Literature:

Bailey, J., & Burch, M. (2011). *Ethics for Behavior Analysts: 2nd Expanded Edition.* Taylor & Francis.

Cooper, J. O., Heron, T. E., & Heward, W. L. (2007). *Applied behavior analysis.* (2nd Ed.) Pearson Prentice Hall.

Foxx, R. M. (1982). *Decreasing behaviors of severely retarded and autistic persons.* Champaign, IL: Research Press.

Houten, R., Axelrod, S., Bailey, J. S., Favell, J. E., Foxx, R. M., Iwata, B. A., & Lovaas, O. I. (1988). The right to effective behavioral treatment. *Journal of Applied Behavior Analysis, 21*(4), 381-384.

Related Lessons:

D-01 Use positive and negative reinforcement

D-17 Use appropriate parameters and schedules of punishment

D-19 Use combinations of reinforcement with punishment and extinction

E-11 Use pairing procedures to establish new conditioned reinforcers and punishers

G-07 Practice within one's limits of professional competence in applied behavior analysis, and obtain consultation, supervision, and training, or make referrals as necessary

J-10 When a behavior is to be decreased, select an acceptable alternative behavior to be established or increased

FK-19 Unconditioned punishment

FK 20 Conditioned punishment

Notes:

Write another example:

Questions to ask your supervisor:

D-17 USE APPROPRIATE PARAMETERS AND SCHEDULES OF PUNISHMENT.

Definitions:

Punishment: "Occurs when stimulus change immediately follows a response and decreases the future frequency of that type of behavior in similar conditions." (Cooper Heron, & Heward, 2007)*

Legislation and agency policies limit the use of punishment. Lerman and Vorndran (2002) suggested that punishment may be considered if:

- The challenging behavior produces serious physical harm and has to be suppressed quickly
- Reinforcement based treatments have not reduced the problem behavior to socially acceptable levels or
- The reinforcer maintaining the challenging behavior cannot be identified or withheld

BACB Labels specific considerations regarding punishment in the ethical guideline 4.08

4.08 Considerations Regarding Punishment Procedures.

- Behavior analysts recommend reinforcement rather than punishment whenever possible.
- If punishment procedures are necessary, behavior analysts always include reinforcement procedures for alternative behavior in the behavior-change program.
- Before implementing punishment-based procedures, behavior analysts ensure that appropriate steps have been taken to implement reinforcement-based procedures unless the severity or dangerousness of the behavior necessitates immediate use of aversive procedures.
- Behavior analysts ensure that aversive procedures are accompanied by an increased level of training, supervision, and oversight. Behavior analysts must evaluate the effectiveness of aversive procedures in a timely manner and modify the behavior-change program if it is ineffective. Behavior analysts always include a plan to discontinue the use of aversive procedures when no longer needed. (BACB, 2014, p.12-13)

Ethical Considerations Related to Punishment as outlined by Cooper, Heron, and Heward (2007)

- The right to safe and humane treatment
- Least restrictive alternative
- Right to effective treatment

Footnotes

- Positive punishment may also be described as a type of aversive control
- Negative side effects include: emotional or aggressive reactions, behavioral contrast, escape and avoidance of the punisher, modeling of inappropriate behavior and the overuse associated with negative reinforcement of the person presenting the punisher (Cooper, Heron, & Heward, 2007)

Example:

Appropriate Use of Punishment as outlined by Cooper, Heron, and Heward (2007)

1. Conduct a functional assessment
2. Attempt reinforcement based strategies (behavior as above does not reach socially acceptable levels)
3. Conduct punisher assessment
4. Ensure informed consent is given
5. Include reinforcement based strategies with punishment procedures
6. Ensure all staff are trained in the procedure and monitored closely
7. Use punishers of sufficient quality and magnitude
8. Use varied punishers
9. Deliver punisher at the beginning of a behavioral sequence
10. Punish each instance of the behavior Initially
11. Shift to intermittent schedule gradually
12. If delay in punishment use mediation
13. Supplement punishment with complementary interventions
14. Be prepared for negative side effects
15. Collect data, graph and evaluate daily
16. Discontinue procedure if a decrease in behavior is not observed

Write another example:

Questions to ask your supervisor:

Lerman, D. C., & Vorndran, C. M. (2002). On the status of knowledge for using punishment: Implications for treating behavior disorders. *Journal of Applied Behavior Analysis, 35*(4), 431-464.

Iwata, B. A. (1988). The development and adoption of controversial default technologies. *The Behavior Analyst, 11*(2), 149.

Related Lessons:
D-16 Use positive and negative punishment
D-15 Identify punishers
D-19 Use combinations of reinforcement with punishment and extinction
E-11 Use pairing procedures to establish new conditional reinforcers and punishers
G-07 Practice within one's limits of professional competence in applied behavior analysis, and obtain consultation, supervision, and training, or make referrals as necessary
J-10 When behavior is to be decreased, select an acceptable alternative behavior to be established or increased
FK-19 Unconditioned punishment
FK 20 Conditioned punishment
FK 21 Schedules of reinforcement and punishment
FK 38 Behavioral contrast

Notes:

Relevant Literature:
Bailey, J., & Burch, M. (2011). *Ethics for Behavior Analysts: 2nd Expanded Edition.* Taylor & Francis.

Cooper, J. O., Heron, T. E., & Heward, W. L. (2007). *Applied behavior analysis.* (2nd Ed.) Pearson Prentice Hall.

Foxx, R. M. (1982). *Decreasing behaviors of severely retarded and autistic persons.* Champaign, IL: Research Press.

Houten, R., Axelrod, S., Bailey, J. S., Favell, J. E., Foxx, R. M., Iwata, B. A., & Lovaas, O. I. (1988). The right to effective behavioral treatment. *Journal of Applied Behavior Analysis, 21*(4), 381-384.

C – 02 STATE AND PLAN FOR THE POSSIBLE UNWANTED EFFECTS OF PUNISHMENT.

Definition:

Punishment is one such technique that is sometimes used to change or shape behavior. While this technique can be effective, there may be unwanted or undesirable effects of this treatment option.

Punishment may also have unwanted effects with regards to an individual's future learning. It may not appropriately generalize to new situations requiring further intervention. When used as the sole intervention in a treatment package, it fails to teach an individual an alternative behavior to engage in and consequently individuals may revert back to old behaviors without a replacement strategy. These behaviors may diminish temporarily only to be subject to a "recovery of responding" (Catania, 1998) at a later period of time.

As a result, the majority of those in the field agree that "punishment be limited to those situations in which other interventions have failed (May, Risley, Twardosz, Friedman, Bijou, Wexler et al., 1975). Iwata et. Al, 1994 found that "reinforcement approaches to behavior reduction were just as effective as punishment approaches" and that if a functional analysis of the problem behavior was done, the need for the use of punishment procedures was greatly reduced.

During the supervision process, be diligent in choosing interventions, which are based on reinforcement and not solely on punishment. The function of a problem behavior should always be assessed before making decisions regarding an individual's program to ensure effective treatment. If a team has deemed that punishment is necessary as a part of a treatment package, it is important to state any potential unwanted effects of any procedure being utilized and to attempt to plan for these. These are some general guidelines to consider when planning for these effects:

- A team should always adhere to the "Fair Pair Rule" when using punishment. This states that a "practitioner should choose one or more alternatives to increase for every behavior targeted for reduction" (White and Haring, 1980).
- Be sure to plan for continuation of the procedure to different environments, staff and stimuli (any and all that apply).
- Avoid modeling any behavior which you do not want the adult or child to imitate
- The team should develop a contingency plan for managing aggression or extreme emotional responses (should they occur) and have safety measures in place to avoid accidental injury to the individual.

- The team should develop a plan to manage any escape/avoidant behaviors that may occur
- Be aware the effects of punishment can be difficult to predict. Staff may need to adjust the plan over time if the effects are not therapeutic or effective.

Example:

- For instance, those individuals who are being treated using punishment procedures may become aggressive (Azrin & Holz, 1966) or may have strong emotional reactions to such measures.
- An adult or child may become subject to negative modeling (such as imitating scolding or hitting behavior).
- Those treated through the use of punishment may seek out escape/avoidance of the punisher or the contingencies surrounding punishment.
- In extreme cases, the use of punishment can result in harm or injury to the child or adult.

Write another example:

Questions to ask your supervisor:

Relevant Literature:

Azrin, N.H., & Holz, W.C. (1966). Punishment. In W.K. Honig (Ed), *Operant Behavior: Areas of Research and Application*. New York: Appleton-Century-Crofts.

Catania, C.A. (1998). *Learning*. Upper Saddle River, NJ: Prentice-Hall, Inc.

Cooper J.O, Heron T.E, Heward W.L. (2007). *Applied behavior analysis* (2nd ed.) Upper Saddle River, NJ: Pearson.

Iwata, B. A., Dorsey, M. F., Slifer, K. J., Bauman, K. E. and Richman, G. S. (1994). Toward a Functional Analysis of Self-injury. *Journal of Applied Behavior Analysis*, 27: 197–209.

May, J. G., Risley, T. R., Twardosz, S., Friedman, P., Bijou, S., Wexler, D., et al. (1975). Guidelines for the use of behavioral procedures in state programs for the retarded. *NARC Monograph*, M. R. Research, 1.

White, O.R. & Haring, N.G. (1980). *Exceptional Teaching* (2nd ed.). Columbus, O.H.: Charles E. Merrill.

Related Lessons:

C-02 State and plan for the possible unwanted effects of punishment.

D-16 Use positive and negative punishment.

D-17 Use appropriate parameters and schedules of punishment.

D-19 Use combinations of reinforcement with punishment and extinction.

E-07 Plan for behavioral contrast effects.

FK-31 Behavioral contingencies

Notes:

Segment 6 – Scorecard
Conditioning

☐ Presentation (2-5 minutes)

E 11
☐ Assessment
☐ SAFMED learned to fluency
☐ Workbook boxes completed

FK 13
☐ Assessment
☐ SAFMED learned to fluency
☐ Workbook boxes completed

FK 14
☐ Assessment
☐ SAFMED learned to fluency
☐ Workbook boxes completed

FK 15
☐ Assessment
☐ SAFMED learned to fluency
☐ Workbook boxes completed

FK 16
☐ Assessment
☐ SAFMED learned to fluency
☐ Workbook boxes completed

FK 24
☐ Assessment
☐ SAFMED learned to fluency
☐ Workbook boxes completed

FK 35
☐ Assessment
☐ SAFMED learned to fluency
☐ Workbook boxes completed

Segment 6 – Individual Supervision Agenda

Supervisor: _____ **Supervisee:** _____

Meeting Date: _____ **Time of meeting – From:** _____ **To:** _____

This document covers supervisory period from ____/____/____ **to** ____/____/____

1. Pass-in/Review Homework:

    Did the Supervisee satisfactorily complete this homework assignment?   Yes / No

- If not, what is needed to complete assignment? Describe below.

2. Task List items addressed (E 11; FK 13-16; 24, 35)

3. Definitions/SAFMEDs learned

    ☐ Flashcard(s) created   Was supervisee fluent with definitions? Yes ☐ No ☐

4. Discussion topics or activities completed during this meeting:

Evaluation of Supervisee's Performance (Record: S- "Satisfactory"; NI- "Needs Improvement"; U- "Unsatisfactory"; or NA- "Not Applicable")			
Arrived on time for meeting		Gave examples as needed	
Completed Homework Assigned		Accepted supervisory feedback appropriately	
Referred to literature/readings		Answered all questions thoroughly	
Maintained professional communication during supervision meeting			
Overall evaluation of supervisee performance during this meeting *(Circle one—use code above)*		S NI U	
If "NI" or "U", please list corrective steps needed to achieve a score of "S"			

5. Homework assigned for next meeting

6. Closing questions/feedback

Segment 6 – Group Supervision Meeting Agenda

- <u>Meeting Topic</u>: Conditioning

- <u>Task List Items Reviewed</u>:

o E-11: Use pairing procedures to establish new conditioned reinforcers.

o FK-13: Reflexive relations (US-UR).

o FK-14: Respondent conditioning.

o FK-15: Operant conditioning.

o FK-16: Respondent-operant interactions.

o FK-24: Stimulus control.

o FK-35: Stimulus discrimination.

1. Housekeeping
    - Upon entry to meeting have supervisees hand in the previous week's homework assignment and discuss several "Housekeeping Items" related to supervision.
    - Take attendance for the meeting.
    - State the duration of today's meeting (90 minutes).
    - Distribute BACB® experience forms to supervisees.

2. Task List Lesson and Discussion
    - Discuss task list item E-11: Use pairing procedures to establish new conditioned reinforcers.
    - Discuss task list item FK-13: Reflexive relations (US-UR).
    - Discuss task list item FK-14: Respondent conditioning.
    - Discuss task list item FK-15: Operant conditioning.
    - Discuss task list item FK-16: Respondent-operant interactions.
    - Discuss task list item FK-24: Stimulus control.
    - Discuss task list item FK-35: Stimulus discrimination.

3. Homework Review
    - Review homework that was assigned at the previous supervision meeting.

4. Questions
    - Answer any questions related to the homework or topics discussed.

5. Closing Notes
    - *Assign Homework (task list boxes, presentation) from today's segment, due at next group meeting*
    - Close the meeting by inviting supervisees to request topics to be covered in upcoming meetings.

FK-13 REFLEXIVE RELATIONS (US-UR)

Definition (Reflexive relations):

[blank box]

(Cooper, Heron, & Heward, 2007).

☐ Flashcard created   ☐ Learned to fluency

Examples:
- Air blowing in eye (US) → blinking (UR)
- Cold/low temperature (US) → shivering (UR)
- Hot/high temperature (US) → sweating (UR)
- Food in mouth (US) → salivation (UR)
- Hot surface (US) → move hand away (UR)

Relevant Literature:

Bijou, S. W., & Baer, D. M. (1961). *Child Development: Volume 1. A Systematic and Empirical Theory.* New York, NY: Appleton-Century-Crofts.

Cooper, J. O., Heron, T. E., & Heward, W. L. (2007). Basic concepts. *Applied Behavior Analysis* (pp. 24-46). Upper Saddle River, NJ: Pearson Prentice Hall.

Pavlov, I. P. (1927). *Conditioned Reflexes: An Investigation of the Physiological Activity of the Cerebral Cortex.* London: Oxford University Press.

Related Lessons:

FK-14 Respondent conditioning (CS-CR)

FK-15 Operant conditioning

FK-16 Respondent-operant interaction

-

Notes:

Write another example:

[blank box]

Questions to ask your supervisor:

[blank box]

FK-14 RESPONDENT CONDITIONING (CS-CR).

Definition (Reflex):

(Catania, 1998).
☐ Flashcard created   ☐ Learned to fluency

Definition (Respondent conditioning):

(Cooper, Heron, & Heward, 2007).
☐ Flashcard created   ☐ Learned to fluency

Examples:

Pavlov's experiments consisted of a group of dogs who were trained to salivate at the sound of a metronome started just prior to feeding them. Before initial training, the presence of food (US) elicited salivation (UR), but the metronome (NS) was not paired with this response. After numerous trials of food being paired with the sound of the metronome, the dogs began salivating whenever they heard the metronome. After being paired with the presentation of food for several trials, the metronome became a conditioned stimulus (CS) and a conditioned reflex (CR) was elicited.

Roger usually drinks soda every day for lunch. When drinking soda, the sugar (US) inside his blood elicits the release of insulin from his pancreas (UR). Now, when he opens the soda, the snap of the can (CS) starts to elicit the release of insulin (CR) before he takes a drink.

Write another example:

Questions to ask your supervisor:

Relevant Literature:

Catania, A.C. (1998). Learning (4th Ed.), Upper Saddle River, NJ. Prentice-Hall, Inc.

Cooper, J.O., Heron, T.E. & Heward W.L. (2007). *Applied Behavior Analysis* (2nd Ed.), Upper Saddle River, NJ. Pearson Prentice Hall. 29-31 (Figure 2.1), 33 (Table 2.3), 393, 606.

Skinner, B.F. (1984). The Evolution of Behavior. *Journal of the Experimental Analysis of Behavior*, 41, 2, 217-221.

Poling, A., & Braatz, D. (2001). Principles of learning: Respondent and operant conditioning and human behavior. *Handbook of organizational performance: Behavior analysis and management*, 23-49.

Skinner, B.F. (1938). The behavior of organisms: an experimental analysis. Oxford, England: Appleton-Century. (457 pp.)

Pavlov, I.P. (1928). Lectures on conditioned reflexes: Twenty-five years of objective study of the higher nervous activity (behaviour) of animals. (Horsley, G.W., Trans.). New York, NY, US: Liverwright Publishing Corporation. (414 pp.).

Related Lessons:
FK-10: Behavior, response, response class.
FK-13: Reflexive relations (US-UR).
FK-15: Operant conditioning
FK-16: Respondent-operant interactions
FK-17: Unconditioned reinforcement
FK-24: Stimulus control
FK-26: Unconditioned motivating operations
FK-35: Stimulus discrimination

Notes:

FK-15 OPERANT CONDITIONING.

Definition (Operant conditioning):

(Cooper, Heron, & Heward, 2007).
☐ Flashcard created   ☐ Learned to fluency

Example:
- A rat is deprived of food. The rat walks near a specific part of their cage and receives food. As a result, the future probability of the rat walking toward that area of the cage increases.

- A child hits his sibling when fighting over a toy. The child is sent to timeout. As a result, the future probability of hitting their sister decreases.

Write another example:

Questions to ask your supervisor:

Relevant Literature:

Cooper, J.O., Heron, T. E., & Heward, W. L. (2007). *Applied behavior analysis*. Upper Saddle River, NJ: Pearson Education.

McAllister, L. W., Stachowiak, J. G., Baer, D. M., & Conderman, L. (1969). The application of operant conditioning techniques in a secondary school classroom. *Journal of Applied Behavior Analysis*, 2(4), 277-285.

Related Lessons:

- B-01 Use the dimensions of applied behavior analysis (Baer, Wolf, & Risley, 1968) to evaluate whether interventions are behavior analytic in nature.
- B-03 Systematically arrange independent variables to demonstrate their effects on dependent variables.
- D-21 Use differential reinforcement (e.g., DRO, DRA, DRI, DRL, DRH).
- E-01 Use interventions based on manipulation of antecedents, such as motivating operations and discriminative stimuli.
- G-01 Review records and available data at the outset of the case.
- G-02 Consider biological/medical variables that may be affecting the client.
- G-03 Conduct a preliminary assessment of the client in order to identify the referral problem.
- G-04 Explain behavioral concepts using nontechnical language.
- G-05 Describe and explain behavior, including private events, in behavior-analytic (non-mentalistic) terms.
- G-06 Provide behavior-analytic services in collaboration with others who support and/or provide services to one's clients
- G-08 Identify and make environmental changes that reduce the need for behavior analysis services.
- I-02 Define environmental variables in observable and measurable terms.
- I-03 Design and implement individualized behavioral assessment procedures.
- I-04 Design and implement the full range of functional assessment procedures.
- I-05 Organize, analyze, and interpret observed data.
- I-06 Make recommendations regarding behaviors that must be established, maintained, increased, or decreased.
- J-02 Identify potential interventions based on assessment results and the best available scientific evidence.
- J-04 Select intervention strategies based on client preferences.
- J-05 Select intervention strategies based on the client's current repertoires.
- J-06 Select intervention strategies based on supporting environments.
- J-07 Select intervention strategies based on environmental and resource constraints.
- J-08 Select intervention strategies based on the social validity of the intervention.
- J-10 When a behavior is to be decreased, select an acceptable alternative behavior to be established or increased.
- K-03 Design and use competency-based training for persons who are responsible for carrying out behavioral assessment and behavior-change procedures.
- K-05 Design and use systems for monitoring procedural integrity.
- K-06 Provide supervision for behavior-change agents.
- K-07 Evaluate the effectiveness of the behavioral program.
- K-09 Secure the support of others to maintain the client's behavioral repertoires in their natural environments.
- FK-13 reflexive relations (US-UR)
- FK-14 respondent conditioning (CS-CR)
- FK-15 operant conditioning
- FK-24 Stimulus control
- FK-26 unconditioned motivating operation
- FK-31 behavioral contingencies
- FK-33 functional relations

Notes:

FK-16 RESPONDENT-OPERANT-INTER-ACTIONS.

Definition (Respondent Behavior):

[ ]

(Cooper, Heron, & Heward, 2007, p. 703).
☐ Flashcard created   ☐ Learned to fluency

Definition (Operant behavior)

[ ]

(Cooper, Heron, & Heward, 2007, p. 701).
☐ Flashcard created   ☐ Learned to fluency

Operant and respondent behavior interact very commonly. They may occur concurrently when a stimulus both evokes an operant response while at the same time elicits a respondent response on the part of the organism. The procedures involved with what we call operant or respondent conditioning are names of procedures for the ease of use of our field. There are respondent and operant interactions occurring whenever an organism behaves.

Pierce and Cheney (2013) describe it this way: "When biologically relevant stimuli such as food are contingent on an organism's operant behavior, species-characteristic, innate behavior is occasionally elicited at the same time" (p. 194). The presence of stimuli that have been paired with aversive or appetitive stimulation will elicit respondent behavior at the same time operant behavior is occurring to access or avoid those stimuli.

"The neural capacity for operant conditioning arose on the basis of species history; organisms that changed their behavior as result of life experience had an advantage over animals that did not do so" (Pierce & Cheney, 2013, p. 194).

Certain respondent behavior interacts with operant behavior. The effects are often described as motivating operations. For instance, behavior changes before and after meal times, with or without medications, after traumatic events, or disruptions in family life.

Examples:
- After a traumatic event involving physical abuse, every time a male walks into the room, your client "freezes" and does not follow instructions. This could

be due to elicited behavior ("freezing" in the presence of conditioned aversive stimuli) in competition with operant behavior (following instructions).

- A medication, when consumed, will elicit respondent behavior that makes certain things more or less aversive. Consider if your client starts taking a medication to decrease aggression maintained by access to toys. The effect of the medication may decrease the likelihood that toys function as a reinforcer in effect decreasing the amount of aggression. It may increase the likelihood that food functions as a reinforcer.

Write another example:

[ ]

Questions to ask your supervisor:

[ ]

Relevant Literature:
Cooper, J. O., Heron, T. E., & Heward, W. L. (2007). Applied behavior analysis (2nd ed). Upper Saddle River, N.J: Pearson/Merrill-Prentice Hall.
Cheney, C. D., & Pierce, W. D. (Eds.). (2013). Behavior analysis and learning (5th ed). New York, NY: Psychology Press.
Davis, H., & Hurwitz, H. M. B. (Eds.). (1977). Operant-Pavlovian interactions. Hillsdale, N.J.: New York: L. Erlbaum Associates; distributed by the Halsted Press Division of J. Wiley.

Related Lessons:
G-02 Consider biological/medical variables that may be affecting the client.
G-05 Describe and explain behavior, including private events, in behavior-analytic (nonmentalistic) terms.
FK-07 Environmental (as opposed to mentalistic) explanations of behavior
FK-13 reflexive relations (US-UR)
FK-14 respondent conditioning (CS-CR)
FK-15 operant conditioning
Notes:

FK-24 STIMULUS CONTROL.

Definition (Stimulus Control):

(Cooper, Heron, & Heward, 2007).
☐ Flashcard created   ☐ Learned to fluency

Definition (Discriminated Operant):

(Cooper, Heron, & Heward, 2007).
☐ Flashcard created   ☐ Learned to fluency

Definition (Discriminative Stimulus (S^D)):

(Cooper, Heron, & Heward, 2007).
☐ Flashcard created   ☐ Learned to fluency

Example:
Stimulus Control: When the telephone rings, George picks up the receiver. Picking up the receiver is under the stimulus control of a ringing phone.

Discriminated Operant: In the above example, picking up the receiver is the discriminated operant.
Discriminative Stimulus (S^D): In the above example, the telephone's ring is the discriminative stimulus.

Discriminative Stimulus	→	Response	→	Stimulus Change
• "What is your name?"		• "John"		• "That's right, good for you!"

Write another example:

Relevant Literature:
Cooper, J. O., Heron, T. E., & Heward, W. L. (2007). *Applied Behavior Analysis*. 2nd Edition. Pearson Prentice Hall.

Related Lessons:
D-19 Use combinations of reinforcement with punishment and extinction
FK-22 Extinction
FK-29 Distinguish between discriminative stimulus and motivating operation

Notes:

Questions to ask your supervisor:

FK 35 STIMULUS DISCRIMINATION.

Definition (Stimulus discrimination):

Questions to ask your supervisor:

(Cooper, Heron, & Heward, 2007).
☐ Flashcard created   ☐ Learned to fluency

Example:
-   During a tooth brushing routine, a child selects their tooth brush from the cup that holds a number of toothbrushes.
-   You own a small white car and can walk directly to your car after leaving the mall even though there are several small white cars parked around your car.
-   You are taking three graduate level ABA classes. Two of the professors keep track of attendance and incorporate that into your final grade and one professor does not track attendance or incorporate that into your final grade. As a result, you periodically miss this class since that your grade will not be lowered due to attendance and you regularly attend the other two classes.

Write another example:

Relevant Literature:
Cooper, J. O., Heron, T. E., & Heward, W. L. (2007). Stimulus control. *Applied Behavior Analysis* (pp. 392-409). Upper Saddle River, NJ: Pearson Prentice Hall.
Green, G. (2001). Behavior analytic instruction for learners with autism: Advances in stimulus control technology. *Focus on Autism & Other Developmental Disabilities, 16,* 72-85.

Related Lessons:
E-06 Use stimulus equivalence procedures.
FK-11 environment, stimulus, stimulus class
FK-24 stimulus control
FK-34 conditional discriminations
FK-37 stimulus generalization

Notes:

Segment 7 – Scorecard
Types of Measurement

☐ Presentation (2-5 minutes)

A 1
☐ Assessment
☐ SAFMED learned to fluency
☐ Workbook boxes completed

A 5
☐ Assessment
☐ SAFMED learned to fluency
☐ Workbook boxes completed

A 2
☐ Assessment
☐ SAFMED learned to fluency
☐ Workbook boxes completed

A 6
☐ Assessment
☐ SAFMED learned to fluency
☐ Workbook boxes completed

A 3
☐ Assessment
☐ SAFMED learned to fluency
☐ Workbook boxes completed

A 7
☐ Assessment
☐ SAFMED learned to fluency
☐ Workbook boxes completed

A 4
☐ Assessment
☐ SAFMED learned to fluency
☐ Workbook boxes completed

I 1
☐ Assessment
☐ SAFMED learned to fluency
☐ Workbook boxes completed

Segment 7 – Individual Supervision Agenda

Supervisor: _____ **Supervisee:** _____

Meeting Date: _____ **Time of meeting – From:** _____ **To:** _____

This document covers supervisory period from ____/____/____ to ____/____/____

1. Pass-in/Review Homework:

   Did the Supervisee satisfactorily complete this homework assignment?   Yes / No

   • If not, what is needed to complete assignment? Describe below.

2. Task List items addressed (A 1-7; I 1)

3. Definitions/SAFMEDs learned

   ☐ Flashcard(s) created   Was supervisee fluent with definitions? Yes ☐ No ☐

4. Discussion topics or activities completed during this meeting:

Evaluation of Supervisee's Performance			
(Record: S- "Satisfactory"; NI- "Needs Improvement"; U- "Unsatisfactory"; or NA- "Not Applicable")			
Arrived on time for meeting		Gave examples as needed	
Completed Homework Assigned		Accepted supervisory feedback appropriately	
Referred to literature/readings		Answered all questions thoroughly	
Maintained professional communication during supervision meeting			
Overall evaluation of supervisee performance during this meeting (Circle one—use code above)			S NI U
If "NI" or "U", please list corrective steps needed to achieve a score of "S"			

5. Homework assigned for next meeting

6. Closing questions/feedback

Segment 7 – Group Supervision Meeting Agenda

- <u>Meeting Topic</u>: Types of Measurement

- <u>Task List Items Reviewed</u>:
- o   I-01: Define behavior in observable and measurable terms.
- o   A-01: Measure frequency (i.e., count).
- o   A-02: Measure rate (i.e., count per unit time).
- o   A-03: Measure duration.
- o   A-04: Measure latency.
- o   A-05: Measure Interresponse time (IRT).
- o   A-06: Measure percent of occurrence.
- o   A-07: Measure trials to criterion

1. Housekeeping
   - Upon entry to meeting have supervisees hand in the previous week's homework assignment and discuss several "Housekeeping Items" related to supervision.
   - Take attendance for the meeting.
   - State the duration of today's meeting (90 minutes).
   - Distribute BACB® experience forms to supervisees.
2. Task List Lesson and Discussion
   - Discuss task list item I-01: Define behavior in observable and measurable terms.
   - Discuss task list item A-01: Measure frequency (i.e., count).
   - Discuss task list item A-02: Measure rate (i.e., count per unit time.
   - Discuss task list item A-03: Measure duration.
   - Discuss task list item A-04: Measure latency.
   - Discuss task list item A-05: Measure Interresponse time (IRT).
   - Discuss task list item A-06: Measure percent of occurrence.
   - Discuss task list item A-07: Measure trials to criterion.
3. Homework Review
   - Review homework that was assigned at the previous supervision meeting.
4. Questions
   - Answer any questions related to the homework or topics discussed.
5. Closing Notes
   - *Assign Homework (task list boxes, presentation) from today's segment, due at next group meeting*

Close the meeting by inviting supervisees to request topics to be covered in upcoming meetings.

I-01 DEFINE BEHAVIOR IN OBSERVABLE AND MEASUREABLE TERMS.

The importance of defining behavior in observable and measurable terms:

- As Baer, Wolf and Risley said in 1968, "since the behavior of an individual is composed of physical events, its scientific study requires their precise measurement" (p. 93). In order to be scientific in our study of behavior, we must be very clear about what behavior it is we are actually studying. Therefore, the target behavior must be observable and measurable. Cooper, Heron and Heward (2007) also make the point that one of the most basic tenets of science is replication. In order for other scientists to replicate an experiment or study, the definition of the behavior under investigation and how it was measured must be transparent enough, that future replication is possible.

Technically-sound written definitions of target behaviors

- Cooper, Heron, and Heward, (2007), suggest that a good behavioral definition is:
  - ○ **Operational** (it allows the practitioner to obtain complete information about a behavior's occurrence/non-occurrence and allows the accurate application of the procedures.)
- Cooper, Heron and Heward (2007) also state that good definitions increase the likelihood that an accurate *evaluation* of the effectiveness of a study or experiment will be conducted.

Two types of target behavior definitions

- Cooper, Heron, and Heward (2007, p. 65) suggest that there are two types of target behavior definitions:
  - ○ **Functional** (These types of definition label responses as part of the target behavior's response class if they have the same effect upon the environment.)
  - ○ **Topographical** (These types of definition look at the shape or form of the target behavior.)

How to write behavioral definitions

- Cooper, Heron, and Heward (2007) cite Hawkins and Dobes (1977) as giving three characteristics of good written target behavior definitions:
  - ○ Objective (should refer only to observable characteristics of the behavior and environment and shouldn't utilize inferential terms, such as "feeling angry".)
  - ○ Clear (the definition should be readable and unambiguous.)
  - ○ Complete (it should outline the boundaries of what is included as an instance of a response and what is not included.)

Notes:

Write another example:

Questions to ask your supervisor:

Relevant Literature:

Baer, D. M., Wolf, M. M., & Risley, T. R. (1968). Some current dimensions of applied behavior analysis. *Journal of Applied Behavior Analysis, 1*, 91-97.

Cooper, J. O., Heron, T. E., & Heward, W. L. (2007). Applied Behavior Analysis, 2nd ed. Upper Saddle River, New Jersey: Pearson Prentice Hall.

Hawkins, R. P., & Dobes, R. W. (1977). Behavioral definitions in applied behavior analysis: Explicit or implicit? In B. C. Etzel, J. M. LeBlanc, & D. M. Baer (Eds.), New developments in behavioral research: Theory, method, and application (pp. 167-188).

Van Houten, R. (1979). Social Validation: The evolution of standards of competency for target behaviors. *Journal of Applied Behavior Analysis, 26*, 197-203.

Related Lessons:

H-01: Select a measurement system to obtain representative data given the dimensions of the behavior and the logistics of observing and recording
H-02: Select a schedule of observation and recording periods.
I-02: Define environmental variables on observable and measurable terms
J-01: State intervention goals in observable and measurable terms
FK-47: Identify the observable dimensions of behavior (e.g., rate, duration, latency, interresponse time)

A-01 - MEASURE FREQUENCY (I.E., COUNT)

Definition (Frequency):

(Cooper, Heron, & Heward, 2007).
☐ Flashcard created ☐ Learned to fluency

Examples:
- A student is sitting in an hour long class. The student raises their hand 3 times to ask and answer questions during the class. The bell rings once and the student goes to their next class. Frequency of hand raising is 3 per hour.

Write another example:

Relevant Literature:
Cooper, J. O., Heron, T. E., *&* Heward, W. L. (2007). *Applied behavior analysis (2nd ed.). Upper Saddle River, NJ: Pearson.*
Catania, A. C. (2013). *Learning* (5th ed.). Croton-on-Hudson, NY: Sloan.

Related Lessons:
I-01 Define behavior in observable and measurable terms
H-01 Select a measurement system to obtain representative data given the dimensions of the behavior and the logistics of observing and recording
FK-47 Identify the measurable dimensions of behavior (e.g. rate, duration, latency, inter-response time)

Notes:

Questions to ask your supervisor:

A-02 - MEASURE RATE (I.E., RATE PER UNIT TIME)

Definition (Rate):

(Cooper, Heron, & Heward, 2007).
☐ Flashcard created ☐ Learned to fluency

Footnotes
Alternatively, rate is not always defined synonymously with frequency throughout the discipline of behavior analysis. Catania (2013) defines rate as "responses per unit time but frequency as "total responses over a fixed time, over a session of variable duration or, in trial procedure, over a fixed number of trials." Cooper, Heron, & Heward (2007) functionally defines "count" whereas Catania defines "frequency".

Write another example:

Questions to ask your supervisor:

Examples:
- A young child is sitting at a table where there is a bag of potato chips. They eat 8 chips, stand up, and walk to the living room to watch TV for the rest of the hour. Rate of chip eating is 8 per hour.
- Child is playing basketball for 30 minutes. Dribbles 7 times and then practices foul shots. He shoots 15 times and between each shot he dribbles 3 times. Frequency of dribbling is 52 dribbles per 30 minutes.

Relevant Literature:
Catania, A. C. (2013). *Learning* (5th ed.). Croton-on-Hudson, NY: Sloan.
Cooper, J. O., Heron, T. E., & Heward, W. L. (2007). Applied behavior analysis.

Related Lessons:
I-01 Define behavior in observable and measurable terms
H-01 Select a measurement system to obtain representative data given the dimensions of the behavior and the logistics of observing and recording
FK-47 Identify the measurable dimensions of behavior (e.g. rate, duration, latency, interresponse time)

Notes:

A-03 - MEASURE DURATION

Definition (Duration):

(Cooper, Heron, & Heward, 2007).
☐ Flashcard created   ☐ Learned to fluency

Examples:
- Sarah gets a fancy new piece of furniture from one of those Swedish companies. When it arrives, Sarah realizes that it is not assembled. She reads the complicated set of directions and begins putting it together at 2:12pm. Armed with a screwdriver and an Allen wrench, she consistently works to put it together until 3:43pm. Phew! Maybe next time she will order the one that comes fully assembled! The duration of the project was 1 hour and 31 minutes.
- Benny gets a new yo-yo for his birthday and plays with it for 20 minutes after eating his cake and ice cream. He puts it down to play tag with his sister. The duration of yo-yo playing is 20 minutes.

Write another example:

Questions to ask your supervisor:

Relevant Literature:
Cooper, J. O., Heron, T. E., & Heward, W. L. (2007). *Applied behavior analysis (2nd ed.). Upper Saddle River, NJ: Pearson.*
DeLeon, I. G., Iwata, B. A., Conners, J., & Wallace, M. D. (1999). Examination of ambiguous stimulus preferences with duration-based measures. *Journal of Applied Behavior Analysis, 32*(1), 111-114.

Related Lessons:
H-01 Select a measurement system to obtain representative data given the dimensions of the behavior and the logistics of observing and recording.
I-01 Define the behavior in observable and measurable terms
FK-47 Identify the measurable dimensions of behavior (e.g., rate, duration, latency, interresponse time).

Notes:

A - 04 MEASURE LATENCY

Definition (Latency):

```


```

(Cooper, Heron, & Heward, 2007).
☐ Flashcard created   ☐ Learned to fluency

Examples:
- Hitting the snooze button or hitting the break:
- Gertrude is not a "morning person." Her alarm goes off at precisely 5:30AM. She hears the annoying wail but doesn't respond immediately. After 32 seconds of beeping, she whacks the snooze button, rolls over and goes back to sleep. Latency to turning off the alarm is 32 seconds.
- Marty is driving down a country road. Out of no-where a herd of deer dart out in front of his car. It takes Marty 5 seconds from the time he first sees the deer to hit the break. Latency from the time the deer are spotted to applying pressure to the break is 5 seconds.
- Gertrude is not a morning person. Her alarm goes off at precisely 5:30 AM. She does not respond to its annoying wailing and continues to sleep despite the noise. The alarm stops on its own 1 hour later.

Write another example:

```



```

Questions to ask your supervisor:

```



```

Relevant Literature:

Cooper, J. O., Heron, T. E., & Heward, W. L. (2007). *Applied behavior analysis (2nd ed.). Upper Saddle River, NJ: Pearson.*

Thomason-Sassi, J. L., Iwata, B. A., Neidert, P. L., & Roscoe, E. M. (2011). Response latency as an index of response strength during functional analyses of problem behavior. Journal of Applied Behavior Analysis, 44(1), 51-67.

Related Lessons:

H-01 Select a measurement system to obtain representative data given the dimensions of the behavior and the logistics of observing and recording.
I-01 Define the behavior in observable and measurable terms
FK-47 Identify the measurable dimensions of behavior (e.g., rate, duration, latency, interresponse time).

Notes:

A - 05 MEASURE INTERRESPONSE TIME.

Definition (Interresponse time):

(Cooper, Heron, & Heward, 2007).
☐ Flashcard created   ☐ Learned to fluency

Example:
- Sparky loves to bark at passing cars. He hears a car drive by the house and barks. Thirty-seven seconds later another car passes by and Sparky barks again. Interresponse time between barking at the vehicles is thirty-seven seconds.
- Doodles the cat likes to scratch the furniture. She walks over the chair and sinks her claws in. Eleven seconds later Doodles walks over to the couch and begins to scratch again. Interresponse time between scratches is eleven seconds.
- Roger the rooster doesn't know that he's only supposed to crow at dawn. He lets out crows all day long. He is observed to crow at 3:43 in the afternoon. He crows again at 3: 59. Interresponse time between crows is sixteen minutes.

Non-Example:
- Sparky's owner accidentally steps on his tail. Sparky yelps from the pain.

Write another example:

Questions to ask your supervisor:

Relevant Literature:
Blough, D. S. (1963), Interresponse Time as a Function of Continuous Variables: A New Method and Some Data. *Journal of Experimental Analysis Behavior*, 6: 237–246.

Cooper J.O, Heron T.E, Heward W.L. (2007). *Applied behavior analysis* (2nd ed.) Upper Saddle River, NJ: Pearson

Favell, J.E., McGimsey, J.F., & Jones, M.L. (1980). Rapid Eating in the Retarded: Reduction by Nonaversive Procedures. *Behavior Modifications*, 4, 235-239.

Related Lessons:
A-05 Measure Interresponse time (IRT)
I-01 Define behavior in observable and measurable terms
H-01 Select a measurement system to obtain representative data given the dimensions of the behavior and the logistics of observing and recording
FK-47 Identify the measurable dimensions of behavior (e.g. rate, duration, latency, interresponse time).

Notes:

A-06 - MEASURE PERCENT OF OCCURRENCE

Definition (Percent of occurrence):

Cooper, Heron, & Heward, 2007).
☐ Flashcard created   ☐ Learned to fluency

Examples:
- Twelve strangers walk by an elderly man. He greets three of them and ignores the rest. The percent of occurrence of greeting strangers is 25%.
- To compute: Divide number of greetings emitted by the man (3) by the total number of opportunities to greet (12) and multiply that product by 100 to yield a percentage (3/12= 0.25 x 100= 25%).

Non-Examples:
- Twelve strangers walk by an elderly man. He greets three of them and ignores the rest. The percent of occurrence of greeting strangers is 0.25.

Relevant Literature:
Cooper, J. O., Heron, T. E., & Heward, W. L. (2007). *Applied Behavior Analysis* (2nd ed.). Upper Saddle River, NJ: Pearson.

Related Lessons:
I-01 Define behavior in observable and measurable terms
H-01 Select a measurement system to obtain representative data given the dimensions of the behavior and the logistics of observing and recording
FK-47 Identify the measurable dimensions of behavior (e.g. rate, duration, latency, inter-response time)

Notes:

Write another example:

Questions to ask your supervisor:

A-07 – MEASURE TRIALS TO CRITERION

Definition (Trials to criterion):

(Cooper, Heron, & Heward, 2007).
☐ Flashcard created   ☐ Learned to fluency

Example:
- A behavioral interventionist is teaching a child how to brush her teeth. She teaches this using a task analysis that involves backwards chaining. She provides two opportunities per session for the child to complete this skill. Data reflect that it takes the child on average four opportunities before she is able to complete the step being taught independently and to move to the next step in the task analysis.

Relevant Literature:
Cooper, J. O., Heron, T. E., & Heward, W. L. (2007). *Applied Behavior Analysis* (2nd ed.). Upper Saddle River, NJ: Prentice Hall.
Lahey, B. B., & Drabman, R. S. (1974). Facilitation of the acquisition and retention of the sight-word vocabulary through token reinforcement1. *Journal of applied behavior analysis*, 7(2), 307-312.

Related Lessons:
H-01 Select a measurement system to obtain representative data given the dimensions of the behavior and the logistics of observing and recording.
H-03 Select a data display that effectively communicates relevant quantitative relations.

Notes:

Write another example:

Questions to ask your supervisor:

Segment 8 – Scorecard
Continuous versus Discontinuous Measurement

☐ Presentation (2-5 minutes)

A 12
☐ Assessment
☐ SAFMED learned to fluency
☐ Workbook boxes completed

A 13
☐ Assessment
☐ SAFMED learned to fluency
☐ Workbook boxes completed

FK 47
☐ Assessment
☐ SAFMED learned to fluency
☐ Workbook boxes completed

FK 48
☐ Assessment
☐ SAFMED learned to fluency
☐ Workbook boxes completed

Segment 8 – Individual Supervision Agenda

Supervisor: _____ **Supervisee:** _____
Meeting Date: _____ **Time of meeting – From:** _____ **To:** _____
This document covers supervisory period from ____/____/____ **to** ____/____/____

1. Pass-in/Review Homework:

    Did the Supervisee satisfactorily complete this homework assignment?   Yes / No

- If not, what is needed to complete assignment? Describe below.

2. Task List items addressed (A 12-13; FK 47-48)

3. Definitions/SAFMEDs learned

    ☐ Flashcard(s) created   Was supervisee fluent with definitions? Yes ☐ No ☐

4. Discussion topics or activities completed during this meeting:

Evaluation of Supervisee's Performance				
(Record: S- "Satisfactory"; NI- "Needs Improvement"; U- "Unsatisfactory"; or NA- "Not Applicable")				
Arrived on time for meeting		Gave examples as needed		
Completed Homework Assigned		Accepted supervisory feedback appropriately		
Referred to literature/readings		Answered all questions thoroughly		
Maintained professional communication during supervision meeting				
Overall evaluation of supervisee performance during this meeting (Circle one—use code above)			S NI U	
If "NI" or "U", please list corrective steps needed to achieve a score of "S"				

5. Homework assigned for next meeting

6. Closing questions/feedback

Segment 8 – Group Supervision Meeting Agenda

- <u>Meeting Topic</u>: Continuous versus Discontinuous Measurement.

- <u>Task List Items Reviewed</u>:
  - A-12: Design and implement continuous measurement procedures (e.g., event recording).
  - A-13: Design and implement discontinuous measurement procedures (e.g., partial & whole interval, momentary time sampling).
  - FK-47: Identify the measurable dimensions of behavior (e.g., rate, duration, latency, inter-response time).
  - FK-48: State the advantages and disadvantages of using continuous measurement procedures and discontinuous measurement procedures (e.g., partial- and whole-interval recording, momentary time sampling).

1. Housekeeping
    - Upon entry to meeting have supervisees hand in the previous week's homework assignment and discuss several "Housekeeping Items" related to supervision.
    - Take attendance for the meeting.
    - State the duration of today's meeting (90 minutes).
    - Distribute BACB® experience forms to supervisees.

2. Task List Lesson and Discussion
    - Discuss task list item A-12: Design and implement continuous measurement procedures (e.g., event recording).
    - Discuss task list item A-01: Measure frequency (i.e., count).
    - Discuss task list item A-13: Design and implement discontinuous measurement procedures (e.g., partial & whole interval, momentary time sampling).
    - Discuss task list item FK-47: Identify the measurable dimensions of behavior (e.g., rate, duration, latency, inter-response time).
    - Discuss task list item FK-48: State the advantages and disadvantages of using continuous measurement procedures and discontinuous measurement procedures (e.g., partial- and whole-interval recording, momentary time sampling).

3. Homework Review
    - Review homework that was assigned at the previous supervision meeting.

4. Questions
    - Answer any questions related to the homework or topics discussed.

5. Closing Notes
    - *Assign Homework (task list boxes, presentation) from today's segment, due at next group meeting*

Close the meeting by inviting supervisees to request topics to be covered in upcoming meetings.

A-12 DESIGN AND IMPLEMENT CONTINUOUS MEASUREMENT PROCEDURES (E.G., EVENT RECORDING)

Definition (Event Recording):

(Cooper, Heron, & Heward, 2007).

☐ Flashcard created   ☐ Learned to fluency

Examples:
Contexts that are likely to be appropriate for an event recording procedure:

- Property destruction that typically occurs two to five times a week.
- Correct responses to the question, "What do you want?" when asked in at least six distributed trials each day.

Contexts that may be inappropriate for an event recording procedure:

- Vocal Stereotypy that occurs on and off so rapidly that an observer would not be able to accurately determine the start and end of the stereotypy.
- Aggressive behavior in a classroom setting with one teacher, who must conduct instruction, interact with other students, and count hitting behavior that often includes multiple students.
- An observer may increase counting accuracy by using a counting device with low-technology (i.e., masking tape around the wrist for tally marks or a golf-stroke counter or with high technology (i.e., IPad or laptop direct observation programs).

Write another example:

Questions to ask your supervisor:

Relevant Literature:

Cooper, J. O., Heron, T. E., & Heward, W. L. (2007). Applied behavior analysis. Upper Saddle River, NJ: Pearson Education.

Kelly, M. B. (1977). A review of the observational data-collection and reliability procedures reported in the Journal of Applied Behavior Analysis. *Journal of Applied Behavior Analysis, 10*(1), 97-101.

Sasso, G. M., Reimers, T. M., Cooper, L. J., Wacker, D., Berg, W., Steege, M., ... & Allaire, A. (1992). Use of descriptive and experimental analyses to identify the functional properties of aberrant behavior in school settings. *Journal of Applied Behavior Analysis, 25*(4), 809-821.

Related Lessons:

A-09 Evaluate the accuracy and reliability of measurement procedures.

H-01 Select a measurement system to obtain representative data given the dimensions of the behavior and the logistics of observing and recording.

I-01 Define behavior in observable and measurable terms.

FK-47 Identify the measurable dimensions of behavior (e.g. rate, duration, latency, interresponse time).

FK-48 State the advantages and disadvantages of using continuous measurement procedures and discontinuous measurement procedures (e.g. partial- and whole-interval recording, momentary time sampling.)

Notes:

A - 13 DESIGN AND IMPLEMENT DISCONTINUOUS MEASUREMENT PROCEDURES (E.G., PARTIAL & WHOLE INTERVAL RECORDING, MOMENTARY TIME SAMPLING)

Definition:

"Time sampling refers to a variety of methods for observing and recording behavior during intervals or at specific moments in time. The basic procedure involves dividing the observation period into time intervals and then recording the presence or absence of behavior within or at the end of interval. Three forms of time sampling used often by applied behavior analysts are whole-interval recording, partial-interval recording and momentary time sampling (Cooper, Heron and Heward, 2007, p.90)."

Whole-Interval Recording

"Once the interval has ended, the observer records whether the behavior has occurred throughout the *entire* interval. Whole-interval recording tends to underestimate how much a behavior is occurring because the behavior has to be emitted for the entire interval in order to get recorded." (Cooper, Heron and Heward, 2007, p. 90)

Partial-Interval Recording

"With the partial-interval recording method, the time of observation is again divided into intervals and a behavior is recorded as having occurred if it has occurred *at some point* during the interval. Data are usually reported as percentage of intervals." (Cooper, Heron and Heward, 2007, p. 92)

Momentary Time Sampling

"With this type of measurement, a period of time is divided up into intervals and the observer records whether the behavior is occurring at the precise moment the interval ends." (Cooper, Heron and Heward, 2007, p. 93).

Examples:

Whole-Interval Recording:

- *Hand-flapping: student moves one or both hands repeatedly and rapidly by bending at the wrist, such that fingers move more than 2 inches. Non-example: waving hand to say "hello" or "goodbye."*
- An observer divides a 5-minute observation period into intervals of 5 seconds. A student flaps his hands for the *entire* 5-second interval. At the end of the 5-second interval, the observer records the behavior as having occurred.

Partial-Interval Recording:

- *Calling-out behavior in a pupil: student raises voice above conversation level when not called on by teacher.*
- A 30-minute observation period is divided into one-minute intervals. At the end of the one minute interval, the behavior is recorded as having occurred because the pupil called-out after the first 30 seconds of the interval.

Momentary Time Sampling:

- *Movie watching: client is seated, and head and eyes are oriented toward screen.*
- An observer is measuring a client's engagement with a movie across a 2-minute period. The 2-minute period is divided up into 5-second intervals. The observer records the behavior as being present at the end of the first 5-second interval as the client was watching the movie appropriately at that specific point in time.

Write another example:

Questions to ask your supervisor:

Relevant Literature:

Daboul-Meany, M. G., Roscoe, E. M., Bourret, J. C., Ahearn, W. H. (2007). A comparison of momentary time sampling and partial-interval recording for evaluating functional relations. *Journal of Applied Behavior Analysis, 40* (3), 501-514.

Powell, J., Martindale, A., & Kulp, S. (1975). An evaluation of time-sample measures of behavior. *Journal of Applied Behavior Analysis, 8*, 463-469.

Suen, H. K., Ary, D., & Covalt, W. (1991). Reappraisal of momentary time sampling and partial-interval recording. *Journal of Applied Behavior Analysis, 24*, 803-804.

Related Lessons:

A-12: Design and implement continuous measurement procedures (e.g., event recording)

H-01: Select a measurement system to obtain representative data given the dimensions of the behavior and the logistics of observing and recording

I-01: Define the behavior in observable and measurable terms

FK-47: Identify the measurable dimensions of behavior (e.g., rate, duration, latency, interresponse time)

FK-48: State the advantages and disadvantages of using continuous measurement procedures and discontinuous measurement procedures (e.g., partial- and whole-interval recording, momentary time sampling)

Notes:

FK-47 IDENTIFY THE MEASUREABLE DIMENSIONS OF BEHAVIOR.

Definition
(Fundamental measureable dimensions of behavior):

(Cooper, Heron, & Heward, 2007).
☐ Flashcard created   ☐ Learned to fluency

Definition (Temporal extent):

(Cooper, Heron, & Heward, 2007).
☐ Flashcard created   ☐ Learned to fluency

Definition (Repeatability):

(Cooper, Heron, & Heward, 2007).
☐ Flashcard created   ☐ Learned to fluency

Definition (Temporal locus):

(Cooper, Heron, & Heward, 2007).
☐ Flashcard created   ☐ Learned to fluency

Example:

- "I want a cookie" (mand for an item; can also include verbs, use of adjectives, prepositions, pronouns etc.)
- A child says "watch me" after learning how to ride a bike independently (mand for attention)
- Asking questions like "what's your name?" or "where's the phone?" (mand for information)
- Child says, "No!" when parent is about to use blender (mand for avoidance of an aversive)

Write another example:

Questions to ask your supervisor:

Relevant Literature:

Cooper, J. O., Heron, T. E., & Heward, W. L. (2007). *Applied Behavior Analysis.* Upper Saddle River, NJ: Pearson Prentice Hall.

Johnston, J. M., & Pennypacker, H. S. (2011). Strategies and tactics of behavioral research. Routledge. Chicago, IL.

Thomason-Sassi, J. L., Iwata, B. A., Neidert, P. L., & Roscoe, E. M. (2011). Response latency as an index of response strength during functional analyses of problem behavior. *Journal of applied behavior analysis, 44*(1), 51-67.

Worsdell, A. S., Iwata, B. A., & Wallace, M. D. (2002). Duration-based measures of preference for vocational tasks. *Journal of applied behavior analysis, 35*(3), 287-290.

Related Lessons:

A-01: Measure frequency
A-02: Measure duration
A-03: Measure duration
A-04: Measure latency
A-05: Measure interresponse time
A-09: Evaluate accuracy and reliability of measurement procedures
D-21: Differential reinforcement

Notes:

FK-48 STATE THE ADVANTAGES AND DIS-
ADVANTAGES OF USING CONTINUOUS
MEASUREMENT PROCEDURES (E.G., PAR-
TIAL- AND WHOLE-INTERVAL RECORD-
ING, MOMENTARY TIME-SAMPLING).

Definition (Whole-interval recording):

(Cooper, Heron, & Heward, 2007).
☐ Flashcard created   ☐ Learned to fluency

Definition (Momentary Time Sampling):

(Cooper, Heron, & Heward, 2007).
☐ Flashcard created   ☐ Learned to fluency

Definition (Partial-interval recording):

(Cooper, Heron, & Heward, 2007).
☐ Flashcard created   ☐ Learned to fluency

Example:
- Roy's self-injury was at such a high rate that
  the behavior analyst decided to track it using
  partial interval recording to estimate the frequency during specific times.

Write another example:

Cooper, J. O., Heron, T. E., & Heward, W. L. (2007). Applied Behavior Analysis, 2nd ed. Upper Saddle River, New Jersey: Pearson Prentice Hall.

Daboul-Meany, M. G., Roscoe, E. M., Bourret, J. C., Ahearn, W. H. (2007). A comparison of momentary time sampling and partial-interval recording for evaluating functional relations. *Journal of Applied Behavior Analysis, 40* (3), 501-514.

Gardenier, N. C., MacDonald, R., & Green, G. (2004). Comparison of direct observational methods for measuring stereotypic behavior in children with autism spectrum disorders. *Research in Developmental Disabilities, 25*(2), 99-118.

Gunter, P. L., Venn, M. L., Patrick, J., Miller, K. A. & Kelly, L. (2003). Efficacy of using momentary time samples to determine on-task behavior of students with emotional/behavioral disorders. *Education and Treatment of Children, 26*, 400-412.

Powell, J., Martindale, A., & Kulp, S. (1975). An evaluation of time-sample measures of behavior. *Journal of Applied Behavior Analysis, 8*, 463-469.

Suen, H. K., Ary, D., & Covalt, W. (1991). Reappraisal of momentary time sampling and partial-interval recording. *Journal of Applied Behavior Analysis, 24*, 803-804.

Related Lessons:

A-09: Evaluate the accuracy and reliability of measurement procedures

A-12: Design and implement continuous measurement procedures (e.g., event recording)

H-01: Select a measurement system to obtain representative data given the dimensions of the behavior and the logistics of observing and recording

H-02: Select a schedule of observation and recording periods

I-01: Define the behavior in observable and measurable terms

FK-47: Identify the measurable dimensions of behavior (e.g., rate, duration, latency, interresponse time)

FK-48: State the advantages and disadvantages of using continuous measurement procedures and discontinuous measurement procedures (e.g., partial- and whole-interval recording, momentary time sampling)

Notes:

Questions to ask your supervisor:

Segment 9 – Scorecard
Motivating Operations/ Discriminative Stimuli

☐ Presentation (2-5 minutes)

E 1
☐ Assessment
☐ SAFMED learned to fluency
☐ Workbook boxes completed

FK 26
☐ Assessment
☐ SAFMED learned to fluency
☐ Workbook boxes completed

FK 27
☐ Assessment
☐ SAFMED learned to fluency
☐ Workbook boxes completed

FK 28
☐ Assessment
☐ SAFMED learned to fluency
☐ Workbook boxes completed

FK 29
☐ Assessment
☐ SAFMED learned to fluency
☐ Workbook boxes completed

FK 30
☐ Assessment
☐ SAFMED learned to fluency
☐ Workbook boxes completed

Segment 9 – Individual Supervision Agenda

Supervisor: _____ **Supervisee:** _____
Meeting Date: _____ **Time of meeting – From:**_____ **To:**_____
This document covers supervisory period from ____/____/____ **to** ____/____/____

1. Pass-in/Review Homework:

    Did the Supervisee satisfactorily complete this homework assignment?   Yes / No

- If not, what is needed to complete assignment? Describe below.

2. Task List items addressed (E 1; FK 26-30)

3. Definitions/SAFMEDs learned
    ☐ Flashcard(s) created   Was supervisee fluent with definitions? Yes ☐ No ☐

4. Discussion topics or activities completed during this meeting:

Evaluation of Supervisee's Performance
(Record: S- "Satisfactory"; NI- "Needs Improvement"; U- "Unsatisfactory"; or NA- "Not Applicable")

Arrived on time for meeting		Gave examples as needed	
Completed Homework Assigned		Accepted supervisory feedback appropriately	
Referred to literature/readings		Answered all questions thoroughly	

	S	NI	U
Maintained professional communication during supervision meeting			
Overall evaluation of supervisee performance during this meeting *(Circle one—use code above)*	S	NI	U
If "NI" or "U", please list corrective steps needed to achieve a score of "S"			

5. Homework assigned for next meeting

6. Closing questions/feedback

Segment 9 – Group Supervision Meeting Agenda

- <u>Meeting Topic</u>: Motivating Operations/ Discriminative Stimuli

- <u>Task List Items Reviewed</u>:
  - o E-01: Use interventions based on manipulation of antecedents, such as motivating operations and discriminative stimuli.
  - o FK-26: Unconditioned motivating operations.
  - o FK-27: Conditioned motivating operations.
  - o FK-28: Transitive, reflexive, and surrogate motivating operations.
  - o FK-29: Distinguish between the discriminative stimulus and the motivating operation.
  - o FK-30: Distinguish between motivating operation and reinforcement effects.

1. Housekeeping
   - Upon entry to meeting have supervisees hand in the previous week's homework assignment and discuss several "Housekeeping Items" related to supervision.
   - Take attendance for the meeting.
   - State the duration of today's meeting (90 minutes).
   - Distribute BACB® experience forms to supervisees.

2. Task List Lesson and Discussion
   - Discuss task list item E-01: Use interventions based on manipulation of antecedents, such as motivating operations and discriminative stimuli.
   - Discuss task list item FK-26: Unconditioned motivating operations.
   - Discuss task list item FK-27: Conditioned motivating operations.
   - Discuss task list item FK-28: Transitive, reflexive, and surrogate motivating operations.
   - Discuss task list item FK-29: Distinguish between the discriminative stimulus and the motivating operation.
   - Discuss task list item FK-30: Distinguish between motivating operation and reinforcement effects.

3. Homework Review
   - Review homework that was assigned at the previous supervision meeting.

4. Questions
   - Answer any questions related to the homework or topics discussed.

5. Closing Notes
   - *Assign Homework (task list boxes, presentation) from today's segment, due at next group meeting*
   - Close the meeting by inviting supervisees to request topics to be covered in upcoming meetings.

E-01 USE INTERVENTIONS BASED ON MANIPULATION OF ANTECEDENTS, SUCH AS MOTIVATING OPERATIONS AND DISCRIMINATIVE STIMULI.

Definition:

While it is commonly known that behaviors are maintained by consequences, antecedent interventions within an individual's treatment package can often expedite positive behavioral change and mitigate negative effects of consequent strategies (e.g. extinction bursts). Some antecedent strategies include motivating operations, discriminative stimuli, non-contingent reinforcement and usage of high probability request sequences.

Michael (1982) describes motivating operations as "a stimulus change which, (1) given the momentary effectiveness of some particular type of reinforcement (2) increases the frequency of a particular type of response (3) because that stimulus change has been correlated with an increase in the frequency with which that type of response has been followed by that type of reinforcement. Skinner first explored this concept, describing deprivation and satiation to be motivating variables that govern behavior. Simply put, reinforcers obtain most of their reinforcing value depending on the individual's drive to obtain that reinforcer, which is a direct result of deprivation-satiation contingencies. Behavior analysts can affect behavioral change by manipulating motivating operations (e.g. challenging behavior maintained by escape from non-preferred tasks may be mitigated by giving the individual frequent breaks).

Another antecedent strategy is effectively programming for discriminative stimuli. Skinner claimed that virtually all operant behavior falls under stimulus control, asserting that "if all behavior were equally likely to occur on all occasions, the result would be chaotic" (Skinner, 1953, p. 108). It is therefore important for individuals to learn to discriminate between conditions in which specific responses will be reinforced and when these responses will not. Discriminative stimuli evoke behavior "because they have been correlated with increased availability of reinforcement" (Cooper, Heron & Heward, 2007). For instance, teaching a student to mand for a break can be problematic if the student mands for a break continuously throughout the day, thereby yielding very little on-task behavior. However, this can be possibly remedied by the availability of a break is represented by the presence of a break icon (e.g. break icon is the discriminative stimulus, signaling that if the student asks for a break, a break will be granted).

Other antecedent strategies include usage of non-contingent reinforcement and usage of high-probability request sequences. Non-contingent reinforcement is "an antecedent intervention in which stimuli with known reinforcing properties are delivered on a fixed-time or variable-time schedule independent of the learner's behavior" (Cooper, Heron & Heward, 2007). This operates on the principle of motivating operations. By satiating an individual with wants/needs, the individual is no longer motivated to engage in responses that used to generate that want/need (e.g. giving attention to a student every five minutes may abolish attention as a reinforcer, thereby reducing the need to engage in inappropriate attention-seeking behavior). High-probability request sequences are synonymous with the term behavioral momentum. It is "an antecedent intervention in which two to five easy tasks with a known history of learner compliance are presented in quick succession immediately before requesting the target task, the low-p request" (Cooper, Heron & Heward, 2007).

Example:

The motivating operation for one's behavior that has run three miles in the heat is to quench their thirst increasing the value of water as a reinforcer.

- Having no money to put into a vending machine to get a bottle of water is the motivating operation to ask friends for loose change.

- Similarly, after the person drinks an entire bottle of water, water may no longer function as a reinforcer.

Write another example:

Questions to ask your supervisor:

Relevant Literature:

Cooper, J. O., Heron, T. E., & Heward, W. L. (2007). *Applied behavior analysis* (2nd ed.). Upper Saddle River, NJ: Prentice Hall.

Michael, J (1982). Distinguishing between discriminative and motivational functions of stimuli. *Journal of Experimental Analysis of Behavior, 37(1),* 149-155.

Skinner, B. F. (1953). *Science and human behavior.* New York: Macmillan.

Smith, R.G. & Iwata, B.A. (1997). Antecedent influences on behavior disorders. *Journal of Applied Behavior Analysis, 30(2),* 343-375.

Related Lessons:

E-09: Arrange high probability request sequences
FK-26: Unconditioned motivating operations
FK-27: Conditioned motivating operations
FK-29: Distinguish between the discriminative stimulus and the motivating operation.

Notes:

FK-26 UNCONDITIONED MOTIVATING OPERATIONS.

Definition (Unconditioned motivating operations):

(Cooper, Heron, & Heward, 2007).
☐ Flashcard created   ☐ Learned to fluency

Examples:
- Roger has not slept in three days because he has been studying for his chemistry final. Sleep becomes more valuable the more deprived of sleep he gets.

Non-example:
- Roger lost his key to his apartment and cannot get in. The locked door serves as motivation for him to find his key to get into his apartment. The key serves as a reinforcer because his learning history identifies this as the only way to unlock his door and get into his apartment.

Write another example:

Questions to ask your supervisor:

Relevant Literature:
Cooper, J.O., Heron, T.E. & Heward W.L. (2007). *Applied Behavior Analysis* (2nd Ed.), Upper Saddle River, NJ. Pearson Prentice Hall.
Laraway, S., Snycerski, S., Michael, J., & Poling, A. (2001). The abative effect: A new term to describe the action of antecedents that reduce operant responding. *The Analysis of Verbal Behavior*, 18, 101-104.
Lotfizadeh, A.D., Edwards, T.L., Redner, R., & Poling, A. (2012). Motivating operations affect stimulus control: A largely overlooked phenomenon in discrimination learning. *Behavior Analyst*, 35, 1, 89-100.
Michael, J. (1982). Distinguishing between discriminative and motivational functions of stimuli. *Journal of the Experimental Analysis of Behavior*, 37, 149-155.
Michael, J. (2000). Implications and refinements of the establishing operation concept. *Journal of Applied Behavior Analysis*, 33, 401-410.
Ulrich, R.E., & Azarin, N.H. (1962). Reflexive fighting in response to aversive stimulation. *Journal of the Experimental Analysis of Behavior*, 5, 511-520.

Related Lessons:
D-01: Use positive and negative reinforcement.
E-01: Use interventions based on manipulation of antecedents, such as motivating operations and Discriminative stimuli.
I-02: Define environmental variables in observable and measureable terms.
FK-02: Selectionism (phylogenic, ontogenic, cultural)
FK-13: Reflexive relations (US-UR)
FK-14: Respondent conditioning (CS-CR)
FK-17: Unconditioned reinforcement.
FK-19: Unconditioned punishment
FK-27: Conditioned motivating operations.
FK-28: Transitive, reflexive, and surrogate motivating operations.
FK-29: Distinguish between the discriminative stimulus and the motivating operation.
FK-30: Distinguish between motivating operation and reinforcement effects.

Notes:

FK-27 CONDITIONED MOTIVATING OPERATIONS.

Definition (Surrogate CMO):

[ ]

(Cooper, Heron, & Heward, 2007).
☐ Flashcard created   ☐ Learned to fluency

Definition (Reflexive CMO):

[ ]

(Cooper, Heron, & Heward, 2007).
☐ Flashcard created   ☐ Learned to fluency

Definition (Transitive CMO):

[ ]

(Cooper, Heron, & Heward, 2007).
☐ Flashcard created   ☐ Learned to fluency

Example:

Surrogate CMO: A rat is placed in a distinctive environment when food deprived. This is repeated a number of times. Over time, the rat is placed in the same environment when they have not been deprived of food. The distinctive environment and it's relation to a state of food deprivation results in an increase in the value of food as a reinforcer and an increase in the frequency of behavior with a history of producing food. In this example, the distinctive environment is paired with a unconditioned motivating operation (food deprivation). Over time, the distinctive environment functions as a motivating operation in the absence of food deprivation.

Reflexive CMO: The presence of instructional materials often precedes the presentation of instructional tasks. If an individual engages in behavior maintained by access to escape from instructional tasks, in time they may engage in escape maintained behavior in the presence of instructional materials and the removal of these materials may function as a reinforcer. In this example, the instructional materials serve as a CMO-R.

Transitive CMO: A locked door functions as a CMO-T to establish a key as a reinforcer.

Write another example:

[ ]

Questions to ask your supervisor:

Relevant Literature:

Catania, A. C. (1993). Coming to terms with establishing operations. The Behavior Analyst, 16, 219-224. Catania, A. C. (1994). Learning. Englewood Cliffs, NJ: Prentice-Hall. Clark, F. C. (1958). The effects of deprivation and frequency of reinforcement on variable interval responding. Journal of the Experimental Analysis of Behavior, 1, 221-228.

Cooper, J.O., Heron, T.E. & Heward W.L. (2007). *Applied Behavior Analysis* (2nd Ed.), Upper Saddle River, NJ. Pearson Prentice Hall. 384-389.

Endicott, K., & Higbee, T.S. (2007). Contriving motivating operations to evoke mands for information in preschoolers with autism. *Research in Autism Spectrum Disorders*, 1, 3, 210-217.

Hesse, B. (1993). The establishing operation revisited. The Behavior Analyst, 16, 215- 217.

Iwata, B. A., Smith, R. G., & Michael, J. (2000). Current research on the influence of establishing operations on behavior in applied settings. Journal of Applied Behavior Analysis, 33, 411-418.

Lotfizadeh, A.D., Edwards, T.L., Redner, R., & Poling, A. (2012). Motivating operations affect stimulus control: A largely overlooked phenomenon in discrimination learning. *Behavior Analyst*, 35, 1, 89-100.

Michael, J. (1993). Establishing operations. *The Behavior Analyst*, *16*(2), 191.

Related Lessons:

D-01: Use positive and negative reinforcement.

E-01: Use interventions based on manipulation of antecedents, such as motivating operations and Discriminative stimuli.

I-02: Define environmental variables in observable and measureable terms.

FK-02: Selectionism (phylogenic, ontogenic, cultural)

FK-13: Reflexive relations (US-UR)

FK-14: Respondent conditioning (CS-CR)

FK-17: Unconditioned reinforcement.

FK-19: Unconditioned punishment

FK-26: Unconditioned motivating operations.

FK-28: Transitive, reflexive, and surrogate motivating operations.

FK-29: Distinguish between the discriminative stimulus and the motivating operation.

FK-30: Distinguish between motivating operation and reinforcement effects.

Notes:

FK-28 TRANSITIVE, REFLEXIVE, SURROGATE MOTIVATING OPERATIONS.

Definition
(Conditioned Motivating Operations (CMO):

(Cooper, Heron, & Heward, 2007).
☐ Flashcard created   ☐ Learned to fluency

Definition
(Reflexive-Conditioned Motivating Operations (CMO-R):

(Cooper, Heron, & Heward, 2007).
☐ Flashcard created   ☐ Learned to fluency

Definition
Transitive-Conditioned Motivating Operations (CMO-T):

(Cooper, Heron, & Heward, 2007).
☐ Flashcard created   ☐ Learned to fluency

Definition
(Surrogate-Conditioned Motivating Operations (CMO-S):

(Cooper, Heron, & Heward, 2007).
☐ Flashcard created   ☐ Learned to fluency

Example:

(CMO-R) A child engages in escape-maintained problem behavior during matching to sample instruction. In time, the child engages in escape-maintained problem behavior when the materials for matching to sample are brought out, before instruction has begun.

(CMO-T) You walk up to your front door and turn the knob, but the door is locked. You reach into your pocket and grab your keys and unlock the door.

(CMO-S) In the presence of a stimulus that has been paired with a cold environment, the value of stimuli that produce warmth increases.

Write another example:

Questions to ask your supervisor:

Relevant Literature:

Carbone, V.J., Morgenstern, B., Zecchin-Tirri, G., & Kolberg, L. (2007). The role of the reflexive conditioned motivating operation (CMO-R) during discrete trial instruction of children with autism. *Journal of Early and Intensive Behavior Intervention,* 4, 4, 658-680.

Cooper, J.O., Heron, T.E. & Heward W.L. (2007). *Applied Behavior Analysis* (2nd Ed.), Upper Saddle River, NJ. Pearson Prentice Hall. 384-388, 390-391.

Laraway, S., Snycerski, S., Michael, J., & Poling, A. (2003). Motivating operations and terms to describe them: Some further refinements. *Journal of Applied Behavior Analysis*, 36, 3, 407-414.

McGill, P. (1999). Establishing Operations: Implications for assessment, treatment, and prevention of problem behavior. *Journal of Applied Behavior Analysis*, 32, 393-418.

Michael, J. (1993). *Concepts and Principles of Behavior Analysis*. Kalamazoo, MI. Society for the Advancement of Behavior Analysis.

Michael, J. (1993). Establishing Operations. *The Behavior Analyst*, 16, 191-206.

Mineka, S. (1975) Some new perspectives on conditioned hunger. *Journal of Experimental Psychology: Animal Behavior Processes*, 104, 143-148.

Rosales, R., & Rehfeldt, R.A. (2007). Contriving transitive conditioned establishing operations to establish derived manding skills in adults with severe developmental disabilities. *Journal of Applied Behavior Analysis*, 40, 1, 105-121.

Related Lessons:

D-01: Use positive and negative reinforcement.
E-01: Use interventions based on manipulation of antecedents, such as motivating operations and discriminative stimuli.
FK-13: Reflexive relations (US-UR)
FK-14: Respondent conditioning (CS-CR)
FK-15: Operant conditioning
FK-16: Respondent-operant interactions.
FK-18: Conditioned reinforcement.
FK-20: Conditioned punishment
FK-27: Conditioned motivating operations.
FK-29: Distinguish between the discriminative stimulus and the motivating operation
FK-30: Distinguish between motivating operation and reinforcement effects.

Notes:

FK-29 DISTINGUISH BETWEEN THE DISCRIMINATIVE STIMULUS AND THE MOTIVATING OPERATION.

Definition (Discriminative Stimulus):

(Cooper, Heron, & Heward, 2007).
☐ Flashcard created   ☐ Learned to fluency

Definition (Motivating Operations):

(Cooper, Heron, & Heward, 2007).
☐ Flashcard created   ☐ Learned to fluency

Example:

A child often asks their parents to play video games after school. The child's father often says "yes" to this request, while the child's mother says "no" and tells the child to get started on their homework. Over time the child continues to ask their father if they can play video games, but has stopped asking their mother. In this example the presence of the father likely functions as an SD due to the history of requests being granted in his presence, but not in the presence of their mother.

After playing outside for an hour, a child walks into the house and gets a drink of water. In this example, playing outside likely functions as a motivating operation, more specifically as establishing operation, in that it increases the value of water as a reinforce and increases the frequency of behavior with a history of producing water.

A student earns tokens throughout the school day and can trade them in for a preferred item or activity. Usually the student chooses to trade in their tokens for a small snack, accept after lunch. Usually after lunch the student chooses computer over snacks. In this example, consuming food during lunch likely functions as a motivating operation, more specifically an abolishing operation, in that it decreases the value of food as a reinforcer and decreases the frequency of behavior with a history of producing food.

Write another example:

Questions to ask your supervisor:

Notes:

Relevant Literature:

Cooper, J.O., Heron, T. E., & Heward, W. L. (2007). *Applied behavior analysis*. Upper Saddle River, NJ: Pearson Prentice Hall.

Michael, J. (1982). Distinguishing between discriminative and motivating functions of stimuli. Journal of the Experimental Analysis of Behavior, 37, 149–155.

Related Lessons:

E-01 Use interventions based on manipulation of antecedents, such as motivating operations and discriminative stimuli.

G-08 Identify and make environmental changes that reduce the need for behavior analysis services.

I-02 Define environmental variables in observable and measurable terms.

J-04 Select intervention strategies based on client preferences.

J-06 Select intervention strategies based on supporting environments.

J-07 Select intervention strategies based on environmental and resource constraints.

K-09 Secure the support of others to maintain the client's behavioral repertoires in their natural environments.

FK-07 Environmental (as opposed to mentalistic) explanations of behavior

FK-24 Stimulus control

FK-26 unconditioned motivating operation

FK-31 behavioral contingencies

FK-33 functional relations

FK-30 DISTINGUISH BETWEEN MOTIVAT-
ING OPERATION AND REINFORCE-
MENT EFFECTS.

Definition (Motivating Operations):

(Cooper, Heron, & Heward, 2007).
☐ Flashcard created   ☐ Learned to fluency

Definition (Behavior altering effect):

(Cooper, Heron, & Heward, 2007).
☐ Flashcard created   ☐ Learned to fluency

Definition (Value altering effect):

(Cooper, Heron, & Heward, 2007).
☐ Flashcard created   ☐ Learned to fluency

Example:

Being deprived of food or water increases the reinforcing value of food and water (i.e., a value altering effect in which the MO functions as an EO), and there will likely be an increase in the current frequency of all behavior that has previously been reinforced with food and water (i.e., an evocative behavior-altering effect). Conversely, if a large meal was just consumed then it is unlikely that food will be reinforcing (i.e., a value-altering effect in which the MO functions as an AO) and there will be a reduction in the current frequency of all behavior previously reinforced with food (i.e., an abative behavior-altering effect).

This next example can illustrate the difference between MO effects and reinforcement/punishment effects (i.e., repertoire-altering effects). Before leaving for work you realize that it is going to be a cold day. The heater in your car does not work well so you plan ahead by putting a blanket and extra jacket in your car to use if it becomes too cold. During your drive to work, it becomes increasingly cold so you turn on your car heater, put your extra jacket on, and lay the blanket over you so you become much warmer. In this example, there was an increase in the current frequency of all behavior that has been reinforced by becoming warmer (i.e., an evocative behavior-altering effect). For the rest of the winter, to avoid becoming too cold on your drive to work, you leave every morning already wearing an extra jacket and put a blanket on you as soon as you get in the car (i.e., repertoire-altering effect on future behavior).

Write another example:

Questions to ask your supervisor:

Relevant Literature:

Cooper, J. O., Heron, T. E., & Heward, W. L. (2007). Motivating operations. *Applied Behavior Analysis* (pp. 374-391). Upper Saddle River, NJ: Pearson Prentice Hall.

Iwata, B. A., Smith, R. G., & Michael, J. (2000). Current research on the influence of establishing operating on behavior in applied settings. *Journal of Applied Behavior Analysis, 33*, 411-418.

Laraway, S., Snycerski, S., Michael, J., & Poling, A. (2001). The abative effect: A new term to describe the action of antecedents that reduce operant responding. *The Analysis of Verbal Behavior, 18*, 101-104.

Schlinger, H., & Blakely, E. (1987). Function-altering effects of contingency-specifying stimuli. *The Behavior Analyst, 10*, 41-45.

Related Lessons:

E-01 Use interventions based on manipulation of antecedents, such as motivating operations and discriminative stimuli.

FK-25 multiple functions of a single stimulus

FK-26 unconditioned motivating operations

FK-27 conditioned motivating operations

FK-28 transitive, reflexive, surrogate motivating operations

FK-29 distinguish between the discriminative stimulus and the motivating operation

Notes:

Segment 10 – Scorecard
Skill Acquisition I

☐ Presentation (2-5 minutes)

D 3
☐ Assessment
☐ SAFMED learned to fluency
☐ Workbook boxes completed

D 5
☐ Assessment
☐ SAFMED learned to fluency
☐ Workbook boxes completed

D 6
☐ Assessment
☐ SAFMED learned to fluency
☐ Workbook boxes completed

D 7
☐ Assessment
☐ SAFMED learned to fluency
☐ Workbook boxes completed

D 8
☐ Assessment
☐ SAFMED learned to fluency
☐ Workbook boxes completed

E 2
☐ Assessment
☐ SAFMED learned to fluency
☐ Workbook boxes completed

E 6
☐ Assessment
☐ SAFMED learned to fluency
☐ Workbook boxes completed

E 12
☐ Assessment
☐ SAFMED learned to fluency
☐ Workbook boxes completed

E 13
☐ Assessment
☐ SAFMED learned to fluency
☐ Workbook boxes completed

FK 12
☐ Assessment
☐ SAFMED learned to fluency
☐ Workbook boxes completed

FK 34
☐ Assessment
☐ SAFMED learned to fluency
☐ Workbook boxes completed

Segment 10 – Individual Supervision Agenda

Supervisor: _____ **Supervisee:** _____
Meeting Date: _____ **Time of meeting – From:**_____ **To:**_____
This document covers supervisory period from ____/____/____ **to** ____/____/____

1. Pass-in/Review Homework:

    Did the Supervisee satisfactorily complete this homework assignment?   Yes / No

- If not, what is needed to complete assignment? Describe below.

2. Task List items addressed (D 3, 5, 6-8; E 2, 6, 12-13; FK 12, 34)

3. Definitions/SAFMEDs learned

    ☐ Flashcard(s) created   Was supervisee fluent with definitions? Yes ☐ No ☐

4. Discussion topics or activities completed during this meeting:

Evaluation of Supervisee's Performance			
(Record: S- "Satisfactory"; NI- "Needs Improvement"; U- "Unsatisfactory"; or NA- "Not Applicable")			
Arrived on time for meeting		Gave examples as needed	
Completed Homework Assigned		Accepted supervisory feedback appropriately	
Referred to literature/readings		Answered all questions thoroughly	
Maintained professional communication during supervision meeting			
Overall evaluation of supervisee performance during this meeting *(Circle one—use code above)*	S	NI	U
If "NI" or "U", please list corrective steps needed to achieve a score of "S"			

5. Homework assigned for next meeting

6. Closing questions/feedback

Segment 10 – Group Supervision Meeting Agenda

- <u>Meeting Topic</u>: Skill Acquisition I

- <u>Task List Items Reviewed</u>:
  - D-05: Use shaping.
  - FK-12: Stimulus equivalence.
  - E-02: Use discrimination training procedures.
  - FK-34: Conditional discriminations.
  - E-06: Use stimulus equivalence.
  - E-12: Use errorless learning procedures.
  - D-03: Use prompts and prompt fading.
  - E-13: Use Matching-to-sample procedures.
  - D-06: Use chaining.
  - D-07: Use task analysis.
  - D-08: Use discrete trials and free operant arrangements.

1. Housekeeping
   - Upon entry to meeting have supervisees hand in the previous week's homework assignment and discuss several "Housekeeping Items" related to supervision.
   - Take attendance for the meeting.
   - State the duration of today's meeting (90 minutes).
   - Distribute BACB® experience forms to supervisees.

2. Task List Lesson and Discussion
   - Discuss task list item D-05: Use shaping.
   - Discuss task list item FK-12: Stimulus equivalence.
   - Discuss task list item E-02: Use discrimination training procedures.
   - Discuss task list item FK-34: Conditional discriminations.
   - Discuss task list item E-06: Use stimulus equivalence.
   - Discuss task list item E-12: Use errorless learning procedures.
   - Discuss task list item D-03: Use prompts and prompt fading.
   - Discuss task list item E-13: Use Matching-to-Sample procedures.
   - D-06: Use chaining.
   - D-07: Use task analysis.
   - D-08: Use discrete trials and free operant arrangements.

3. Homework Review
   - Review homework that was assigned at the previous supervision meeting.

4. Questions
   - Answer any questions related to the homework or topics discussed.

5. Closing Notes

   - *Assign Homework (task list boxes, presentation) from today's segment, due at next group meeting*

   - Close the meeting by inviting supervisees to request topics to be covered in upcoming meetings.

D-03 USE PROMPTS AND PROMPT FADING.

Definition:

Prompts – "…antecedent stimuli that increase the probability of a desired response" (Piazza, & Roane, 2014, p. 256).

Prompt fading – "…transfer stimulus control from therapist delivered prompts to stimuli in the natural environment that should evoke appropriate responses" (Walker, 2008 cited in Fisher, Piazza, & Roane, 2014, p. 412).

Prompts are used when teaching skills. Prompts can be used when teaching in task analysis, discrete trial, incidental teaching, etc. Prompt fading is important as the learner begins to show competence with the skill being taught. Fading allows the learner to become independent and meet naturalistic reinforcers for his/her behavior.

Prompts are generally divided into two categories: stimulus prompts and response prompts.

Stimulus prompts – "…those in which some property of the criterion stimulus is altered, or other stimuli are added to or removed from the criterion stimulus" (Etzel & LeBlanc, 1979 cited in Fisher, Piazza, & Roane, 2014, p. 256).

Response prompts – "…addition of some behavior on the part of an instructor to evoke the desired learner behavior" (Fisher, Piazza, & Roane, 2014, p. 256).

Examples:

- Stimulus Prompts: stimulus shaping and stimulus fading.
- Response Prompts: most-to-least prompting, least-to-most prompting, and time delay prompts.

Write another example:

Questions to ask your supervisor:

Relevant Literature:

Etzel, B. C., & LeBlanc, J. M. (1979). The simplest treatment alternative: The law of parsimony applied to choosing appropriate instructional control and errorless-learning procedures for the difficult-to-teach child. *Journal of Autism and Developmental Disorders, 9*(4), 361-382.

Fisher, W. W., Piazza, C. C., & Roane, H. S. (2014). *Handbook of applied behavior analysis.* New York: Guilford Press.

Walker, G. (2008). Constant and progressive time delay procedures for teaching children with autism: A literature review. *Journal of Autism and Developmental Disorders, 38*(2), 261-275.

Related Lessons:

D-04 Use modeling and imitation training.
D-05 Use shaping.
D-06 Use chaining.
D-07 Conduct task analyses.
D-08 Use discrete-trial and free-operant arrangements.
E-01 Use interventions based on manipulation of antecedents, such as motivating operations and discriminative stimuli.
E-02 Use discrimination training procedures.
E-13 Use matching-to-sample procedures.
FK-24 stimulus control

Notes:

D-05 USE SHAPING.

Definition (Shaping):

[ ]

(Cooper, Heron, & Heward, 2007).
☐ Flashcard created   ☐ Learned to fluency

Example:

Bernice's baby boy is beginning to babble. She has been trying to get him to say, "Mama." While playing with him she happens to catch him making the "mmmm" sound. She smiles and praises him for making the vocalization. Over the next several days she continues to applaud him when he makes this sound. After a few weeks she observes the baby making a "ma" noise. She praises him more enthusiastically giving him tickles. Although she still continues to commend him for making the "mmm" sound, the social reinforcement delivered for saying "ma" is differentially delivered. Some time later she catches him babbling "ma ma ma." She praises him excitedly proclaiming, "You said 'Mama'," giving him big hugs and kisses. Verbal praise and affection is almost exclusively delivered for saying "ma ma ma" now. Eventually the baby who continually hears him mother say "Mama" (and not "ma ma ma") echoes his mother when she gives the verbal model. She demonstrates the highest level of excitement for this vocalization and the baby continues to emit this response.

Petunia is pet sitting for a friend. On her way out the door the cat, Mr. Boots, escapes outside. Petunia tries to call the feline back indoors, but every time she gets near him, Mr. Boots runs away. Petunia has an idea. She places a bowl of cat food outside. Mr. Boots goes to the bowl but only when he thinks the coast is clear. Over the next few days, she successively moves the bowl of food closer to the front door. On the fourth day, Petunia puts the bowl just inside of the doorway. Mr. Boots takes the bait. While he gobbles down the food, Petunia, who had been hiding nearby shuts the door and captures the beloved cat.

Non-example:
- Bernice's baby has gotten bigger. While looking at a picture book she points out a picture of a farm animal. She tells him that this is a cow and that the cow says, "moo." The baby immediately echoes the word "moo" and Bernice

praises him. He continues to say "moo" when seeing pictures of cows in other books as well.
Write another example:

[ ]

Questions to ask your supervisor:

[ ]

Relevant Literature:

Cooper J.O, Heron T.E, Heward W.L. (2007). *Applied behavior analysis* (2nd ed.) Upper Saddle River, NJ: Pearson.

Lovaas O.I. The autistic child: Language development through behavior modification. New York: Irvington; 1977.

Newman, B., Reinecke, D., & Ramos, M. (2009). Is a Reasonable Attempt Reasonable? Shaping Versus Reinforcing Verbal Attempts of Preschoolers with Autism. *The Analysis of Verbal Behavior*, 25(1), 67–72.

Pryor, K. (1999). Don't Shoot the Dog [rev. ed.]. New York: Bantam.

Ricciardi, J. N., Luiselli, J. K., & Camare, M. (2006). Shaping approach responses as intervention for specific phobia in a child with autism. Journal of Applied Behavior Analysis, 39(4), 445-448.

Skinner, B. F. (1979). *The shaping of a behaviorist: Part two of an autobiography.* New York: New York University Press.

Related Lessons:

D-01: Use positive and negative reinforcement
D-05: Use Shaping
D-21: Use differential reinforcement
FK -41: Contingency-shaped behavior

Notes:

D-06 USE CHAINING.

Definition (Behavior chain):

(Cooper, Heron, & Heward, 2007).
☐ Flashcard created   ☐ Learned to fluency

Definition (Behavior chain characteristics):

(Cooper, Heron, & Heward, 2007).
☐ Flashcard created   ☐ Learned to fluency

Example:
Brad is going to teach show tying to one of his students. He decides to use a forward chain and writes down all the smaller steps involved in tying ones shoes. This successfully and systematically helps his student learn to tie their shoes.

Non-Example:
Joe decides to use video modeling to help his student learn to tie their shoes. He has them watch the video daily and then model what they learned from that video in an attempt to have them learn how to tie their shoes.

Write another example.

Questions to ask your supervisor:

Relevant Literature:
Cooper, J.O., Heron, T.E. & Heward W.L. (2007). *Applied Behavior Analysis* (2nd Ed.), Upper Saddle River, NJ. Pearson Prentice Hall. 435-453, 589.

Catania, A.C. (1998). Learning (4th Ed.), Upper Saddle River, NJ. Prentice-Hall, Inc. 44, 82, 124, 380.

Libby, M.E., Weiss, J.S., Bancroft, S., & Ahearn, W.A. (2008).A comparison of most-to-least and least-to-most prompting on the acquisition of solitary play skills. *Behavior Analytic Practices*, 1, 1, 37-43.

Kayser J. E, Billingsley F. F, & Neel R. S. (1986). A comparison of in-context and traditional instructional approaches: Total task, single trial versus backward chaining, multiple trials. *Journal of the Association for the Severely Handicapped*. 11, 28–38.

Spooner F. (1984). Comparisons of backward chaining and total task presentation in training severely handicapped persons. *Education and Training of the Mentally Retarded*. 19, 15–22.

Reynolds, G.S. (1975). *A primer of operant conditioning* (Rev. Ed.) Glenview, IL.:. Scott, Foresman.

McWilliams, R., Nietupski, J., & Hamre-Nietupski, S. (1990). Teaching complex activities to students with moderate handicaps through the forward chaining of shorter total cycle response sequences. *Education and Training in Mental Retardation*, 25, 3, 292-298.

Test, D.W., Spooner, F., Keul, P.K., & Grossi, T. (1990). Teaching adolescents with severe disability to use the public telephone. *Behavior Modification*, 14, 157-171.

Snell, M.E. & Brown, F. (2006). *Instruction of students with severe disabilities* (6th ed.) Upper Saddle River, NJ. Prentice Hall.

Related Lessons:
A-07: Measure trials to criterion.
D-03: Use prompts and prompt fading.
D-04: Use modeling and imitation training.
D-05: Use shaping.
E-01: Use interventions based on manipulation of antecedents (e.g., motivating operations & discriminative stimuli).
E-02: Use discrimination training procedures.
I-01: Define behavior in observable and measureable terms.
J-03: Select intervention strategies based on task analysis.
FK-10: Behavior, response, response class.

Notes:

D-07 CONDUCT TASK ANALYSES

Definition (Task analysis):

(Cooper, Heron, & Heward, 2007).
☐ Flashcard created   ☐ Learned to fluency

Examples:

Accessing an iPhone 5s
1. Press home key (circle)
2. Slide finger across bottom of screen, from left to right, over text that reads "slide to unlock"
3. Enter passcode

Washing a Cup
1. Turn on tap
2. Pick up sponge and put dish soap on sponge
3. Put down dish soap
4. Pick up dirty cup, scrub outside rim, sides, and base of cup with sponge
5. Scrub inside, base, and rim of cup with sponge
6. Put sponge down
7. Rinse cup with warm water
8. Place cup on drying rack
9. Rinse excess soap out of sponge
10. Turn off tap
11. Put sponge in holder/in sink

Write another example:

Questions to ask your supervisor:

Relevant Literature:

Cooper, J. O., Heron, T. E., & Heward, W. L. (2007). *Applied behavior analysis*. (2nd Ed.) Upper Saddle River, NJ. : Pearson Prentice Hall.

Resnick, L. B., Wang, M. C., & Kaplan, J. (1973). Task analysis in curriculum design: a hierarchically sequenced introductory mathematics curriculum. *Journal of Applied Behavior Analysis*, *6*(4), 679-709.

Bancroft, S. L., Weiss, J. S., Libby, M. E., & Ahearn, W. H. (2011). A comparison of procedural variations in teaching behavior chains: Manual guidance, trainer completion, and no completion of untrained steps. *Journal of applied behavior analysis*, *44*(3), 559-569.

Jerome, J., Frantino, E. P., & Sturmey, P. (2007). The effects of errorless learning and backward chaining on the acquisition of internet skills in adults with developmental disabilities. *Journal of applied behavior analysis*, *40*(1), 185-189.

Slocum, S. K., & Tiger, J. H. (2011). An assessment of the efficiency of and child preference for forward and backward chaining. *Journal of applied behavior analysis*, *44*(4), 793-805.

Related Lessons:
D-03 Use prompts and prompt fading
D-05 Use shaping
D-06 Use chaining

Notes:

D-08 USE DISCRETE-TRIALS AND FREE-OPERANT ARRANGEMENTS

Definition (Free-operant):

(Baer & Fowler, 1984).
☐ Flashcard created   ☐ Learned to fluency

Definition (Discrete-trial/Rate of response):

(Cooper, Heron, & Heward, 2007).
☐ Flashcard created   ☐ Learned to fluency

Definition (Free-operant/Discrete-trial Comparison):

(Mazur 2002).
☐ Flashcard created   ☐ Learned to fluency

Example:
-    Bill is presented with an array of 3 shapes and his teacher states, "show me the circle". Bill points to the circle and his teacher tells him he did a great job.

Non-example:
-    Bill's teacher gives him a worksheet on matching shapes to pictures. She tells him to complete the worksheet and then hand it in to her so she can review it.

Write another example:

Questions to ask your supervisor:

Relevant Literature:
Cooper, J.O., Heron, T.E. & Heward W.L. (2007). *Applied Behavior Analysis* (2nd Ed.), Upper Saddle River, NJ. Pearson Prentice Hall. 77-78, chapters 11-23, 25-28.

Otto, J. (2003). Discrete trial procedures vs. free-operant procedures. Retrieved from http://old.dickmalott.com/students/undergradprogram/psy3600/discrete_vs_free.html.

Malott, R.W., & Trojan, E.A. (2003). *Principles of Behavior.* (5th Ed.), Upper Saddle River, NJ. Pearson Prentice Hall. Chapter 17.

Mazur, J.E. (2002), Learning and Behavior (5th Ed.) Upper Saddle River, NJ. Pearson Prentice Hall.

Related Lessons:
A-01: Measure frequency (i.e., count).
A-02: Measure rate (i.e., count per unit time).
A-07: Measure trials to criterion.
D-03: Use prompts and prompt fading.
E-01: Use interventions based on manipulation of antecedents, such as motivating operations and discriminative stimuli.
E-12: Use errorless learning procedures.
H-01: Select a measurement system to obtain representative data given the dimensions of the behavior and the logistics of observing and recording.
FK-10: Behavior, response, response class.
FK-11: Environment, stimulus, stimulus class
FK-47: Identify the measureable dimensions of behavior (e.g., rate, duration, latency, inter-response time).

Notes:

E-02 USE DISCRIMINATION TRAINING.

Definition:

Discrimination training procedures involve "reinforcing or punishing a response in the presence of one stimulus and extinguishing it or allowing it to recover in the presence of another stimulus" (Malott &Trojan Suarez, 2004). There are typically two competing contingencies when discrimination training occurs. The first contingency involves an S-delta (i.e., signals that a specified response will not be reinforced or punished when in the presence of a specified stimulus). The second contingency involves a discriminative stimulus (i.e., signals that a specified response will be reinforced in the presence of a specific stimulus condition). When discrimination training occurs, a specified response will no longer be reinforced in the presence of an S-delta, however, that same response will be reinforced in the presence of a discriminative stimulus. The goal of discrimination training is to reinforce responses in certain stimulus conditions so that they occur more frequently when those stimulus conditions are present and over time, the response will no longer occur in the presence of the S-delta. When discrimination training is successful, the learner can discriminate which antecedent stimulus conditions will result in greater reinforcement for a given response.

Examples:

Discrimination training can be used to teach an individual when it is and is not appropriate to take a break, when or where it is acceptable to engage in self-stimulatory behaviors, what items in the kitchen can be accessed without asking for permission, and so on. Discrimination training procedures are evident in basic instructional lessons such as teaching a child to identify colors to seemingly natural situations such as only scheduling clients on days allowed by funding sources because this results in you being paid for your services.

Carl's teacher determines attention is reinforcing his speaking out in class. Carl's teacher teaches Carl to ask questions when there is a green card present on the board, and not to ask questions when there is a red card on the board. She does this by only delivering attention to Carl when the green card is present on the board, and ignoring Carl when the red card is present.

Write another example:

Questions to ask your supervisor:

Relevant Literature:

Cooper, J. O., Heron, T. E., & Heward, W. L. (2007). Stimulus Control. *Applied Behavior Analysis* (pp. 392-409). Upper Saddle River, NJ: Pearson Prentice Hall.

Malott, R. W., & Trojan Suarez, E.A. (2004). Discrimination. *Principles of Behavior* (pp. 206-225). Upper Saddle River, NJ: Pearson Prentice Hall.

Taylor-Santa, C., Sidener, T. M., Carr, J. E., & Reeve, K. F. (2014). A discrimination training procedure to establish conditioned reinforcers for children with autism. *Behavioral Intervention, 29*, 157-176.

Related Lessons:

D-08 Use discrete-trial and free-operant arrangements
E-01 Use interventions based on manipulation of antecedents, such as motivating operations and discriminative stimuli.
E-03 Use instructions and rules
E-13 Use matching-to-sample procedures
J-11 Program for stimulus and response generalization
FK-11 environment, stimulus, stimulus class
FK-24 stimulus control
FK-25 multiple functions of a single stimulus
FK-35 stimulus discrimination

Notes:

E-06 USE STIMULUS EQUIVALENCE PROCEDURES.

Definition:

In the field of applied behavior analysis, a number of procedures have been used to teach new concepts. One of these procedures is known as stimulus equivalence. In 1971, Murray Sidman discovered that a previously untaught, unreinforced stimuli could come under stimulus control through its pairing with other stimuli which were explicitly taught (Sidman, 1971). This concept revolutionized the field as it demonstrated a new way of teaching that could potentially reduce the amount of time needed to teach a new class of stimuli. "Behavior analysts define stimulus equivalence by testing stimulus-stimulus relations. A positive demonstration of all three behavioral tests (i.e. reflexivity, symmetry, and transitivity) is necessary to meet the definition of an equivalence relation among a set of arbitrary stimuli." (Cooper, Heron, & Heward, 2007).

- Reflexivity describes the action of selecting a stimulus that is matched to itself in the absence of training and reinforcement (A=A). For instance an individual is shown three pictures; a penny, a nickel, and a dime. When given an identical picture of a penny, he matches it to the identical picture of a penny in the array (Sidman, 1994).

- Symmetry describes the reversibility of the sample stimulus and a comparison stimulus (A=B and B=A). For instance an individual who is taught to select the picture of a penny (out of an array of 3), when the word penny is given, would also be able to choose the comparison spoken word *penny* shown the picture of the penny without being previously taught this correlation (Sidman, 1994).

- Transitivity is the most crucial test for demonstrating stimulus equivalence. A third, untrained relation emerges as a result of being taught the first two relations. (A=C and C=A) "is a product of training the other two stimulus-stimulus relations" (Cooper, Heron, & Heward, 2007).

Example:

- The following equation demonstrates the basic principles of stimulus equivalence:

If A = B, and B = C, then A = C. (Sidman & Tailby, 1982)

When using stimulus equivalence, decide what relations are to be taught (i.e. spoken word to picture, picture to written word, drawing to real-life picture, etc.). Decide which order the conditional relations are to be taught. Teach the relations A=B and B=C to mastery criteria. Once mastery criteria are met for the first two relations, test for reflexivity, symmetry, and transitivity using the same criteria. If the participant demonstrates these relations without having been previously been taught them, they will have acquired the third relation C=A that demonstrates the most important test for stimulus equivalence.

Write another example:

Questions to ask your supervisor:

Relevant Literature:

Cooper J.O, Heron T.E, Heward W.L. (2007). *Applied behavior analysis* (2nd ed.) Upper Saddle River, NJ: Pearson

Sidman, M. (1971) Reading and auditory-visual equivalences. *Journal of Speech & Hearing Research*, Volume 14(1), 5-13.

Sidman, M. (1994). *Equivalence Relations and Behavior: A Research Story*. Boston: Author's Cooperative.

Sidman, M. and Tailby, W. (1982). Conditional Discrimination Vs. Matching to Sample: An Expansion of the Testing Paradigm. *Journal of Experimental Analysis Behavior*, 37: 5–22.

Related Lessons:

E-06 Use stimulus equivalence procedures.

E-13 Use matching-to-sample procedures.

FK-11 environment, stimulus, stimulus class

FK-12 stimulus equivalence

FK-13 reflexive relations (US-UR)

FK-24 stimulus control

FK-28 transitive, reflexive, surrogate motivating operations

FK-35 stimulus discrimination

Notes:

E-12 USE ERRORLESS LEARNING PROCEDURES.

Definition:

Errorless learning - an "approach whereby the task is manipulated to eliminate/reduce errors. Tasks are executed in such a way that the subject is unlikely to make errors" (Fillingham, Hodgson, Sage, & Ralph, 2003, p. 339).

Errorless learning techniques include most-to-least prompt fading or stimulus shaping/fading techniques. Prompts are removed gradually as the individual becomes more adept with the skill, thereby reducing the likelihood of errors. To apply errorless learning, behavioral strategies utilized may include: response prevention (e.g., only S+ is presented allowing for only correct responding or physical guidance is provided with instruction so incorrect responses are not possible); verbal prompt fading; modeling; stimulus fading (e.g. emphasizing a physical dimension of the stimuli to evoke a correct response such as by illuminating the correct selection, S+, and presenting the incorrect selection, S-, in a dimmer format); or stimulus shaping (e.g. increasing likelihood of correct responding by gradually changing the shape of the stimulus to maintain correct responding).

The advantages of errorless learning include that it removes negative side effects involved with trial-and-error learning and that it is proven particularly effective among individuals that suffer from brain damage or have a developmental disorder. The disadvantages include cost, time-intensity, and maybe considered less natural than trial-and-error learning (Mueller, Palkovic & Maynard, 2007).

Example:

Trial-and-error learning, being presented with stimuli in which both the correct selection (S+) and incorrect selection (S-) are available, can lead to adverse side effects due to the possibility of incorrect responding and failure to access reinforcers. Research has shown that this can result in aggression, negative emotional responses and stimulus overselectivity (Mueller et al., 2007).

Write another example:

Questions to ask your supervisor:

Relevant Literature:

Fillingham, J.K,, Hodgson, C., Sage, K., & Ralph, M.A. (2003). The application of errorless learning to aphasic disorders: A review of theory and practice. *Neuropsychological Rehabiliation, 13*(3), 337-363.

Mueller, M.M., Palkovic, C.M., & Maynard, C.S. (2007). Errorless learning: review and practical application for teaching children with pervasive developmental disorders. *Psychology in the Schools, 44*(7), 691-700.

Terrace, H.S. (1963). Discrimination learning with and without "errors". *Journal of the Experimental Analysis of Behavior, 6*(1), 1-27.

Related Lessons:

D-03 Use prompts and prompt fading
D-04 Use modeling and imitation training
FK-24 Stimulus control
Notes:

E-13 USE MATCHING-TO-SAMPLE PROCEDURES.

Definition:
Matching-to-sample - "A procedure for investigating conditional relations and stimulus equivalence. A matching-to-sample trial begins with the participant making a response that presents or reveals the sample stimulus; next, the sample stimulus may or may not be removed, and two or more comparison stimuli are presented. The participant then selects one the comparison stimuli. Responses that select a comparison stimulus that matches the sample stimulus are reinforced, and no reinforcement is provided for responses selecting the nonmatching comparison stimuli" (Cooper, Heron, & Heward, 2007, p. 699).

Example:
A teacher presents a student with a picture of an apple. The teacher then lays out three other picture cards away from the original picture of an apple. One picture card depicts an apple, the second picture card depicts a banana, and the final picture card depicts an orange. The teacher holds up the initial picture card depicting an apple and states, "match". The student takes the picture of an apple and places it on top of the corresponding picture of an apple. The teacher says, "Great job" and gives the student a high five.

Write another example:

Cooper, J.O., Heron, T.E. & Heward W.L. (2007). *Applied Behavior Analysis* (2nd Ed.), Upper Saddle River, NJ. Pearson Prentice Hall. 398-401.

Cumming, W.W. & Berryman, R. (1965). The complex discriminated operant: Studies of matching-to-sample and related problems. In D.I. Mostofsky (Ed.), *Stimulus Generalization* (pp. 284-333). Palo Alto, CA: Stanford University Press.

Fields, L., Garrutto, M., & Watanabe, M. (2010). Varieties of stimulus control in matching-to-sample: A kernel analysis. *The Psychological Record*, 60, 3-26.

Sidman, M., Wilson-Morris, M., & Kirk, B. (1986). Matching-to-sample procedures and the development of equivalence relations: The role of naming. *Analysis and Interventions in Developmental Disabilities*, 6, 1, 1-19.

Related Lessons:
D-03: Use prompts and prompt fading.
D-08: Use discrete-trials and free-operant arrangements.
E-02: Use discrimination training procedures.
E-06: Use stimulus equivalence procedures.
E-12: Use errorless learning procedures.

Notes:

Questions to ask your supervisor:

FK-12 STIMULUS EQUIVALENCE.

Definition (Stimulus Equivalence):

(Cooper, Heron, & Heward, 2007).
☐ Flashcard created   ☐ Learned to fluency

Definition (Reflexivity):

(Cooper, Heron, & Heward, 2007).
☐ Flashcard created   ☐ Learned to fluency

Definition (Symmetry):

(Cooper, Heron, & Heward, 2007).
☐ Flashcard created   ☐ Learned to fluency

Definition (Transitivity):

(Cooper, Heron, & Heward, 2007).
☐ Flashcard created   ☐ Learned to fluency

Examples:
- When learner responds without prior reinforcement and training that A=A (exhibiting reflexivity) and if A=B, then B must also = A (exhibiting symmetry) and finally that if A=B and B=C, then C must also equal A (exhibiting transitivity).
- *Reflexivity*: Without prior reinforcement or training, when shown a picture of a dog and given a picture of the same dog, a rat, and a cow, student matches the picture of the two dogs (e.g. A=A).

- *Symmetry:* Student is taught that when given the written word *dog* to select the picture of a dog. Without further reinforcement or training, when given the picture of the dog, student selects the written word *dog* (e.g. If A=B, then B=A).

- *Transitivity*: Student is taught that when given the written word *dog* to select the picture of the dog (e.g. A=B). Student is also taught to select the picture of the dog when hearing the spoken word *dog* (e.g. B=C). Without further reinforcement or training, student selects the written word *dog* after hearing the spoken word *dog* (e.g. C=A).

Non-Examples:
- When learner responds without prior reinforcement and training that A=A (exhibiting reflexivity) and if A=B, then B must also equal A (exhibiting symmetry) but cannot show that if A=B and B=C, then C must also equal A (failure to exhibit transitivity).

Write another example:

Questions to ask your supervisor:

Relevant Literature:
Cooper, J. O., Heron, T. E., & Heward, W. L. (2007). *Applied behavior analysis* (2nd ed.). Upper Saddle River, NJ: Prentice Hall.
Sidman, M. (1997). Equivalence relations. Journal of the Experimental Analysis of Behavior, 68(2), 258-266.

Sidman, M. (2009). Equivalence relations and behavior: An introductory tutorial. *The Analysis of verbal behavior, 25*(1), 5.

Related Lessons:
- E-06 Use Stimulus equivalence procedures
- E-13 Use matching-to-sample procedures

Notes:

FK-34 CONDITIONAL DISCRIMINATIONS.

Definition (Conditional discriminations):

(Cooper, Heron, & Heward, 2007).
☐ Flashcard created   ☐ Learned to fluency

Definition (Conditional relations):

(Carrigan & Sidman, 1992).
☐ Flashcard created   ☐ Learned to fluency

Definition (Functional relation):

(Sidman, 1994).
☐ Flashcard created   ☐ Learned to fluency

Example:

In a matching-to-sample trial, "A" is given as the conditional sample and is then presented in a series of five letters "z", "k", "a", "t", and "b." By correctly matching "A" to "a" the learner is discriminating stimuli and selecting the correct comparison that will be reinforced. The learner's response will not be reinforced if a stimulus other than "a" is selected. In this example, the conditional sample "A" reflects the contextual stimulus as it creates a context for which stimulus to discriminate.

Write another example:

Relevant Literature:

Bush, K. M., Sidman, M., & De Rose, T. (1989). Contextual control of emergent equivalence relations. Journal of the Experimental Analysis of Behavior, 51, 29-45.

Carrigan, P. F., & Sidman, M. (1992). Conditional discrimination and equivalence relations: A theoretical analysis of control by negative stimuli. Journal of the Experimental Analysis of Behavior, 58, 183 204.

Cooper, J. O., Heron, T. E., & Heward, W. L. (2007). Stimulus control. *Applied Behavior Analysis* (pp. 392-409). Upper Saddle River, NJ: Pearson Prentice Hall.

Johnson. C. & Sidman, M. (1993). Conditional discrimination and equivalence relations: Control by negative stimuli. *Journal of the Experimental Analysis of Behavior, 59*, 333-347.

Sidman, M. (1994). *Equivalence relations and behavior: A research story.* Boston, MA: Author's Cooperative.

Questions to ask your supervisor:

Related Lessons:
E-06 Use stimulus equivalence procedures.
FK-11 environment, stimulus, stimulus class
FK-24 stimulus control
FK-35 stimulus discrimination
FK-37 stimulus generalization
J-14 Arrange instructional procedures to promote generative learning (i.e., derived relations).

Notes:

Segment 11 – Scorecard
Skill Acquisition II

☐ Presentation (2-5 minutes)

D 4
☐ Assessment
☐ SAFMED learned to fluency
☐ Workbook boxes completed

D 14
☐ Assessment
☐ SAFMED learned to fluency
☐ Workbook boxes completed

F 3
☐ Assessment
☐ SAFMED learned to fluency
☐ Workbook boxes completed

F 4
☐ Assessment
☐ SAFMED learned to fluency
☐ Workbook boxes completed

F 5
☐ Assessment
☐ SAFMED learned to fluency
☐ Workbook boxes completed

F 6
☐ Assessment
☐ SAFMED learned to fluency
☐ Workbook boxes completed

F 7
☐ Assessment
☐ SAFMED learned to fluency
☐ Workbook boxes completed

J 10
☐ Assessment
☐ SAFMED learned to fluency
☐ Workbook boxes completed

Segment 11 – Individual Supervision Agenda

Supervisor: _____ **Supervisee:** _____

Meeting Date: _____ **Time of meeting – From:**_____ **To:**_____

This document covers supervisory period from ____/____/____ **to** ____/____/____

1. Pass-in/Review Homework:

   Did the Supervisee satisfactorily complete this homework assignment?   Yes / No

   • If not, what is needed to complete assignment? Describe below.

2. Task List items addressed (D 4, 14; F 3-7; J 10)

| |
| |

3. Definitions/SAFMEDs learned

   ☐ Flashcard(s) created   Was supervisee fluent with definitions? Yes ☐ No ☐

| |
| |

4. Discussion topics or activities completed during this meeting:

Evaluation of Supervisee's Performance			
(Record: S- "Satisfactory"; NI- "Needs Improvement"; U- "Unsatisfactory"; or NA- "Not Applicable")			
Arrived on time for meeting		Gave examples as needed	
Completed Homework Assigned		Accepted supervisory feedback appropriately	
Referred to literature/readings		Answered all questions thoroughly	
Maintained professional communication during supervision meeting			

	S	NI	U
Overall evaluation of supervisee performance during this meeting *(Circle one—use code above)*	S	NI	U
If "NI" or "U", please list corrective steps needed to achieve a score of "S"			

5. Homework assigned for next meeting

| |
| |

6. Closing questions/feedback

| |
| |

Segment 11 – Group Supervision Meeting Agenda

- <u>Meeting Topic</u>: Skill Acquisition II

- <u>Task List Items Reviewed</u>:
- D-14: Use listener training.
- D-04: Use modeling and imitation training.
- F-03: Use direct instruction.
- F-04: Use precision teaching.
- F-05: Use personalized systems of instruction (PSI).

- F-06: Use incidental teaching.
- F-07: Use functional communication training.
- J-10: When a behavior is to be decreased, select an acceptable alternative behavior to be established or increased.

1. Housekeeping
    - Upon entry to meeting have supervisees hand in the previous week's homework assignment and discuss several "Housekeeping Items" related to supervision.
    - Take attendance for the meeting.
    - State the duration of today's meeting (90 minutes).
    - Distribute BACB® experience forms to supervisees.

2. Task List Lesson and Discussion
    - Discuss task list item D-14: Use listener training.
    - Discuss task list item D-04: Use modeling and imitation training.
    - Discuss task list item F-03: Use direct instruction.
    - Discuss task list item F-04: Use precision teaching.
    - Discuss task list item F-05: Use personalized systems of instruction (PSI).
    - Discuss task list item F-06: Use incidental teaching.
    - Discuss task list item F-07: Use functional communication training.
    - Discuss task list item J-10: When a behavior is to be decreased, select an acceptable alternative behavior to be established or increased.

3. Homework Review
    - Review homework that was assigned at the previous supervision meeting.

4. Questions
    - Answer any questions related to the homework or topics discussed.

5. Closing Notes
    - *Assign Homework (task list boxes, presentation) from today's segment, due at next group meeting*
    - Close the meeting by inviting supervisees to request topics to be covered in upcoming meetings.

D-04 USE MODELING AND IMITATION TRAINING

Definition (Imitation):

[ ] Flashcard created   [ ] Learned to fluency

(Cooper, Heron, & Heward, 2007).

Definition (Modeling):

(Cooper, Heron, & Heward, 2007).
[ ] Flashcard created   [ ] Learned to fluency

Example:
- A therapist sits across from his student Zeke in the preschool classroom. The therapist prompts the student to "do this," and claps her hands. Zeke responds within two seconds of the therapist's prompt and claps. The therapist responds by adding a token to Zeke's token board.
- During job training, the job coach, Flora, demonstrates to her new employee, Fauna, how to turn the copy machine off at the end of the workday. Fauna then immediately flicks the switch, demonstrating that she understands the expectation. Flora praises Fauna for paying attention.

Non-Example:
- A therapist sits across from his student Zeke in the preschool classroom. The therapist prompts the student to "do this," and claps her hands. Zeke does not imitate the model and reinforcement is not delivered. Later during the day Zeke excitedly claps his hands when his favorite song is playing on the TV.

Write another example:

Questions to ask your supervisor:

Relevant Literature:

Baer, D. M., Peterson, R. F. and Sherman, J. A. (1967), The development of imitation by reinforcing behavioral similarity to a model. *Journal of the Experimental Analysis Behavior*, 10: 405–416.

Cooper J.O, Heron T.E, Heward W.L. (2007). *Applied behavior analysis* (2nd ed.) Upper Saddle River, NJ: Pearson.

Striefel, S., Bryan, K. S. and Aikins, D. A. (1974), Transfer of stimulus control from motor to verbal stimuli. *Journal of Applied Behavior Analysis*, 7: 123–135.

Related Lessons:
D-04 Use modeling and imitation training.

Notes:

D-14 USE LISTENER TRAINING.

Definition:

Listener – "someone who provides reinforcement for verbal behavior" (Cooper, Heron, & Heward, 2007, p. 698)

Part of being involved in a verbal community is reinforcing the behavior of speakers. There are several methods for training someone to respond as a listener. Skills such as vocal imitation (echoic), following instructions, answering questions (intraverbal), conversation skills (intraverbal), indicating objects, etc., all require listener behavior.

Sundberg discusses a distinction between intraverbal and listener responding. "If the child's response were verbal, then it would classified as intraverbal... but if the response were nonverbal it would be classified as listener behavior (or often termed receptive language or receptive labeling)" (Sundberg, 2008).

There are multiple protocols for receptive language training (cf., Fabrizio & Moors, 2001; Leaf & McEachin, 1999; Lovaas, 2003; Maurice, Green, & Luce, 1996). In a review of teaching receptive language to children with autism, Pelios and Sucharzewski (2004) point out that one must consider antecedent manipulations (e.g., within-stimulus prompts, keeping stimulus short, using topographically dissimilar responses) and consequence manipulations (e.g., rich reinforcement schedules, token economies, performance based breaks). Also, they recommend systematically programming specific antecedent and consequence manipulations and requiring specific response requirements.

Example:
- A teacher conducting receptive language training tells her student "sit down" the student sits down and the teacher praises the student. The teacher then says "clap hands" the student claps hands and the teacher praises the student.
- A teacher presents an array of fruit and says to the student, "give me the apple." The student gives the teacher the apple and the teacher gives the student a token.

Write another example:

Questions to ask your supervisor:

Relevant Literature:

Cooper, J. O., Heron, T. E., & Heward, W. L. (2007). *Applied behavior analysis*. Upper Saddle River, NJ: Pearson Prentice Hall.

Fabrizio, M. S. (2001). *A Brief Overview of Fluency-Based Instruction for Learners with Autism*. Fabrizio/Moors Consulting, Seattle, Washington.

Leaf, R., & McEachin, J. (1999). *A work in progress: Behavior management strategies and a curriculum for intensive behavioral treatment of autism*. New York: DRL Books, LLC.

Lovaas, O. I. (2003). *Teaching individuals with developmental delays: Basic intervention techniques*. Austin, TX: Pro-Ed.

Maurice C, Green G, Luce S, editors. Behavioral intervention for young children with autism: A manual for parents and professionals. Austin, TX: Pro-Ed; 1996.

Pelios, L. V., & Sucharzewski, A. (2004). Teaching receptive language to children with autism: A selective overview. *The Behavior Analyst Today, 4*(4), 378.

Schlinger, H. D. (2008). Listening Is Behaving Verbally. *The Behavior Analyst,31*(2), 145–161.

Sundberg, M. L. (2008). VB-MAPP Verbal Behavior Milestones Assessment and Placement Program: a language and social skills assessment program for children with autism or other developmental disabilities: guide. Concord, CA: AVB Press.

Related Lessons:
D-10 Use echoic training.
D-13 Use intraverbal training.
FK-43 Echoics
FK-44 Mands
FK-45 Tacts
FK-46 Intraverbals

Notes:

F-03 USE DIRECT INSTRUCTION.

Definition:
Direct instruction - a teaching method "…emphasizing the use of specified teacher directions, programmed instruction and presentation of materials, examples, and prompts, the use of reinforcement and mastery learning principles, regular and direct assessment, and teaching prerequisite skills." (Callahan, Shukla-Mehta, & Wie, 2010, p. 78).

Direct instruction was developed to improve academic skills of elementary school students with learning challenges. This model of instructional design was proposed by Engelmann and Becker (Becker, et al., 1975). Direct instruction relies on scripted lessons implemented by a directly trained teacher provided to small-group of learners. These scripted lessons include a lot of examples and non-examples. Students respond in unison when asked by a teacher and practice skills in groups until reaching a mastery level. Students and teachers systematically measure and teachers analyze students' performance. Those who follow the DI model believe that the learner knows better; that all children can be taught. If a student fails, this is teacher's fault. Additionally, the process of teaching includes hierarchy of instruction complexity: basic skills should be taught before advancing to more complex skills.

Write another example:

Questions to ask your supervisor:

Callahan, K., Shukla-Mehta, S., MaGee, S., & Wie, M. (2010). ABA vs. TEACCH: The case for defining and validating comprehensive treatment models in autism. *Journal of Autism and Developmental Disorders*, 40, 1, 74-88.

Cooper, J. O., Heron, T. E., & Heward, W. L. (2007). *Applied behavior analysis.* (2nd ed.). Upper Saddle River, NJ: Pearson Education.

Moran, D.J. & Mallot, R.W. (2004). *Evidence Based Educational Methods.* (1st ed.). San Diego, CA: Elsevier Academic Press. pp. 81-91.

Ledford, J.R., Lane, J.D., Elam, K.L., & Wolery, M. (2012). Using response-prompting procedures during small group direct-instruction: Outcomes and procedural variations. *American Journal on intellectual and Developmental Disabilities*, 117, 5, 413-434.

Gersten, R., & Keating, T. (1987). Long-term benefits from direct instruction. *Educational Leadership*, 44, 6, 28-31.

Gersten, R., Keating, T., & Becker, W. (1988). The continued impact of the direct instruction model: Longitudinal studies of follow through students. *Education and Treatment of Children*, 11, 4, 318-327.

Gersten, R., Woodward, J., & Darch, C. (1986). Direct instruction: A research-based approach to curriculum design and teaching. *Exceptional Children*, 53, 1, 17-31.

Graves, A. W. (1986). Effects of direct instruction and meta-comprehension training on finding main ideas. *Learning Disabilities Research*, 1, 2, 90-100.

Related Lessons:
A-07: Measure trials to criterion.
D-03: Use prompts and prompt fading.
D-08: Use discrete trials and free-operant arrangements.
J-02: Identify potential interventions based on assessment results and the best available scientific evidence.
J-11: Program for stimulus and response generalization.
J-12: Program for maintenance.
J-14: Arrange instructional procedures to promote generative learning (i.e., derived learning).

Notes:

F-04 USE PRECISION TEACHING.

Precision teaching is a methodology of teaching which involves measuring performance of a learner and making changes based on these data. Precision teaching was proposed by Ogden Lindsley in 1964 in an article "Direct Measurement and Prosthesis of Retarded Behavior".

There are four steps of precision teaching process:

1. **Pinpoint** - means to describe an actual movement which a learner needs to perform in a specific time interval to show an improvement on learning behavior.
2. **Record** - means that a learner or a teacher collect data on pinpointed behavior regularly and display these data graphically using the Standard Celeration Chart (the SCC).
3. **Change** - means that the teacher analyzes the data using guidelines of analyzing the SCC (Graf & Lindsley, 2002) and quickly makes changes in a current instructional method if needed.
4. **Try Again** - means that the teacher keeps exploring the best instructional methods for those learners who need more help and provides the learners with the opportunities to practice until the mastery level.

Precision teaching follows four principles described by Kubina (2012): "(i) a focus on observable behavior, (ii) the use of frequency as data metric, (iii) graphing student performance data on a Standard Celeration Chart, and (iv) making decisions based on performance data" (As cited in Cooper, Heron, Heward, 2007, p. 142).

Example:

- A teacher's objective is to teach a student to say and write an answer when vocally asked simple math problems questions. The teacher will record how many times a student answers correctly in one minute interval. These data will be collected over the next several weeks and progress will be charted using a Standard Celebration Chart. Decisions about the teaching procedure will be made depending on the performance data.

Non- example:

- A teacher's objective is to teach students to solve simple math problems. Percent correct are collected across the quarter. At the end of the quarter a report card will be sent to the student's home.

Relevant Literature:

Cooper, J. O., Heron, T. E., & Heward, W. L. (2007). *Applied behavior analysis*. Upper Saddle River, NJ: Pearson Education, 139-144.

Cooper, J.O. (2000). Tutoring Joe: Winning with the precision teaching team. In W.L. Heward (ed.) *Exceptional Children: An introduction to special education* (6th ed.) Upper Saddle River, NJ: Merrill, 268-270.

Kerr, K.P., Smyth, P., & McDowell, C. (2003). Precision teaching children with autism: Helping design effective programmes. *Early Childhood Development and Care*, 173, 4, 399-410.

Hughes, J.C., Beverley, M., & Whitehead, J. (2007). Using precision teaching to increase the fluency of word reading with problem readers. *European Journal of Behavior Analysis*, 8, 221-238.

Kubina, R. M. (2012). *Precision teaching book*. [S.l.]: Greatness Achieved Pub Co.

Kubina, R.M., Morrison, R., & Lee, D.L. (2002). Benefits of adding precision teaching to behavioral interventions for students with autism. *Behavioral Interventions*, 17, 233-246.

Potts, L., Eshleman, J.W., & Cooper, J.O. (1993). Ogden R. Lindsley and the historical development of precision teaching. *The Behavior Analyst*, 2, 16, 177-189.

Related Lessons:

A-01: Measure frequency (i.e., count)
A-07: Measure trials to criterion.
F-03: Use Direction Instruction
H-01: Select a measurement system to obtain representative data given the dimensions of the behavior and the logistics of observing and recording.
H-02: Select a schedule of observation and recording periods.
H-03: Select a data display that effectively communicates relevant quantitative relations.
H-04: Evaluate changes in level, trend, and variability.
H-05: Evaluate temporal relations between observed variables (within and between sessions, times series).
J-15: Base decision-making on data displayed in various formats.
FK-33: Functional relations.

Notes:

Write another example:

Questions to ask your supervisor:

F-05 USE PERSONALIZED SYSTEMS OF INSTRUC-
TION (PSI).

Personalized system of instruction (PSI) was created by
Fred S. Keller. PSI uses self-paced modules with study
guides to help direct students' learning. Proctors are
used to help students with the material and lectures are
not as common compared to traditional teaching formats. PSI focuses on self-paced learning by the student
rather than teacher directed instruction. Specific criteria
on mastery tests are required before moving on to the
next module. Keller (1968) summarized his writings
from 1967 describing features of this type of training:

1. The go-at-your-own-pace component
2. The unit-perfection requirement for advancement
3. The use of lectures and demonstrations sparingly but
not for critical information
4. The promotion of written word in teacher-student
communication
5. The use of proctors for repeated testing, immediate
scoring, answering questions, and personal-social part
of the educational process

Relevant Literature:

Axelrod, S. (1992). Disseminating an effective educational technology. *Journal of Applied Behavior Analysis*, 1, 25, 31-35.

Buskist, W., Cush, D., & DeGrandpre, R. J. (1991). The
life and times of PSI. *Journal of Behavioral Education*,
1, 215–234.

Keller, F. S. (1994). The Fred S. Keller School: CABAS
at work. *The Current Repertoire*, 10, 3–4.

Keller, F. S. (1968). Goodbye, teacher. *Journal of Applied
Behavior Analysis*, 1, 79–89.

Keller, F. S., & Sherman, G. (1982). *The PSI handbook.*
Lawrence, KS: TRI Publications.

Twyman, J.S. (1992). The Fred S. Keller School. *Journal
of Applied Behavior Analysis*, 4, 31, 695-701.

Eyre, H.L. (2007) Keller's personalized system of instruction: Was it fleeting fancy or is there a revival
on the horizon? The Behavior Analyst, 8, 3, 317-
324.

Related Lessons:
F-01: Use self-management strategies.
F-04: Use precision teaching.
J-14: Arrange instructional procedures to promote gen-
erative learning (i.e., derived relations).

Notes:

Write another example:

Questions to ask your supervisor:

F-06 USE INCIDENTAL TEACHING.

Definition:

Incidental teaching - When the "instructor assesses the child's ongoing interests, follows the child's lead, restricts access to high interest items, and constructs a lesson within the natural context, with a presumably more motivated child." (Anderson & Romanczyk, 1999, p. 169)

Incidental teaching requires an instructor to use moments in the natural environment as teaching opportunities. It can be used to teach language based skills, social skills, play skills, or other skills as well.

Example:

- Todd often struggles to initiate play with his peers during recess. His teacher decided to go over and prompt Todd to introduce himself to Mike and ask him to play a game.

Non-example:

Rich wanted to help teach Todd multiplication, so he gave him a worksheet and sat down with him to go through the problems one by one.

Write another example:

Questions to ask your supervisor:

Relevant Literature:

Anderson, S. R., & Romancyzk, R. G. (1999). Early intervention for young children with autism: Continuum-based behavioral models. *Journal of the Association for Persons with Severe Handicaps*, 24, 162–173.

Cooper, J. O., Heron, T. E., & Heward, W. L. (2007). *Applied behavior analysis*. Upper Saddle River, NJ: Pearson Education, 448, 542, 634.

Hart, B. & Risley, T.R. (1975) Incidental teaching of language in the preschool. *Journal of Applied Behavior Analysis*, 8, 4, 411-420.

McGee, G.G., & Daly, T. (2007). Incidental Teaching of Age-Appropriate Social Phrases to Children with Autism. *Research and Practice for Persons with Severe Disabilities*, 32, 112-123.

McGee, G.G., Morrier, M.J., & Daly, T. (1999) An Incidental Teaching Approach to Early Intervention for Toddlers with Autism. *Research and Practice for Persons with Severe Disabilities*, 24, 133-146.

McGee, G. G., Krantz, P. J., Mason, D., & McClannahan, L. E. (1983). A modified incidental-teaching procedure for autistic youth: acquisition and generalization of receptive object labels. Journal of Applied Behavior Analysis, 16(3), 329–338.

Related Lessons:

B-03: Systematically arrange independent variables to demonstrate their effects on dependent variables.

D-04: Use modeling and imitation training.

D-05: Use shaping.

D-11: Use mand training.

J-06: Select intervention strategies based on supporting environments.

J-11: Program for stimulus and response generalization. FK-44: Mands.

Notes:

F-07 USE FUNCTIONAL COMMUNICATION TRAINING.

Definition:

Functional communication training (FCT) - "…an application of differential reinforcement of alternative behaviors (DRA) because the intervention develops an alternative communicative response as an antecedent to diminish the problem behavior" (Fisher, Kuhn, & Thompson, 1998, p. 543).

The alternative response can include vocalizations, sign language, communication boards and devices, picture cards, or gestures.

Carr and Durand (1985) used a two-step process to demonstrate how to deliver FCT. First they completed a functional behavior assessment to identify the stimuli with known reinforcing properties that maintain the problem behavior, and second, they used those stimuli as reinforcers to develop an alternative behavior to replace the problem behavior.

Guidelines for the effective use of functional communication training include providing a dense schedule of reinforcement, fading prompts, and the appropriate reinforcement schedule thinning after the response is at strength.

Example:

Rob was throwing books at his teacher every time he was asked to do a math worksheet. After completing a functional analysis, Rob's teacher found throwing books was maintained by access to escape. Rob was taught to ask for a break when he was doing math instead of throwing something at his teacher. This response, paired with pre-teaching and prompt fading, helped replace the problematic behavior.

Write another example:

Questions to ask your supervisor:

Relevant Literature:

Cooper, J. O., Heron, T. E., & Heward, W. L. (2007). *Applied behavior analysis.* Upper Saddle River, NJ: Pearson Education, 494-496.

Durand, V.M. (1999). Functional communication training using assistive devices: Recruiting natural communities of reinforcement. *Journal of Applied Behavior Analysis, 32,* 247-267.

Carr, E.G., & Durand, V.M. (1985). Reducing behavior problems through functional communication training. *Journal of Applied Behavior Analysis, 18,* 111-126.

Durand, V.M, & Carr, E.G. (1992). An analysis of maintenance following functional communication training. *Journal of Applied Behavior Analysis, 25,* 777-794.

Fisher, W.W., Kuhn, D.E., & Thompson, R.H. (1998). Establishing discriminative control of responding using functional and alternative reinforcers during functional communication training. *Journal of Applied Behavior Analysis, 31,* 543-560.

Hanley, G.P., Iwata, B.A., & Thompson, R.H. (2001). Reinforcement schedule thinning following treatment with functional communication training. *Journal of Applied Behavior Analysis, 34,* 17-38.

Related Lessons:

D-02: Use appropriate parameters and schedules of reinforcement.
D-03: Use prompts and prompt fading.
D-04: Use modeling and imitation training.
D-05: Use shaping.
D-10: Use echoic training.
D-11: Use mand training.
D-21: Use differential reinforcement (e.g., DR0, DRA, DRI, DRL, DRH)
E-01: Use interventions based on manipulation of antecedents, such as motivating operations and discriminative stimuli.
I-03: Design and implement individualized behavioral assessment procedures.
I-04: Design and implement the full range of functional assessment procedures.

Notes:

J-10 WHEN A BEHAVIOR IS TO BE DE-
CREASED, SELECT AN ACCEPTABLE AL-
TERNATIVE BEHAVIOR TO ESTAB-
LISHED OR INCREASED.

Definition:

**Differential reinforcement of alternative be-
havior (DRA)** - "a procedure for decreasing
problem behavior in which reinforcement is delivered for a behavior that serves as desirable alternative to the behavior targeted for reduction and
withheld following instances of the problem behavior" (Cooper, Heron & Heward, 2007, p. 693).
When choosing a replacement behavior, it is often
recommended to look at behavior that would
serve the same function or would meet the same
reinforcers for the problem behavior. This response could be using vocal-verbal behavior, ex-
changing a symbol, using sign language, or another
form of communication. Consider the pros and
cons of each mode. How quickly can the response
be taught? Is it likely to be less or more effortful
than the problem behavior? Will the new response
meet reinforcement in natural settings?

Initially, the response to be taught should be reinforced on a continuous reinforcement schedule to
ensure that the individual makes steady contact
with the reinforcer and that this new replacement
behavior occurs often and becomes strengthened
in the individual's repertoire. Once the new response is at strength, the DRA schedule should be
thinned to reflect reinforcement rates that occur in
the natural environment (e.g., a child learning to
request for a break in lieu of eloping will not likely
be granted a break every time he/she asks for one
in a typical classroom environment).

Some considerations when utilizing DRA include
resurgence of challenging behavior when DRA
schedules are thinned. There are several techniques that can be utilized to decrease this occurrence: increase the response requirement of the alternative response (e.g., if the alternate response is
to ask for a break, allow a break only after completion of a set amount of work), provide a delay for
reinforcement for the alternative response (e.g.,
provide a break after several minutes), decrease
availability of alternative response materials (e.g. if
break is requested utilizing a break card, limit
amount of breaks or decrease presentation), and
usage of a multiple schedule of reinforcement such
as providing more reinforcement for completing
work than for asking for a break (Sweeney & Shahan, 2013).

Notes:

Write another example:

Questions to ask your supervisor:

Relevant Literature:
Athen, E.S., & Vollmer, T.R., (2010). An investigation of
differential reinforcement of alternative behavior without
extinction. *Journal of Applied Behavioral Analysis, 43(4)*, 569-
589.
Cooper, J. O., Heron, T. E., & Heward, W. L. (2007). *Applied behavior analysis* (2nd ed.). Upper Saddle River, NJ:
Prentice Hall.
Sweeney, M.M., & Shahan, T.A., (2013). Effects of high,
low, and thinning rates of alternative reinforcement on response elimination and resurgence. *Journal of the Experimental Analysis of Behavior, 100(1)*, 102-116.
Vollmer, T. R., Roane, H. S., Ringdahl, J. E., & Marcus, B.
A. (1999). Evaluating treatment challenges with differential reinforcement of alternative behavior. *Journal of Applied
Behavior Analysis, 32*(1), 9-23.

Related Lessons:
D-02 Use appropriate parameters and schedules of rein-
forcement.
D-18. Use Extinction.
D.-19 Use combinations of reinforcement with punish-
ment and extinction.
I-06 Make recommendations regarding behaviors that
must be established, maintained, increased or decreased.
J-06 Select intervention strategies based on supporting en-
vironments.
J-07 Select intervention strategies based on environmental
and resource constraints.

Segment 12 – Scorecard
Research Design I

☐ Presentation (2-5 minutes)

A 10
☐ Assessment
☐ SAFMED learned to fluency
☐ Workbook boxes completed

A 11
☐ Assessment
☐ SAFMED learned to fluency
☐ Workbook boxes completed

B 3
☐ Assessment
☐ SAFMED learned to fluency
☐ Workbook boxes completed

B 10
☐ Assessment
☐ SAFMED learned to fluency
☐ Workbook boxes completed

B 11
☐ Assessment
☐ SAFMED learned to fluency
☐ Workbook boxes completed

Segment 12 – Individual Supervision Agenda

Supervisor: _____ **Supervisee:** _____

Meeting Date: _____ **Time of meeting – From:**_____ **To:**_____

This document covers supervisory period from ____/____/____ to ____/____/____

1. Pass-in/Review Homework:

    Did the Supervisee satisfactorily complete this homework assignment?   Yes / No

- If not, what is needed to complete assignment? Describe below.

2. Task List items addressed (A 10-11; B 3, 10-11)

| |
| |

3. Definitions/SAFMEDs learned

    ☐ Flashcard(s) created   Was supervisee fluent with definitions? Yes ☐ No ☐

| |
| |

4. Discussion topics or activities completed during this meeting:

Evaluation of Supervisee's Performance			
(Record: S- "Satisfactory"; NI- "Needs Improvement"; U- "Unsatisfactory"; or NA- "Not Applicable")			
Arrived on time for meeting		Gave examples as needed	
Completed Homework Assigned		Accepted supervisory feedback appropriately	
Referred to literature/readings		Answered all questions thoroughly	
Maintained professional communication during supervision meeting			
Overall evaluation of supervisee performance during this meeting *(Circle one—use code above)*			S NI U
If "NI" or "U", please list corrective steps needed to achieve a score of "S"			

5. Homework assigned for next meeting

| |
| |

6. Closing questions/feedback

| |
| |

Segment 12 – Group Supervision Meeting Agenda

- <u>Meeting Topic</u>: Research Design I

- <u>Task List Items Reviewed</u>:
  o A-10: Design, plot, and interpret data using equal-interval graphs.
  o A-11: Design, plot, and interpret data using a cumulative record.
  o B-03: Systematically arrange independent variables to demonstrate their effects on dependent variables.
  o B-10: Conduct a component analysis to determine the effective components of an intervention package.
  o B-11: Conduct a parametric analysis to determine the effective values of an independent variable.

1. Housekeeping
   - Upon entry to meeting have supervisees hand in the previous week's homework assignment and discuss several "Housekeeping Items" related to supervision.
   - Take attendance for the meeting.
   - State the duration of today's meeting (90 minutes).
   - Distribute BACB® experience forms to supervisees.
2. Task List Lesson and Discussion
   - Discuss task list item A-10: Design, plot, and interpret data using equal-interval graphs.
   - Discuss task list item A-11: Design, plot, and interpret data using a cumulative record.
   - Discuss task list item B-03: Systematically arrange independent variables to demonstrate their effects on dependent variables.
   - Discuss task list item B-10: Conduct a component analysis to determine the effective components of an intervention package.
   - Discuss task list item B-11: Conduct a parametric analysis to determine the effective values of an independent variable.
3. Homework Review
   - Review homework that was assigned at the previous supervision meeting.
4. Questions
   - Answer any questions related to the homework or topics discussed.
5. Closing Notes
   - *Assign Homework (task list boxes, presentation) from today's segment, due at next group meeting*
   - Close the meeting by inviting supervisees to request topics to be covered in upcoming meetings.

A - 10 DESIGN, PLOT, AND INTERPRET DATA USING EQUAL-INTERVAL GRAPHS

Definition:
"In applied behavior analysis, each point on a line graph shows the level of some quantifiable dimension of the target behavior (i.e. the dependent variable) in relation to a specified point in time and/or environmental condition." (Cooper, Heron, & Heward, p. 129)*

The behavior analyst defines behavior in quantifiable, observable terms to measure consistently and accurately. The behavior is measured in terms of a pertinent aspect of behavior that can be counted or assessed across observers. When data are plotted, the patterns they make provide for a visual analysis of levels of the behavior (shown on the vertical, y-axis) as the behavior occurs at a specific point in time or environmental condition (shown on a horizontal, x-axis). Graphs are drawn with the y-axis in a two-thirds ratio to the x-axis in order to enable accurate comparison of intervention results across graphs. The analysis interprets levels of data points, directions (trend), and stability or variability of data paths within a single condition or viewed across different conditions. These factors help an analyst assess if an individual is responding to intervention efforts in a therapeutic or non-therapeutic direction. As a result of this systematic interpretation of results, the analyst continues treatment strategies or alters them until the line graph shows consistent behavior change in a therapeutic direction.

Examples:
Designing an equal interval line graph (Cooper, et al., 2007, pp 144-149) with example of visual analysis of data within and across conditions*:
Approximate ratio of y to x-axis is 2:3
The target behavior to measure was the percent (dimension) of math homework (varied number of problems assigned) a student completed each morning when math homework was assigned (session). Lowest possible percent of homework completed was zero and highest possible percent (100 %) is shown at equal intervals of outside tick parks. Before intervention began, John showed a baseline pattern of completing between zero and 10% of his assigned math homework. Zero value is raised above the x-axis to see data points clearly.
Baseline lasted 4 sessions in a non-therapeutic pattern. Conditions changed from baseline to intervention between Session 4 and 5. The intervention included John's teacher praising him each day that he returned any part of his math homework assigned. In the first session of intervention, John turned in 10% of his homework. The second day after receiving teacher

praise, John increased his completed amount of homework to 40% of the assignment. John did not always increase the percent of homework completed each day that math homework was given. The intervention data path shows an increasing trend overall throughout the intervention condition of teacher praise for math homework completion. Although data showed some variability, John reached criteria of at least 90% of math

homework completed for 3 consecutive days on the 12th day of teacher praise for his efforts to return homework.

Figure 2 – Percent of daily math homework John completed in September

*AB designs can show relations between baseline and intervention responding but cannot be used to show cause and effect.

Write another example:

Questions to ask your supervisor:

Relevant Literature:

Alberto, P. A., & Troutman, A. C. (2012). *Applied behavior analysis for teachers*. Pearson Higher Ed.American Psychological Association, 2010.

Cooper, J. O., Heron, T. E., & Heward, W. L. (2007). *Applied behavior analysis*. (2nd ed.). Upper Saddle River, NJ. Pearson: Prentice Hall.

Gast, D. L., & Ledford, J. R. (Eds.). (2010). *Single subject research methodology in behavioral sciences*. Routledge.

Vanselow, N. R., & Bourret, J. C. (2012). Online Interactive Tutorials for Creating Graphs with Excel 2007 or 2010. *Behavior analysis in practice, 5*(1), 40.

Notes:

Related Lessons:

H-01 Select a measurement system to obtain representative data given the dimensions of the behavior and the logistics of observing and recording.

H-02 Select a schedule of observation and recording periods.

H-03 Select a data display that effectively communicates relevant quantitative relations.

H-04 Evaluate changes in level, trend, and variability.

I-05 Organize, analyze, and interpret observed data.

FK-47 Identify the measurable dimensions of behavior (e.g. rate, duration, latency, interresponse time)

J-15 Base decision-making on data displayed in various formats.

A-11 DESIGN, PLOT, AND INTERPRET DATA USING A CUMULATIVE RECORD TO DISPLAY DATA

Definition (Cumulative record):

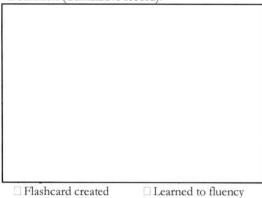

☐ Flashcard created   ☐ Learned to fluency

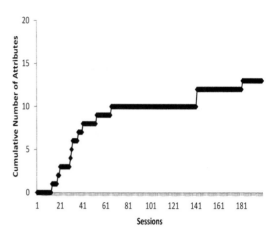

Example:
The cumulative record below indicates the number of attributes learned by a first grade student. The overall response rate is 13 attributes across 181 sessions. In general, data in this graph suggests that there was a fairly slow rate of acquisition. However, the slope is much steeper between sessions 1 and 61, indicating that the rate of acquisition was quicker during the first part of the intervention.

Write another example:

Questions to ask your supervisor:

Relevant Literature:
Cooper, J. O., Heron, T. E., & Heward, W. L. (2007). Constructing and interpreting graphic displays of behavioral data. *Applied Behavior Analysis* (pp. 126-157). Upper Saddle River, NJ: Pearson Prentice Hall.
Ferster, C. B., & Skinner, B. F. (1957). Schedules of reinforcement. New York, NY: Appleton-Century-Crofts.

Related Lessons:
A-10 Design, plot, and interpret data using equal-interval graphs.
H-01 Select a measurement system to obtain representative data given the dimensions of the behavior and the logistics of observing and recording.
H-02 Select a schedule of observation and recording periods.
H-03 Select a data display that effectively communicates relevant quantitative relations.
H-04 Evaluate changes in level, trend, and variability.
H-05 Evaluate temporal relations between observed variables (within &between sessions, time series).

Notes:

B — 03 SYSTEMATICALLY ARRANGE INDE-
PENDENT VARIABLES TO DEMON-
STRATE THEIR EFFECTS ON DEPEND-
ENT VARIABLES.

Definition (Independent variable):

(Cooper, Heron, & Heward, 2007).
☐ Flashcard created   ☐ Learned to fluency

Definition (Dependent variable guidelines):

(Horner et al., 2005).
☐ Flashcard created   ☐ Learned to fluency

Definition (Dependent variable):

(Cooper, Heron, & Heward, 2007).
☐ Flashcard created   ☐ Learned to fluency

Definition (Experimental Control):

(Horner et al., 2005).
☐ Flashcard created   ☐ Learned to fluency

Example:

A student consistently disrupts group activities. When given visuals for appropriate behavior (i.e., quiet voice, calm body) paired with gestural redirection, disruptive behavior in group lessons decreases. The teacher then takes the visuals away for a week to see if fading these supports would be an option. The gestural redirection for inappropriate behavior is still in place. The student's disruptive behavior remains low. When the redirection is removed the following week. The student engages in increased disruptive behavior during this week, so the teacher decides to continue the gestural prompts and the disruptive behavior decreases again.

Non-Example:

A student with attention deficits consistently disrupts group activities. His teacher occasionally uses the visuals for appropriate behavior outlined in the BSP and the disruptive behavior does not decrease.

Write another example:

Questions to ask your supervisor:

Relevant Literature:

Cooper, J.O., Heron, T.E. & Heward W.L. (2007). *Applied Behavior Analysis* (2nd Ed.), Upper Saddle River, NJ. Pearson Prentice Hall.

Horner, R.H., Carr, E.G., Halle, J., McGee, G., Odom, S., Wolery, M. (2005). The Use of Single-Subject Research to Identify Evidence-Based Practice in Special Education. *Exceptional Children*, 71, 2, 165-179.

Related Lessons:

B-04: Use withdrawal/reversal designs
B-05: Use alternating treatments (i.e., multi-element) designs
B-06: Use changing criterion designs
B-07: Use multiple baseline designs
B-09: Conduct a component analysis to determine the effective components of an intervention package
B-11: Conduct a parametric analysis to determine the effective values of an independent variable.
H-04: Evaluate changes in level, trend, and variability.
I-01: Define behavior in observable and measurable terms.

Notes:

B – 10 CONDUCT A COMPONENT ANALYSIS TO DETERMINE THE EFFECTIVE COMPONENTS OF AN INTERVENTION PACKAGE.

Definition (Component analysis):

(Cooper, Heron, & Heward, 2007.
  ☐ Flashcard created   ☐ Learned to fluency

Example:
An experiment that compares response blocking with and without redirection.
An experiment that compares differential reinforcement of alternative behavior with and without extinction
An experiment that removes one procedure at a time from a treatment package consisting of three procedures (e.g., Token system, response cost and extinction) and compares responding under each condition to responding during implementation of the full treatment package.

Write another example:

Questions to ask your supervisor:

Relevant Literature:

Cooper, J. O., Heron, T. E., & Heward, W. L. (2007). *Applied behavior analysis (2nd ed.). Upper Saddle River, NJ: Pearson.*

Hardesty, S. L., Hagopian, L. P., McIvor, M. M., Wagner, L. L., Sigurdsson, S. O., & Bowman, L. G. (2014). Effects of specified performance criterion and performance feedback on staff behavior: A component analysis. *Behavior Modification, 38*(5), 760-773. doi:10.1177/0145445514538280

Ward-Horner, J., & Sturmey, P. (2010). Component analyses using single-subject experimental designs: A review. *Journal of Applied Behavior Analysis, 43*(4), 685-704. doi:10.1901/jaba.2010.43-685

Ward-Horner, J., & Sturmey, P. (2012). Component analysis of behavior skills training in functional analysis. *Behavioral Interventions, 27*(2), 75-92. doi:10.1002/bin.1339

Related Lessons:
B-03 Systematically arrange independent variables to demonstrate their effects on dependent variables

Notes:

B – 11 CONDUCT A PARAMETRIC ANALYSIS TO DETERMINE THE EFFECTIVE VALUES OF AN INDEPENDENT VARIABLE.

Questions to ask your supervisor:

Definition (Parametric analysis):

(Cooper, Heron, & Heward, 2007).
☐ Flashcard created   ☐ Learned to fluency

Examples:
An experiment designed to analyze different magnitudes of a punishment procedure to determine the least intrusive magnitude of a stimulus to decrease behavior.
An experiment designed to analyze the optimal quality of attention necessary to reinforce appropriate behavior

Write another example:

Relevant Literature:
Cooper, J. O., Heron, T. E., & Heward, W. L. (2007). *Applied behavior analysis (2nd ed.). Upper Saddle River, NJ: Pearson.*
Lerman, D. C., & Iwata, B. A. (1996). A methodology for distinguishing between extinction and punishment effects associated with response blocking. *Journal of Applied Behavior Analysis, 29,* 231-233.
Lerman, D. C., Kelley, M. E., Vorndran, C. M., Kuhn, S. C., & LaRue, R. J. (2002). Reinforcement magnitude and responding during treatment with differential reinforcement. *Journal of Applied Behavior Analysis, 35*(1), 29-48.

Related Lessons:
B-03 Systematically arrange independent variables to demonstrate their effects on dependent variables

Notes:

Segment 13 – Scorecard
Research Design II

☐ Presentation (2-5 minutes)

B 4
☐ Assessment
☐ SAFMED learned to fluency
☐ Workbook boxes completed

B 5
☐ Assessment
☐ SAFMED learned to fluency
☐ Workbook boxes completed

B 6
☐ Assessment
☐ SAFMED learned to fluency
☐ Workbook boxes completed

B 7
☐ Assessment
☐ SAFMED learned to fluency
☐ Workbook boxes completed

B 8
☐ Assessment
☐ SAFMED learned to fluency
☐ Workbook boxes completed

B 9
☐ Assessment
☐ SAFMED learned to fluency
☐ Workbook boxes completed

Segment 13 – Individual Supervision Agenda

Supervisor: _____ **Supervisee:** _____

Meeting Date: _____ **Time of meeting – From:**_____ **To:**_____

This document covers supervisory period from ____/____/____ **to** ____/____/____

1. Pass-in/Review Homework:

   Did the Supervisee satisfactorily complete this homework assignment?   Yes / No

- If not, what is needed to complete assignment? Describe below.

2. Task List items addressed (B 4-9)

```



```

3. Definitions/SAFMEDs learned

    ☐ Flashcard(s) created   Was supervisee fluent with definitions? Yes ☐ No ☐

```



```

4. Discussion topics or activities completed during this meeting:

Evaluation of Supervisee's Performance		
(Record: S- "Satisfactory"; NI- "Needs Improvement"; U- "Unsatisfactory"; or NA- "Not Applicable")		
Arrived on time for meeting	Gave examples as needed	
Completed Homework Assigned	Accepted supervisory feedback appropriately	
Referred to literature/readings	Answered all questions thoroughly	
Maintained professional communication during supervision meeting		
Overall evaluation of supervisee performance during this meeting *(Circle one—use code above)*	S	NI	U
If "NI" or "U", please list corrective steps needed to achieve a score of "S"		

5. Homework assigned for next meeting

```



```

6. Closing questions/feedback

```



```

Segment 13 – Group Supervision Meeting Agenda

- <u>Meeting Topic</u>: Research Design II

- <u>Task List Items Reviewed</u>:
  - B-04: Use withdrawal/reversal designs
  - B-05: Use alternating treatments (i.e., multi-element) designs
  - B-07: Use multiple baseline designs.
  - B-08: Use multiple probe designs.
  - B-06: Use changing criterion designs.
  - B-09: Use combinations of design elements.

1. Housekeeping
   - Upon entry to meeting have supervisees hand in the previous week's homework assignment and discuss several "Housekeeping Items" related to supervision.
   - Take attendance for the meeting.
   - State the duration of today's meeting (90 minutes).
   - Distribute BACB® experience forms to supervisees.

2. Task List Lesson and Discussion
   - Discuss task list item B-04: Use withdrawal/reversal designs
   - Discuss task list item B-05: Use alternating treatments (i.e., multi-element) designs
   - Discuss task list item B-07: Use multiple baseline designs.
   - Discuss task list item B-08: Use multiple probe designs.
   - Discuss task list item B-06: Use changing criterion designs.
   - Discuss task list item B-09: Use combinations of design elements.

3. Homework Review
   - Review homework that was assigned at the previous supervision meeting.

4. Questions
   - Answer any questions related to the homework or topics discussed.

5. Closing Notes
   - *Assign Homework (task list boxes, presentation) from today's segment, due at next group meeting*
   - Close the meeting by inviting supervisees to request topics to be covered in upcoming meetings.

B – 04 USE WITHDRAWAL/REVERSAL DESIGNS.

Definition (Withdrawal Design):

(Cooper, Heron, & Heward, 2007).
☐ Flashcard created   ☐ Learned to fluency

Definition (Reversal Design):

(Cooper, Heron, & Heward, 2007).
☐ Flashcard created   ☐ Learned to fluency

Footnotes:

Some authors exclusively use the term reversal design for studies in which the contingency is reversed (or switched to another behavior) as in DRO and DRA/DRI reversal techniques and the term withdrawal design for studies that employ an A-B-A-B approach where the A signifies baseline condition and B the treatment condition (Cooper, Heron, & Heward, 2007).

A multiple treatment reversal design can also be used to compare the effects of two or more treatment conditions to baseline and/or to the other treatments (e.g., ABABA-CAC, ABABCBCB) (Cooper, Heron, & Heward, 2007).

Example:

- An experiment that entails exposing a participant to a condition of no programmed reinforcement for a work task (baseline) until steady state is achieved, then exposes a participate to a condition in which they earn stickers contingent on a work task (intervention) and then repeats these two conditions respectively.

- An experiment in which baseline consists of the reinforcement of challenging behavior and the treatment consists of differential reinforcement of an alternative/replacement behavior and both conditions are replicated at least twice.

Write another example:

Questions to ask your supervisor:

Relevant Literature:

Anderson, C. M., & Long, E. S. (2002). Use of a structured descriptive assessment methodology to identify variables affecting problem behavior. *Journal of Applied Behavior Analysis, 35*(2), 137-154.

Baer, D. M., & Wolf, M. M. (1970). Recent examples of behavior modification in preschool settings. *Behavior modification in clinical psychology*, 5-12.

Cooper, J. O., Heron, T. E., & Heward, W. L. (2007). *Applied behavior analysis (2nd ed.).* Upper Saddle River NJ: Pearson.

Falcomata, T. S., Roane, H. S., Hovanetz, A. N., Kettering, T. L., & Keeney, K. M. (2004). An evaluation of response cost in the treatment of inappropriate vocalizations maintained by automatic reinforcement. *Journal of Applied Behavior Analysis, 37*(1), 83-87.

Lerman, D. C., Kelley, M. E., Vorndran, C. M., Kuhn, S. A., & LaRue, R. H. (2002). Reinforcement magnitude and responding during treatment with differential reinforcement. *Journal of Applied Behavior Analysis, 35*(1), 29-48.

Related Lessons:

B-03 Systematically arrange independent variables to demonstrate their effects on dependent variables

J-09 Identify and address practical and ethical considerations when using experimental designs to demonstrate treatment effectiveness.

Notes:

B – 05 USE ALTERNATING TREATMENTS (I.E., MULTIELEMENT) DESIGNS.

Definition (Alternating treatment design):

(Cooper, Heron, & Heward, 2007).
☐ Flashcard created   ☐ Learned to fluency

Example:
An experiment that entails conducting DRA and no programmed treatment during alternating sessions to compare treatment to the no treatment.
- An experiment that entails conducting DRI, DRO and DRA on alternating days to compare all treatments to each other.

Write another example:

Questions to ask your supervisor:

Relevant Literature:
Barbetta, P. M., Heron, T. E., & Heward, W. L. (1992). Effects of active student response during error correction on the acquisition, maintenance, and generalization of sight words by students with developmental disabilities. *Journal of applied behavior analysis, 26*(1), 111-119.

Barlow, D. H., & Hayes, S. C. (1979). Alternating treatments design: One strategy for comparing the effects of two treatments in a single subject. *Journal of Applied Behavior Analysis, 12*(2), 199-210.

Cooper, J. O., Heron, T. E., & Heward, W. L. (2007). *Applied Behavior Analysis (2nd ed.)*. Upper Saddle River, NJ: Pearson Prentice Hall.

Iwata, B.A., Dorsey, M. F., Slifer, K .J. Bauman, K. E., & Richman, G. S. (1994).Toward a functional analysis of self-injury. *Journal of Applied Behavior Analysis, 27*, 197-209. (Reprinted from *Analysis and Intervention in Developmental Disabilities, 2*, 3-20, 1982).

Martens, B. K., Lochner, D. G., & Kelly, S. Q. (1992). The effects of variable-interval reinforcement on academic engagement: A demonstration of matching theory. *Journal of Applied Behavior Analysis, 25*(1), 143-151.

Singh, J., & Singh, N. N. (1985). Comparison of word-supply and word-analysis error-correction procedures on oral reading by mentally retarded children. *American Journal of Mental Deficiency*.

Ulman, J. D., & Sulzer-Azaroff, B. (1975). Multielement baseline design in educational research. *Behavior analysis: Areas of research and application*, 377-391.

Related Lessons:
B-03 Systematically arrange independent variables to demonstrate their effects on dependent variables
J-09 Identify and address practical and ethical considerations when using experimental designs to demonstrate treatment effectiveness

Notes:

B – 06 USE CHANGING CRITERION DESIGNS.

Definition (Changing criterion design):

(Cooper, Heron, & Heward, 2007).
☐ Flashcard created   ☐ Learned to fluency

Definition (Changing criterion design and guide-

(Hartmann & Hall, 1976).
☐ Flashcard created   ☐ Learned to fluency

Example:
- Jim created a classwide reinforcement program to increase the vocabulary test scores of a 1st grade class. He wanted to make sure that the reinforcement program was effective so he set specific score criterion for the class, to monitor their progress. Average baseline test scores were 55 % correct for the entire class. Jim set the first criterion phase at 70% of the test questions answered correctly for the entire class. After 4 weeks, the class met these criteria for 3 consecutive tests, so Jim set the classroom performance criterion to 80% of the test questions answered correctly. This time the class met the criterion in 3 weeks and Jim increased the criterion to 90%. Once again, the class met these criteria for 3 consecutive tests. Jim concluded that his intervention was likely responsible for the change in test scores, since the test score reliably increased when the criteria were altered and required a greater score.

Non-Example:
- John created a reinforcement program to increase Larry's rate of answering questions during class. After 3 weeks, the data indicated that Larry was answering more questions appropriately in class. However, there was a new teacher in the classroom and other variables that may have accounted for this change. John wanted to see if the program was increasing this behavior, so he decided to remove the reinforcement program for a week to see if Larry's rate of answering questions decreased.

Write another example:

Questions to ask your supervisor:

Relevant Literature:

Cooper, J.O., Heron, T.E. & Heward W.L. (2007). *Applied Behavior Analysis* (2nd Ed.), Upper Saddle River, NJ. Pearson Prentice Hall.

Hartmann, D.P. & Hall, R.V. (1976). The changing criterion design. *Journal of Applied Behavior Analysis*, 9, 4, 527-532.

McDougall, D. (2005). The range-bound changing criterion design. *Behavioral Interventions*, 20, 2, 129-137.

McLaughlin, T.F. (1983). An examination and evaluation of single subject designs used in behavior analysis research in school settings. *Educational Research Quarterly*, 7, 4, 35-42.

Hall, R.V., & Fox, R.G. (1977). Changing criterion designs: An alternative applied behavior analysis procedure. In B.C. Etzel, J.M. LeBlanc, & D.M. Baer (Eds.). *New developments in behavioral research: Theory, method, and application* (pp. 151-166). Hillsdale, NJ: Erlbaum.

Allen, K.D., & Evans, J.H. (2001). Exposure-based treatment to control excessive blood glucose monitoring. *Journal of Applied Behavior Analysis*, 34, 497-500.

Related Lessons:

B-04: Use withdrawal/reversal designs

B-05: Use alternating treatments (i.e., multi-element) designs

B-07: Use multiple baseline designs

B-09: Conduct a component analysis to determine the effective components of an intervention package

B-11: Conduct a parametric analysis to determine the effective values of an independent variable.

H-04: Evaluate changes in level, trend, and variability.

I-01: Define behavior in observable and measureabl e terms

Notes:

B – 07 USE MULTIPLE BASELINE DESIGNS.

Definition (Multiple baseline design):

(Cooper, Heron, & Heward, 2007).
☐ Flashcard created   ☐ Learned to fluency

Definition (Multiple baseline design variations and uses):

(Carr, 2005).
☐ Flashcard created   ☐ Learned to fluency

Example:

- Rod conducted an FBA on Billy's aggression and property destruction. Both behaviors were determined to be maintained by escape from demands. Rod decided to implement the same intervention for each behavior using a multiple baseline design because they both served the same function and a reversal would possibly reestablish the dangerous behavior after therapeutic effects were observed.

Non-Example:

- Bob wanted to determine the effects of response blocking and redirection on hand flapping with one of his students. He implemented this procedure and once it proved effective, decided to eliminate the intervention to determine if this procedure was the likely cause of the behavior decrease.

Write another example:

Questions to ask your supervisor:

Relevant Literature:

Barger-Anderson, R., Domaracki, J.W., Kearney-Vaku-lick, N., & Kubina, R.M. (2004). Multiple baseline designs: The use of a single-case experimental design in literacy research. *Reading Improvement*, 41, 4, 217.

Carr, J.E. (2005). Recommendations for reporting multiple-baseline designs across participants. Behavioral Interventions, 20, 3, 219-224.

Cooper, J.O., Heron, T.E. & Heward W.L. (2007). *Applied Behavior Analysis* (2nd Ed.), Upper Saddle River, NJ. Pearson Prentice Hall.

Harris, F.N., & Jenson, W.R. (1985). Comparisons of multiple-baseline across persons designs and AB designs with replication: Issues and confusions. *Behavioral Assessment*, 7, 2, 121,127.

Harvey, M.T., May, M.E., & Kennedy, C.H. (2004) Nonconcurrent multiple baseline designs and the evaluation of educational systems. *Journal of Behavioral Education*, 13, 4, 267-276.

Watson, P.J., & Workman, E.A. (1981), The non-concurrent multiple baseline across-individuals design: An extension of the traditional multiple baseline design. *Journal of Behavior Therapy and Experimental Psychology*, 12, 3, 257-259.

Zhan, S. & Ottenbacher, K.J. (2001). Single subject research designs for disability research. Journal of Disability and Rehabilitation, 23, 1, 1-8.

Related Lessons:

B-03: Systematically arrange independent variables to demonstrate their effects on dependent variables.

B-04: Use withdrawal/reversal designs.

B-08: Use multiple probe designs.

B-09: Use combinations of design elements.

B-10: Conduct a component analysis to determine the effective components of an intervention package.

B-11: Conduct a parametric analysis to determine the effective values of an independent variable.

E-01: Use interventions based on manipulation of antecedents, such as motivating operants and discriminative stimuli

H-03: Select a data display that effectively communicates relevant quantitative relations.

I-05: Organize, analyze, and interpret observed data.

FK-33: Functional relations.

Notes:

B – 08 USE MULTIPLE PROBE DESIGNS.

Definition (Multiple Probe Design):

(Gast & Spriggs, 2010).
☐ Flashcard created   ☐ Learned to fluency

Example:
- Multiple probe designs are particularly useful for researchers and teachers in educational settings to efficiently demonstrate results of instructional interventions when teaching across functionally different new skills (behaviors), across multiple students (participants), or across different sets of skills (conditions).

- Multiple probe designs might not be appropriate if assessing the effects of intervention on severe behaviors that result in injury or property destruction because of the requirement that intervention be delayed across each tier while a person continues to engage in severe behaviors with lasting consequences.

Write another example:

Questions to ask your supervisor:

Relevant Literature:

Cooper, J.O., Heron, T.E. & Heward W.L. (2007). *Applied Behavior Analysis* (2nd Ed.), Upper Saddle River, NJ. Pearson Prentice Hall.

Gast, D. L., & Spriggs, A. D. (2010). Visual analysis of graphic data. In D. L. Gast (Ed.), *Single subject research methodology in behavioral sciences*. New York: Routledge.

Horner, R. D., & Baer, D. M. (1978). Multiple-probe technique: A variation of the multiple baseline. *Journal of Applied Behavior Analysis, 11*(1), 189-196.

Thompson, T. J., Braam, S. J., & Fuqua, R. W. (1982). Training and generalization of laundry skills: A multiple probe evaluation with handicapped persons. *Journal of applied behavior analysis, 15*(1), 177-182.

Related Lessons:

B-03 Systematically arrange independent variables to demonstrate their effects on dependent variables.

B-07 Use multiple baselines designs.

H-01 Select a measurement system to obtain representative data given the dimensions of the behavior and the logistics of observing and recording.

H-02 Select a schedule of observation and recording periods.

H-04 Evaluate changes in level, trend, and variability.

I-05 Organize, analyze, and interpret observed data.

FK-36 response generalization

Notes:

B – 09 USE COMBINATIONS OF DESIGN ELEMENTS.

Definition:

[blank box]

Questions to ask your supervisor:

[blank box]

When designing an experiment it is sometimes useful to combine experimental design elements to strengthen the demonstration of experimental control. For instance it may be valuable to combine a multiple baseline design with a reversal design. In 1985, Alexander used a multiple baseline across students with reversal design to evaluate the effects of a study skill training procedure. Johnston and Pennypacker (2009) point out that experimenters often combine and intermingle many different types of designs as necessary. Categorizing types of designs is really a more valuable thing for the student than it is for the researcher. Murray Sidman in *Tactics of Scientific Research* says that it is not valuable to say that there are rules to follow when designing an experiment. He says "this would be disastrous" (Sidman, 1960/1988, p. 214). Simply put, he says, "The fact is that *there are no rules of experimental design*" (Sidman, 1960/1988, p. 214). The most important thing is that the experiment is designed to answer some question we have about the natural world. Sidman says, "We conduct experiments to find out something we do not know" (Sidman, 1960/1988, p.214).

Examples:

- Colón, et al. (2012) used a nonconcurrent multiple baseline design across participants to analyze the effects of verbal operant training on appropriate vocalizations and vocal stereotypy. RIRD was implemented and examined using a reversal design for each participant exposed to their procedure.

Write another example:

[blank box]

Relevant Literature:

Alexander, D. F. (1985). The effect of study skill training on learning disabled students' retelling of expository material. *Journal of applied behavior analysis*, *18*(3), 263-267.

Colón, C. L., Ahearn, W. H., Clark, K. M., & Masalsky, J. (2012). The effects of verbal operant training and response interruption and redirection on appropriate and inappropriate vocalizations. *Journal of applied behavior analysis*, *45*(1), 107-120.

Cooper, J. O., Heron, T. E., & Heward, W. L. (2007). *Applied behavior analysis*. Upper Saddle River, NJ: Pearson Education.

Iwata, B. A., Wallace, M. D., Kahng, S., Lindberg, J. S., Roscoe, E. M., Conners, J., ... & Worsdell, A. S. (2000). Skill acquisition in the implementation of functional analysis methodology. *Journal of Applied Behavior Analysis*, *33*(2), 181-194.

Johnston, J. M., & Pennypacker, H. S. (2009). *Strategies and tactics of behavioral research*. Routledge.

Related Lessons:

B-03 Systematically arrange independent variables to demonstrate their effects on dependent variables.
B-07 Use multiple baselines designs.
H-01 Select a measurement system to obtain representative data given the dimensions of the behavior and the logistics of observing and recording.
I-05 Organize, analyze, and interpret observed data.

Notes:

Segment 14 – Scorecard
Measurement: Applications and Considerations

☐ Presentation (2-5 minutes)

H 1
☐ Assessment
☐ SAFMED learned to fluency
☐ Workbook boxes completed

H 2
☐ Assessment
☐ SAFMED learned to fluency
☐ Workbook boxes completed

H 3
☐ Assessment
☐ SAFMED learned to fluency
☐ Workbook boxes completed

H 4
☐ Assessment
☐ SAFMED learned to fluency
☐ Workbook boxes completed

H 5
☐ Assessment
☐ SAFMED learned to fluency
☐ Workbook boxes completed

I 2
☐ Assessment
☐ SAFMED learned to fluency
☐ Workbook boxes completed

Segment 14 – Individual Supervision Agenda

Supervisor: _____ **Supervisee:** _____
Meeting Date: _____ **Time of meeting – From:** _____ **To:** _____
This document covers supervisory period from ____/____/____ to ____/____/____

1. Pass-in/Review Homework:
   Did the Supervisee satisfactorily complete this homework assignment?   Yes / No

   - If not, what is needed to complete assignment? Describe below.

2. Task List items addressed (H 1-5; I 2)

3. Definitions/SAFMEDs learned
   ☐ Flashcard(s) created   Was supervisee fluent with definitions? Yes ☐ No ☐

4. Discussion topics or activities completed during this meeting:

Evaluation of Supervisee's Performance				
(Record: S- "Satisfactory"; NI- "Needs Improvement"; U- "Unsatisfactory"; or NA- "Not Applicable")				
Arrived on time for meeting		Gave examples as needed		
Completed Homework Assigned		Accepted supervisory feedback appropriately		
Referred to literature/readings		Answered all questions thoroughly		
Maintained professional communication during supervision meeting				
Overall evaluation of supervisee performance during this meeting *(Circle one—use code above)*			S NI U	
If "NI" or "U", please list corrective steps needed to achieve a score of "S"				

5. Homework assigned for next meeting

6. Closing questions/feedback

Segment 14 – Group Supervision Meeting Agenda

- <u>Meeting Topic</u>: Measurement: Applications and Considerations

- <u>Task List Items Reviewed</u>:
o H-01: Select a measurement system to obtain representative data given the dimensions of the behavior and the logistics of observing and recording.
o H-02: Select a schedule of observation and recording periods.
o H-03: Select a data display that effectively communicates relevant quantitative relations.
o H-04: Evaluate changes in level, trend, and variability.
o H-05: Evaluate temporal relations between observed variables.
o I-02: Define environmental variables in observable and measurable terms.

1. Housekeeping
    - Upon entry to meeting have supervisees hand in the previous week's homework assignment and discuss several "Housekeeping Items" related to supervision.
    - Take attendance for the meeting.
    - State the duration of today's meeting (90 minutes).
    - Distribute BACB® experience forms to supervisees.

2. Task List Lesson and Discussion
    - Discuss task list item H-01: Select a measurement system to obtain representative data given the dimensions of the behavior and the logistics of observing and recording.
    - Discuss task list item H-02: Select a schedule of observation and recording periods.
    - Discuss task list item H-03: Select a data display that effectively communicates relevant quantitative relations.
    - Discuss task list item H-04: Evaluate changes in level, trend, and variability.
    - Discuss task list item H-05: Evaluate temporal relations between observed variables.
    - Discuss task list item I-02: Define environmental variables in observable and measurable terms.

3. Homework Review
    - Review homework that was assigned at the previous supervision meeting.

4. Questions
    - Answer any questions related to the homework or topics discussed.

5. Closing Notes
    - *Assign Homework (task list boxes, presentation) from today's segment, due at next group meeting*
    - Close the meeting by inviting supervisees to request topics to be covered in upcoming meetings.

H-01 SELECT A MEASUREMENT SYSTEM TO OBTAIN REPRESENTATIVE DATA GIVEN THE DIMENSIONS OF THE BEHAVIOR AND THE LOGISTICS OF OBSERVING AND RECORDING.

Assessment and treatment decisions of behavior analysts rely on data. A behavior analyst can design and implement effective treatments only when the data accurately represent the behavior of interest (validity) and have been reliably recorded as they are observed. To accomplish this goal, behavior analysts choose behaviors and dimensions of those behaviors to facilitate accurate and consistent recording within a given context for each client. Behavior analysts measure "three fundamental properties, or dimensional quantities" (Cooper et al., 2007, p. 75) of behavior:

- Repeatability--Behavior can be counted in the same way each time it occurs.

- Temporal extent--Behavior can be measured in relation to time.

- Temporal locus—Behavior occurs in relation to other behaviors.

First, identify which of these three properties will provide the most accurate method for quantifying behavior. Then, decides what dimension of behavior to measure, such as a count of occurrences, frequency of behavior per unit of time, duration, latency, or other. Last, decide who will record the behavior and in what context. If a preferred measurement system is unlikely to be effectively implemented, then the analyst has to reconsider definitions or recording circumstances in order to obtain adequate and accurate data for decision-making.

Examples:

- A teacher is asked to record the number of times a student yells out inappropriate language in class each day. Since the time the student spends in class varies widely during the week, the behavior analyst designed a measurement system to record rate (number of occurrences divided by time in class) of yelling out inappropriate language. With these data, the behavior analyst can compare the student's behavior across time of unequal durations.

- A parent is committed to accurately recording data to show duration of a child's tantrums, but found that she was not always in close proximity with the child when the behavior begins. The behavior analyst identifies two conditions during the day when the mother can accurately record duration of each tantrum (the first 30 minutes after school and the last 30 minutes before bedtime). The mother records duration of total tantruming behavior during each 30 mimute-observation twice a day.

Write another example:

Questions to ask your supervisor:

Relevant Literature:

Cooper, J.O., Heron, T. E., & Heward, W. L. (2007). *Applied behavior analysis*. Upper Saddle River, NJ: Pearson Education.

Gast, D. L. (2010). *Single subject research methodology in behavioral sciences*. New York: NY: Routledge.

Related Lessons:

A-01 Measure frequency

A-02 Measure rate (i.e., count per unit time).

A-03 Measure duration

A-04 Measure latency

A-09 Evaluate the accuracy and reliability of measurement procedures.

A-10 Design, plot, and interpret data using equal-interval graphs.

D-05 Use shaping.

H-02 Select a schedule of observation and recording periods.

H-03 Select a data display that effectively communicates relevant quantitative relations.

H-04 Evaluate changes in level, trend, and variability.

H-05 Evaluate temporal relations between observed variables (within & between sessions, time series).

I-01 Define behavior in observable and measurable terms.

I-05 Organize, analyze, and interpret observed data.

K-07 Evaluate the effectiveness of the behavioral program.

FK-33 functional relations

FK-41 contingency-shaped behavior

FK-47 Identify the measurable dimensions of behavior (e.g. rate, duration, latency, interresponse time)

FK-48 State the advantages and disadvantages of using continuous measurement procedures and discontinuous measurement procedures (e.g. partial- and whole-interval recording, momentary time sampling.)

Notes:

H-02 SELECT A SCHEDULE OF OBSERVATION AND RECORDING PERIODS.

BCBAs select the most appropriate forms of measurement. The target behavior should have a clear and observable operational definition so that it can be recorded during a period of observation. Using a consistent measurement procedure and schedule of observation will help ensure that the data are truly reflective of the target behavior you want to measure. Specify a time interval (or observation period) for recording data. Additionally, time intervals used in interval recording should remain consistent across observations (e.g., if you collect data on a target behavior during a 15 minute observation using 30-second partial intervals then you should use the same procedure on subsequent observations). If you change any aspect of the operational definition, observational period, or measurement procedures, explain the change when presenting data.

Example:
- If your client's parent reported that aggression only happens when the client is asked to brush their teeth, then you want to ensure that you can observe the client during times they are asked to brush their teeth.
- An instructor wanted to use the PLACHECK measurement procedure to record his students' involvement in an in-class group assignment. It would be appropriate to collect these data when students separate into groups and start the assignment. Recording data during the lecture or a test would not be an appropriate observation period.

Write another example:

Questions to ask your supervisor:

Relevant Literature:
Cooper, J. O., Heron, T. E., & Heward, W. L. (2007). Measuring behavior. *Applied Behavior Analysis* (pp. 72-101). Upper Saddle River, NJ: Pearson Prentice Hall.
Bailey, J. & Burch, M. (2010). *25 Essential Skills and Strategies for the Professional Behavior Analyst: Expert Tips for Maximizing Consulting Effectiveness.* New York, NY: Routledge.

Related Lessons:
A-01 Measure frequency (i.e., count).
A-02 Measure rate (i.e., count per unit time).
A-03 Measure duration.
A-04 Measure latency.
A-05 Measure interresponse time (IRT).
A-06 Measure percent of occurrence.
A-07 Measure trials to criterion.
A-12 Design and implement continuous measurement procedures (e.g., event recording).
A-13 Design and implement discontinuous measurement procedures (e.g., partial & whole interval, momentary time sampling).
A-14 Design and implement choice measures.
FK-47 Identify the measurable dimensions of behavior (e.g., rate, duration, latency, interresponse time).
FK-48 State the advantages and disadvantages of using continuous measurement procedures and discontinuous measurement procedures (e.g., partial- and whole-interval recording, momentary time sampling).
Notes:

H-03 SELECT A DATA DISPLAY THAT EFFECTIVELY COMMUNICATES RELEVANT QUANTITATIVE RELATIONS.

Behavior change is an ongoing process that must be continuously evaluated. This evaluation occurs through an analysis of data that reflects the quantifiable form of the behavior of interest. However, understanding the extent of behavior change can be difficult if one is looking at raw data alone. As such, behavior analysts use graphic displays to analyze, interpret, and communicate the results of behavior interventions (Cooper, Heron, & Heward, 2007). The most common graphic displays include line graphs, bar graphs, cumulative records, Standard Celeration charts, and scatterplots. The clinical utility of each graphic display varies so it is important to select the graphic display that will most accurately illustrate what the behavior analyst wants to understand.

Cooper et al. (2007) outlines the following purposes for the different graphic displays.

Line graphs are the most common form of graphic display and can be used to (1) show multiple dimensions of one behavior, (2) two or more different behaviors, (3) a behavior under different conditions, (4) changes in the target behavior relative to the manipulation of an independent variable, (5) and the behavior of multiple learners.

Bar graphs are typically used to (1) display discrete data that cannot be captured by an underlying dimension reflected on a horizontal axis and (2) provide an easy comparison of variables during different conditions.

Cumulative records are useful when the behavior analyst wants to (1) illustrate the total number of responses made over time, (2) the graph is used as a means to provide feedback to the learner, (3) the behavior of interest can only occur once during the specified measurement period, and (4) an analysis of a specific instance during an experiment is warranted.

The Standard Celeration Chart is a semilogarithmic chart that is used to reflect a linear measure of change across time. Lastly, scatterplots illustrate the comparative distribution of discrete measures in a data set and can be useful to uncover relationships across different subsets of data.

Example:
- If you want to see data paths across three behaviors and different intervention conditions, then a line graph is the most appropriate graphic display.
- Your client has rapidly acquired several language targets. A cumulative record can illustrate acquisition and is more efficient than creating a line graph for each acquired language target.

Questions to ask your supervisor:

Relevant Literature:
Cooper, J. O., Heron, T. E., & Heward, W. L. (2007). Constructing and interpreting graphic displays of behavioral data. *Applied Behavior Analysis* (pp. 126-157). Upper Saddle River, NJ: Pearson Prentice Hall.

Parsonson, B. S., & Baer, D. M. (1978). The analysis and presentation of graphic data. In T. R. Kratochwill (Ed.), *Single subject research: Strategies for evaluating change* (pp. 101-165). New York, NY: Academic Press.

Related Lessons:
A-10 Design, plot, and interpret data using equal-interval graphs.
A-11 Design, plot, and interpret data using a cumulative record to display data.
A-12 Design and implement continuous measurement procedures (e.g., event recording).
FK-47 Identify the measurable dimensions of behavior (e.g., rate, duration, latency, interresponse time).
B-03 Systematically arrange independent variables to demonstrate their effects on dependent variables.
H-04 Evaluate changes in level, trend, and variability.
H-05 Evaluate temporal relations between observed variables (within &between sessions, time series).

Notes:

Write another example.

H 04 EVALUATE CHANGES IN LEVEL, TREND, AND VARIABILITY.

Definition (Level):

(Cooper, Heron, & Heward, 2007).
☐ Flashcard created   ☐ Learned to fluency

Definition (Trend):

(Cooper, Heron, & Heward, 2007).
☐ Flashcard created   ☐ Learned to fluency

Definition (Variability)

(Cooper, Heron, & Heward, 2007).
☐ Flashcard created   ☐ Learned to fluency

Example:
- Rich sneaks candy from home and eats it in class. His teacher catches him one day and he stops eating candy in the classroom. However, he now asks to go to the bathroom every morning and eats candy in the bathroom where the teacher cannot see him.

Write another example:

Questions to ask your supervisor:

Relevant Literature:

Cooper, J. O., Heron, T. E., & Heward, W. L. (2007). *Applied Behavior Analysis*, (2nd ed.) Upper Saddle River, New Jersey: Pearson Prentice Hall.

Keohane, D. D., & Greer, R. D. (2005). Teachers' use of a verbally governed algorithm and student learning. *International Journal of Behavioral and Consultation Therapy, 1*, 249-268.

Lindsley, O. R. (1985). *Quantified trends in the results of behavior analysis*. Presidential address at the Eleventh Annual Convention of the Association for Behavior Analysis, Columbus, OH.

McCain, L. J., & McCleary, R. (1979). The statistical analysis of the simple interrupted time series quasi-experiment. In T. D. Cook & D. T. Campbell (Eds.), *Quasi -experimentation: Design and analysis issues for field settings*. Chicago: Rand McNally.

White, O. (2005). Trend lines. In G. Sugai & R. Horner (Eds.), *Encyclopedia of behavior modification and cognitive behavior therapy, Volume 3: Educational applications*. Pacific Grove, CA; Sage Publications.

Related Lessons:
A-10: Design, plot, and interpret data using equal-interval graphs
A-11: Design, plot, and interpret data using a cumulative record to display data
H-03: Select a data display that effectively communicates relevant quantitative relations
H-04: Evaluate changes in level, trend, and variability
I-01: Define behavior in observable and measurable terms
I-05: Organize, analyze, and interpret observed data
FK-47: Identify the measurable dimensions of behavior (e.g., rate, duration, latency, interresponse time)

Notes:

H-05 EVALUATE TEMPORAL RELATIONS BETWEEN OBSERVED VARIABLES (WITHIN & BETWEEN SESSIONS, TIME SERIES).

Behavior analysts can analyze data across several **temporal relations** prior to visual inspection. "The manner in which data are aggregated before transforming them into a visual display serves an equally influential role in data analysis" (Fahmie & Hanley, 2008, p. 320). Such aggregation occurs with the use of within-session, between-session in time series data.

Between-session analysis involves plotting total number of occurrences of a dependent variable within some unit of time (i.e., sessions) and visually inspecting point-by-point (i.e., session-by-session). Another prevalent type of aggregation occurrences of behavior is **within-session data** (likely due to its universal application).

Within-sessing data can be analyzed via the observation of data as it changes throughout the duration of the session or at specific times during the session. Fahmie and Hanley (2008) outlined eight conditions under which within-session data are valuable:

4. Description of naturally occurring behavioral relations (descriptive assessment)
5. Determination of behavioral function (functional analyses)
6. Detection of within-session trends
7. Safeguard clients from any risks associated with prolonged session exposure
8. Creation of sufficient data for analysis following abbreviated data collection
9. Determination of observation session duration
10. Clarification of counterintuitive response patterns
11. Understanding behavioral processes

There are several methods of within-session data analysis. In the descriptive assessment literature, within-session data are calculated via conditional probabilities to determine possible temporal relations between behavior and environmental events (e.g., occurrence/nonoccurrence of putative reinforcer delivery) (Vollmer, Borrero, Wright, Camp, & Lalli, 2001). In the functional analysis literature, within-session data have been used to compare the utility of two types of functional analyses (e.g., trial-based versus multi-element) (Kahng & Iwata, 1999; LaRue et al., 2010). Moreover, within-session data have been used in an effort to further analyze unclear results following an unclear analysis of full session data (Call & Mevers, 2014; Kahng & Iwata, 1999; Payne et al., 2014; Roane, Lerman, Kelley, & Van-Camp, 1999; Vollmer, Marcus, Ringhdahl & Roane, 1995; Vollmer et. al., 1993). For example, Kahng &

Iwata (1999) compared full 15-minute functional analysis session data with within-session data by plotting the first session of each condition into a minute-by-minute observation period. One of their findings was that within-session data clarified unclear (absence of function) results of the full session data.

In another example, Payne et al., (2014) analyzed within-session data in different manner by comparing data when the putative establishing operation (EO) was present versus when the putative EO was absent across the last five 10-minute sessions of each condition. The results generated from the within-session data analysis was used to develop a second experimental analysis that clarified the function of the behavior for the two participants.

Write another example.

Questions to ask your supervisor:

Iwata, B. A., Wallace, M. D., Kahng, S., Lindberg, J. S., Roscoe, E. M., Conners, J., & Worsdell, A. S. (2000). Skill acquisition in the implementation of functional analysis methodology. *Journal of Applied Behavior Analysis, 33*(2), 181-194.

Krause, T. R., Seymour, K. J., & Sloat, K. C. M. (1999). Long-term evaluation of a behavior-based method for improving safety performance: a meta-analysis of 73 interrupted time-series replications. *Safety Science, 32*(1), 1-18.

LaRue, R. H., Lenard, K., Weiss, M. J., Bamond, M., Palmieri, M., & Kelley, M. E. (2010). Comparison of traditional and trial-based methodologies for conducting functional analyses. *Research in Developmental Disabilities, 31*(2), 480-487.

Payne, S. W., Dozier, C. L., Neidert, P. L., Jowet, E. S., & Newquist, M. H. (2014). Using Additional Analyses to Clarify the Functions of Problem Behavior: An Analysis of Two Cases. *Education and Treatment of Children, 37*(2), 249-275.

Roane, H. S., Lerman, D. C., Kelley, M. E., & Van Camp, C. M. (1999). Within-session patterns of responding during functional analyses: The role of establishing operations in clarifying behavioral function. *Research in Developmental Disabilities, 20*(1), 73-89.

Tryon, W. W. (1982). A simplified time-series analysis for evaluating treatment interventions. *Journal of applied behavior analysis, 15*(3), 423-429.

Vollmer, T. R., Borrero, J. C., Wright, C. S., Camp, C. V., & Lalli, J. S. (2001). Identifying possible contingencies during descriptive analyses of severe behavior disorders. *Journal of Applied Behavior Analysis, 34*(3), 269-287.

Vollmer, T. R., Iwata, B. A., Zarcone, J. R., Smith, R. G., & Mazaleski, J. L. (1993). Within-session patterns of self-injury as indicators of behavioral function. *Research in Developmental Disabilities, 14*(6), 479-492.

Vollmer, T. R., Marcus, B. A., Ringdahl, J. E., & Roane, H. S. (1995). Progressing from brief assessments to extended experimental analyses in the evaluation of aberrant behavior. *Journal of Applied Behavior Analysis, 28*(4), 561-576.

Relevant Literature:

Call, N. A. and Lomas Mevers, J. E. (2014), The Relative Influence of Motivating Operations for Positive and Negative Reinforcement on Problem Behavior During Demands. *Behavioral Interventions*, 29: 4–20. doi: 10.1002/bin.1374

Fahmie, T. A., & Hanley, G. P. (2008). Progressing Toward Data Intimacy: A Review of Within-Session Data Analysis. *Journal of Applied Behavior Analysis, 41*(3), 319.

Hartmann, D. P., Gottman, J. M., Jones, R. R., Gardner, W., Kazdin, A. E., & Vaught, R. S. (1980). Interrupted time-series analysis and its application to behavioral data. *Journal of Applied Behavior Analysis, 13*(4), 543-559.

Related Lessons:

H-01 Select a measurement system to obtain representative data given the dimensions of the behavior and the logistics of observing and recording.
H-04 Evaluate changes in level, trend, and variability.
I-05 Organize, analyze and interpret observed data
J-15 Base decision-making on data displayed in various formats
FK-47 Identify the measurable dimensions of behavior (e.g., rate, duration, latency, interresponse time).

Notes:

I-02 DEFINE ENVIRONMENTAL VARIA-
      BLES   IN   OBSERVABLE   AND
      MEASUREABLE TERMS.

<u>The importance of defining environmental variables in
observable and measurable terms</u>

- As Cooper, Heron, and Heward (2007) state, in order to achieve a high level of treatment integrity in
  an experiment, it is of utmost importance to "develop complete and precise operational definitions
  of the treatment procedures" (Cooper, Heron, &
  Heward, 2007, p. 235). In the same way that it is
  critical to define target behavior in observable and
  measurable terms, so is the case with defining environmental variables.

- Baer, Wolf, and Risley (1968) stress that the "technological" dimension of Applied Behavior Analysis
  refers simply to the fact that "the techniques making up a particular behavioral application are completely identified and described"(Baer, Wolf, & Risley, 1968, p. 95). As such, the techniques, or environmental variables being manipulated, must be defined in observable and measurable terms to meet
  the technological dimension of applied behavior
  analysis (Cooper, Heron, & Heward, 2007).

- However, historically, operationally defining independent variables has not been conducted to the
  standard required for a science of behavior that
  seeks to achieve the technological dimension of applied behavior analysis*. It has also not been done
  to the same standard as that of the dependent variables (Johnston & Pennypacker, 1980; Peterson,
  Homer & Wonderlich, 1982; Gresham, Gansle &
  Noell, 1993). In 1982 Peterson, Homer and Wonderlich called for researchers to measure the independent variables in a more stringent manner. Unfortunately, an assessment of this area later on by
  Gresham, Gansle and Noell (1993) found that this
  had not been accomplished.

- <u>Defining environmental variables in observable and
  measurable terms</u>

- It is believed that environmental variable definitions
  should be written to meet the same standards as
  those required to be met by *target behavior* definitions
  (Gresham, Gansle & Noell, 1993). They should be
  "clear, concise, unambiguous, and objective"
  (Cooper, Heron & Heward, 2007, p. 235).

- Gresham *et al.* (1993, p. 261) suggest that independent variable definitions can be made along four dimensions: spatial, verbal, physical and temporal.

<u>Example Definition</u>

- Gresham *et al.* (1993, pp. 261-262) give an example
  of an adequate definition of an independent variable, a time-out procedure, provided by Mace, Page,
  Ivancic and O'Brien (1986).

  o Immediately following the occurrence of a target
     behavior (temporal dimension), (b) the therapist
     said, "No, go to time-out" (verbal dimension), (c)
     led the child by the arm to a prepositioned time-out
     chair (physical dimension), and (d) seated the child
     facing the corner (spatial dimension). (e) If the
     child's buttocks were raised from the time-out chair
     or if the child's head was turned more than 45° (spa-
     tial dimension), the therapist used the least amount
     of force necessary to guide compliance with the
     time-out procedure (physical dimension). (f) At the
     end of 2 min (temporal dimension), the therapist
     turned the time-out chair 45° from the corner
     (physical and spatial dimensions) and walked away
     (physical dimension).

- Gresham *et al.*, (1993, p. 262) argued that a failure
  to define operational variables along these four dimensions, as done so by Mace, Page, Ivancic and
  O'Brien (1986), makes "replication and external validation of behavior-analytic investigations difficult."

Write another example:

Questions to ask your supervisor:

Relevant Literature:

Baer, D. M., Wolf, M. M., & Risley, T. R. (1968). Some current dimensions of applied behavior analysis. *Journal of Applied Behavior Analysis, 1*, 91-97.

Cooper, J. O., Heron, T. E., & Heward, W. L. (2007). *Applied Behavior Analysis*, 2nd ed. Upper Saddle River, New Jersey: Pearson Prentice Hall.

Gresham, F. M., Gansle, K. A. & Noell, G. H. (1993). Treatment integrity in applied behavior analysis with children. *Journal of Applied Behavior Analysis, 26*, 257-263.

Johnston, J., & Pennypacker, H. S. (1980). *Strategies and tactics of human behavioral research.* Hillsdale, N.J.: Erlbaum.

Peterson, L., Homer, A. L., Wonderlich, S. A. (1982). The integrity of independent variables in behavior analysis. *Journal of Applied Behavior Analysis, 15*, 477-492.

Related Lessons:

B-11: Conduct a parametric analysis to determine the effective values of an independent variable
I-01: Define behavior in observable and measurable terms
I-04: Design and implement the full range of functional assessment procedures
J-01: State intervention goals in observable and measurable terms
FK-07: Environmental (as opposed to mentalistic explanations of behavior)
FK-11: Environment, stimulus, stimulus class
FK-33: Functional relations

Footnotes
* See Baer, Wolf & Risley (1968) for more information on the seven dimensions of Applied Behavior Analysis.

Notes:

Segment 15 – Scorecard
Treatment Integrity and Fidelity Measures

☐ Presentation (2-5 minutes)

A 8
☐ Assessment
☐ SAFMED learned to fluency
☐ Workbook boxes completed

A 9
☐ Assessment
☐ SAFMED learned to fluency
☐ Workbook boxes completed

I 5
☐ Assessment
☐ SAFMED learned to fluency
☐ Workbook boxes completed

K 5
☐ Assessment
☐ SAFMED learned to fluency
☐ Workbook boxes completed

K 7
☐ Assessment
☐ SAFMED learned to fluency
☐ Workbook boxes completed

Segment 15 – Individual Supervision Agenda

Supervisor: _____ **Supervisee:** _____
Meeting Date: _____ **Time of meeting – From:** _____ **To:** _____
This document covers supervisory period from ____/____/____ **to** ____/____/____

1. Pass-in/Review Homework:
   Did the Supervisee satisfactorily complete this homework assignment?   Yes / No

   • If not, what is needed to complete assignment? Describe below.

2. Task List items addressed (A 8, 9; I 5; K 5, 7)

3. Definitions/SAFMEDs learned
   ☐ Flashcard(s) created   Was supervisee fluent with definitions? Yes ☐ No ☐

4. Discussion topics or activities completed during this meeting:

Evaluation of Supervisee's Performance			
(Record: S- "Satisfactory"; NI- "Needs Improvement"; U- "Unsatisfactory"; or NA- "Not Applicable")			
Arrived on time for meeting		Gave examples as needed	
Completed Homework Assigned		Accepted supervisory feedback appropriately	
Referred to literature/readings		Answered all questions thoroughly	
Maintained professional communication during supervision meeting			
Overall evaluation of supervisee performance during this meeting *(Circle one—use code above)*			S NI U
If "NI" or "U", please list corrective steps needed to achieve a score of "S"			

5. Homework assigned for next meeting

6. Closing questions/feedback

Segment 15 – Group Supervision Meeting Agenda

- <u>Meeting Topic</u>: Treatment Integrity and Fidelity Measures

- <u>Task List Items Reviewed</u>:
  - A-08: Assess and interpret Interobserver agreement.
  - A-09: Evaluate the accuracy and reliability of measurement procedures.
  - I-05: Organize, analyze, and interpret observed data.
  - K-05: Design and use systems for monitoring procedural integrity.
  - K-07: Evaluate the effectiveness of the behavioral program.

1. Housekeeping
   - Upon entry to meeting have supervisees hand in the previous week's homework assignment and discuss several "Housekeeping Items" related to supervision.
   - Take attendance for the meeting.
   - State the duration of today's meeting (90 minutes).
   - Distribute BACB® experience forms to supervisees.

2. Task List Lesson and Discussion
   - Discuss task list item A-08: Assess and interpret Interobserver agreement.
   - Discuss task list item A-09: Evaluate the accuracy and reliability of measurement procedures.
   - Discuss task list item I-05: Organize, analyze, and interpret observed data.
   - Discuss task list item K-05: Design and use systems for monitoring procedural integrity.
   - Discuss task list item K-07: Evaluate the effectiveness of the behavioral program.

3. Homework Review
   - Review homework that was assigned at the previous supervision meeting.

4. Questions
   - Answer any questions related to the homework or topics discussed.

5. Closing Notes
   - *Assign Homework (task list boxes, presentation) from today's segment, due at next group meeting.*
   - Close the meeting by inviting supervisees to request topics to be covered in upcoming meetings.

A-08 – ASSESS AND INTERPRET INTEROBSERVER AGREEMENT

Definition (Interobserver agreement):

(Cooper, Heron, & Heward, 2007).

☐ Flashcard created   ☐ Learned to fluency

Definition (Four types of interobserver agreement):

(Johnston & Pennypacker, 2009).

☐ Flashcard created   ☐ Learned to fluency

Examples:

- John is conducting a functional analysis (FA) on aggression in one of his students. He has asked Mary to observe the behavior and record data simultaneously with him to calculate Interobserver agreement. He plans on conducting a 5-minute session with 30, 10-second intervals. He plans to use interval agreement IOA. He records 4 instances of aggression during the FA in the 21st, 22nd, 23rd and 24th interval. Mary records 4 instances in the 21st, 22nd, 23rd, and 25th interval. He calculates IOA to be 97% or 29/30 intervals.

Non-examples:

- John is conducting a functional analysis on aggression in one of his students. He asks Mary to come in and observe but does not provide her with a data recording sheet to take data on the behavior. At the end of the session he asks Mary if she saw any aggression during the session.

Relevant Literature:

Boyce, T.E., Carter, N., & Neboschick, H. (2000). An Evaluation of Intraobserver Reliability versus Interobserver Agreement. *European Journal of Behavior Analysis*, 1, 2, 107-114.

Cooper, J.O., Heron, T.E. & Heward W.L. (2007). *Applied Behavior Analysis* (2nd Ed.), Upper Saddle River, NJ. Pearson Prentice Hall. 113-122.

Johnston, J. M., & Pennypacker, H. S. (2009). Strategies and tactics of behavioral research.

Watkins, M.W. & Pacheco, M. (2000). Interobserver Agreement in Behavioral Research: Importance and Calculation. Journal of Behavioral Education, 10, 4, 205-212.

Related Lessons:

A-01: Measure Frequency (i.e., count)

A-09: Evaluate the accuracy and reliability of measurement procedures.

B-02: Review and interpret articles from the behavior-analytic literature.

G-06: Provide behavior-analytic services in collaboration with others who support and/or provide services to one's clients.

H-02: Select a schedule of observation and recording periods.

I-01: Define behavior in observable and measureable terms.

I-05: Organize, analyze, and interpret observed data.

J-09: Identify and address practical and ethical considerations when using experimental designs to demonstrate treatment effectiveness.

K-05: Design and use systems for monitoring procedural integrity.

Notes:

Write another example:

Questions to ask your supervisor:

A - 09 EVALUATE THE ACCURACY AND RELIABILITY OF MEASUREMENT PROCEDURES

Definition (Reliability of measurement):

(Cooper, Heron, & Heward, 2007).
☐ Flashcard created   ☐ Learned to fluency

Relevant Literature:
Cooper, J. O., Heron, T. E., & Heward, W. L. (2007). Improving and assessing the quality of behavioral measurement. *Applied Behavior Analysis* (pp. 102-124). Upper Saddle River, NJ: Pearson Prentice Hall.

Johnston, J. M., & Pennypacker, H. S. (1993a). *Strategies and tactics for human behavioral research* (2nd ed.). Hillsdale, NJ Erlbaum.

Example:

Accuracy: You and a friend decide to go on a 5-mile run. Your friend tells you that she can monitor the distance because her legs always start to hurt once she runs 5 miles. You, being a data-driven behavior analyst, decide that your friend's measurement procedure might not be the most accurate so you use your smart phone app to track the distance. Your measurement system will likely reveal a better estimate of the true value of the distance you ran.

Reliability: Using the example for accuracy, both measures can be reliable if at the end of the run your friend tells you that you must have run 5 miles because her legs hurt and your app indicates you ran 5 miles.

Related Lessons:
A-01 Measure frequency (i.e., count).
A-02 Measure rate (i.e., count per unit time).
A-03 Measure duration.
A-04 Measure latency.
A-05 Measure interresponse time (IRT).
A-06 Measure percent of occurrence.
A-07 Measure trials to criterion.
A-08 Assess and interpret interobserver agreement.
H-01 Select a measurement system to obtain representative data given the dimensions of the behavior and the logistics of observing and recording.
H-02 Select a schedule of observation and recording periods.

Notes:

Write another example:

Questions to ask your supervisor:

I-05 ORGANIZE, ANALYZE, AND INTER-
PRET OBSERVED DATA.

Organize the data
- Once data have been collected in their raw format, it is then important to organize the data into a format that is easy to analyze (Cooper, Heron & Heward, 2007). The most effective way to do this, and the most common method utilized by Behavior Analysts, is to visually display the data in a **graph** (Cooper, Heron, & Heward, 2007).
- As Parsonson and Baer (1978, p. 134) said "the function of the graph is to communicate…..in an attractive manner, descriptions and summaries of the data that enable rapid and accurate analysis of the facts" (cited from Cooper, Heron & Heward, 2007, p. 128).
- The visual formats most often used by behavior analysts are line graphs, bar graphs, cumulative records, semilogarithmic charts and scatterplots* (Cooper, Heron & Heward, 2007).

Analyze and interpret observed data
- Behavior analysts use a systematic form of assessing graphically displayed data called **visual analysis** (Cooper, Heron & Heward, 2007).
- Visual analysis encompasses examining each of three characteristics in a graphic display of data, both within and across the different conditions and phases of an experiment. These three characteristics are:
  - The level of the data
  - The extent and type of variability in the data
  - The trends in the data
- Johnston and Pennypacker (1993b, p. 320) recommend that the viewer should carefully examine the graph's overall construction, paying attention to details such as the axis labels and the scaling of each axis, prior to attempting to interpret the data. They argue "it's impossible to interpret graphic data without being influenced by various characteristics of the graph itself" (cited from Cooper, Heron & Heward, 2007, p. 149).

Visual analysis within conditions
- Within given conditions, examination needs to occur to determine a few relevant factors (Cooper, Heron & Heward, 2007):
  - The number of data points in each condition (in general, the more measurements of the dependent variable there are per unit of time, the more confidence one can have in the data).
  - Variability (A high degree of variability usually indicates little control has been achieved over the factors influencing behavior).
  - Level (examined in terms of its absolute value within a condition, the degree of stability/variability and the extent of change from one level to another).
  - Trend (the trend indicates whether a particular behavior has increased, decreased or has neither increased nor decreased within a condition).

Visual analysis between conditions
- After examining the data within each condition or phase of a study, visual analysis now proceeds to examining the data between conditions (Cooper, Heron & Heward, 2007):
  - Comparison needs to be made between the different conditions of the level, trend and variability of the data (Cooper, Heron & Heward, 2007, p. 154).
  - The data are examined in terms of the overall level of performance between conditions; generally when there is no overlap of data points between the highest values in one condition and the lowest values in another condition, there is a strong likelihood that the behavior changed from one condition to the next (Cooper, Heron & Heward, 2007, p. 154).

Once an "examination and comparison of changes in level, trend and variability between conditions has occurred, a comparison needs to be made of performance across *similar* conditions" (Cooper, Heron & Heward, 2007, p. 155). If a behavior change is found to have occurred over the course of an intervention, the next question to be asked is, "was the behavior change a result of the intervention?" (Cooper, Heron & Heward, 2007, p. 155).

Write another example:

Relevant Literature:

Cooper, J. O., Heron, T. E., & Heward, W. L. (2007). *Applied Behavior Analysis*, 2nd ed. Upper Saddle River, New Jersey: Pearson Prentice Hall.

Fisher, W. W. Piazza, C. C. & Roane, H. S. (2011). *Handbook of Applied Behavior Analysis*. New York: The Guildford Press.

Johnston, J., & Pennypacker, H. S. (1993b). *Readings for Strategies and tactics of behavioral research* (2nd ed.). Hillsdale, NJ: Erlbaum.

Parson, B. S. & Baer, D. M. (1978). The analysis and presentation of graphic data. In T. R. Kratochwill (Ed.), *Single subject research: Strategies for evaluating change* (p. 101 – 165). New York: Academic Press.

Related Lessons:

A-10: Design, plot and interpret data using equal-interval graphs

A-11: Design, plot and interpret data using a cumulative record to display data

B-04: Use withdrawal/reversal designs

B-05: Use alternating treatments (i.e., multielement) designs

B-06: Use changing criterion designs

B-07: Use multiple baseline designs

B-08: Use multiple probe designs

B-09: Use combinations of design elements

J-15: Base decision-making on data displayed in various formats

Footnotes

* See Cooper, Heron & Heward (2007), pages 129 – 154 for more information on these graphic displays.

Notes:

Questions to ask your supervisor:

K-05 DESIGN AND USE SYSTEMS FOR MONITORING PROCEDURAL INTEGRITY.

Definitions:

Procedural Integrity - "The extent to which the independent variable is applied exactly as planned and described and no other unplanned variables are administered inadvertently along with the planned treatment" (Cooper Heron, & Heward, 2007, pp. 706-707).

Treatment Drift - "An undesirable situation in which the independent variable of an experiment is applied differently during later stages than it was at the outset of the study" (Cooper Heron, & Heward, 2007, p. 706).

Low treatment integrity is not only bad for research (confounding, cannot interpret the results) but can also lead to inconsistencies and poor outcomes in treatments. These can be related to many factors such as experimenter bias (unfair advantage to see positive results), staff implementing only procedures they favor, treatment too difficult to implement, poor staff training, or staff turnover.

Systems to Avoid Treatment Drift

- Precise operational definition
- Make behavioral plan simple and easy to administer
- Provide competency-based training (use behavior skills training)
- Assess treatment integrity

Assessing Treatment Integrity

- Provide a brief checklist of each of the components in the treatment plan
- May be self-monitored but important to conduct inter-rater reliability
- Establish a schedule to complete the treatment integrity
- Graph the percent of treatment integrity and monitor to ensure treatment drift does not occur

Write another example:

Questions to ask your supervisor:

Relevant Literature:

Cooper, J. O., Heron, T. E., & Heward, W. L. (2007). Applied behavior analysis: 2nd Edition. Pearson Education, Inc.

Johnston, J. M., & Pennypacker, H. S. (2011). *Strategies and tactics of behavioral research.* Routledge.

Wolery, M. (1994). Procedural fidelity: A reminder of its functions. *Journal of Behavioral Education, 4*(4), 381-386.

Related Lessons:

F-01 Use self-management strategies

H-03 Select a schedule of observation and recording periods

H-04 Select a data display that effectively communicates relevant qualitative relations

H-04 Evaluate changes in level, trend and variability

K-03 Design and use competency-based training for persons who are responsible for carrying out behavioral assessment and behavior-change procedures

K-04 Design and use effective performance monitoring and reinforcement systems

Footnotes:

Also called procedural fidelity, treatment integrity, procedural reliability, or treatment adherence

Notes:

K-07 EVALUATE THE EFFECTIVENESS OF THE BEHAVIORAL PROGRAM.

In the field of applied behavior analysis, it is crucial to have ongoing evaluation of the effectiveness of behavior programs. This helps to ensure that the most effective treatments are being offered to a client based on ethical practices, the most current research, and the individual's needs.

Birnbrauer (1999) lists the following steps for evaluating the effectiveness of treatment:

1. Describe the exact purposes of the treatment – what is it intended to achieve?
2. Describe exactly how the treatment is conducted –there should be no mystery or secrecy about the methods and procedures being used.
3. Describe how treatment effects were measured – what numerical data were collected and how were they collected?
4. Show before and after data collected by independent, unbiased evaluators
5. Show follow up data –do the persons maintain gains? Do they continue to improve? Do they regress?

"The data obtained throughout a behavior change program or a research study are the means for that contract; they form the empirical basis for every important decision: to continue with the present procedure, to try a different intervention, or to reinstitute a previous condition" (Cooper, Heron, & Heward, 2007, p. 167). It is important that if there is evidence of behavioral regression or that the treatment package is ineffective, that the team re-evaluate, make changes or adjustments, or discontinue a behavioral program entirely. It is unethical to continue a behavioral program that is deemed ineffective.

Write another example:

Questions to ask your supervisor:

Relevant Literature:

Bailey, J., & Burch, M. (2011). *Ethics for Behavior Analysts: 2nd Expanded Edition.* Taylor & Francis.

Birnbrauer, J.S (1999). How to Evaluate Intervention Programs. Cambridge Center for Behavioral Studies, Inc.

Cooper J.O, Heron T.E, Heward W.L. (2007). *Applied behavior analysis* (2nd ed.) Upper Saddle River, NJ: Pearson.

Related Lessons:

B-01 Use the dimensions of applied behavior analysis (Baer, Wolf, &Risley, 1968) to evaluate whether interventions are behavior analytic in nature.

FK-47 Identify the measurable dimensions of behavior (e.g., rate, duration, latency, interresponse time).

G-01 Review records and available data at the outset of the case.

H-01 Select a measurement system to obtain representative data given the dimensions of the behavior and the logistics of observing and recording.

I-01 Define behavior in observable and measurable terms.

I-05 Organize, analyze, and interpret observed data.

I-06 Make recommendations regarding behaviors that must be established, maintained, increased, or decreased.

J-01 State intervention goals in observable and measurable terms.

K-07 Evaluate the effectiveness of the behavioral program.

Notes:

Segment 16 – Scorecard
Verbal Behavior

☐ Presentation (2-5 minutes)

D 9
☐ Assessment
☐ SAFMED learned to fluency
☐ Workbook boxes completed

D 10
☐ Assessment
☐ SAFMED learned to fluency
☐ Workbook boxes completed

D 11
☐ Assessment
☐ SAFMED learned to fluency
☐ Workbook boxes completed

D 12
☐ Assessment
☐ SAFMED learned to fluency
☐ Workbook boxes completed

D 13
☐ Assessment
☐ SAFMED learned to fluency
☐ Workbook boxes completed

F 8
☐ Assessment
☐ SAFMED learned to fluency
☐ Workbook boxes completed

FK 43
☐ Assessment
☐ SAFMED learned to fluency
☐ Workbook boxes completed

FK 44
☐ Assessment
☐ SAFMED learned to fluency
☐ Workbook boxes completed

FK 45
☐ Assessment
☐ SAFMED learned to fluency
☐ Workbook boxes completed

FK 46
☐ Assessment
☐ SAFMED learned to fluency
☐ Workbook boxes completed

Segment 16 – Individual Supervision Agenda

Supervisor: _____ **Supervisee:** _____
Meeting Date: _____ **Time of meeting – From:**_____ **To:**_____
This document covers supervisory period from ____/____/____ to ____/____/____

1. Pass-in/Review Homework:

     Did the Supervisee satisfactorily complete this homework assignment?   Yes / No

   • If not, what is needed to complete assignment? Describe below.

2. Task List items addressed (D 9-13; F 8; FK 43-46)

3. Definitions/SAFMEDs learned
     ☐ Flashcard(s) created   Was supervisee fluent with definitions? Yes ☐ No ☐

4. Discussion topics or activities completed during this meeting:

Evaluation of Supervisee's Performance			
(Record: S- "Satisfactory"; NI- "Needs Improvement"; U- "Unsatisfactory"; or NA- "Not Applicable")			
Arrived on time for meeting		Gave examples as needed	
Completed Homework Assigned		Accepted supervisory feedback appropriately	
Referred to literature/readings		Answered all questions thoroughly	
Maintained professional communication during supervision meeting			
Overall evaluation of supervisee performance during this meeting *(Circle one—use code above)*		S NI U	
If "NI" or "U", please list corrective steps needed to achieve a score of "S"			

5. Homework assigned for next meeting

6. Closing questions/feedback

Segment 16 – Group Supervision Meeting Agenda

- <u>Meeting Topic</u>: Verbal Behavior

- <u>Task List Items Reviewed</u>:
o   D-09: Use verbal operants as a basis for language assessment.
o   D-10: Use echoic training.
o   D-11: Use mand training.
o   D-12: Use tact training.
o   D-13: Use intraverbal training.

o   F-08: Use augmentative communication systems.
o   FK-43: Echoics.
o   FK-44: Mands.
o   FK-45: Tacts.
o   FK-46: Intraverbals.

1.   Housekeeping
   - Upon entry to meeting have supervisees hand in the previous week's homework assignment and discuss several "Housekeeping Items" related to supervision.
   - Take attendance for the meeting.
   - State the duration of today's meeting (90 minutes).
   - Distribute BACB® experience forms to supervisees.

2.   Task List Lesson and Discussion
   - Discuss task list item D-09: Use verbal operants as a basis for language assessment.
   - Discuss task list item D-10: Use echoic training
   - Discuss task list item D-11: Use mand training.
   - Discuss task list item D-12: Use tact training.
   - Discuss task list item D-13: Use intraverbal training.
   - Discuss task list item F-08: Use augmentative communication systems.
   - Discuss task list item FK-43: Echoics.
   - Discuss task list item FK-44: Mands.
   - Discuss task list item FK-45: Tacts.
   - Discuss task list item FK-46: Intraverbals.

3.   Homework Review
   - Review homework that was assigned at the previous supervision meeting.

4.   Questions
   - Answer any questions related to the homework or topics discussed.

5.   Closing Notes
   - *Assign Homework (task list boxes, presentation) from today's segment, due at next group meeting*
   - Close the meeting by inviting supervisees to request topics to be covered in upcoming meetings.

D-09 USE THE VERBAL OPERANTS AS A BASIS FOR LANGAUGE ASSESSMENT.

Definition:

In the field of applied behavior analysis extensive research has been done on the development of verbal behavior.

"Verbal behavior involves social interactions between speakers and listeners, whereby speakers gain access to reinforcement and control their environment through the behavior of listeners" (Cooper, Heron, & Heward, 2007). Verbal operants are the basic units of this exchange.

In 1957 B.F. Skinner identified six elementary verbal operants in his book on *Verbal Behavior*. These included mands, tacts, intraverbals, echoics, textuals, and transcription. "Skinner's analysis suggests that a complete verbal repertoire is composed of each of the different elementary operants, and separate speaker and listener repertoires" (Cooper, Heron, & Heward, 2007).

Since Skinner described these operants, those in the field have applied these concepts to both language assessment and training. In order to evaluate whether or not specific language training is necessary, a variety of standardized tools have been used to test an individual's receptive and expressive language abilities.

Although these tests provide some good information, they may fail to identify deficits in one or more of the six verbal operant areas. Some children who may be proficient in tacting (such as labeling things in their environment such as letters and numbers) may fail to make appropriate mands for desired items (Cooper, Heron & Heward, 2007). In this case it is important for behavior analysts to use a combination of approaches or less standardized methods to assess these needs. It may be helpful to observe the individual in their natural environment and take data on their verbal interactions.

Ask questions such as:

- What is the frequency of and complexity of mands?
- What it the frequency and complexity of tacting behavior?
- Will the child or individual demonstrate echoic behavior when prompted?
- Does the child or individual engage in intraverbal behavior with known caregivers?
- Can or will the child or individual read words that are written down for him?
- Can or will the child or individual write down words that are said to him?

Example:

Tact: labeling things in their environment such as letters and numbers.

Standardized assessments of verbal behavior include but are not limited to: the Peabody Picture Vocabulary Test III (Dunn & Dunn, 1997), the Comprehensive Receptive and Expressive Vocabulary Test (Hammill & Newcomer, 1997), the Assessment of Basic Language and Learning Skills (ABLLS) (Partington & Sundberg, 1998), the Verbal Behavior Milestones Assessment and Placement Program (VB-MAPP) and the CELF-4 (Semel, Wiig, & Secord, 2003).

Write another example:

Questions to ask your supervisor:

Relevant Literature:

Cooper J.O., Heron T.E., Heward W.L. (2007). *Applied behavior analysis* (2nd ed.) Upper Saddle River, NJ: Pearson

Hammill, D., & Newcomer, P.L. (1997). *Test of language development-3*. Austin, TX: Pro-Ed.

Partington, J. W., & Sundberg, M. L. (1998). *Assessment of basic language and learning skills. (The ABLLS): an assessment for language delayed students*. Pleasant Hill, CA: Behavior Analysts, Inc.

Semel, E., Wiig, E. H., & Secord, W. A. (2003). *Clinical evaluation of language fundamentals, fourth edition (CELF-4). Toronto, Canada: The Psychological Corporation/A Harcourt Assessment Company.*

Skinner, B.F. (1957). *Verbal Behavior*. New York: Appleton-Century.

Sundberg, M. L. (2008) *Verbal behavior milestones assessment and placement program: The VB-MAPP*. Concord, CA: AVB Press.

Sundberg, M.L. & Partington, J.W. (1998). *Teaching language to children with autism or other developmental disabilities*. Pleasant Hill, CA: Behavior Analysts, Inc.

Related Lessons:

D-10 Use echoic training.
D-11 Use mand training.
D-12 Use tact training.
D-13 Use intraverbal training.
D-14 Use listener training.
FK-43 Echoics
FK-44 Mands
FK-45 Tacts
FK-46 Intraverbals

Notes:

D-10 USE ECHOIC TRAINING.

Definition:

Echoics are units of verbal behavior that are, "evoked by a verbal discriminative stimulus that has point-to point correspondence and formal similarity with the response" (Cooper, Heron, & Heward, 2014). Repeating words, phrases, or other auditory verbal units is common for all speakers in day-to-day speech (Sundberg, 2008).

Echoic training, sometimes referred to as vocal imitation training, is a procedure in which a caregiver or teacher emits a sound and a listener echoes or repeats what has been said (Skinner, 1957). Reinforcement (either social, tangible or other) is often delivered after the correct utterance is given.

When using echoic training, the trainer should:
1. Deliver the verbal discriminative stimulus (the word, sound or phrase you intend them to repeat).
2. Provide positive reinforcement for responses that have point-to-point similarity to the target response.

Examples:

- Echoic training can be used to teach a variety of skills such as:
- Mands-such as when you give a child a full verbal model of the appropriate way to ask for another cup of milk "I want milk" and he repeats this phrase.
- Tacts- such as telling a classroom full of Spanish students that the word for dog is "perro" and asking them to repeat this word back to you.
- Intraverbal behavior- such as an elementary school teaching modeling the fill in of the word "star" after saying "Twinkle, twinkle little _____" and pausing.

Write another example:

Relevant Literature:

Drash, P. W., High, R. L., & Tudor, R. M. (1999). Using mand training to establish an echoic repertoire in young children with autism. *The Analysis of Verbal Behavior*, 16, 29–44.

Cooper J.O, Heron T.E, Heward W.L. (2014). *Applied behavior analysis*. Upper Saddle River, NJ: Pearson.

Kodak, T., & Clements, A. (2009). Acquisition of Mands and Tacts with Concurrent Echoic Training. *Journal of Applied Behavior Analysis*, 42(4), 839–843.

Mirenda, P. (2008). A Comparison of Stimulus-Stimulus Pairing, Standard Echoic Training, and Control Procedures on the Vocal Behavior of Children with Autism. *The Analysis of Verbal Behavior*, 24(1), 123–133.

Sundberg, M. L. (2008). *Verbal Behavior Milestones Assessment and Placement Program*. Concorde, CA: AVB Press

Skinner, B.F. (1957). *Verbal Behavior*. New York: Appleton-Century

Related Lessons:

D-01 Use positive and negative reinforcement.
D-04 Use modeling and imitation training.
FK-43 Echoics

Notes:

Questions to ask your supervisor:

D-11 USE MAND TRAINING.

Definition:

Mands are important in the development of language in children. The development of a mands allows an individual to communicate their wants and needs, including basic needs such as food and water, to those around them. When an early learner fails to develop a mand repertoire, they may not be able to effectively communicate with others and may not be able to access these reinforcers. This can lead to frustration, learned helplessness, or a variety of other maladaptive behaviors such aggression, self-injurious behavior social withdrawal or tantrums (Cooper, Heron, & Heward, 2007).

When mands fail to develop typically, it is crucial begin language training. Cooper, Heron and Heward (2007) suggest teaching mands before all other types of verbal behavior as manding allows an individual to gain access to their wants and needs. During early training a variety of mands should be taught so that the child learns to differentiate their response based on their current needs and MO. Instructors should focus on teaching bids for edibles and tangibles before making other requests. Sundberg & Partington (1998) suggest that teachers should use a combination of "prompting, fading and differential reinforcement to transfer control from stimulus variables to motivative variables" (Cooper, Heron, & Heward, 2007). It is important that both the echoic prompt and the non-verbal stimulus be faded out for mand training to be effective.

When using mand training:

Establish a likely MO (motivating operation). This may be done formally through preference assessment procedures or more informally through observations or caregiver report. It is important that a child be motivated to make a request for mand training to be effective.

- _Note:_ It may be helpful to ensure that a reinforcer has been withheld prior to training to ensure that it is potent. For instance a child who has just recently eaten is not as likely to be motivated to request food.
- Enrich the environment with potential reinforcers (things that the child generally seems to prefer such as foods and toys).
- Wait for the child to initiate or show interest in the nonverbal stimulus (the child reaches for an item, emits some sort of vocalization, points to it, etc.).
- Use an echoic prompt to label the non-verbal stimulus. Successively reinforce closer and closer approximations to the target verbal response and follow with specific reinforcement (the requested item).
- Once the client is able to imitate the verbal model in the presence of the stimulus, gradually fade out the echoic prompt to establish the response "under the multiple control of the MO and the nonverbal stimulus" Cooper, Heron, & Heward, 2007).
- Finally the presentation of the non-verbal stimulus should also be faded out so that the response is only under the control of the MO. This helps to ensure that the individual can make the request regardless of whether or not the item is physically present within the environment.

- Gradually increase the verbal requirement over time so that the child is making more complex and specific requests ("I want the chocolate cookie.").

Example:
- Rachel wants a cookie, but does not know how to ask. So instead she has a long tantrum and screams, "cookie, cookie, cookie". This goes on for several days, so her teacher's decide to train her on how to ask for a cookie appropriately instead of engaging in tantrum behavior.

Write another example:

Questions to ask your supervisor:

Relevant Literature:

Cooper J.O, Heron T.E, Heward W.L. (2007). _Applied behavior analysis_ (2nd ed.) Upper Saddle River, NJ: Pearson Prentice Hall.

Drash, P. W., High, R. L., & Tudor, R. M. (1999). Using mand training to establish an echoic repertoire in young children with autism. _The Analysis of Verbal Behavior, 16,_ 29–44.

Skinner, B.F. (1957). _Verbal Behavior._ New York: Appleton-Century.

Sundberg, M. L., Loeb, M., Hail, L., & Eigenheer, P. (2002). Contriving establishing operations to teach mands for information. The Analysis of Verbal Behavior, 18, 14-28

Sundberg, M.L., & Partington, J.W. (1998). _Teaching language to children with autism or other developmental disabilities._ Pleasant Hill, CA: Behavior Analysts, Inc.

Related Lessons:

FK-44 Mands

Notes:

D-12 USE TACT TRAINING.

Definition:
Practitioners may use a variety of techniques to teach language when working with clients. Tact training is one such technique in which a consumer may be taught to label "objects, actions, properties of objects and actions, prepositional relations, abstractions, private events, and so on" (Cooper, Howard, & Heron, 2007). "The goal of teaching is to bring a verbal response under nonverbal stimulus control" (Cooper, Howard, & Heron, 2007).

When using tact training:
- Ensure that the listener is attending. Make sure that they are looking in your direction, are making eye contact and that the environment isn't too noisy or distracting.
- Pair the presentation of nonverbal stimulus that you would like to train with an echoic model.
- Pause to allow the listener to process the information and wait for a response.
- Provide differential reinforcement for responses that are closer and closer approximations to the verbal model.

Note: It may be difficult to differentially reinforce the tacting of events that cannot be shared by both instructor and student, such as private events like pain, as the instructor may not be able to adequately able to label them (Cooper, Howard, & Heron, 2007). For this reason it is recommended that initial tact training be done with objects or actions that can be directly observed.

Once the client is able to imitate the verbal model in the presence of the stimulus, gradually fade out the verbal model so that only the stimulus itself sets the occasion for the response.

Example:
Initially a practitioner pairs a nonverbal stimulus (such as snow falling outside of one's window) with an echoic model "snow." The imitation of this verbal model is differentially reinforced. Over time this echoic is faded out so that only the presence of the nonverbal stimulus (the snow) sets the occasion for the consumer to label "snow" in the absence of a verbal model. A time delay procedure, in which the practitioner gradually delays the presentation of the echoic model after the nonverbal stimulus appears, may be helpful in fading out the verbal model.

Notes:

Write another example:

Questions to ask your supervisor:

Relevant Literature:
Cooper J.O., Heron T.E, Heward W.L. (2007). *Applied behavior analysis* (2nd ed.) Upper Saddle River, NJ: Pearson
Skinner, B.F. (1957). *Verbal Behavior*. New York: Appleton-Century.
Sundberg, M. L., & Michael, J. (2001). The value of Skinner's analysis of verbal behavior for teaching children with autism. *Behavior Modification*, 25, 698-724.
Sundberg, M.L., & Partington, J.W. (1998). *Teaching language to children with autism or other developmental disabilities*. Pleasant Hill, CA: Behavior Analysts, Inc.

Related Lessons:
D-12 Use Tact Training
FK-45 Tacts

D-13 USE INTRAVERBAL TRAINING.

Definition:
"Many children with autism, developmental disabilities, or other language delays suffer from defective or non-existent intraverbal repertoires, even though some can emit hundreds of mands, tacts, and receptive responses" (Cooper, Heron, & Heward, 2007).

Although typically developing children generally acquire this type of language on their own, some learners may not acquire this type of language without specific training in the skill. In such cases, intraverbal training may be recommended. Prior to starting intraverbal training, the learner must have a acquired a variety of pre-requisite skills such as being able to mand, tact, engage in echoic behavior or imitation, to receptively identify stimuli, and to do match to sample tasks (Sundberg & Partington, 1998). The goal is not to teach new language, but to bring words or phrases that are currently under nonverbal stimulus control entirely under verbal stimulus control (Cooper, Heron, & Heward, 2007). For instance, a child who has previously learned to tact or echo the word "cow" when they see a picture of a cow, may learn to then say "cow" when his teacher has asked, "What says moo?"

It is recommended that simple intraverbal interactions that are appropriate to the child's developmental age be taught before more complicated responses. Fill in the blank relations are often the easiest to teach first (Cooper et al., 2007). For instance, a learner may be taught to fill in the word "star" after someone has delivered the line "Twinkle, twinkle little _____." A teacher may start by using visual stimuli and then gradually fade out these prompts as the child is successful so that only the verbal stimulus is presented.

Since intraverbal behavior is reinforced by generalized conditioned reinforcement (i.e., social reinforcement via praise, eye contact, body language, etc.) it may be challenging to motivate some students initially to engage in the desired response. Trainers may need to initially pair specific reinforcement (such as a crayon after the child has responded "crayon" when asked, "What do you color with?") initially and then fade this over time (Cooper et al., 2007).

Varying both the verbal stimuli and the verbal responses over time will help to strengthen these responses (Cooper et al., 2007).

When using intraverbal training:
- Be sure that the desired verbal responses are already in the child's or individual's repertoire
- Ensure that the listener is attending. Make sure that they are looking in your direction, are making eye contact and that the environment isn't too noisy or distracting.

- Deliver the verbal stimulus (i.e. "The itsy bitsy _____.") and pause. Initially pair the verbal response with a nonverbal stimulus that can be faded out over time (such as a picture of a spider or spider puppet).
- Provide reinforcement for correct responding. Specific reinforcement such as providing edibles, access to the spider puppet, etc. should be faded over time so that social reinforcement becomes the reinforcing consequence.
- Once simple intraverbal relations have been established, teach the child to respond to variations to the verbal stimulus ("Who went up the water spout?") or respond with more complexity.

Examples:
- For instance a child who has learned to respond "bear" when asked, "What is your favorite toy?" may then learn to respond with more complexity such as "blue bear" or "my blue bear with the purple hat." The teacher can also vary the verbal prompt such as asking, "What toy do you like the most?" which is simply another way of phrasing "what is your favorite toy," and is a part of the same stimulus class.

Write another example:

Questions to ask your supervisor:

Relevant Literature:

Cooper J.O., Heron T.E, Heward W.L. (2007). *Applied behavior analysis* (2nd ed.) Upper Saddle River, NJ: Pearson

Partington, J. W., & Bailey, J. S. (1993). Teaching intraverbal behavior to preschool children. *The Analysis of Verbal Behavior, 11*, 9–18.

Skinner, B.F. (1957). *Verbal Behavior.* New York: Appleton-Century.

Sundberg, M.L. & Partington, J.W. (1998). *Teaching language to children with autism or other developmental disabilities.* Pleasant Hill, CA: Behavior Analysts, Inc.

Vedora, J., Meunier, L., & Mackay, H. (2009). Teaching Intraverbal Behavior to Children with Autism: A Comparison of Textual and Echoic Prompts. *The Analysis of Verbal Behavior, 25*(1), 79–86.

Related Lessons:
D-13 Use Intraverbal Training
FK-46 Intraverbals

Notes:

F-08 USE AUGMENTATIVE COMMUNICATION SYSTEMS.

"A set of procedures and processes by which an individual's communication skills (i.e., production as well as comprehension) can be maximized for functional and effective communication. It involves supplementing or replacing natural speech and/or writing with aided (e.g. picture communication symbols, line drawing, Blissymbols, and tangible objects) and/or unaided symbols (e.g. manual signs, gestures, and finger spelling)" (American Speech-Language-Hearing Association, 2002).

Augmentative communication includes any modality that supplements a person with difficulties engaging in spoken language. This can include gestures, sign language, PECS, electronic devices, picture books, etc...

The use of augmentative communication should be considered as a way to allow the user to access reinforcement from the natural environment. Often functionally equivalent responses can be taught to replace problematic behavior therefore leading to a decrease in that behavior (Durand, 1999).

Teaching of functional communication using augmentative communication devices should be taught using the same strategies to teach other skills (prompt fading, reinforcement considerations, generalization considerations, etc.)

Augmentative communication systems should not be confused with the long-discredited "facilitated communication" which is a pseudoscientific attempt at getting people with developmental disabilities to communicate.

Example:
- Bill uses pictures to tell his teachers when he wants.
- Ralph is eating snack and signs "more" to his teacher after running out of crackers to eat. She gladly hands him more and praises him for using his words.
- Hillary uses an app on a tablet device that generates speech sounds so others respond to her.

Non-examples:
- Bill wants more crackers so tells his teacher, "I want some more, please." using spoken word.
- Bill wants more crackers so he hits his fist on the table and screams. His teacher says, "Oh, you're still hungry? Here are a few more crackers".

Write another example:

Questions to ask your supervisor:

Relevant Literature:

American Speech-Language-Hearing Association. (2002). Augmentative and alternative communication: knowledge and skills for service delivery [Knowledge and Skills]. Available from www.asha.org/policy.

Charlop-Christy, M. H., Carpenter, M., Le, L., LeBlanc, L. A., & Kellet, K. (2002). Using the picture exchange communication system (PECS) with children with autism: Assessment of PECS acquisition, speech, social-communicative behavior, and problem behavior. *Journal of applied behavior analysis, 35*(3), 213-231.

Dattilo, J., & Camarata, S. (1991). Facilitating conversation through self-initiated augmentative communication treatment. *Journal of Applied Behavior Analysis, 24*(2), 369-378.

Jacobson, J. W., Mulick, J. A., & Schwartz, A. A. (1995). A history of facilitated communication: Science, pseudoscience, and antiscience science working group on facilitated communication. *American Psychologist, 50*(9), 750.

Durand, V. M. (1999). Functional communication training using assistive devices: recruiting natural communities of reinforcement. *Journal of Applied Behavior Analysis, 32*(3), 247.

Mirenda, P., Iacono, T., & Williams, R. (1990). Communication options for persons with severe and profound disabilities: State of the art and future directions. *Journal of the Association for Persons with Severe Handicaps.*

Related Lessons:
D-03: Use prompts and prompt fading.
D-04: Use modeling and imitation training.
D-05: Use shaping.
F-07: Use functional communication training
Notes:

FK-43 ECHOICS.

Definition (Echoic):

[   ]

(Cooper, Heron, & Heward, 2007).
☐ Flashcard created   ☐ Learned to fluency

Examples:
- Mrs. Platypus is instructing her 3rd grade class on their math facts. She holds up a card stating that, "three times nine is eighteen". She then restates the fact asking the class to repeat. The class says, "three times nine is eighteen" in unison. Mrs. Platypus praises the students for their repetition.

- Mr. Penguin is a kindergarten teacher. He is working with one student on his reading skills. He shows little Timmy the letter R. He tells him that the letter R makes the "rrr" sound and asks him to repeat. Little Timmy says, "rrr," and Mr. Penguin comments, "Nice job Timmy."

-

- Mrs. Dodo the art teacher needs one of her students to run to the office and get some supplies. One of the children volunteers. She tells him that she needs him to get, "Crayons, markers, and paint." He repeats, "Crayons, markers, and paint." "Exactly," Mrs. Dodo says sending him on his way.

Non-examples:
- Mrs. Platypus is still working on math facts with her class. She holds up the math fact

$4x9=$ and asks the students to give the answer. Susie Q raises her hand and answers "thirty-six."

Write another example:

[   ]

Questions to ask your supervisor:

[   ]

Relevant Literature:
Cooper J.O, Heron T.E, Heward W.L. (2007). *Applied behavior analysis*. (2nd Ed.). Upper Saddle River, NJ: Pearson.

Sundberg, M. L. (2008). *Verbal Behavior Milestones Assessment and Placement Program*. Concorde, CA: AVB Press

Skinner, B.F. (1957). *Verbal Behavior*. New York: Appleton-Century.

Related Lessons:
D-04 Use modeling and imitation training.
D-10 Use echoic training.

Notes:

FK-44 MANDS.

Definition (Mand):

(Cooper, Heron, & Heward, 2007).
☐ Flashcard created   ☐ Learned to fluency

Example:
- "I want a cookie" (mand for an item; can also include verbs, use of adjectives, prepositions, pronouns etc.)
- A child says "watch me" after learning how to ride a bike independently (mand for attention)
- Asking questions like "what's your name? or "where's the phone?" (mand for information)
- Child says "no!" when parent is about to use blender (mand for avoidance of an aversive)

Write another example:

Questions to ask your supervisor:

Relevant Literature:

Cooper, J. O., Heron, T. E., & Heward, W. L. (2007). *Applied behavior analysis*. (2nd Ed.) Upper Saddle River, NJ: Pearson Prentice Hall.

Laraway, S., Snycerski, S., Michael, J., & Poling, A. (2003). Motivating operations and terms to describe them: Some further refinements. *Journal of Applied Behavior Analysis, 36*(3), 407-414.

Michael, J. (1988). Establishing operations and the mand. *The Analysis of Verbal Behavior, 6*, 3.

Sundberg, M. L., & Michael, J. (2001). The benefits of Skinner's analysis of verbal behavior for children with autism. *Behavior Modification, 25*(5), 698-724.

Sweeney-Kerwin, E. J., Carbone, V. J., O'Brien, L., Zecchin, G., & Janecky, M. N. (2007). Transferring control of the mand to the motivating operation in children with autism. *The Analysis of verbal behavior, 23*(1), 89.

Related Lessons:
D-09 verbal operant as a basis for language assessment
D-11 use mand training
FK 27 Conditioned motivating operations
FK 28 Transitive, reflexive, surrogate motivating operations

Notes:

FK-45 TACTS.

Definition (Tact):

Write another example:

(Cooper, Heron, & Heward, 2007).

☐ Flashcard created   ☐ Learned to fluency

Questions to ask your supervisor:

Example:

- Dexter walks outside with his mother and sees birds in a tree. "Robins," he says. "You're right. Those are robins," Dexter's mom says. "Robins" is a tact.
- Hector is in the store shopping for Valentine's Day. He sees a variety of flowers before noticing the ones he wants to buy. "Red roses," Hector says quietly to himself. "Red roses" in this context is likely a tact.
- Chester goes to his friends Superbowl party. Upon scanning the array of delicious apps and snacks on the counter, he hones in on one that is his favorite. "Ooh, buffalo chicken dip," he comments. "Buffalo chicken dip" would be likely a tact in this context.

Non-Example:

- Dexter is thinking about buying some cookies the next time he goes to the supermarket. He writes the word "cookies" down on his shopping list.

Relevant Literature:

Cooper J.O, Heron T.E, Heward W.L. (2007). *Applied behavior analysis* (2nd ed.) Upper Saddle River, NJ: Pearson.

Skinner, B.F. (1957). *Verbal Behavior.* New York: Appleton-Century.

Related Lessons:

D-12 Use tact training.

Notes:

FK-46 INTRAVERBALS.

Definition (Intraverbals):

(Cooper, Heron, & Heward, 2007).

☐ Flashcard created   ☐ Learned to fluency

Example:

- A new employee shows up for his first day on the job. The man in the cubical next to him asks, "What is your name?" "Harvey," the man replies." Saying, "Harvey," is an intraverbal in that context.

- Hanks boss stops his office to let him know that his sales were "outstanding this week." "Thanks. I really put in some long hours," Hank noted, "Thanks," is an intraverbal in that context.

Non-Example:

- The phone in the office rings. Harvey picks up the phone and answers "Hello." There is no one on the line so he hangs up and gets back to work.

Write another example:

Relevant Literature:

Cooper J.O, Heron T.E, Heward W.L. (2007). *Applied behavior analysis* (2nd ed.) Upper Saddle River, NJ: Pearson.

Partington, J. W., & Bailey, J. S. (1993). Teaching intraverbal behavior to preschool children. *The Analysis of Verbal Behavior*, *11*, 9.

Skinner, B.F. (1957). *Verbal Behavior*. New York: Appleton-Century.

Related Lessons:
D-13 Use intraverbal training

Notes:

Segment 17 – Scorecard
Interventions

☐ Presentation (2-5 minutes)

C 3
☐ Assessment
☐ SAFMED learned to fluency
☐ Workbook boxes completed

J 1
☐ Assessment
☐ SAFMED learned to fluency
☐ Workbook boxes completed

J 2
☐ Assessment
☐ SAFMED learned to fluency
☐ Workbook boxes completed

J 3
☐ Assessment
☐ SAFMED learned to fluency
☐ Workbook boxes completed

J 5
☐ Assessment
☐ SAFMED learned to fluency
☐ Workbook boxes completed

J 6
☐ Assessment
☐ SAFMED learned to fluency
☐ Workbook boxes completed

J 7
☐ Assessment
☐ SAFMED learned to fluency
☐ Workbook boxes completed

J 8
☐ Assessment
☐ SAFMED learned to fluency
☐ Workbook boxes completed

FK 22
☐ Assessment
☐ SAFMED learned to fluency
☐ Workbook boxes completed

Segment 17 – Individual Supervision Agenda

Supervisor: _____ **Supervisee:** _____
Meeting Date: _____ **Time of meeting – From:** _____ **To:** _____
This document covers supervisory period from ____/____/____ **to** ____/____/____

1. Pass-in/Review Homework:

    Did the Supervisee satisfactorily complete this homework assignment?   Yes / No

- If not, what is needed to complete assignment? Describe below.

2. Task List items addressed (C 3, J 1-3, 5-8; FK 22)

3. Definitions/SAFMEDs learned

    ☐ Flashcard(s) created   Was supervisee fluent with definitions? Yes ☐ No ☐

4. Discussion topics or activities completed during this meeting:

Evaluation of Supervisee's Performance		
(Record: S- "Satisfactory"; NI- "Needs Improvement"; U- "Unsatisfactory"; or NA- "Not Applicable")		
Arrived on time for meeting	Gave examples as needed	
Completed Homework Assigned	Accepted supervisory feedback appropriately	
Referred to literature/readings	Answered all questions thoroughly	
Maintained professional communication during supervision meeting		
Overall evaluation of supervisee performance during this meeting (Circle one—use code above)	S NI U	
If "NI" or "U", please list corrective steps needed to achieve a score of "S"		

5. Homework assigned for next meeting

6. Closing questions/feedback

Segment 17 – Group Supervision Meeting Agenda

- <u>Meeting Topic</u>: Interventions

- <u>Task List Items Reviewed</u>:
  - C-03: State and plan for the possible unwanted effects of extinction.
  - J-01: State intervention goals in observable and measurable terms.
  - J-02: Identify potential interventions based on assessment results and the best available scientific evidence.
  - J-03: Select intervention strategies based on task analysis.J-05: Select intervention strategies based on the client's current repertoires.
  - J-05: Select intervention strategies based on the client's current repertoires.
  - J-06: Select intervention strategies based on supporting environments.
  - J-07: Select intervention strategies based on environmental and resource constraints.
  - J-08: Select intervention strategies based on the social validity of the intervention.
  - FK-22: Extinction.

1. Housekeeping
   - Upon entry to meeting have supervisees hand in the previous week's homework assignment and discuss several "Housekeeping Items" related to supervision.
   - Take attendance for the meeting.
   - State the duration of today's meeting (90 minutes).
   - Distribute BACB® experience forms to supervisees.

2. Task List Lesson and Discussion
   - Discuss task list item C-03: State and plan for the possible unwanted effects of extinction.
   - Discuss task list item J-01: State intervention goals in observable and measurable terms.
   - Discuss task list item J-02: Identify potential interventions based on assessment results and the best available scientific evidence.
   - Discuss task list item J-03: Select intervention strategies based on task analysis.
   - Discuss task list item J-05: Select intervention strategies based on the client's current repertoires.
   - Discuss task list item J-06: Select intervention strategies based on supporting environments.
   - Discuss task list item J-07: Select intervention strategies based on environmental and resource constraints.
   - Discuss task list item J-08: Select intervention strategies based on the social validity of the intervention.
   - Discuss task list item FK-22: Extinction.

3. Homework Review
   - Review homework that was assigned at the previous supervision meeting.

4. Questions
   - Answer any questions related to the homework or topics discussed.

5. Closing Notes

   - *Assign Homework (task list boxes, presentation) from today's segment, due at next group meeting*

   - Close the meeting by inviting supervisees to request topics to be covered in upcoming meetings.

C – 03 STATE AND PLAN FOR THE POSSIBLE UNWANTED EFFECTS OF EXTINCTION.

Definition:

Extinction "occurs when reinforcement of a previously rein-forced behavior is discontinued; as a result the frequency of that behavior decreases in the future." (Cooper, Heron & Howard, 2007) Extinction renders target behavior useless and is often a significant component contributing to the ef-fectiveness of a behavioral program. However, extinction should be used with caution. Research has shown that there are two common side effects that may occur when extinction is utilized; these include an extinction burst, defined as "an immediate increase in the frequency of the response after the removal of the positive, negative, or automatic reinforce-ment" (Cooper, Heron & Howard, 2007), and extinction-in-duced aggression. Studies have compared withdrawal of rein-forcement as an aversive event and responses to extinction are similar to attack responses in laboratory subjects exposed to aversive stimulation, such as heat, shocks and physical blows. (Lerman et al., 1999) Extinction should not be used as a singular intervention when self-injury or aggression is severe and cannot be prevented and appropriate safe-guards cannot be put in place. Other considerations include extinction being inappropriate in settings where maladaptive behaviors are likely to be imitated by others (e.g. in a classroom setting) and when extinction is not feasible.

Research has shown that there are other behavioral strategies that can be utilized to mitigate the unwanted effects of ex-tinction. These include using differential reinforcement of al-ternative behavior in conjunction with extinction procedures. In situations in which using extinction is not possible, re-search has shown that by manipulating reinforcement sched-ules and reinforcement parameters (e.g. quality, duration, im-mediacy of reinforcement) to favoring appropriate behavior rather than problem behavior, problem behavior has also been shown to decrease. (Athens & Vollmer, 2010).

Example:

- If an individual engages in physical aggression for at-tention, response-blocking may be enough to reinforce the individual's behavior.

Write another example.

Questions to ask your supervisor:

Relevant Literature:

Athen, E.S., & Vollmer, T.R., (2010). An investigation of dif-ferential reinforcement of alternative behavior without extinction. *Journal of Applied Behavioral Analysis, 43(4)*, 569-589.

Cooper, J. O., Heron, T. E., & Heward, W. L. (2007). *Applied behavior analysis* (2nd ed.). Upper Saddle River, NJ: Pren-tice Hall.

Lerman, D.C., & Iwata, B.A., (1995). Prevalence of the ex-tinction burst and its attenuation during treatment. *Jour-nal of Applied Behavioral Analysis, 28(1)*, 93-94.

Lerman, D.C., Iwata, B.A., & Wallace, M.D., (1999). Side ef-fects of extinction: Prevalence of bursting and aggres-sion during the treatment of self-injurious behavior. *Journal of Applied Behavioral Analysis, 32 (1)*, 1-8.

Related Lessons:

D-02 Use appropriate parameters and schedules of reinforce-ment.

D-18. Use Extinction.

D.-19 Use combinations of reinforcement with punishment and extinction.

E-01 Use interventions based on manipulation of anteced-ents, such as motivating operations and discriminative stim-uli.

E-08 Use the matching law and recognize factors influencing choice.

G-06 Provide behavior-analytic services in collaboration with others who support and/or provide services to one's clients.

I-06 Make recommendations regarding behaviors that must be established, maintained, increased or decreased.

J-05 Select intervention strategies based on the client's cur-rent repertoires.

J-06 Select intervention strategies based on supporting envi-ronments.

J-07 Select intervention strategies based on environmental and resource constraints.

J-09 Identify and address practical and ethical considerations when using experimental designs to demonstrate program ef-fectiveness.

J-10 When a behavior is to be decreased, select an acceptable alternative behavior to be established or increased.

Notes:

J-01 STATE INTERVENTION GOALS IN OB-SERVEABLE AND MEASUREABLE TERMS.

"Target behaviors are selected for study in applied behavior analysis because of their importance to the people involved. Applied behavior analysts attempt to increase, maintain, and generalize adaptive, desirable behaviors and decrease the occurrence of maladaptive, undesirable behaviors" (Cooper, Heron, & Heward, 2007, p. 69).

Van Houten (1979) cited in Cooper et al. (2007, p. 69) suggests "two basic approaches to determining socially valid goals: (a) Assess the performance of people judged to be highly competent, and (b) experimentally manipulate different levels of performance to determine empirically which produces optimal results. Regardless of the method used, specifying treatment goals before intervention begins providing a guideline for continuing or terminating treatment. Further, setting objective, predetermined goals helps to eliminate disagreements or biases among those involved in evaluating a program's effectiveness."

Examples:
- The intervention goal: Client's aggression will decrease by 80% of baseline levels across 5 consecutive school days. Staff will record every instance of hitting across the school day on the data collection sheet.
- The intervention goal: Client will expressively identify 10 different colors with 80% accuracy, across 3 consecutive days. Staff will record data on correct and incorrect responses.

Write another example:

Questions to ask your supervisor:

Relevant Literature:
Cooper, J. O., Heron, T. E., & Heward, W. L. (2007). *Applied behavior analysis*. Upper Saddle River, NJ: Pearson Education.
Houten, R. V. (1979). Social validation: The evolution of standards of competency for target behaviors. *Journal of Applied Behavior Analysis, 12*(4), 581-591

Related Lessons:
B-01 Use the dimensions of applied behavior analysis (Baer, Wolf, & Risley, 1968) to evaluate whether interventions are behavior analytic in nature.
I-01 Define behavior in observable and measurable terms.
I-02 Define environmental variables in observable and measurable terms.
FK-07 Environmental (as opposed to mentalistic) explanations of behavior

Notes:

J-02 IDENTIFY POTENTIAL INTERVEN-IONS BASED ON ASSESSMENT RE-SULTS AND THE BEST AVAILABLE SCIENTIFIC EVIDENCE.

"Interventions should be functionally equivalent to problem behavior" (Cooper, Heron, & Heward, 2007, p. 513). In other words, the intervention should serve as a more appropriate way of accessing a specific function than the interfering behavior. "One effective way to design interventions is to review confirmed hypotheses to determine how the ABC contingency can be altered to promote more positive behavior" (Cooper, et al., 2007, p. 513). In other words if you can change the antecedents or consequences associated with a problem behavior, you may be able to decrease occurrences of that behavior.

Wolf (1978) recommended that interventions should be assessed based on appropriateness and the potential social significance of the outcomes. Specific social validity assessments can be conducted "to help choose and guide (behavior change) program developments and applications" (Baer & Schwartz, 1991, p. 231).

Results of an FBA can help determine which interventions would not be appropriate to decrease the target behavior. Once assessments are completed, monitor the progress of the interventions put in place and conduct follow up assessments regularly. Any intervention program should be based on techniques found in behavior analytic literature. This ensures that the intervention is a proven technology and has stood up to experimental manipulation and decreased or increased similar types of behavior.

In regard to assessments that are not based on the function of the behavior, (i.e., adaptive assessments, verbal behavior assessments, cognitive assessments) a profile of strengths and weaknesses as well as standard scores and rankings are typically provided once the assessment is completed. The areas that present as weaknesses should typically be addressed first based on their social significance to the client. Once these areas have been identified, appropriate interventions can be put into place to build the client's missing repertoires and skill base.

Example:
George completed an FBA on Sam's instances of aggression in the classroom. The hypothesized function for this behavior was escape from demands. George created an intervention plan that would allow Sam to functionally ask for breaks to briefly escape work demands.

Write another example:

Questions to ask your supervisor:

Relevant Literature:

Baer, D.M. & Schwartz, I.S. (1991). If reliance on epidemiology were to become epidemic, we would need to assess its social validity. *Journal of Applied Behavior Analysis*, 24, 321-334.

Cooper, J.O., Heron, T.E. & Heward W.L. (2007). *Applied Behavior Analysis* (2nd Ed.), Upper Saddle River, NJ. Pearson Prentice Hall. 55-65, 237-240, 513-523, 623-624.

Gresham, F., Watson, T.S., & Skinner, C.H. (2001). *Functional Behavioral Assessment: Principals, Procedures, and Future Directions.* School Psychology Review, 30, 2, 156-172.

Lerman, D.C., Iwata, B.A., Smith, R.G., Zincone, J.R., & Vollmer, T.R. (1994). Transfer of behavioral function as a contributing factor in treatment relapse. *Journal of Applied Behavior Analysis*, 27, 357-370.

Related Lessons:

E-01: Use interventions based on manipulation of antecedents, such as motivating operations & discriminative stimuli.
I-01: Define behavior in observable and measurable terms.
I-02: Define environmental variables in observable and measurable terms.
I-04: Design and implement the full range of functional assessment procedures.
I-06: Make recommendations regarding behaviors that must be established, maintained, increased, or decreased.
J-01: State intervention goals in observable and measurable terms.
J-02: Identify potential interventions based on assessment results and the best available scientific evidence.
J-10: When a behavior is to be decreased, select an acceptable alternative behavior to be established or increased.

Notes:

J-03 SELECT INTERVENTION STRATEGIES BASED ON TASK ANALYSIS.

What are the options for intervention strategies when it comes to teaching a chain of behavior through a task analysis?

- Once a person's baseline level has been assessed (through the single or multiple-opportunity method*) to determine what components of the task analysis he/she can perform, the appropriate intervention strategy needs to be selected. Cooper, Heron & Heward (2007) suggest there are four appropriate intervention strategies which practitioners can choose from; forward chaining, total-task chaining, and backward chaining.

- Cooper, Heron and Heward (2007, p. 446) argue that research to date does not suggest a clear answer to the question "which chaining strategy to use?" As such, it is very important to examine the results of the baseline level assessment, to consider the client and how they learn best, and what the different intervention strategies can offer in different situations, in order to select the most appropriate method.

Total-task chaining

- If the client performs quite a few steps in the task analysis but is not performing them in the correct sequence, the most appropriate method to choose would probably be total-task chaining.

- Total-task chaining would also be an appropriate intervention strategy to select when the client has generalized motor imitation and moderate to severe disabilities (Test et al., 1990, cited from Cooper, Heron & Heward, 2007).

- When the chain is quite short and not too complex, this may also be an appropriate teaching method to utilize (Cooper, Heron & Heward, 2007).

Forward chaining

- This approach may be more appropriate to use when the client has demonstrated more proficiency with the *first* couple of steps in the chain and/or the last steps in the chain are more complex to complete.

- It may also be useful to use this approach when it is necessary to link smaller chains into larger ones. For example, if you have a skill such as bed making and this is made up of perhaps four/five skill clusters, forward chaining is a useful method to link the skill clusters altogether (Cooper, Heron & Heward, 2007).

Backward chaining

- Backward chaining may be more appropriate to use when the client has demonstrated more proficiency with the *last* couple of steps in the chain and/or steps that appear earlier in the chain are more complex to complete.

Write another example:

Questions to ask your supervisor:

Relevant Literature:

Cooper, J. O., Heron, T. E., & Heward, W. L. (2007). *Applied Behavior Analysis*, 2nd ed. Upper Saddle River, New Jersey: Pearson Prentice Hall.

Kazdin, A. E. (2001). *Behavior Modifications in applied settings* (6th ed). Belmont, CA: Wadsworth.

Miltenberger, R. G. (2001). *Behavior Modification: Principles and procedures* (2nd ed). Belmont, CA: Wadsworth/Thomson Learning.

Test, D. W., Spooner, F. Keul, P. K., & Grossi, T. (1990). Teaching adolescents with severe disability to use the public telephone. *Behavior Modification, 14,* 157-171. Cited from, Cooper, J. O., Heron, T. E., & Heward, W. L. (2007, p. 446). *Applied Behavior Analysis*, 2nd ed. Upper Saddle River, New Jersey: Pearson Prentice Hall.

Related Lessons:

D-06: Use chaining
D-07: Conduct task analyses
J-02: Identify potential interventions based on assessment results and the best available scientific evidence.
J-05: Select intervention strategies based on the client's current repertoire

Footnotes

* Please see task list item D-07 for more information on conducting task analyses
* Please see task list item D-06 for a more detailed description of the different chaining procedures.

Notes:

J-05 SELECT INTERVENTION STRATEGIES BASED ON CLIENT'S CURRENT REPERTOIRES.

The importance of considering the client's current repertoires

- Basing intervention strategies on the client's current repertoires is a key foundation of what behavior analysts do. It is imperative that prior to implementing any type of intervention or strategy with a client, the behavior analyst is extremely clear about what the client already does and can therefore, consider possible intervention strategies. Noell, Call, and Ardoin (2011) state that "one of the considerable challenges in teaching arises from identifying not only the behaviors that are prerequisites for the target response, but also the level of skill proficiency needed to set the occasion for teaching the target skill" (Noell, Call, & Ardoin, 2011, cited from Fisher, Piazza, & Roane, 2011, p. 251).

The importance of accurate assessments

- In order to assess a client's current repertoires, it is imperative that these repertoires are properly assessed. For example, assessments to evaluate the presence of a particular skill or repertoire should take place in a variety of different environments, with many different examples of stimuli, with the antecedent presented in a variety of different ways, and with many different people presenting the skill. Novel examples of the skill should also be tested. Noell *et al.* (2011) emphasize this point by suggesting that "assessment of behavior under varied conditions in a manner that tests consequences should be an element of any pre-teaching assessment" (Noell, Call & Ardoin, 2011, cited from Fisher, Piazza & Roane, 2011, p. 255).

Once assessments of the client's current repertoires are complete

- Once the assessment stage is complete, it is then appropriate to select possible intervention strategies. As Noell *et al.* (2011) propose it is important at this point that behavior analysts "keep the long-term view in mind" (Noell, Call & Ardoin, 2011, cited from Fisher, Piazza &Roane, 2011, p. 266). We should be attempting to "not bring individual operants under stimulus control" but instead "help clients and students develop the complex, flexible repertoires that are adaptive, that remain in contact with reinforcement, and that confer adaptive advantage and endure" (Noell, Call & Ardoin, 2011, cf. Fisher, Piazza & Roane, 2011, p. 266).

Write another example:

Questions to ask your supervisor:

Relevant Literature:

Fisher, W. W., Piazza, C. C., & Roane, H. S. (Eds.). (2011). *Handbook of applied behavior analysis.* Guilford Press.

Noell, G. H., Call, N. A. & Ardoin, S. P. (2011). Building complex repertoires from discrete behaviors by establishing stimulus control, behavioral chains, and strategic behavior.

Shapiro, E. S. (1996). *Academic skills problems: Direct assessment and intervention* (2nd ed.). New York: Guildford Press.

Related Lessons:

D-09: Use the verbal operants as a basis for language assessment.

G-03: Conduct a preliminary assessment of the client in order to identify the referral problem.

I-03: Design and implement individualized behavioral assessment procedures.

J-03: Select intervention strategies based on task analysis.

I-04: Design and implement the full range of functional assessment procedures.

J-02: Identify potential interventions based on assessment results and the best available scientific evidence.

J-06: Select intervention strategies based on supporting environments

J-07: Select intervention strategies based on environmental and resource constraints

J-08: Select intervention strategies based on the social validity of the intervention

Notes:

J-06 SELECT INTERVENTION STRATEGIES BASED ON SUPPORTING ENVIRON-MENTS.

"Achieving optimal generalized outcomes requires thoughtful, systematic planning. This planning begins with two major steps: (1) selecting target behaviors that will meet natural contingencies of reinforcement, and (2) specifying all desired variations of the target behavior and the settings/situations in which it should (and should not) occur after instruction has ended" (Cooper, Heron, & Heward, 2007, p. 623). In other words, an intervention must be selected that will allow the client to access reinforcement in a specific environment. If that is not possible, then alternative interventions should be explored.

Ayllon and Azrin (1968) state that an important rule of thumb is to choose interventions that will help produce reinforcement after the intervention is discontinued. The intervention should support the student until they can access naturally existing contingencies (i.e., verbal praise from a teacher) and then more intensive, contrived contingencies should be systematically faded. The goal of most intervention programs is to teach a skill and then fade support so the client can implement that skill across settings.

Cooper, Heron, & Heward (2007, p. 626) identify 5 strategic approaches to promote generalized behavior change.
1. Teach the full range of relevant stimulus conditions and response requirements (i.e., teaching sufficient stimulus and response examples based on the setting)
2. Make the instructional setting similar to the generalization setting. (i.e., program common stimuli and teach loosely)
3. Maximize the target behavior's contact with reinforcement in the generalization setting. (i.e., ask people in the generalization setting to reinforce the target behavior, teach the learner to recruit reinforcement, and teach the target behavior to levels of performance required by natural existing contingencies of reinforcement.)
4. Mediate generalization. (i.e., teach self-management skills and contrive a mediating stimulus)
5. Train to generalize. (i.e., reinforce response variability and instruct the learner to generalize)

Example:
George set up a token economy for Bill that systematically increased the number of responses needed to earn a token. After some time, Bill was earning tokens for completing an entire worksheet rather than earning a token for each question answered. This allowed Bill to independently complete worksheets in his general education classroom without a paraprofessional by his side giving him tokens after each answer.

Write another example:

Questions to ask your supervisor:

Relevant Literature:

Ayllon, T., & Azrin, N.H. (1968). *The token economy: A motivational system for therapy and rehabilitation.* New York: Appleton-Century-Crofts.

Baer, D.M. (1999). *How to plan for generalization* (2nd ed.). Austin, TX.: Pro-Ed.

Cooper, J.O., Heron, T.E. & Heward W.L. (2007). *Applied Behavior Analysis* (2nd Ed.), Upper Saddle River, NJ. Pearson Prentice Hall. 55-65, 623-624, 652.

Snell, M.E., & Brown. F. (2006). *Instruction of students with severe disabilities* (6th ed.). Upper Saddle River, NJ: Prentice Hall.

Stokes, T.F., & Baer, D.M. (1977). An implicit technology of generalization. *Journal of Applied Behavior Analysis, 10,* 349-367.

Stokes, T.F., & Osnes, P.G. (1989). An operant pursuit of generalization. *Behavior Therapy, 20,* 337-355.

Related Lessons:
G-08: Identify and make environmental changes that reduce the need for behavior analysis services.
J-07: Select intervention strategies based on environmental and resource constraints.
J-08: Select intervention strategies based on the social validity of the intervention.
J-11: Program for stimulus and response generalization
J-12: Program for maintenance.
K-07: Evaluate the effectiveness of the behavioral program.
K-09: Secure the support of others to maintain the client's behavioral repertoires in their natural environments.

Notes:

J-07 SELECT INTERVENTION STRATEGIES BASED ON ENVIRONMENTAL AND RESOURCE CONTRAINTS.

Definition:
"The independent variable should be evaluated not only in terms of its effects on the dependent variable, but also in terms of its social acceptability, complexity, practicality, and cost" (Cooper, Heron, & Heward, 2007).

One method for determining the feasibility of an intervention is by asking consumers (parents, teachers, administrators) to rate the social validity of the client's performance. Questions that are typically posed to consumers before interventions are implemented include asking the consumer how reasonable they feel the intervention is, asking the consumer's willingness to implement the intervention strategies, asking if the consumer would be willing to change the environment to implement the intervention, asking how disruptive the intervention may be to the natural environment, asking how costly it would be to implement the intervention, asking if there will be any discomfort in the client when implementing these procedures, and asking if carrying out the intervention will fit with the classroom or setting routines (Reimers & Wacker, 1988 cited from Cooper et al., 2007)

Example:
Rob has decided to implement a reinforcement program based on appropriate responses rather than a fixed time DRO program. He understands that there is no paraprofessional in the classroom to help run the program and the teacher has other educational duties so she cannot run a timer and deliver reinforcement consistently enough for a rigorous DRO.

Write another example:

Questions to ask your supervisor:

Cooper, J.O., Heron, T.E. & Heward W.L. (2007). *Applied Behavior Analysis* (2nd Ed.), Upper Saddle River, NJ. Pearson Prentice Hall. 240 (Figure 10.5), 250, 652, 674-676.

Hawkins, R.P. (1984). What is "meaningful" behavior change in a severely/ profoundly retarded learner: The view of a behavior analytic parent. In W.L. Heward, T.E. Heron, D.S. Hill, & J. Trap-Porter (Eds.), Focus on behavior analysis in education (pp. 282-286). Upper Saddle River, NJ: Prentice-Hall/Merrill.

Reimers, T.M., & Wacker, D.P. (1988). Parent's ratings of the acceptability of behavior treatment recommendations made in an outpatient clinic: A preliminary analysis of the influence of treatment effectiveness. *Behavioral Disorders*, 14, 7-15.

Wolf, M.M. (1978). Social Validity: The case for subjective measurement or how applied behavior analysis is finding its heart. *Journal of Applied Behavior Analysis*, 11, 203-214.

Related Lessons:
C-01: State and plan for the possible unwanted effects of reinforcement.
G-06: Provide behavior-analytic services in collaboration with others who support and/or provide services to one's clients.
G-08: Identify and make environmental changes that reduce the need for behavior analysis services.
I-01: Define behavior in observable and measureable terms.
1-02: Define environmental variables in observable and measureable terms.
J-06: Select intervention strategies based on supporting environments.
J-08: Select intervention strategies based on the social validity of the intervention.
K-07: Evaluate the effectiveness of the behavioral program.
K-09: Secure the support of others to maintain the client's behavioral repertoires in their natural environments.
FK-11: Environment, stimulus, stimulus class.

Notes:

J-08 SELECT INTERVENTION STRATEGIES BASED ON THE SOCIAL VALIDITY OF THE INTERVENTION.

A distinguishing characteristic of applied behavior analysis is assessing an individual's functioning within the context of natural environments. This applied aspect focuses the behavior analyst on identifying meaningful goals and acceptable methods for intervention that will increase the individual's independence and level of functioning in natural settings. The behavior analyst sets intervention goals that comply with stated preferences of the individual client, goals of those who live and work with the individual, and consider how typical individuals function in similar environments. Analysts seek goals that are socially valid and intervention methods that are not only scientifically validated strategies for accomplishing those goals, but strategies that can be expected to be implemented consistently and with fidelity by those who will apply the strategies. Although an intervention might be effective in a clinical, controlled setting, the behavior analyst must consider intervention limitations related to "social acceptability, complexity, practicality, and cost. Regardless of their effectiveness, treatments that are perceived by practitioners, parents, and/or clients as unacceptable or undesirable for whatever reason are unlikely to be used" (Cooper et al, 2007, p. 250).

Examples:
A child hits her six month-old sister even when their parents model and reinforce appropriate behaviors toward the baby. The parents find it difficult to avoid explaining to the child, at the same time that they block her physically, reasons her behaviors are unkind and even dangerous. The behavior analyst talks to the parents about how the parent's explanations might be reinforcing the big sister aggression. The parents and the analyst increase the opportunities they have to individually attend to the child during appropriate play throughout the day. The parents ask the analyst to help them design a structured plan to teach appropriate sibling behaviors through language, modeling, literature, role play, movies, and increased reinforcement for appropriate behaviors of the sister toward her younger sibling.

A man hits his head and pulls at his ears with such force that he has required emergency medical care. At the beginning of treatment, the behavior analyst recommends that the man be given access to a helmet to prevent significant injury when he is not adequately staffed to stop his behavior. His family is against the man appearing in public with a protective helmet. The behavior analyst explains the reasons such equipment might be important for protecting the man from harm when his 1:1 staff person is distracted by driving a car or interacting with clerks or others in the community. The analyst and the family agree that until interventions stops the severe self-injury, the man will participate in community activities with a helmet unless a family member accompanies staff in the community with him.

Write another example:

Questions to ask your supervisor:

Relevant Literature:
Cooper, J.O., Heron, T. E., & Heward, W. L. (2007). *Applied behavior analysis.* Upper Saddle River, NJ: Pearson Education.

Fawcett, S. B. (1991). Social validity: A note on methodology. *Journal of Applied Behavior Analysis, 24*(2), 235-239.

Wolf, M. M. (1978). Social validity: The case for subjective measurement or how applied behavior analysis is finding its heart. *Journal of applied behavior analysis, 11*(2), 203-214.

Related Lessons:
G-06 Provide behavior-analytic services in collaboration with others who support and/or provide services to one's clients
G-08 Identify and make environmental changes that reduce the need for behavior analysis services.
I-06 Make recommendations regarding behaviors that must be established, maintained, increased, or decreased.
J-04 Select intervention strategies based on client preferences.
J-05 Select intervention strategies based on the client's current repertoires.
J-06 Select intervention strategies based on supporting environments.
J-12 Program for maintenance.
K-02 Identify the contingencies governing the behavior of those responsible for carrying out behavior-change procedures and design interventions accordingly.
K-03 Design and use competency-based training for persons who are responsible for carrying out behavioral assessment and behavior-change procedures.
K-09 Secure the support of others to maintain the client's behavioral repertoires in their natural environments.

Notes:

FK-22 EXTINCTION

Definition (Extinction):

```



```

(Cooper, Heron, & Heward, 2007).
☐ Flashcard created   ☐ Learned to fluency

Examples:

A young woman at a group home was observed to scream loudly every time she was instructed to wash her hands. Each time she began screaming, she was allowed to avoid the task for an average of ten minutes or escape the task altogether. A behavioral analyst instructed group home staff to put this behavior on extinction. After being instructed to wash her hands, group home staff physically guided her to comply even if she began screaming. After a week, screaming decreased to near zero levels.

Different types of extinction:

Extinction of behavior maintained by positive reinforcement: This occurs when behavior to access tangibles, activities, and/or attention is no longer reinforced.

Extinction of behavior maintained by negative reinforcement: This occurs when behavior to avoid/escape an aversive stimulus/event is no longer reinforced.

Extinction of behavior maintained by automatic reinforcement: This occurs when behavior that provides a natural and automatic sensory consequence is no longer reinforced. (i.e., a child is blocked each time he raises both hands above his mid-line to engage in hand-flapping.)

Non-example:

A young woman at a group home was observed to scream loudly every time she was instructed to wash her hands. Each time she began screaming, she was allowed to avoid the task for an average of ten minutes or escape the task altogether. When she engaged in screaming, group home staff would tell her that if she stopped screaming and complied she would be given chips, a preferred food.

Write another example:

```



```

Questions to ask your supervisor:

```



```

Relevant Literature:

Cooper, J. O., Heron, T. E., & Heward, W. L. (2007). *Applied behavior analysis* (2nd ed.). Upper Saddle River, NJ: Prentice Hall.

Lerman, D. C., Iwata, B. A., & Wallace, M. D. (1999). Side effects of extinction: prevalence of bursting and aggression during the treatment of self-injurious behavior. *Journal of Applied Behavior Analysis, 32*(1), 1-8.

Magee, S. K., & Ellis, J. (2000). Extinction effects during the assessment of multiple problem behaviors. *Journal of Applied Behavior Analysis, 33*(3), 313-316.

Related Lessons:

C-03 State and plan for unwanted effects of extinction
D-18. Use Extinction.
D.-19 Use combinations of reinforcement with punishment and extinction.

Notes:

Segment 18 – Scorecard
Assessment

☐ Presentation (2-5 minutes)

G 1
☐ Assessment
☐ SAFMED learned to fluency
☐ Workbook boxes completed

I 4
☐ Assessment
☐ SAFMED learned to fluency
☐ Workbook boxes completed

G 3
☐ Assessment
☐ SAFMED learned to fluency
☐ Workbook boxes completed

I 6
☐ Assessment
☐ SAFMED learned to fluency
☐ Workbook boxes completed

I 3
☐ Assessment
☐ SAFMED learned to fluency
☐ Workbook boxes completed

J 13
☐ Assessment
☐ SAFMED learned to fluency
☐ Workbook boxes completed

Segment 18 – Individual Supervision Agenda

Supervisor: _____ **Supervisee:** _____

Meeting Date: _____ **Time of meeting – From:** _____ **To:** _____

This document covers supervisory period from ____/____/____ **to** ____/____/____

1. Pass-in/Review Homework:

    Did the Supervisee satisfactorily complete this homework assignment?   Yes / No

- If not, what is needed to complete assignment? Describe below.

2. Task List items addressed (G 1, 3; I 3-4, 6; J 13)

3. Definitions/SAFMEDs learned

    ☐ Flashcard(s) created   Was supervisee fluent with definitions? Yes ☐ No ☐

4. Discussion topics or activities completed during this meeting:

Evaluation of Supervisee's Performance				
(Record: S- "Satisfactory"; NI- "Needs Improvement"; U- "Unsatisfactory"; or NA- "Not Applicable")				
Arrived on time for meeting		Gave examples as needed		
Completed Homework Assigned		Accepted supervisory feedback appropriately		
Referred to literature/readings		Answered all questions thoroughly		
Maintained professional communication during supervision meeting				
Overall evaluation of supervisee performance during this meeting *(Circle one—use code above)*				S NI U
If "NI" or "U", please list corrective steps needed to achieve a score of "S"				

5. Homework assigned for next meeting

6. Closing questions/feedback

Segment 18 – Group Supervision Meeting Agenda

- <u>Meeting Topic</u>: Assessment

- <u>Task List Items Reviewed</u>:
  - o G-03: Conduct a preliminary assessment of the client in order to identify the referral problem.
  - o G-01: Review records and available data at the outset of the case.
  - o I-03: Design and implement individualized behavioral assessment procedures.
  - o I-04: Design and implement the full range of functional assessment procedures.
  - o I-06: Make recommendations regarding behaviors that must be established, maintained, increased, or decreased.
  - o J-13: Select behavioral cusps as goals for intervention when appropriate.

1. Housekeeping
    - Upon entry to meeting have supervisees hand in the previous week's homework assignment and discuss several "Housekeeping Items" related to supervision.
    - Take attendance for the meeting.
    - State the duration of today's meeting (90 minutes).
    - Distribute BACB® experience forms to supervisees.

2. Task List Lesson and Discussion
    - Discuss task list item G-03: Conduct a preliminary assessment of the client in order to identify the referral problem.
    - Discuss task list item G-01: Review records and available data at the outset of the case.
    - Discuss task list item I-03: Design and implement individualized behavioral assessment procedures.
    - Discuss task list item I-04: Design and implement the full range of functional assessment procedures.
    - Discuss task list item I-06: Make recommendations regarding behaviors that must be established, maintained, increased, or decreased.
    - Discuss task list item J-13: Select behavioral cusps as goals for intervention when appropriate.

3. Homework Review
    - Review homework that was assigned at the previous supervision meeting.

4. Questions
    - Answer any questions related to the homework or topics discussed.

5. Closing Notes
    - *Assign Homework (task list boxes, presentation) from today's segment, due at next group meeting*
    - Close the meeting by inviting supervisees to request topics to be covered in upcoming meetings.

G-01 REVIEW RECORDS AND AVAILABLE DATA AT THE OUTSET OF THE CASE.

An important part of understanding the client you are working with is to take time to review the treatment history of this individual. There are records related to a medical history that would be beneficial to see. This would include medical procedures, medications, and any current health concerns. It's also important to get the history of treatment related to psychological/behavioral intervention as well.

Gresham, Watson, Steuart, & Skinner in 2001 recommend that FBAs should include a record review to understand more about the history of the client as well as information regarding previous interventions.

Matson (2010) summarized this position by saying "The behavior analyst should carefully review records relating to previous attempts to change potential target behaviors. Records indicating previous success with related target behaviors or a history of limited impact on a behaviour despite well-planned and faithfully implemented change programmes may be useful in selecting change targets which can be achieved within meaningful timescales" (p. 35).

Write another example.

Relevant Literature:

Gresham, F. M., Watson, T. S., Steuart, T., & Skinner, C. H. (2001). Functional Behavioral Assessment: Principles, Procedures, and Future Directions. School Psychology Review, 30(2), 156–172.

Matson, J. L. (Ed.). (2010). *Applied Behavior Analysis for Children with Autism Spectrum Disorders* (2009 edition). New York: Springer.

Related Lessons:

G-01 Review records and available data at the outset of the case.

G-02 Consider biological/medical variables that may be affecting the client.

G-03 Conduct a preliminary assessment of the client in order to identify the referral problem.

G-04 Explain behavioral concepts using nontechnical language.

G-05 Describe and explain behavior, including private events, in behavior-analytic (nonmentalistic) terms.

G-06 Provide behavior-analytic services in collaboration with others who support and/or provide services to one's clients.

G-07 Practice within one's limits of professional competence in applied behavior analysis, and obtain consultation, supervision, and training, or make referrals as necessary.

I-03 Design and implement individualized behavioral assessment procedures.

I-04 Design and implement the full range of functional assessment procedures.

K-01 Provide for ongoing documentation of behavioral services.

Notes:

Questions to ask your supervisor:

G-03 CONDUCT A PRELIMINARY ASSESS- MENT OF THE CLIENT IN ORDER TO IDENTIFY THE REFERRAL PROBLEM.

Definition:

Behavioral assessment - "A form of assessment that involves a full range of inquiry methods (observation, interview, testing, and the systematic manipulation of antecedent or consequent variables) to identify proba- ble antecedent and consequent controlling varia- bles. Behavioral assessment is designed to discover re- sources, assets, significant others, competing contin- gencies, maintenance and generality factors, and possi- ble reinforcers and/or punishers that surround the po- tential target behavior" (Cooper, Heron, & Heward, 2007, p. 691).

Five Phases of a Behavioral Assessment

Hawkins (1979) described behavioral assessment as be- ing funnel shaped, beginning with a broad scope and then moving to a narrow focus.

1. Screening and general disposition
2. Defining and quantifying problems or goals
3. Pinpointing the target behavior
4. Monitoring progress
5. Follow-up

The preliminary assessment consists of the first 3 phases of this model. It is the broad gathering of in- formation needed in order to pinpoint the target be- havior. Once the target behavior is selected, a formal functional behavioral assessment is required.

Preliminary Assessment

Assessment Methods*

1. Interviews (client and significant others)
2. Checklists
3. Standardized Tests
4. Direct Observations

Write another example:

Social Significance

Before selecting a target behavior, it is important to re- flect on how important the behavior change is for the client, not to others around the client. The rational for the behavior change must be critically ana- lyzed. Cooper, Heron, and Heward (2007) suggest the following methods for determining the social signifi- cance of the target behavior

- Is the behavior likely to produce reinforcement in the natural environment?
- Is the skill useful?
- Will it increase the individual's access to new re- inforcing environments?
- Will it allow more social interaction?
- Is it a pivotal behavior?
- Is it a behavior cusp?
- Is it age-appropriate?
- If it is a behavior to be eliminated?
- What is the replacement skill?
- Is the identified behavior actually problematic?
- Is this the identified behavior just reports or is it real?

Prioritizing Target Behaviors

If a number of target behaviors are selected which are socially significant, it is then important to prioritize the target behavior ensuring dangerous behavior is tar- geted first. Other guidelines are listed by Cooper, Heron, and Heward (2007) as the following:

- Pose a danger to client or others?
- How often does it occur?
- How longstanding is the problem?
- Will changing the behavior produce higher rates of reinforcement?
- What is the importance related to overall inde- pendence?
- Will changing the behavior reduce negative atten- tion?
- Will changing the behavior produce positive at- tention?
- How likely is success of changing the behavior?
- How much will it cost to change the behavior?

Defining the Target Behavior

Before beginning, the target behavior must be objec- tively and concisely defined in a clear concrete observ- able manner.

Setting the Criteria for Behavior Change

Goals must be socially meaningful to the person's life.

Questions to ask your supervisor:

Relevant Literature:

Bailey, J., & Burch, M. (2011). *Ethics for Behavior Analysts: 2nd Expanded Edition.* Taylor & Francis.

Cooper, J. O., Heron, T. E., & Heward, W. L. (2007). Applied behavior analysis: 2nd Edition. Pearson Education, Inc.

Hawkins, R. P. (1979). The functions of assessment: Implications for selection and development of devices for assessing repertoires in clinical, educational, and other settings. *Journal of Applied Behavior Analysis, 12*(4), 501-516.

Linehan, M. M. (1977). Issues in behavioral interviewing. *Behavioral assessment: New directions in clinical psychology. New York: Brunner/Mazel.*

Houten, R. V. (1979). Social validation: The evolution of standards of competency for target behaviors. *Journal of Applied Behavior Analysis, 12*(4), 581-591.

Related Lessons:

I-01 Define behavior in observable and measurable terms

I-02 Define environmental variables in observable and measurable terms

J-01 State intervention goals in observable and measurable terms

Notes:

I-03 DESIGN AND IMPLEMENT INDIVIDUAL-IZED BEHAVIORAL ASSESSMENT PROCEDURES.

"Behavioral assessment involves a variety of methods including direct observations, interviews, checklists, and tests to identify and define targets for behavior change" (Cooper, Heron, & Heward, 2007, p. 49).

"Applied behavior analysis uses the methods of FBA to identify antecedent and consequent events and to use this information in designing interventions to change socially significant behaviors (Gresham, Watson, & Skinner, 2001, p. 157)."

"FBA is designed to obtain information about the purpose (function) a behavior serves for a person....FBA is used to identify the type and source of reinforcement for challenging behaviors as the basis for intervention efforts... (Cooper et al., 2007, p. 501)."

"Once the function of behavior is determined, this information is used to design interventions to reduce problem behaviors and to facilitate positive behaviors" (Gresham et al., 2001, p. 158).

The first step in the process is to define the target behaviors that the assessment will focus on. These behaviors are typically identified by teachers, therapists, or caregivers due to their interference with learning, adaptive functioning, and overall quality of life. In following the principles of ABA, the behaviors targeted for assessment must be socially significant.

Another direct method of determining the function of a behavior is to conduct a functional analysis. This involves systematic manipulation of the environment, while controlling variables to evoke the target behavior under conditions representing each possible function. The typical functions of behavior include access to attention, access to tangible items, escape from demands, and automatic reinforcement. During a functional analysis, each function is assessed to determine if they are maintaining the target behavior. FA is considered to be the most reliable source for determining the function of a behavior, but may not be feasible in some settings due to the time it takes to conduct, safety implications (depending on the severity of the target behavior), and resources needed to conduct each experimental phase.

Other methods used to gather information about the function of target behaviors in a behavioral assessment include a thorough review of the client's previous records (academic reports, past evaluations, behavior support plans, IEP's, etc.), the use of behavioral rating scales such as the FAST (functional analysis screening tool), MAS (Motivational Assessment Scale), or PBQ (Problem Behavior Questionnaire), structured interviews with caregivers (i.e., functional assessment interview form), direct observation in the target environment (i.e., home, school, community), behavior data collection and analysis, and A-B-C data collection and analysis. These indirect assessments should be used to inform an experimental functional analysis. They are not designed to determine the function of a response on their own.

Once the direct and indirect assessments are completed, this information is analyzed and the BCBA makes recommendations for intervention based on the results of assessments.

Example:
Rich is completing an FBA on the aggression of one of his students. After teacher interviews, the completion of rating scales, and several observations in various settings, Rich hypothesizes that the function of aggression is escape from demands. He uses this information to create an intervention plan to decrease aggression at school.

Write another example:

Questions to ask your supervisor:

Iwata, B. A., Dorsey, M. F., Slifer, K. J., Bauman, K. E., & Richman, G. S. (1994). Toward a functional analysis of self-injury. *Journal of applied behavior analysis, 27*(2), 197-209.

O'Neill, R., Horner, R., Albin, R., Storey, K., & Sprague, J. (1997). *Functional assessment and program development for problem behaviors.* Pacific Grove, CA: Brooks/Cole.

Sprague, J., Sugai, G. & Walker, H. (1998). *Antisocial Behavior in Schools.* In T.S. Watson & F.M. Gresham (Eds). *Handbook of child behavior therapy* (pp. 451-474). New York: Pleunum Press.

Witt, J., Daly, E., & Noell, G.H. (2000). *Functional Assessment: A step by step guide to solving academic and behavior problems.* Longmont, CO. Sopris West.

Related Lessons:

B-03: Systematically arrange independent variables to demonstrate their effects on dependent variables.

E-01: Use interventions based on manipulation of antecedents, such as motivating operations and discriminative stimuli.

G-01: Review records at the outset of a case.

G-04: Conduct a preliminary assessment of the client in order to identify the referral problem.

G-05: Describe and explain behavior, including private events, in behavior-analytic (non-mentalistic) terms.

G-08: Identify and make environmental changes that reduce the need for behavior analysis services.

H-02: Select a schedule of observation and recording periods.

I-01: Define behavior in observable and measurable terms.

I-02: Define environmental variables in observable and measurable terms.

I-04: Design and implement the full range of functional assessment procedures.

I-06: Make recommendations regarding behaviors that must be established, maintained, increased, or decreased.

J-01: State intervention goals in observable and measurable terms.

J-02: Identify potential interventions based on assessment results and the best available scientific evidence.

J-10: When a behavior is to be decreased, select an acceptable alternative behavior to be established or increased.

Notes:

Relevant Literature:

Carr, E. (1993). Behavior analysis is not ultimately about behavior. *The Behavior Analyst,* 16, 47-49.

Cooper, J.O., Heron, T.E. & Heward W.L. (2007). *Applied Behavior Analysis* (2nd Ed.), Upper Saddle River, NJ. Pearson Prentice Hall. 49-71, 300, 335-336, 364-366, 457, 459-460, 499-524.

Gresham, F., Watson, T.S., & Skinner, C.H. (2001). *Functional Behavioral Assessment: Principals, Procedures, and Future Directions.* School Psychology Review, 30, 2, 156-172.

I-04 DESIGN AND IMPLEMENT THE FULL RANGE OF FUNCTIONAL ASSESSMENT PROCEDURES.

Definitions:

Functional behavior assessment (FBA) - "A systematic method of assessment for obtaining information about the purposes (functions) a problem behavior serves for a person; results are used to guide the design of an intervention for decreasing the problem behavior and increasing appropriate behavior" (Cooper, Heron, & Heward, 2007, p. 696).

Functional analysis (FA) - "An analysis of the purposes of problem behavior, wherein antecedents and consequences representing those in the person's natural routines are arranged within an experimental design so that their separate effects on problem behavior can be observed and measured" (Cooper, Heron, & Heward, 2007, p. 696).* The FA is considered to be best practice standard in conducting a functional assessment (Hanley, Iwata, & McCord 2003).

Descriptive assessment - "Direct observation of problem behavior and the antecedent and consequent events under naturally occurring conditions" (Cooper, Heron, & Heward, 2007, p. 693).* The advantages are that the information yields what happens in the individual's natural environment, does not disrupt the individual's routine, and provides information for designing a functional analysis. The disadvantages of these assessments are false positives due to behavior maintained by intermittent reinforcement or the presence of antecedent and consequent events which are often present but have no functional relation, the time required in taking data, and inaccurate data collection. Also, there is little correspondence between descriptive analysis outcomes being compared to functional analysis outcomes (Pence, Roscoe, Bourret, and Ahearn, 2009)

Indirect assessment - "Structured interviews, checklists, rating scales, or questionnaires used to obtain information from people who are familiar with the person exhibiting the problem behavior" (Cooper, Heron, & Heward, 2007, p. 697). The advantages of indirect assessments are that the forms can yield valuable information and are convenient. The disadvantage is the lack of research supporting the reliability of these measurements.

The ethical guidelines of BACB requires BCBAs to conduct a functional assessment according to 3.01 Behavior-Analytic Assessment. RBT

(a) Behavior analysts conduct current assessments prior to making recommendations or developing behavior-change programs. The type of assessment used is determined by clients' needs and consent, environmental parameters, and other contextual variables. When behavior analysts are developing a behavior-reduction program, they must first conduct a functional assessment.

(b) Behavior analysts have an obligation to collect and graphically display data, using behavior-analytic conventions, in a manner that allows for decisions and recommendations for behavior-change program development (BACB, 2014, p.8).

Role of Functional Behavior Assessment as outlined by Cooper, Heron, and Heward (2007).

- Identifies antecedent variables that may be altered to prevent problem behaviors.
- Identifies reinforcement contingencies which can be altered so problem behavior no longer receives reinforcement.
- Identifies reinforcers for alternative replacement behavior.
- Reduces the reliance on default technologies such as punishment.

Conducting a functional behavior assessment as outlined by Cooper, Heron, and Heward (2007).

- Conduct indirect assessments
- Conduct a descriptive assessment
- Analyze data from the indirect and descriptive assessment and create a hypotheses
- Test conditions the data suggest may be contributing to the behavior using a functional analysis
- Develop intervention strategies based on the results.

Write another example:

Questions to ask your supervisor:

http://www.bacb.com/Download-files/BACB_Compliance_Code.pdf.

Cooper, J. O., Heron, T. E., & Heward, W. L. (2007). Applied Behavior Analysis: 2nd Edition. Pearson Education, Inc.

Hanley, G. P., Iwata, B. A., & McCord, B. E. (2003). Functional analysis of problem behavior: A review. *Journal of Applied Behavior Analysis*, *36*(2), 147-185.

Iwata, B. A., Pace, G. M., Dorsey, M. F., Zarcone, J. R., Vollmer, T. R., Smith, R. G. Willis, K. D. (1994). The functions of self-injurious behavior: An experimental-epidemiological analysis. *Journal of Applied Behavior Analysis*, *27*(2), 215–240.

Pence, S. T., Roscoe, E. M., Bourret, J. C., & Ahearn, W. H. (2009). Relative contributions of three descriptive methods: Implications for behavioral assessment. *Journal of Applied Behavior Analysis*, *42*(2), 425-446.

Sasso, G. M., Reimers, T. M., Cooper, L. J., Wacker, D., Berg, W., Steege, M. & Allaire, A. (1992). Use of descriptive and experimental analyses to identify the functional properties of aberrant behavior in school settings. *Journal of Applied Behavior Analysis*, *25*(4), 809-821.

Related Lessons:

B-03 Systematically arrange independent variables to demonstrate their effects on dependent variables

B-05 Use alternating treatment designs

E-01 Use interventions based on manipulation of antecedents, such as motivating operations and discriminative stimuli

H-01 Select a measurement system to obtain representative data given the dimensions of the behavior and the logistics of observing and recording

H-03 Select a data display that effectively communicates relevant quantitative relations

H-05 Evaluate temporal relations between observed variables

I-03 Design and implement individualized behavioral assessment procedures

Footnotes:

*Functional analysis may also be called an analog analysis or experimental analysis.

*Descriptive analysis may also be called direct assessment.

Relevant Literature:

Baer, D. M., Wolf, M. M., & Risley, T. R. (1987). Some still-current dimensions of applied behavior analysis. *Journal of Applied Behavior Analysis*, *20*(4), 313-327.

Behavior Analyst Certification Board (BACB) Behavior Analyst Certification Board professional and ethical compliance code for behavior analysts. 2014.   Retrieved   from

Notes:

I-06 MAKE RECOMMENDATIONS REGARDING BEHAVIORS THAT MUST BE ESTABLISHED, MAINTAINED, INCREASED, OR DECREASED.

Hawkins (1984, p. 284) (cited from Cooper, Heron & Heward, 2007, p. 56) defined habilitation as "the degree to which the person's repertoire maximizes short and long term reinforcers for that individual and for others, and minimizes short and long term punishers."

When determining what behaviors to target, one can use the relevance of behavior rule (Ayllon and Azrin, 1968) as a guide. This rule states that a target behavior should only be selected if it is likely to produce reinforcement for the client in their natural environment. Another key factor is deciding if the behavior will generalize to other settings and be sustainable once the behavior change program has ended.

Cooper et al. (2007) provide some considerations when choosing a target behavior to increase, decrease, or maintain. These include:

1. Does this behavior pose any danger to the client or others?
2. How many opportunities will the person have to use this new behavior? Or how often does this problem behavior occur?
3. How long-standing is the problem or skill deficit?
4. Will changing the behavior produce higher rates of reinforcement for the person?
5. What will be the relative importance of this target behavior to the future skill development and independent functioning?
6. Will changing this behavior reduce negative attention from others?
7. Will the new behavior produce reinforcement for significant others?
8. How likely is success in changing this target behavior?
9. How much will it cost to change this behavior?

Example:
Dave has decided to implement an intervention to increase a student's compliance. He chose this because lack of compliance interferes with the student's ability to learn new skills and access reinforcement by completing their work and daily routines.

Write another example:

Questions to ask your supervisor:

Relevant Literature:

Ayllon, T. & Azrin, N.H. (1968). *The token economy: A motivational system for therapy and rehabilitation.* New York: Appleton-Century-Crofts.

Cooper, J.O., Heron, T.E. & Heward W.L. (2007). *Applied Behavior Analysis* (2nd Ed.), Upper Saddle River, NJ. Pearson Prentice Hall. 55-65, 237-238.

Hawkins, R.P. (1984) What is "meaningful" behavior change in a severely/profoundly retarded learner: The view of a behavior analytic parent. In W.L. Heward, T.E. Heron, D.S. Hill, & J. Trap-Porter (Eds.) *Focus on behavior analysis in education.* (pp. 282-286). Upper Saddle River, NJ: Prentice-Hall/ Merrill.

Hawkins, R.P. (1986) Selection of target behaviors. In R.O. Nelson & S.C. Hayes (Eds.), *Conceptual foundations of behavioral assessment* (pp. 331-385). New York: Guilford Press.

Rosales-Ruiz, J. & Baer, D.M. (1997). Behavioral cusps: A developmental and pragmatic concept for behavior analysis. *Journal of Applied Behavior Analysis*, 30, 533-544.

Related Lessons:

B-01: Use the dimensions of applied behavior analysis (Baer, Wolf, & Risley, 1968) to evaluate whether interventions are behavior analytic in nature.

G-03: Conduct a preliminary assessment of the client in order to identify the referral problem.

G-05: Describe and explain behavior, including private events, in behavior analytic (non-mentalistic) terms.

I-01: Define behavior in observable and measurable terms.

J-01: State intervention goals in observable and measurable terms.

J-05: Select intervention strategies based on the client's current repertoires.

J-08: Select intervention strategies based on the social validity of the intervention.

J-10: When a behavior is to be decreased, select an acceptable alternative behavior to be established or increased.

J-13: Select behavioral cusps as goals for intervention when appropriate.

FK-10: Behavior, response, response class.

Notes:

J-13 SELECT BEHAVIORAL CUSPS AS GOALS FOR INTERVENTION WHEN APPROPRIATE.

"A behavior that has consequences beyond the change itself, some of which may be considered important…What makes a behavior change a cusp is that it exposes the individual's repertoire to new environments, especially new reinforcers and punishers, new contingencies, new responses, new stimulus controls, and new communities of maintaining or destructive contingencies. When some or all of these events happen, the individual's repertoire expands; it encounters a differentially selective maintenance of the new as well as some old repertoires, and perhaps that leads to some further cusps." (Rosales-Ruiz & Baer, 1997, p. 534).

Bosch and Fuqua (2001) cited 5 criteria for a behavior to be considered a behavioral cusp. "They stated that a behavior might be a cusp if it meets one or more of five criteria: "(a) access to new reinforcers, contingencies, and environments; (b) social validity; (c) generativeness; (d) competition with inappropriate responses; and (e) number and the relative importance of people affected." (Bosch & Fuqua, 2001, p. 125 via Cooper et al., 2007, p. 59).

Examples:
Common behavioral cusps include crawling, reading, imitation skills, walking, talking, and writing. These skills set the stage for the client to develop and learn many other skills (i.e., reading allows a client to access leisure material, access information, and is necessary in regards to reading street and safety signs, and accessing various other forms of reinforcement).

Relevant Literature:
Cooper, J.O., Heron, T.E. & Heward W.L. (2007). *Applied Behavior Analysis* (2nd Ed.), Upper Saddle River, NJ. Pearson Prentice Hall. 58-59.

Rosales-Ruiz, J., & Baer, D. M. (1997). Behavioral cusps: A developmental and pragmatic concept for behavior analysis. *Journal of Applied Behavior Analysis*, 30, 533–544.

Bosch, S. & Fuqua, R.W. (2001). Behavioral cusps: a model for selecting target behaviors. *Journal of Applied Behavior Analysis*, 34(1), 123-125.

Related Lessons:
G-08: Identify and make environmental changes that reduce the need for behavior analysis services.
I-01: Define behavior in observable and measurable terms.
I-06: Make recommendations regarding behaviors that must be established, maintained, increased, or decreased.
J-01: State intervention goals in observable and measurable terms.
J-08: Select interventions based on the social validity of the intervention.
J-14: Arrange instructional procedures to promote generative learning (i.e., derived relations).
FK-10: Behavior, response, response class.

Notes:

Write another example:

Questions to ask your supervisor:

Segment 19 – Scorecard
Behavioral Contingencies

☐ Presentation (2-5 minutes)

E 3
☐ Assessment
☐ SAFMED learned to fluency
☐ Workbook boxes completed

FK 31
☐ Assessment
☐ SAFMED learned to fluency
☐ Workbook boxes completed

F 1
☐ Assessment
☐ SAFMED learned to fluency
☐ Workbook boxes completed

FK 32
☐ Assessment
☐ SAFMED learned to fluency
☐ Workbook boxes completed

G 4
☐ Assessment
☐ SAFMED learned to fluency
☐ Workbook boxes completed

FK 41
☐ Assessment
☐ SAFMED learned to fluency
☐ Workbook boxes completed

FK 25
☐ Assessment
☐ SAFMED learned to fluency
☐ Workbook boxes completed

FK 42
☐ Assessment
☐ SAFMED learned to fluency
☐ Workbook boxes completed

Segment 19 – Individual Supervision Agenda

Supervisor: _____ **Supervisee:** _____
Meeting Date: _____ **Time of meeting – From:**_____ **To:**_____
This document covers supervisory period from ____/____/____ to ____/____/____

1. Pass-in/Review Homework:

   Did the Supervisee satisfactorily complete this homework assignment?   Yes / No

- If not, what is needed to complete assignment? Describe below.

2. Task List items addressed (E 3; F 1; G 4; FK 25, 31-32, 41-42)

3. Definitions/SAFMEDs learned
    □ Flashcard(s) created   Was supervisee fluent with definitions? Yes □ No □

4. Discussion topics or activities completed during this meeting:

Evaluation of Supervisee's Performance
(Record: S- "Satisfactory"; NI- "Needs Improvement"; U- "Unsatisfactory"; or NA- "Not Applicable")

Arrived on time for meeting		Gave examples as needed	
Completed Homework Assigned		Accepted supervisory feedback appropriately	
Referred to literature/readings		Answered all questions thoroughly	
Maintained professional communication during supervision meeting			
Overall evaluation of supervisee performance during this meeting *(Circle one—use code above)*		S NI U	
If "NI" or "U", please list corrective steps needed to achieve a score of "S"			

5. Homework assigned for next meeting

6. Closing questions/feedback

Segment 19 – Group Supervision Meeting Agenda

- <u>Meeting Topic</u>: Behavioral Contingencies

- <u>Task List Items Reviewed</u>:

o FK-31: Behavioral contingencies.	o FK-25: Multiple functions of a single stimulus.
o F-01: Use self-management strategies.	o FK-31 Behavioral contingencies
o G-04: Explain behavioral concepts using nontechnical language.	o FK-32: Contiguity.
	o FK-41: Contingency shaped behavior.
o E-03: Use instructions and rules.	o FK-42: Rule governed behavior.

1. Housekeeping
    - Upon entry to meeting have supervisees hand in the previous week's homework assignment and discuss several "Housekeeping Items" related to supervision.
    - Take attendance for the meeting.
    - State the duration of today's meeting (90 minutes).
    - Distribute BACB® experience forms to supervisees.

2. Task List Lesson and Discussion
    - Discuss task list item FK-31: Behavioral contingencies.
    - Discuss task list item F-01: Use self-management strategies.
    - Discuss task list item G-04: Explain behavioral concepts using nontechnical language.
    - Discuss task list item E-03: Use instructions and rules.
    - Discuss task list item FK-25: Multiple functions of a single stimulus.
    - Discuss task list item FK-31 Behavioral contingencies
    - Discuss task list item FK-32: Contiguity.
    - Discuss task list item FK-41: Contingency shaped behavior.
    - Discuss task list item FK-42: Rule governed behavior.

3. Homework Review
    - Review homework that was assigned at the previous supervision meeting.

4. Questions
    - Answer any questions related to the homework or topics discussed.

5. Closing Notes
    - *Assign Homework (task list boxes, presentation) from today's segment, due at next group meeting*
    - Close the meeting by inviting supervisees to request topics to be covered in upcoming meetings.

E-03 USE INSTRUCTIONS AND RULES.

Definition:

Rules are descriptions of behavioral contingencies (e.g., "Putting a sweater on when it is cold outside will help you stay warm"). When rules are followed, behavior can come under the control of delayed or indirect consequences therefore resulting in rule-governed behavior. Malott and Trojan-Suarez (2004) suggest that all instructions involve rules. It is argued that rules function as reinforcement-based or punishment-based discriminative stimuli (Malott & Trojan-Suarez, 2004). Skinner (1969) referred to rules, instructions, advice, and laws as contingency-specifying stimuli, describing the

$$S^D : R \rightarrow S^r$$ relations of everyday life.

Evidence that behavior is the result of instructional control or rule following is provided if: (1) there is no obvious or immediate consequence of the behavior; (2) the delivery of the consequence following the behavior exceeds 30 seconds; (3) behavior changes without reinforcement; (4) a substantial increase in the rate of behavior occurs following one instance of direct contact with reinforcement; and (5) the rule exists but no consequence (including automatic reinforcement) exists following the behavior (Cooper, Heron, & Heward, 2007).

Example:

Incomplete rules (e.g., "Stop it") provide minimal instruction (e.g., stop) and imply an outcome (e.g., you might get in trouble).

Write another example:

Questions to ask your supervisor:

Relevant Literature:

Cooper, J. O., Heron, T. E., & Heward, W. L. (2007). Positive reinforcement. *Applied Behavior Analysis* (pp. 256-290). Upper Saddle River, NJ: Pearson Prentice Hall.

Hayes, S. C. (2004). *Rule-Governed Behavior: Cognition, Contingencies & Instructional Control.* Oakland, CA: Context Press.

Malott, R. W., & Trojan Suarez, E.A. (2004). Analogs to reinforcement and avoidance part 1. *Principles of Behavior* (pp. 377-393). Upper Saddle River, NJ: Pearson Prentice Hall.

Malott, R. W., & Trojan Suarez, E.A. (2004). Analogs to reinforcement and avoidance part 2. *Principles of Behavior* (pp. 394-409). Upper Saddle River, NJ: Pearson Prentice Hall.

Skinner, B. F. (1969). *Contingencies of reinforcement: A theoretical analysis.* New York: Appleton-Centrury-Crofts.

Related Lessons:

D-01 Use positive and negative reinforcement.

D-16 Use positive and negative punishment.

K-02 Identify the contingencies governing the behavior of those responsible for carrying out behavior-change procedures and design interventions accordingly.

FK-30 distinguish between motivating operation and reinforcement effects

FK-31 behavioral contingencies

FK-33 functional relations

FK-41 contingency-shaped behavior

FK-42 rule-governed behavior

Notes:

F-01 USE SELF-MANAGEMENT STRATEGIES.

Definition:

Self-management - "…behavior that a person emits to influence another behavior" (Cooper, Heron, & Heward, 2007, p. 577).

Skinner (1953) first outlined the idea of self-management with his theories on self-control. He defined self-control as, "When a man controls himself, chooses a course of action, thinks out the solution to a problem, or strives towards an increase in self-knowledge, he is behaving. He controls himself precisely as he would control the behavior of anyone else- through the manipulation of variables of which behavior is a function" (pp. 228-229).

"All self-control- or self-management- tactics can be operationalized in terms of two behaviors: (a) the target behavior a person wants to change (Skinner's controlled response) and (b) the self-management behavior (Skinner's controlling response) emitted to control the target behavior" (Cooper et al., 2007, p. 577).

Applications include "helping a person be more effective and efficient in his daily life, replacing bad habits with good ones, accomplishing difficult tasks, and achieving personal goals" (Cooper et al., 2007, p. 579).

Example:

- Skipping lunch (controlling behavior) to enjoy all three courses of your dinner (controlled behavior).
- Leaving a bag of garbage near the front door (controlling behavior) to remind you to take it to the dumpster next time you leave the house (controlled behavior).

Agran, M. (Ed.) (1997). *Self-directed learning: Teaching self-determination skills.* Pacific Grove, CA. Brooks/Cole.

Baum, W.M. (2005). *Understanding behaviorism: Science, behavior, and culture* (2nd ed.). Malden, MA. Blackwell Publishing.

Cooper, J. O., Heron, T. E., & Heward, W. L. (2007). *Applied behavior analysis.* (2nd ed.) Upper Saddle River, NJ: Pearson Education, 576-612, 646, 648-650.

Epstein, R. (1997). Skinner as self-manager. *Journal of Applied Behavior Analysis,* 30, 545-568.

Kazdin, A.E. (2001). *Behavior modification in applied settings* (6th ed.). Belmont, CA. Wadsworth.

Skinner, B.F. (1953). *Science and human behavior.* New York: MacMillan, pp. 228-240.

Thoreson, C.E., & Mahoney, M.J. (1974). *Behavioral self-control.* New York: Holt, Rinehart, & Winston.

Watson, D.L., & Tharp, R.G. (2007). *Self-directed behavior: Self-modification for personal adjustment* (9th ed.). Belmont, CA. Wadsworth/Thompson Learning.

Related Lessons:

B-03: Systematically arrange independent variables to demonstrate their effects on dependent variables.

F-02: Use token economies and other conditioned reinforcement systems.

I-01: Define behavior in observable and measurable terms.

I-06: Make recommendations regarding behaviors that must be established, maintained, increased, or decreased.

J-01: State intervention goals in observable and measurable terms.

J-02: Identify potential interventions based on assessment results and the best available scientific evidence.

J-10: When a behavior is to be decreased, select an acceptable alternative behavior to be established or increased.

FK-18: Conditioned reinforcement.

FK-20: Conditioned punishment.

FK-31: Behavioral contingencies.

Notes:

Write another example:

Questions to ask your supervisor:

G-04 EXPLAIN BEHAVIORAL CONCEPTS USING NONTECHNICAL LANGUAGE.

It is important for a behavior analyst to have a strong verbal repertoire when speaking about the science of behavior analysis. Jargon used in journals, universities, and with other behavior analysts is valuable to promote effective action on the part of the listener with precise discriminative control.

That being said, Skinner wrote that we should choose words for the effects they have on the listener (Skinner, 1957) and unless that listener has extensive training in behavior analysis, our use of technical language will "fall on deaf ears" and not produce effective action. When speaking with client family members, friends, or professionals from other closely related fields, it is important to remember that your verbal behavior is for the benefit of your audience. Bailey (1991) describes this phenomenon well:

"In our zeal to be scientific, we have stressed the need to match the requirements of science in our writing and publishing. Although this has given us much-needed academic credibility (faculty can be promoted and tenured by publishing in JABA) it doesn't help at all in selling our technology to the masses" (p. 446)

During the supervision process, spend considerable amounts of time, working on precise definitions for technical terms. This benefits the supervisees in several ways. It allows him/her to behave effectively as a listener and speaker when interacting with other behavior analysts in the field. It will also promote accurate translations to nontechnical language. If a precise definition is practiced, a less technical, more layperson-friendly definition will be easier to describe and it will be more likely to be accurate.

Write another example.

Questions to ask your supervisor:

Relevant Literature:

Bailey, J. S. (1991). Marketing behavior analysis requires different talk. *Journal of Applied Behavior Analysis, 24*(3), 445-448.

Lindsley, O. R. (1991). From technical jargon to plain English for application. *Journal of Applied Behavior Analysis, 24*(3), 449-458.

Malott, R. W. (1992). Should we train applied behavior analysts to be researchers?. *Journal of applied behavior analysis, 25*(1), 83-88.Skinner B.F. Verbal behavior. New York: Appleton-Century-Crofts; 1957.

Related Lessons:

G-06 Provide behavior-analytic services in collaboration with others who support and/or provide services to one's clients.

I-06 Make recommendations regarding behaviors that must be established, maintained, increased, or decreased.

J-06 Select intervention strategies based on supporting environments.

J-07 Select intervention strategies based on environmental and resource constraints.

K-01 Provide for ongoing documentation of behavioral services.

K-03 Design and use competency-based training for persons who are responsible for carrying out behavioral assessment and behavior-change procedures.

K-08 Establish support for behavior-analytic services from direct and indirect consumers.

K-09 Secure the support of others to maintain the client's behavioral repertoires in their natural environments.

Notes:

FK-25 MULTIPLE FUNCTIONS OF A SINGLE STIMULUS.

The same stimulus may serve multiple functions depending on the context. For instance, an aversive stimulus can function as a positive punisher or a negative reinforcer depending on whether it is added or removed contingent on a response. An appetitive stimulus can function as a positive reinforcer or a negative punisher depending on whether it is added or removed contingent on a response.

In a behavior chain, a stimulus can function as a discriminative stimulus and a reinforcer depending on how much of the chain has been completed. Behavior chains are described by Catania as "a sequence of discriminated operants such that responses during one stimulus are followed by other stimuli that reinforce those responses and set the occasion for the next ones" (Catania, 2013, p. 431).

Respondent behavior interacts with operant behavior in ways that can cause a single stimulus to be an eliciting stimulus for respondent behavior as well as a discriminative stimulus for operant behavior. For example, when seeing your best friend arrive to your home for a visit, this may elicit respondent behavior one might describe as "excitement". Seeing your friend may also serve as a discriminative stimulus for waving at him/her.

Example:
When seeing your best friend arrive to your home for a visit, this may elicit respondent behavior one might describe as "excitement". Seeing your friend may also serve as a discriminative stimulus for waving at him/her.

Write another example:

Relevant Literature:
Catania, A. C. (2013). *Learning* (5th ed.). Cornwall-on-Hudson, NY: Sloan Pub.

Catania, A. C., & Overmier, J. B. (1971). Discriminative stimulus functions of drugs: Interpretations. In *Stimulus properties of drugs* (pp. 149-160). Springer New York.

Bullock, C. E., & Hackenberg, T. D. (2015). The several roles of stimuli in token reinforcement. Journal of the Experimental Analysis of Behavior, 103(2), 269–287. http://doi.org/10.1002/jeab.117

Related Lessons:
FK-24 Stimulus control
FK-29 Distinguish between the discriminative stimulus and the motivating operation
FK-35 Stimulus discrimination
FK-37 Stimulus generalization

Notes:

Questions to ask your supervisor:

FK-31 BEHAVIORAL CONTINGENCIES.

Definition (three term contingency):

Example:
When John has not eaten in a while he asks his caregiver for a snack. When John asks he's given a snack. In this case the antecedents are food deprivation and the presence of someone who can provide food. The behavior would be the request for a snack and the consequence is being provided with a snack.

Write another example:

(Moxley, 2004).

☐ Flashcard created   ☐ Learned to fluency

Definition (three term contingency):

(Cooper, Heron, & Heward, 2007).

☐ Flashcard created   ☐ Learned to fluency

Questions to ask your supervisor:

Relevant Literature:

Azrin, N.H. & Holz, W.C. (1966). Punishment. In W.K. Honig (Ed.), *Operant Behavior: Areas of research and application* (pp. 380-447). New York: Appleton-Century-Crofts.

Cooper, J.O., Heron, T.E. & Heward W.L. (2007). *Applied Behavior Analysis* (2nd Ed.), Upper Saddle River, NJ. Pearson Prentice Hall. 35, 41-42, 258-259, 261, 263-265, 292-294, 331 (Figure 14.2).

Glenn, S.S., Ellis, J., & Greenspoon, J. (1992). On the revolutionary nature of the operant as a unit of behavioral selection. *American Psychologist*, 47, 1329-1336.

Michael, J. (2004). *Concepts and Principles of Behavior Analysis* (rev. ed.) Kalamazoo, MI: Society for the Advancement of Behavior Analysis.

Skinner, B.F. (1969). *Contingencies of reinforcement: A theoretical analysis.* (pp. 7, 114) New York: Appleton-Century-Crofts.

Moxley, R.A. (2004). Pragmatic selectionism: The philosophy of behavior analysis. *The Behavior Analyst Today*, 5, 108-125.

Sulzer-Azaroff, B., & Mayer, G.R. (1977). *Applying behavior analysis procedures with children and youth.* New York: Holt, Rinehart, & Winston.

Vollmer, T.R. (2002). Punishment happens: Some comments on Lerman and Vorndran's review. *Journal of Applied Behavior Analysis*, 35, 469-473.

Vollmer, T.R. & Iwata, B.A. (1991). Establishing Operations and reinforcement effects. *Journal of Applied Behavior Analysis*, 24, 279-291.

Related Lessons:

B-01: Use the dimensions of applied behavior analysis (Baer, Wolf, & Risley, 1968) to evaluate whether interventions are behavior analytic in nature.

E-01: Use interventions based on manipulation of antecedents, such as motivating operations and discriminative stimuli.

G-04: Explain behavioral concepts using nontechnical language.

I-01: Define behavior in observable and measureable terms.

I-02: Define environmental variables in observable and measureable terms.

FK-10: Behavior, response, response class

FK-11: Environment, stimulus, stimulus class.

FK-15: Operant Conditioning

FK-21: Schedules of reinforcement and punishment

FK-27: Conditioned motivating operations.

FK-30: Distinguish between motivating operation and reinforcement effects.

FK-33: Functional relations

FK-34: Conditional discriminations

FK-35: Stimulus discrimination

FK-41: Contingency-shaped behavior

Notes:

FK-32 CONTIGUITY.

Definition (three term contingency):

(Catania, 1998).

☐ Flashcard created   ☐ Learned to fluency

Relevant Literature:

Buehner, MJ. (2005). Contiguity and Covariation in Human Causal Inference. *Learning and Behavior*, 33, 230–238.

Catania, A. C. (1998). Learning (4th ed.). Upper Saddle River, NJ: Prentice Hall.

Shanks, D.R., Pearson, S.M., & Dickinson A. (1989). Temporal Contiguity and the Judgment of Causality by Human Subjects. *Quarterly Journal of Experimental Psychology*, 41B, 139–159

Related Lessons:
FK-14 respondent conditioning (CS-CR)
FK-24 stimulus control
FK-32 contiguity
FK-36 response generalization

Notes:

Example:

- Perseus wears his favorite lucky socks to the Patriots game for the first time. On the same day he wears his socks the team wins the game.
- Dr. Zeus is working in an experimental lab with rats. He trips on a banana peel immediately after a rat pulled a level in the operant chamber.
- Perseus also loves to play Monopoly. He needs a 4 to land on free parking. He blows on the dice and says "come on 4!" He rolls a 4.

Write another example:

Questions to ask your supervisor:

FK-41   CONTINGENCY-SHAPED   BEHAV-
IOR.

Definition (Contingency-shaped behavior):

(Cooper, Heron, & Heward, 2007).

☐ Flashcard created   ☐ Learned to fluency

Examples:
-   Melvin puts a dollar into the soda machine
    and pushes the cola button. Seconds later a
    can of soda comes out. He opens the soda and
    drinks it. He buys 3 more drinks from the
    same machine that week.
-   Simon's friend Ernest is a prankster. Ernest
    shakes up a can of soda and offers Simon a
    drink. The can sprays him in the face and
    soaks his clothing. The next time Ernest of-
    fers a soda, Simon is hesitant to accept. Alt-
    hough he'd like to open the soda and drink it,
    he hands it back expecting another explosive
    surprise.
-   Thirsty Floyd finds a 12 pack of old sodas in
    the storeroom. He cracks a can and starts to
    drink. Unfortunately, the soda has gone bad.
    Floyd gets sick from drinking the soda. In the
    future Floyd avoids drinking old sodas.

Non-Example:
-   Horace's mom tells him that drinking soda is
    bad for him. Horace avoids drinking soda in
    the future.

Write another example:

Questions to ask your supervisor:

Relevant Literature:
Cooper J.O, Heron T.E, Heward W.L. (2007). *Applied
    behavior analysis* (2nd ed.) Upper Saddle River, NJ:
    Pearson
Malott, R. & Trojan-Suarez, E. (2004) *Principles of Behav-
    iour*. New Jersey: Pearson Prentice Hall.
Michael, J. (2004). *Concepts and Principles of Behavior Anal-
    ysis (*rev. ed.). Kalamazoo, MI: Society for the
    Advancement of Behavior Analysis.

Related Lessons:
E-04 Use contingency contracting (i.e., behavioral con-
tracts).
FK-42 Rule-governed behavior

Notes:

FK-42 RULE-GOVERNED BEHAVIOR.

Definition (Rule-governed behavior):

(Cooper, Heron, & Heward, 2007).
☐ Flashcard created   ☐ Learned to fluency

Example:
- Matilda's mother told her that if she gets all of her homework done this week that she will take her out for ice cream on Saturday. It is only Wednesday and Matilda still hasn't finished all of the work. This is a new contingency for Matilda, but when Saturday arrived, all of her homework was done.
  - Felicia has never put a metal fork in the toaster before but her dad told her that she could be electrocuted if she tried to get her bagel out that way. She always gets a wooden spoon to get the bagel out.

Non-Example:
- Matilda's mother told her that if she gets all of her homework done this week that she will take her out for ice cream on Saturday. It is only Wednesday and Matilda still hasn't finished all of the work. Her mother brings her to get ice cream every week that she gets her homework done. When Saturday arrived, all of her homework was done.

Write another example:

Questions to ask your supervisor:

Relevant Literature:

Cooper J.O, Heron T.E, Heward W.L. (2007). *Applied behavior analysis* (2nd ed.) Upper Saddle River, NJ: Pearson

Malott, R. W. (1988). Rule-governed behavior and behavioral anthropology. *The Behavior Analyst, 11*(2), 181–203.

Malott, R.W., & Garcia, M.E. (1991). The role of private events in rule-governed behavior. In L.J. Hayes & P. Chase (Eds.), *Dialogues on verbal behavior* (pp. 237-254). Reno, NV: Context Press.

Schlinger Jr, H. D. (1990). A reply to behavior analysts writing about rules and rule-governed behavior. *The Analysis of Verbal Behavior*, 8, 77.

Skinner, B.F. (1969). *Contingencies of reinforcement: A Theoretical Analysis.* New York: Appleton-Century-Crofts.

Related Lessons:
E-04 Use contingency contracting (i.e., behavioral contracts).
FK-41 Contingency-shaped behavior

Notes:

Segment 20 – Scorecard
Laws and Principles

☐ Presentation (2-5 minutes)

E 7
☐ Assessment
☐ SAFMED learned to fluency
☐ Workbook boxes completed

E 8
☐ Assessment
☐ SAFMED learned to fluency
☐ Workbook boxes completed

E 9
☐ Assessment
☐ SAFMED learned to fluency
☐ Workbook boxes completed

E 10
☐ Assessment
☐ SAFMED learned to fluency
☐ Workbook boxes completed

FK 38
☐ Assessment
☐ SAFMED learned to fluency
☐ Workbook boxes completed

FK 39
☐ Assessment
☐ SAFMED learned to fluency
☐ Workbook boxes completed

FK 40
☐ Assessment
☐ SAFMED learned to fluency
☐ Workbook boxes completed

Segment 20 – Individual Supervision Agenda

Supervisor: _____ **Supervisee:** _____
Meeting Date: _____ **Time of meeting – From:**_____ **To:**_____
This document covers supervisory period from ____/____/____ to ____/____/____

1. Pass-in/Review Homework:

Did the Supervisee satisfactorily complete this homework assignment?   Yes / No

- If not, what is needed to complete assignment? Describe below.

2. Task List items addressed (E 7-10; FK 38-40)

3. Definitions/SAFMEDs learned
   ☐ Flashcard(s) created   Was supervisee fluent with definitions? Yes ☐ No ☐

4. Discussion topics or activities completed during this meeting:

Evaluation of Supervisee's Performance		
(Record: S- "Satisfactory"; NI- "Needs Improvement"; U- "Unsatisfactory"; or NA- "Not Applicable")		
Arrived on time for meeting	Gave examples as needed	
Completed Homework Assigned	Accepted supervisory feedback appropriately	
Referred to literature/readings	Answered all questions thoroughly	
Maintained professional communication during supervision meeting		
Overall evaluation of supervisee performance during this meeting *(Circle one—use code above)*	S NI U	
If "NI" or "U", please list corrective steps needed to achieve a score of "S"		

5. Homework assigned for next meeting

6. Closing questions/feedback

Segment 20 – Group Supervision Meeting Agenda

- <u>Meeting Topic</u>: Laws and Principles

- <u>Task List Items Reviewed</u>:
- o E-07: Plan for behavioral contrast effects.
- o E-08: Use the matching law and recognize factors influencing choice.
- o E-09: Arrange high-probability request sequences.
- o E-10: Use the Premack principle.
- o FK-38: Behavioral contrast.
- o FK-39: Behavioral momentum.
- o FK-40: Matching law.

1. Housekeeping
    - Upon entry to meeting have supervisees hand in the previous week's homework assignment and discuss several "Housekeeping Items" related to supervision.
    - Take attendance for the meeting.
    - State the duration of today's meeting (90 minutes).
    - Distribute BACB® experience forms to supervisees.

2. Task List Lesson and Discussion
    - Discuss task list item E-07: Plan for behavioral contrast effects.
    - Discuss task list item E-08: Use the matching law and recognize factors influencing choice.
    - Discuss task list item E-09: Arrange high-probability request sequences.
    - Discuss task list item E-10: Use the Premack principle.
    - Discuss task list item FK-38: Behavioral contrast.
    - Discuss task list item FK-39: Behavioral momentum.
    - Discuss task list item FK-40: Matching law.

3. Homework Review
    - Review homework that was assigned at the previous supervision meeting.

4. Questions
    - Answer any questions related to the homework or topics discussed.

5. Closing Notes
    - *Assign Homework (task list boxes, presentation) from today's segment, due at next group meeting*
    - Close the meeting by inviting supervisees to request topics to be covered in upcoming meetings.

E-07 PLAN FOR BEHAVIORAL CONTRAST EF-FECTS.

Definition:

George Reynolds first presented behavioral contrast in 1961. He defined behavioral contrast as "an increase in the rate of responding in one component of a multiple schedule when certain changes occur in the other component" (p. 60).

Cooper, Heron and Heward state that behavioral contrast "can occur as a function of a change in reinforcement or punishment density on one component of a multiple schedule" (p. 337).

It is important to consider *prior* to beginning an intervention, whether behavioral contrast may occur as a result of that planned intervention. If behavioral contrast is a possibility; then planning for its occurrence is crucial.

Cooper, Heron and Heward (2007, p. 338) suggest that one way to minimize or completely prevent the contrast effects of punishment is to plan the intervention so that the consequence is consistently applied to the target behavior across all relevant environments and stimulus conditions. All those involved in the client's life that may be required to deliver the consequence, will need to be thoroughly trained to ensure its consistent implementation.

Additionally, reinforcement will need to be minimized, or where possible, withheld, when the target behavior has occurred. Similarly, training will need to be provided to all those involved so that the client isn't receiving reinforcement when the target behavior is emitted.

Example:

- A pigeon pecks a backlit key, which alternates between blue and green. Reinforcement is delivered on the same schedule on both keys, and the bird pecks at approximately the same rate regardless of the key's color. However, this changes so that responses on one component of the schedule are punished, i.e., pecks on the blue key are punished because reinforcement is not delivered, but pecks on the other (green) key continue to produce reinforcement. As a result, rate of responding decreases on the blue key and rate of responding on the green key increases, even though no more reinforcement is delivered from the green key than before. (Cooper, Heron, Heward, 2007).

Write another example:

Relevant Literature:

Cooper, J. O., Heron, T. E., & Heward, W. L. (2007). Applied Behavior Analysis, 2nd ed. Upper Saddle River, New Jersey: Pearson Prentice Hall.

Fagan, J. W. (1978). Behavioral contrast in infants. *Infant behavior and development, 2,* 101-112.

Hantula, D. A., & Crowell, C. R. (1994). Behavioral contrast in a two-option analogue task of financial decision making. *Journal of Applied Behavior Analysis, 27,* 607-617.

McSweeney, F. K., & Weatherly, J. N. (1998). Habituation to the reinforcer may contribute to multiple-schedule behavioral contrast. *Journal of the Experimental Analysis of Behavior, 69,* 199-221.

Reynolds, G. S. (1961a). Behavioral contrast. *Journal of Experimental Analysis of Behavior, 4,* 57 – 71.

Reynolds, G. S. (1963). Some limitations on behavioral contrast and induction during successive discrimination. *Journal of Experimental Analysis of Behavior, 6,* 131-139.

Tarbox, J., & Parrott Hayes, L. (2005). Verbal behavior and behavioral contrast in human subjects. *The Psychological Record, 55,* 419-437.

Weatherly, J. N., Melville, C. L., & McSweeney, F. K. (1996). Picking, pecking, and pressing: A cross-species demonstration of behavioral contrast. *The Psychological Record, 46,* 351-372.

Weatherly, J. N., King, B. M., Arthur, E. I. L. (2002). Rats' level pressing for 1% sucrose and food-pellet reinforcement: In search of negative behavioral contrast. *The Psychological Record, 52,* 507-529.

Related Lessons:

C-02: State and plan for the possible unwanted effects of punishment

D-15: Identify punishers

D-16: Use positive and negative punishment

D-17: Use appropriate parameters and schedules of punishment

D19: Use combinations of reinforcement with punishment and extinction

J-10: When a behavior is to be decreased, select an acceptable alternative behavior to be established or increased.

K-02: Identify the contingencies governing the behavior of those responsible for carrying out behavior-change procedures and design interventions accordingly

FK-38: Behavioral contrast

FK-40: Matching law

Notes:

E-08 USE THE MATCHING LAW AND RECOGNIZE FACTORS INFLUENCED BY CHOICE.

Definition:

"When two or more concurrent-interval schedules are available, the relative rate of response matches (or equals) the relative rate of reinforcement. More generally, the matching law states that the distribution of behavior between (or among) alternative sources of reinforcement is equal to the distribution of reinforcement for these alternatives" (Pierce & Cheney, 2013)

Choice is defined as "…the emission of one of two or more alternative and, usually, incompatible responses" (Catania, 2007).

Organisms are constantly confronted with making choices; the allocation of responding is based upon the probability of reinforcement for that response. There are also other variables known to effect response allocation such as magnitude of reinforcement, quality of reinforcement, delay to reinforcement, and duration of reinforcement (Baum, 1974). If a variable that is affecting responding on a particular option cannot be identified, this is known as *bias*.

Multiple basic and applied studies with humans and non-humans have demonstrated that behavior is allocated to response options based on reinforcement schedules available on those options (Baum, 1974; Borrero & Vollmer, 2002; Epling & Pierce, 1983)

Of note, there is debate about the status of the matching law as a convenient description vs. a fundamental property of behavior (c.f., Catania, 1981; Killeen, 2015, Rachlin, 1971)

Examples:

An example of bias might be a right-handed person responding on an option to the right side. This variable and others are accounted for using different coefficients in the matching law.

Baum, W. M. (1974). On two types of deviation from the matching law: Bias and undermatching. *Journal of the experimental analysis of behavior, 22*(1), 231.

Baum, W. M. (1979). Matching, undermatching, and overmatching in studies of choice. *Journal of the experimental analysis of behavior, 32*(2), 269.

Borrero, J. C., & Vollmer, T. R. (2002). An application of the matching law to severe problem behavior. *Journal of Applied Behavior Analysis, 35*(1), 13-27.

Catania, A. C. (2007). Learning (Interim. *4ª. Ed.) USA: Sloan Publishing.*

Catania, A. C. (2012). Discussion: The flight from experimental analysis. *European Journal of Behavior Analysis13*, 165-176.

Cooper, J. O., Heron, T. E., & Heward, W. L. (2007). *Applied behavior analysis.* Upper Saddle River, NJ: Pearson Education.

Epling, W. F., & Pierce, W. D. (1983). Applied behavior analysis: New directions from the laboratory. *The Behavior Analyst, 6*(1), 27.

Herrnstein, R. J. (1961). Relative and absolute strength of response as a function of frequency of reinforcement. *Journal of the experimental analysis of behavior, 4*(3), 267.

Killeen, P. R. (2015). The logistics of choice. Jrnl Exper Analysis Behavior. doi: 10.1002/jeab.156

Pierce, W. D., & Cheney, C. D. (2013). *Behavior analysis and learning.* Psychology Press.

Rachlin, H. (1971). On the tautology of the matching law. *Journal of the Experimental Analysis of Behavior, 15*(2), 249-251.

Related Lessons:

A-14 Design and implement choice measures.

Notes:

Write another example:

Questions to ask your supervisor:

E-09 ARRANGE HIGH PROBABILITY REQUEST SEQUENCES.

Definitions:

Using a high-probability (high-p) request sequence involves presenting a series of requests that the individual has a history of following before presenting a target request (low-p). The following is recommended in order to maximize the effectiveness of the high-p request sequence: (1) tasks/requests should already be in the learner's repertoire (i.e., the skill is considered mastered); (2) high-p requests should be presented rapidly; (3) the first low-p request should be presented immediately after reinforcement for high-p compliance; and (4) and salient reinforcers should be used for low-p requests (Cooper, Heron, & Heward, 2007). It is also recommended to avoid using low-difficulty tasks immediately after a maladaptive behavior that was triggered by a high-difficulty task (Sailors, Guess, Rutherford, & Baer, 1968). In the initial stages of acquisition of a low-p request, increasing the number of high-p requests increases the effectiveness of the high-p request sequence (Mace, 1996). High-p request sequences are helpful in reducing the reinforcing value of escape from requests and the maladaptive behaviors that often occur when low-p requests are presented. The high-p request sequence is synonymous with interspersal training and behavioral momentum (Cooper, Heron, & Heward, 2007).

Example:

- Brett is starting to become noncompliant and swiping materials off of his desk. To get him back on track, the teacher starts presenting trials of letter identification. This is an easy task for Brett and one he has mastered. After ten trials, the teacher presents the previous demand and Brett begins working again without interfering behaviors.

Write another example:

Questions to ask your supervisor:

Relevant Literature:

Cooper, J. O., Heron, T. E., & Heward, W. L. (2007). Antecedent interventions. *Applied Behavior Analysis* (2nd Ed.). (pp. 486-499). Upper Saddle River, NJ: Pearson Prentice Hall.

Davis, C. A., & Reichle, J. (1996). Variant and invariant high-probability requests: Increasing appropriate behaviors in children with emotional-behavioral disorders. *Journal of Applied Behavior Analysis, 29,* 471-482.

Mace, F. C. (1996). In pursuit of general behavioral relations. *Journal of Applied Behavior Analysis, 29,* 557-514.

Sailor, W., Guess, D., Rutherford, G., & Baer, D. M. (1968). Control of tantrum behavior by operant techniques during experimental verbal training. *Journal of Applied Behavior Analysis, 1*(3), 237-243.

Related Lessons:

D-01 Use positive and negative reinforcement.

D-02 Use appropriate parameters and schedules of reinforcement.

E-01 Use interventions based on manipulation of antecedents, such as motivating operations and discriminative stimuli.

E-10 Use the Premack principle.

Notes:

E-10 USE THE PREMACK PRINCIPLE

Definitions:

"The Premack principle is a principle of reinforcement which states that an opportunity to engage in more probable behaviors (or activities) will reinforce less probable behaviors (or activities). For example, if a child often plays computer games (more probable) and avoids completing math problems (less probable), we might allow her to play the computer after (contingent upon) completing 15 math problems. Prior to the introduction of the Premack principle, systems of reinforcement were viewed as the contingency between a stimulus and behavior. The Premack principle expanded the existing reinforcement contingency of stimulus behavior to include contingencies between two behaviors. This principle is often referred to as "grandma's rule" because grandmothers (or any caregivers) often apply this principle: "you have to eat your vegetables (less probable) before you can have dessert (more probable)." (Barton, 2013)

In education, the Premack principle is the basis for "first/then" strategies. "First/then" strategies consist of a teacher telling a student "First *X*, then *Y*" with *X* being a less preferred activity or task demand and *Y* being a more preferred activity contingent on the completion of *X*.

This principle uses preferred activities as reinforcers to help increase engagement in less preferred activities or demands.

Example:

- A father tells his teenage son, "When you have finished washing the dishes, you can watch TV."

Write another example:

Questions to ask your supervisor:

Relevant Literature:

Azrin, N. H., Vinas, V., & Ehle, C. T. (2007). Physical activity as reinforcement for classroom calmness of ADHD children: A preliminary study. *Child & Family Behavior Therapy, 29, 2*, 1-8.

Barton, E.E. (2013). Premack's Principle. In *Encyclopedia of Autism Spectrum Disorders.* Volkmar, F.R. (Ed.) (p. 2345) Springer New York: New York, NY.

Cooper, J.O., Heron, T.E. & Heward W.L. (2007). *Applied Behavior Analysis* (2nd Ed.), Upper Saddle River, NJ. Pearson Prentice Hall. 271-273, 277.

Mazur, J.E. (1975). The Matching Law and Quantifications Related to Premack's Principle. *Journal of Experimental Psychology: Animal Behavior Processes*, 1, 4, 374-386.

Sigafoos, J. (2005). From Premack to PECS: 25 Years of Progress in Communication Intervention for Individuals with Developmental Disabilities. *Educational Psychology*, 25, 6, 601-607.

Welsh, D.H., Bernstein, D.J., & Luthans, F. (1992). Application of the Premack Principle of Reinforcement to the Quality Performance of Service Employees. Journal of Organizational Behavior Management, 13, 1, 9.

Related Lessons:

D-01: Use positive and negative reinforcement

D-02: Use appropriate parameters and schedules of reinforcement.

I-07: Design and conduct preference assessments to identify putative reinforcers.

J-02: Identify potential interventions based on assessment results and the best available scientific evidence.

Notes:

FK-38 BEHAVIORAL CONTRAST

Definitions (Behavioral contrast):

(Cooper, Heron, & Heward, 2007).

☐ Flashcard created   ☐ Learned to fluency

Example:

- Rich sneaks candy from home and eats it in class. His teacher catches him one day and he stops eating candy in the classroom. However, he now asks to go to the bathroom every morning and eats candy in the bathroom where the teacher cannot see him.

Write another example:

Questions to ask your supervisor:

Relevant Literature:

Cooper, J.O., Heron, T.E. & Heward W.L. (2007). *Applied Behavior Analysis* (2nd Ed.), Upper Saddle River, NJ. Pearson Prentice Hall. 337-338, 349.

Gross, A.M. & Drabman, R.S. (1981) Behavioral contrast and behavior therapy. *Behavior Therapy*, 12, 2, 231-246.

Koegel, R.L. & Williams, J.A. (1980). Behavioral contrast and generalization across settings in the treatment of autistic children. *Journal of Experimental Child Psychology*, 30, 3, 422-437.

Nevin, J.A. (1992). Behavioral contrast and behavioral momentum. *Journal of Experimental Psychology: Animal Behavior Processes*, 18, 2, 126-133.

Reynolds, G.S. (1961) Behavioral Contrast. *Journal of the Experimental Analysis of Behavior*, 4, 1, 57-71.

Related Lessons:

C-01: State and plan for the possible unwanted effects of reinforcement.
C-02: State and plan for the possible unwanted effects of punishment.
D-01: Use positive and negative reinforcement.
D-02: Use appropriate parameters and schedules of reinforcement.
D-15: Use positive and negative punishment.
D-16: Identify and use punishers.
D-17: Use appropriate parameters and schedules of punishment.
D-19: Use combinations of reinforcement with punishment and extinction.
E-07: Plan for behavioral contrast effects.
FK-18: Conditioned reinforcement
FK-20: Conditioned punishment
FK-21: Schedules of reinforcement and punishment

Notes:

FK-39 BEHAVIORAL MOMENTUM

Definition:
Behavioral momentum is defined as "a metaphor to describe a rate of responding and its resistance to change following an alteration in reinforcement conditions" (Cooper, Heron, & Heward, 2007).

"In classical physics, momentum is defined as the product of velocity and mass. Translating metaphorically, behavioral momentum is the product of response rate and resistance to change" (Nevin, 1992, p. 302).

Response rate had been used as the measure of response rate for many years. With the introduction of behavioral momentum, Nevin challenges this and describes resistance to change as a better way to measure response strength. (1974)

There is a common misconception that behavioral momentum is synonymous with the high-p request sequence. According to Nevin, the field should be cautious when describing behavioral momentum this way (Nevin, 1996).

Example:
- "If you are working at the computer, and you keep working even though you are called to dinner that is an example of behavioral momentum" (Pierce & Cheney, 2013, p. 134).

- A student is coloring at his desk. The teacher asks him to come down to the rug to listen to a story. He continues to color for a few more seconds.

- James is watching TV. His remote stops working. He continues to push the button despite the battery being dead.

Write another example:

Relevant Literature:
Brandon, P. K., & Houlihan, D. (1997). Applying behavioral theory to practice: An examination of the behavioral momentum metaphor. *Behavioral Interventions, 12*(3), 113-131.
Cooper, J. O., Heron, T. E., & Heward, W. L. (2007). *Applied behavior analysis.* Upper Saddle River, NJ: Pearson Education.
Nevin, J. A. (1974). Response strength in multiple schedules. *Journal of the Experimental Analysis of Behavior, 21*(3), 389–408. doi:10.1901/jeab.1974.21-389
Nevin, J. A. (1992). An integrative model for the study of behavioral momentum. *Journal of the Experimental Analysis of Behavior, 57*(3), 301.
Nevin, J. A. (1996). The Momentum of Compliance. *Journal of Applied Behavior Analysis, 29*(4), 535–547.
Nevin, J. A., Mandell, C., & Atak, J. R. (1983). The analysis of behavioral momentum. *Journal of the Experimental analysis of behavior, 39*(1), 49.

Related Lessons:
E-09 Arrange high-probability request sequences.
FK-10 behavior, response, response class

Notes:

FK-40 MATCHING LAW

Definition (Matching law):

(Catania, 2007).

☐ Flashcard created   ☐ Learned to fluency

Example:
- Herrnstein (1961) described pigeon's distribution of responding on concurrent schedules of reinforcement. He found the relation between absolute rate of reinforcement and the absolute rate of responding is a linear function that passes through the origin. In other words, if rate of reinforcement and rate of responding are plotted on the x and y axis the result is close to a line that passes through the origin with the slope of 1. The matching equation can be denoted as follows:

-

-

$$\frac{B_a}{(B_a + B_b)} = \frac{R_a}{(R_a + R_b)}$$

The term B_a is behavior measured as rate of response for behavior a, and B_b is behavior measured as rate of response for behavior b. The term R_a is the scheduled rate or reinforcement for response a, and R_b is the scheduled rate of reinforcement for response b.

Mace, Neef, Shade, and Mauro (1994) found special education high school students spent time on math problems, arranged in different stacks, that was equal to the relative rate of reinforcement for completing math problems from the different stacks.

Borrero and Vollmer (2002), after conducting functional analyses to find maintaining variables for problem behavior, found that proportional rates of problem behavior relative to problem behavior matched the proportional rate of reinforcement for 4 individuals with disabilities.

Write another example:

Questions to ask your supervisor:

Relevant Literature:

Baum, W. M. (1974). Choice in free-ranging wild pigeons. *Science, 185*(4145), 78-79.

Borrero, J. C., & Vollmer, T. R. (2002). An application of the matching law to severe problem behavior. *Journal of Applied Behavior Analysis, 35*(1), 13-27.

Conger, R., & Killeen, P. (1974). Use of concurrent operants in small group research: A demonstration. *Pacific Sociological Review*, 399-416.

Herrnstein, R. J. (1961). Relative and absolute strength of response as a function of frequency of reinforcement. *Journal of the experimental analysis of behavior, 4*(3), 267.

Mace, F. C., Neef, N. A., Shade, D., & Mauro, B. C. (1994). Limited matching on concurrent-schedule reinforcement of academic behavior. *Journal of Applied Behavior Analysis, 27*(4), 585.

Matthews, L. R., & Temple, W. (1979). Concurrent schedule assessment of food preference in cows. *Journal of the Experimental Analysis of Behavior, 32*(2), 245-254.

Poling, A. (1978). Performance of rats under concurrent variable-interval schedules of negative reinforcement. *Journal of the Experimental Analysis of Behavior, 30*(1), 31-36.

Related Lessons:

A-14 Design and implement choice measures.
B-03 Systematically arrange independent variables to demonstrate their effects on dependent variables.
E-08 Use the matching law and recognize factors influencing choice.
G-04 Explain behavioral concepts using nontechnical language.

Notes:

Segment 21 – Scorecard
Maintaining Professional Standards/Ethics

☐ Presentation (2-5 minutes)

B 2
☐ Assessment
☐ SAFMED learned to fluency
☐ Workbook boxes completed

G 8
☐ Assessment
☐ SAFMED learned to fluency
☐ Workbook boxes completed

D 18
☐ Assessment
☐ SAFMED learned to fluency
☐ Workbook boxes completed

J 9
☐ Assessment
☐ SAFMED learned to fluency
☐ Workbook boxes completed

G 2
☐ Assessment
☐ SAFMED learned to fluency
☐ Workbook boxes completed

J 15
☐ Assessment
☐ SAFMED learned to fluency
☐ Workbook boxes completed

Segment 21 – Individual Supervision Agenda

Supervisor: _____ **Supervisee:** _____
Meeting Date: _____ **Time of meeting – From:**_____ **To:**_____
This document covers supervisory period from ____/____/____ **to** ____/____/____

1. Pass-in/Review Homework:
   Did the Supervisee satisfactorily complete this homework assignment?   Yes / No
   - If not, what is needed to complete assignment? Describe below.
2. Task List items addressed (B 2; D 18, G 2, 8; J 9, 15)

3. Definitions/SAFMEDs learned
   ☐ Flashcard(s) created   Was supervisee fluent with definitions? Yes ☐ No ☐

4. Discussion topics or activities completed during this meeting:

Evaluation of Supervisee's Performance				
(Record: S- "Satisfactory"; NI- "Needs Improvement"; U- "Unsatisfactory"; or NA- "Not Applicable")				
Arrived on time for meeting		Gave examples as needed		
Completed Homework Assigned		Accepted supervisory feedback appropriately		
Referred to literature/readings		Answered all questions thoroughly		
Maintained professional communication during supervision meeting				
Overall evaluation of supervisee performance during this meeting (Circle one—use code above)			S NI U	
If "NI" or "U", please list corrective steps needed to achieve a score of "S"				

5. Homework assigned for next meeting

6. Closing questions/feedback

Segment 21 – Group Supervision Meeting Agenda

- <u>Meeting Topic</u>: Maintaining Professional Standards/Ethics

- <u>Task List Items Reviewed</u>:
- B-02: Review and interpret articles from the behavior analytic literature.
- D-18: Use extinction
- J-09: Identify and address practical and ethical considerations when using experimental designs to demonstrate treatment effectiveness
- J-15: Base decision making on data displayed in various formats.
- G-02: Consider biological/medical variables that may be affecting the client.
- G-08: Identify and make environmental changes that reduce the need for behavior analysis services.

1. Housekeeping
   - Upon entry to meeting have supervisees hand in the previous week's homework assignment and discuss several "Housekeeping Items" related to supervision.
   - Take attendance for the meeting.
   - State the duration of today's meeting (90 minutes).
   - Distribute BACB® experience forms to supervisees.

2. Task List Lesson and Discussion
   - Discuss task list item B-02: Review and interpret articles from the behavior analytic literature.
   - Discuss task list item D-18: Use extinction
   - Discuss task list item J-09: Identify and address practical and ethical considerations when using experimental designs to demonstrate treatment effectiveness
   - Discuss task list item J-15: Base decision making on data displayed in various formats.
   - Discuss task list item G-02: Consider biological/medical variables that may be affecting the client.
   - Discuss task list item G-08: Identify and make environmental changes that reduce the need for behavior analysis services.

3. Homework Review
   - Review homework that was assigned at the previous supervision meeting.

4. Questions
   - Answer any questions related to the homework or topics discussed.

5. Closing Notes
   - *Assign Homework (task list boxes, presentation) from today's segment, due at next group meeting*
   - Close the meeting by inviting supervisees to request topics to be covered in upcoming meetings.

B – 02 REVIEW AND INTERPRET ARTICLES FROM THE BEHAVIOR-ANALYTIC LITERATURE.

Definition:

Applied behavior analysis is an applied science that develops its technology via the discovery of environmental variables that produce socially significant behavior change. The process of putting the science into practice begins with basic researchers discovering the principles of behavior that are then tested on socially significant behavior by applied researchers and then ultimately implemented by practitioners (Cooper, Heron, & Heward, 2007). Whether a behavior analyst is solely a practitioner or a practitioner and a researcher, it is important that they maintain close contact with the scientific literature and its possible applications by regularly reviewing and critically interpreting articles from the behavior analytic literature.

When engaging in a review of the literature it is useful to consider the criteria that define applied behavior analysis which are outlined by Baer, Wolf, & Risley (1987). These criteria referred to as the seven dimensions (applied, behavioral, analytic, technological, conceptually systematic, effective and generality) can not only assist in determining if an intervention meets the standards of applied behavior analysis but it can also conclude whether a research intervention is prepared to translate into practice or if further investigation is necessary prior to effective clinical implementation.

Cooper, Heron and Heward (2007), assert that "scientific knowledge is built on above all, empiricism - the practice of objective observations of the phenomena of interest." Therefore, a behavior analyst should also remain objective when reviewing and interpreting articles. Furthermore, it is important to remain objective when conducting visual analyses of the data to determine the extent that a functional relation is demonstrated. To assist in this process, Johnston and Pennypacker (2009) suggest that a behavior analyst have extensive experience with graphical analyses both as a designer and a reader. They also note that the first step to analyzing behavioral data is to ask whether the data presentation is straightforward and productive toward the research question by orienting to the graph's scale, axes and legend. Next, one should conduct a visual analysis by acknowledging the number of data points, variability, level and trend for each experimental condition followed by a visual analysis across conditions and then across participants to draw comparisons and begin to establish conclusions (Cooper, Heron, & Heward, 2007).

A behavior analyst's ability to critically and empirically analyze the literature requires a thorough understanding of the science and acknowledgment of the bidirectional relationship between research and practice.

Example:

When reviewing an article it is important to make an unbiased interpretation regarding whether or not experimental control (internal validity) was established by acknowledging possible subject, setting, measurement and/or independent variable confounds (Cooper, Heron, & Heward, 2007).

Write another example:

Questions to ask your supervisor:

Relevant Literature:

Baer, D. M., Wolf, M. M., & Risley, T. R. (1968). Some current dimensions of applied behavior analysis. *Journal of applied behavior analysis*, 1(1), 91-97.

Cooper, J. O., Heron, T. E., & Heward, W. L. (2007). *Applied Behavior Analysis* (2nd ed.). Upper Saddle River, NJ: Pearson Prentice Hall.

Johnston, J. M. (2009). Pennypacker Jr. Strategies and tactics of behavioral research.

Related Lessons:

B-01: Use the dimensions of applied behavior analysis (Baer, Wolf, & Risley, 1968) to evaluate whether interventions are behavior-analytic in nature.

I-05: Organize, analyze, and interpret observed data.

FK-04: Empiricism.

FK-09: Distinguish between the conceptual analysis of behavior, experimental analysis of behavior, applied behavior analysis, and behavioral service delivery.

FK-33: Functional relations.

Notes:

D-18 USE EXTINCTION.

Definition:

As a behavioral intervention, extinction "involves eliminating the reinforcement contingency maintaining a response" and has "been used successfully to reduce the frequency of a variety of behavioral disorders" (Lerman & Iwata, 1995). To use extinction effectively, behavioral analysts must first determine the reinforcer maintaining an individual's behavior. Once the reinforcer is determined, extinction can be utilized by preventing the behavior from achieving the same function, thereby rendering the behavior ineffective at producing reinforcement. There are three common procedures for extinction: extinction of behavior maintained by positive reinforcement, extinction of behavior maintained by negative reinforcement and extinction of behavior maintained by automatic reinforcement.

While often effective when used correctly, extinction may produce unwanted side effects. These include extinction bursts, initial increases in target behavior as the individual engages in an increased rate of behavior to access previous reinforcers and extinction-induced aggression. Also, you may see an increase in unwanted novel behavior. To be effective, it is crucial to withhold all reinforcers maintaining the problem behavior and to provide frequent opportunities for the individual's behavior to contact new reinforcement contingencies (e.g. problem behavior no longer produces reinforcement while replacement behavior produces does produce reinforcement). This may not always be feasible (e.g. If an individual engages in aggression to gain attention from others, even response blocking may sufficiently reinforce this behavior). It is often not advised for use in environments when problem behaviors are likely to be imitated by others (e.g. in classroom settings), when harm to the individual or others cannot be prevented such as with severe aggression or self-injury and when behaviors are too disruptive to others or occur at high frequencies and cannot be managed effectively.

Extinction should also not be used as singular intervention. When coupled with differential reinforcement strategies, studies have shown the unwanted effects of extinction can be reduced significantly (Athens & Vollmer, 2010).

Example:
- Teaching an individual an appropriate means to gain attention while putting inappropriate attention-seeking behavior on extinction allows the individual to gain access to previous reinforcers, thereby mitigating the aversive effects of extinction.

Write another example:

Questions to ask your supervisor:

Relevant Literature:

Cooper, J. O., Heron, T. E., & Heward, W. L. (2007). *Applied behavior analysis* (2nd ed.). Upper Saddle River, NJ: Prentice Hall.

Lerman, D.C., & Iwata, B.A., (1995). Prevalence of the extinction burst and its attenuation during treatment. *Journal of Applied Behavioral Analysis, 28(1),* 93-94.

Athen, E.S., & Vollmer, T.R., (2010). An investigation of differential reinforcement of alternative behavior without extinction. *Journal of Applied Behavioral Analysis, 43(4),* 569-589.

Related Lessons:
C-03 State and plan for unwanted effects of extinction
D-18. Use Extinction.
D-19 Use combinations of reinforcement with punishment and extinction
J-06 Select intervention strategies based on supporting environments
J-07 Select intervention strategies based on environmental and resource constraints
J-09 Identify and address practical and ethical considerations when using experimental designs to demonstrate program effectiveness.
J-10 When a behavior is to be decreased, select an acceptable alternative behavior to be established or increased.
Notes:

G-02 CONSIDER BIOLOGICAL/MEDICAL VARIABLES THAT MAY BE AFFECTING THE CLIENT.

The Behavior Analyst Certification Board (BACB) instructs that a "behavior analyst recommends seeking a medical consultation if there is any reasonable possibility that a referred behavior influenced by medical or biological variables" in section **3.02 Medical Consultation, of the BACB** professional and ethical compliance code for behavior analysts **(2014)**

This is relevant both in research and practice. Therefore, the first step in the assessment process should be to determine whether the problem may be due to a medical/biological issue and whether a medical evaluation has been completed (Cooper, Heron & Heward, 2007). Failure to rule out medical needs would be unethical as it would delay potentially necessary medical treatment that may even prove life threatening dependent on the medical concerns or the severity of the challenging behavior.

Possible pain related disorders or other medical/biological disorders that restrict an individual's ability to engage in appropriate behavior should be investigated. Some relevant behavioral topics correlated with a high likelihood of medical and biological causes are feeding disorders, toileting challenges (e.g., encopresis and incontinence), sleep problems and self-injury. Take self-injury for example; studies have shown that self-injurious behavior (SIB) has been maintained by pain attenuation which, can be categorized as automatic negative reinforcement behavior (Carr & Smith, 1995; O'Reilly, 1997). In detail, an increase in painful stimulation is an establishing operation (EO), thereby increasing behavior that has been reinforced by pain reduction.

Aside from the common examples presented above, it is possible that any form of challenging behavior could be a result of an underlying medical or biological issue. For example, aggressive behavior may also be related to pain related disorders which act as an EO (Carr et al., 2003; Skinner, 1953). The argument has also been made that aggressive behavior in response to painful stimulation may be respondent behavior (Ulrich & Azrin, 1962). Furthermore, Kennedy and Meyer (1996) found that the occurrence of allergy symptoms and sleep deprivation were correlated with an increase in escape maintained challenging behavior.

Relevant Literature:

Behavior Analyst Certification Board (BACB) Behavior Analyst Certification Board professional and ethical compliance code for behavior analysts. 2014. Retrieved from http://www.bacb.com/Downloadfiles/BACB_Compliance_Code.pdf.

Carr, E. G., Smith, C. E., Giacin, T. A., Whelan, B. M., & Pancari, J. (2003). Menstrual discomfort as a biological setting event for severe problem behavior: Assessment and intervention. *Journal Information, 108*(2).

Carr, E. G., & Smith, C. E. (1995). Biological setting events for self-injury. *Mental Retardation and Developmental Disabilities Research Reviews, 1*(2), 94-98.

Cooper, J. O., Heron, T. E., & Heward, W. L. (2007). *Applied behavior analysis (2nd ed.).* Upper Saddle River, NJ: Pearson.

Kennedy, C. H., & Meyer, K. A. (1996). Sleep deprivation, allergy symptoms, and negatively reinforced problem behavior. *Journal of Applied Behavior Analysis, 29*(1), 133-135.

O'Reilly, M. F. (1997). Functional analysis of episodic self-injury correlated with recurrent otitis media. *Journal of Applied Behavior Analysis, 30*(1), 165-167.

Skinner, B. F. (1953). *Science and human behavior.* Simon and Schuster.

Ulrich, R. E., & Azrin, N. H. (1962). Reflexive fighting in response to aversive stimulation. *Journal of the Experimental Analysis of Behavior, 5*(4), 511.

Related Lessons:

G-01 Review records and available data at the outset of the case.

G-03 Conduct a preliminary assessment of the client in order to identify the referral problem.

G-06 Provide behavior-analytic services in collaboration with others who support and/or provide services to one's clients.

G-07 Practice within one's limits of professional competence in applied behavior analysis, and obtain consultation, supervision, and training, or make referrals as necessary.

FK-13 reflexive relations (US-UR)

FK-26 unconditioned motivating operations

Notes:

Write another example:

Questions to ask your supervisor:

G-08 IDENTIFY AND MAKE ENVIRONMENTAL CHANGES THAT REDUCE THE NEED FOR BEHAVIOR ANALYSIS SERVICES.

"Behavior analysis is a science of studying how we can arrange our environments so they make very likely the behaviors we want to be probably enough, and they make unlikely the behaviors we want to be improbable" (Cooper, Heron, & Heward, 2007, p. 15). The behavior analyst assesses the nature of the fit between an individual and the environment in which he/she functions using a three-part contingency (antecedent, behavior, consequences) structure of events. In this process, the analyst identifies motivating operations associated with antecedent events and the consequences that maintain problem behaviors or prevent adequate development of adaptive behaviors. This information can be used to identify relatively uncomplicated proactive environmental changes that will improve the functioning of the individual. As a result of the individual's increased access to positive reinforcement, more intrusive behavior interventions may be less necessary.

Examples:
- Parents found it difficult to get their daughter ready for the school bus on time. They decided they would try giving her time to shower at night instead of in the morning. They added showering to her regular nighttime routine and the daughter not only got to the school bus on-time but began to go to sleep earlier after the expanded nighttime routine.
- A student refused to sit in his seat at school. An occupational therapist suggested a gel filled wedge for the student's chair and the student not only remained seated in one class, but chose to use the wedge in all of his classes.

Write another example.

Questions to ask your supervisor:

Relevant Literature:
Cooper, J.O., Heron, T.E. & Heward W.L. (2007). *Applied Behavior Analysis* (2nd Ed.), Upper Saddle River, NJ. Pearson Prentice Hall.

Related Lessons:
B-02 Review and interpret articles from the behavior-analytic literature.
D-21 Use differential reinforcement (e.g., DRO, DRA, DRI, DRL, DRH).
E-01 Use interventions based on manipulation of antecedents, such as motivating operations and discriminative stimuli.
E-03 Use instructions and rules.
I-03 Design and implement individualized behavioral assessment procedures.
I-05 Organize, analyze, and interpret observed data.
I-06 Make recommendations regarding behaviors that must be established, maintained, increased, or decreased.
J-04 Select intervention strategies based on client preferences.
J-05 Select intervention strategies based on the client's current repertoires.
J-06 Select intervention strategies based on supporting environments.
J-07 Select intervention strategies based on environmental and resource constraints.
J-08 Select intervention strategies based on the social validity of the intervention.
J-10 When a behavior is to be decreased, select an acceptable alternative behavior to be established or increased.
J-12 Program for maintenance.
K-09 Secure the support of others to maintain the client's behavioral repertoires in their natural environments.
FK-05 Parsimony
FK-06 Pragmatism
FK-23 automatic reinforcement and punishment
FK-26 unconditioned motivating operation
FK-33 functional relations

Notes:

J-09 IDENTIFY AND ADDRESS PRACTICAL AND ETHICAL CONSIDERATONS WHEN USING EXPEIMENTAL DESIGNS TO DEMONSTRATE TREATMENT EFFECTIVENESS.

The general goal of behavioral research is "to demonstrate that measured changes in the target behavior occur because of experimentally manipulated changes in the environment" (Cooper, 2007, p. 160). Without a controlled research design, practitioners cannot claim a causal relation between intervention and behavior change. Practical and ethical concerns limit practitioner's use of experimental designs in most settings. Typical risks associated with controlled research include the need to delay treatment while collecting baseline data or to withdraw interventions that are successful. Each research design has specific risks to participants associated with its application. In applied practice, meaningful, socially valid, and lasting change is the goal. Clients, parents, staff, and teachers prefer the most efficient and effective path toward treatment goals. For such reasons, practitioners seek to show evidence of a correlation rather than a causal relation between changes in a client's behavior and an intervention by providing comparison of patterns of baseline (A) and intervention (B) responding over time. The AB design has poor experimental control but strong practical and ethical value in natural settings.

Examples:

A researcher-practitioner designed a multiple baseline study for a woman who hit and scratched herself. The researcher's review of the first three days of baseline data showed that occurrences of the behavior were highly variable without an obvious pattern of responding. The researcher concluded that further delay of treatment that might decrease a dangerous behavior was not ethical. The researcher knew that the strength of the results of his research would be threatened if he began treatment before he had a clear pattern in baseline responding, but his responsibility to his client, and those close to her, was his primary concern. He regretted not anticipating this possibility by choosing a research design that could have demonstrated experimental control without depending on highly stable baseline responding.

A student's teacher did not want the student to participate in a graduate intern's study because the intern planned to work with the student during classroom reading instruction. Even though the research study was designed to provide a benefit to the student by increasing sight-word reading, the boy's parent refused to sign permission for his participation. The intern realized that social validity was threatened by his original plan and he would have to arrange to work with the student after school or exclude him from the study.

Write another example:

Questions to ask your supervisor:

Relevant Literature:

Cooper, J.O., Heron, T. E., & Heward, W. L. (2007). *Applied behavior analysis.* Upper Saddle River, NJ: Pearson Education.

Gast, D. L. (2010). *Single subject research methodology in behavioral sciences.* New York: NY: Routledge.

Related Lessons:

B-03 Systematically arrange independent variables to demonstrate their effects on dependent variables.

G-08 Identify and make environmental changes that reduce the need for behavior analysis services.

H-03 Select a data display that effectively communicates relevant quantitative relations.

J-02 Identify potential interventions based on assessment results and the best available scientific evidence.

06 Select intervention strategies based on supporting environments.

J-07 Select intervention strategies based on environmental and resource constraints.

J-08 Select intervention strategies based on the social validity of the intervention.

J-10 When a behavior is to be decreased, select an acceptable alternative behavior to be established or increased.

K-02 Identify the contingencies governing the behavior of those responsible for carrying out behavior-change procedures and design interventions accordingly.

K-07 Evaluate the effectiveness of the behavioral program

Notes:

J-15 BASE DECISION MAKING ON DATA DISPLAYED IN VARIOUS FORMATS.

Behavior analysts make decisions during assessment and intervention based on data. Graphic displays (e.g., line graphs, bar graphs, and cumulative graphs) aid accurate and efficient interpretation of quantitative data and facilitate communication with others. "The primary function of a graph is to communicate without assistance from the accompanying text" (Spriggs & Gast, 2010, p. 167). Line graphs are most often used by behavior analysts to show effects and possible functional relations between intervention (independent variable) and a defined behavior (dependent variable). Bar graphs are often used by behavior analysts to summarize or compare discrete aspects of recorded behavior. Cumulative graphs show the rate of change in responding across time. Although they may be used with duration or latency data, they are most often used to show frequency data. Behavior analysts often use tables to summarize data or other information. "An informative table supplements—rather than duplicates—the text" (APA, 2010). As with graphs, a table should communicate efficiently but include enough information to be understood alone without explanations in the text.

Examples:
Example 1: A behavior analyst interprets the effectiveness of a constant time delay procedure for teaching a student 10 sight words using the following line graph:

2: A behavior analyst uses a table to summarize the number of times a child chose a specific toy during seven sessions of free-play with four toys available.

Toy	Chosen 1st	Chosen 2nd	Chosen 3rd	Chosen 4th	Frequency of toy as 1st or 2nd choice
Car	5	2	0	0	7
Blocks	0	3	4	0	3
Bubbles	1	1	3	2	2
Doll	1	1	0	5	2

Example 2 data display:
    Ask supervisee to interpret information in the table to decide which toys she would place in a free time area for this child to enjoy.
    Would you consider adding different types of any one toy to the playtime area based on these data? If so, which type? If not, why not?
    Write a title for this table.

Write another example:

Questions to ask your supervisor:

Relevant Literature:

American Psychological Association. (2010). *Publication manual of the American Psychological Association* (6th ed.). Washington, DC: Author.

Cooper, J. O., Heron, T. E., & Heward, W. L. (2007). *Applied behavior analysis.* Upper Saddle River, NJ: Pearson Education.

Spriggs, A. D., & Gast, D. L. (2010). Visual representation of data. In D. L. Gast (Ed.), *Single subject research methodology in behavioral sciences (pp 166-198).* New York, NY: Routledge.

Related Lessons:

A-10 Design, plot, and interpret data using equal-interval graphs.

A-11 Design, plot, and interpret data using a cumulative record to display data.

A-12 Design and implement continuous measurement procedures (e.g., event recording).

A-14 Design and implement choice measures.

B-03 Systematically arrange independent variables to demonstrate their effects on dependent variables.

H-01 Select a measurement system to obtain representative data given the dimensions of the behavior and the logistics of observing and recording.

H-03 Select a data display that effectively communicates relevant quantitative relations.

H-04 Evaluate changes in level, trend, and variability.

I-05 Organize, analyze, and interpret observed data.

I-07 Design and conduct preference assessments to identify putative reinforcers.

J-01 State intervention goals in observable and measurable terms.

K-04 Design and use effective performance monitoring and reinforcement systems.

FK-33 functional relations

Notes:

Segment 22 – Scorecard
Assessing Preference

☐ Presentation (2-5 minutes)

A 14
☐ Assessment
☐ SAFMED learned to fluency
☐ Workbook boxes completed

F 2
☐ Assessment
☐ SAFMED learned to fluency
☐ Workbook boxes completed

I 7
☐ Assessment
☐ SAFMED learned to fluency
☐ Workbook boxes completed

J 4
☐ Assessment
☐ SAFMED learned to fluency
☐ Workbook boxes completed

Segment 22 – Individual Supervision Agenda

Supervisor: _____ **Supervisee:** _____
Meeting Date: _____ **Time of meeting – From:** _____ **To:** _____
This document covers supervisory period from ____/____/____ **to** ____/____/____

1. Pass-in/Review Homework:

   Did the Supervisee satisfactorily complete this homework assignment?   Yes / No

   • If not, what is needed to complete assignment? Describe below.

2. Task List items addressed (A 14; F 2, I 7; J 4)

```
[                                                                    ]
[                                                                    ]
[                                                                    ]
[                                                                    ]
[                                                                    ]
```

3. Definitions/SAFMEDs learned

   ☐ Flashcard(s) created   Was supervisee fluent with definitions? Yes ☐ No ☐

```
[                                                                    ]
[                                                                    ]
[                                                                    ]
[                                                                    ]
```

4. Discussion topics or activities completed during this meeting:

Evaluation of Supervisee's Performance			
(Record: S- "Satisfactory"; NI- "Needs Improvement"; U- "Unsatisfactory"; or NA- "Not Applicable")			
Arrived on time for meeting		Gave examples as needed	
Completed Homework Assigned		Accepted supervisory feedback appropriately	
Referred to literature/readings		Answered all questions thoroughly	
Maintained professional communication during supervision meeting			
Overall evaluation of supervisee performance during this meeting *(Circle one—use code above)*		S	NI	U
If "NI" or "U", please list corrective steps needed to achieve a score of "S"			

5. Homework assigned for next meeting

```
[                                                                    ]
[                                                                    ]
[                                                                    ]
[                                                                    ]
```

6. Closing questions/feedback

```
[                                                                    ]
[                                                                    ]
[                                                                    ]
[                                                                    ]
```

Segment 22 – Group Supervision Meeting Agenda

- <u>Meeting Topic</u>: Assessing Preference

- <u>Task List Items Reviewed</u>:
  - o A-14: Design and implement choice measures.
  - o F-02: Use token economies and other conditioned reinforcement systems.
  - o I-07: Design and conduct preference assessments to identify putative reinforcers.
  - o J-04: Select intervention strategies based on client preferences.

1. Housekeeping
   - Upon entry to meeting have supervisees hand in the previous week's homework assignment and discuss several "Housekeeping Items" related to supervision.
   - Take attendance for the meeting.
   - State the duration of today's meeting (90 minutes).
   - Distribute BACB® experience forms to supervisees.

2. Task List Lesson and Discussion
   - Discuss task list item A-14: Design and implement choice measures.
   - Discuss task list item F-02: Use token economies and other conditioned reinforcement systems.
   - Discuss task list item I-07: Design and conduct preference assessments to identify putative reinforcers.
   - Discuss task list item J-04: Select intervention strategies based on client preferences.

3. Homework Review
   - Review homework that was assigned at the previous supervision meeting.

4. Questions
   - Answer any questions related to the homework or topics discussed.

5. Closing Notes
   - *Assign Homework (task list boxes, presentation) from today's segment, due at next group meeting*
   - Close the meeting by inviting supervisees to request topics to be covered in upcoming meetings.

A - 14 DESIGN AND IMPLEMENT CHOICE MEASURES

Definition (Stimulus Preference Assessment):

(Cooper, Heron, & Heward, 2007).
☐ Flashcard created   ☐ Learned to fluency

Definition
(Multiple Stimulus Without Replacement Assessment):

(Cooper, Heron, & Heward, 2007).
☐ Flashcard created   ☐ Learned to fluency

Definition (Single-Stimulus Preference Assessment):

(Pace, Ivancic, Edwards, Iwata, & Page, 1985).
☐ Flashcard created   ☐ Learned to fluency

Definition (Free-Operant Assessment):

(Roane et al., 1998).
☐ Flashcard created   ☐ Learned to fluency

Definition (Paired Choice Preference Assessment):

(Fisher et al., 1992).
☐ Flashcard created   ☐ Learned to fluency

Definition (Response Restriction Assessment):

(Hanley et al., 2003).
☐ Flashcard created   ☐ Learned to fluency

Definition (Multiple Stimulus Assessment):

(Cooper, Heron, & Heward, 2007).
☐ Flashcard created   ☐ Learned to fluency

Definition (Duration Assessment):

(Hagopian et al., 2001).
☐ Flashcard created   ☐ Learned to fluency

Definition (Concurrent Chains Assessment):

(Hanley, Iwata, & Lindberg, 1999).
☐ Flashcard created   ☐ Learned to fluency

Example:
Bob was trying to find the most reinforcing items for one of his students. He decided to conduct a preference assessment in which he used a timer to track the duration of engagement with various toys and games during recess time. He took the duration of engagement for each item and turned this into a reinforcer hierarchy. This helped his reinforcement program become an instant success.

Write another example:

Questions to ask your supervisor:

Relevant Literature:
Catania, A. C. (2013). *Learning* (5th ed.). Croton-on-Hudson, NY: Sloan.
Cooper, J. O., Heron, T. E., & Heward, W. L. (2007). Applied behavior analysis. Upper Saddle River, NJ: Pearson Education.
Fisher, W., Piazza, C. C., Bowman, L. G., Hagopian, L. P., Owens, J. C., & Slevin, I. (1992). A comparison of two approaches for identifying reinforcers for persons with severe and profound disabilities. *Journal of applied Behavior analysis*, 25(2), 491-498.
Hagopian, L. P., Rush, K. S., Lewin, A. B., & Long, E. S. (2001). Evaluating the predictive validity of a single stimulus engagement preference assessment. *Journal of Applied Behavior Analysis*, 34(4), 475-485.
Hanley, G. P., Iwata, B. A., Lindberg, J. S., & Conners, J. (2003). Response-restriction analysis: I. Assessment of activity preferences. *Journal of Applied Behavior Analysis*, 36(1), 47-58.
Hanley, G. P., Iwata, B. A., & Lindberg, J. S. (1999). Analysis of activity preferences as a function of differential consequences. *Journal of Applied Behavior Analysis*, 32(4), 419-435.
DeLeon, I. G., & Iwata, B. A. (1996). Evaluation of a multiple-stimulus presentation format for assessing reinforcer preferences. *Journal of Applied Behavior Analysis*, 29(4), 519-533.
Pace, G. M., Ivancic, M. T., Edwards, G. L., Iwata, B. A., & Page, T. J. (1985). Assessment of stimulus preference and reinforcer value with profoundly retarded individuals. *Journal of Applied Behavior Analysis*, 18(3), 249-255.
Roane, H. S., Vollmer, T. R., Ringdahl, J. E., & Marcus, B. A. (1998). Evaluation of a brief stimulus preference assessment. *Journal of Applied Behavior Analysis*, 31(4), 605-620.
Smith, R. G., Iwata, B. A., & Shore, B. A. (1995). Effects of subject-versus experimenter-selected reinforcers on the behavior of individuals with profound developmental disabilities. *Journal of Applied Behavior Analysis*, 28(1), 61-71.
Windsor, J., Piché, L. M., & Locke, P. A. (1994). Preference testing: A comparison of two presentation methods. *Research in Developmental Disabilities*, 15(6), 439-455.

Related Lessons:
I-07: Design and conduct preference assessments to identify putative reinforcers.
J-04: Select intervention strategies based on client preferences.

Notes:

F-02 USE TOKEN ECONOMIES AND OTHER CONDITIONED REINFORCEMENT SYSTEMS.

Definition:

Conditioned Reinforcer - "A stimulus change that functions as a reinforcer because of prior pairing with one or more other reinforcers" (Cooper, Heron, & Heward, 2007, p. 692).

"Token economies are used as a method of strengthening a behavior, or increasing its frequency, because the tokens are a way of 'paying' children for completing tasks and the children can then use these tokens to buy desired activities or items" (Miltenberger, 2008, p. 513).

A token economy uses a conditioned reinforcer, or token, as currency for a student to exchange for a backup reinforcer (i.e., tangible items, edibles, activities, etc…) based on earning a certain amount of tokens for desired target behaviors.

The strength of the token is derived from its being paired with other reinforcers (also referred to as a backup reinforcer). If the backup reinforcer loses value due to satiation, the token will subsequently lose its effectiveness.

Miltenberger (2008) listed seven components that need to be defined before implementing a token economy. These include: identifying the desired target behavior to be strengthened, identifying tokens to be used as conditioned reinforcement, identifying backup reinforcers, outlining a reinforcement schedule for token delivery, identifying the amount of tokens needed to exchange for reinforcers, identifying the time and place to exchange tokens, and identifying if a response cost contingency would be necessary for the individual.

Write an example:

Questions to ask your supervisor:

Ayllon, T. & Azrin, N. (1968). *The Token Economy: A Motivational System for Therapy and Rehabilitation.* New York: Appleton Century Crofts.

Cooper, J., Heron, T., & Heward, W. (2007). *Applied Behaviour Analysis.* New Jersey: Pearson Education.

Foxx, R. (1998). A comprehensive treatment program for in-patient adolescents. *Behavioural Interventions, 13,* 67-77.

Hackenberg, T. (2009). Token Reinforcement: A Review and Analysis. *Journal of the Experimental Analysis of Behaviour, 91,* 257-286.

Kazdin, A. (1982). The Token Economy: A Decade Later. *Journal of Applied Behaviour Analysis, 15,* 431-445.

Kazdin, A., & Bootzin, R. (1972). The Token Economy: An Evaluative Review. *Journal of Applied Behaviour Analysis, 5,* 343-372.

Malott & Trojan-Suarez, (2006). *Principles of Behaviour.* New Jersey: Pearson Prentice Hall.

Matson, J. & Boisjoli (2009). The token economy for children with intellectual disability and/or autism: A review. *Research in Developmental Disabilities, 30,* 240-248.

Miltenberger, R. (2008). *Behaviour Modification.* Belmont, CA. Wadsworth Publishing.

Tarbox, R., Ghezzi, P., & Wilson G. (2004). The effects of token reinforcement on attending in a young child with autism. *Behavioural Interventions, 21,* 156-164.

Related Lessons:

C-01: State and plan for the possible unwanted effects of reinforcement.

D-01: Use positive and negative reinforcement.

D-02: Use appropriate parameters and schedules of reinforcement.

D-19: Use combinations of reinforcement with punishment and extinction.

D-21: Use differential reinforcement (e.g., DRO, DRA, DRI, DRL, and DRH).

E-04: Use contingency contracting.

E-05: Use independent, interdependent, and dependent group contingencies.

I-07: Design and conduct preference assessments to identify putative reinforcers.

FK-18: Conditioned reinforcement.

FK-21: Schedules of reinforcement and punishment.

FK-31: Behavioral contingencies.

FK-41: Contingency-shaped behavior

Notes:

I-07 DESIGN AND CONDUCT PREFERENCE ASSESSMENTS TO IDENTIFY PUTATIVE REINFORCERS.

Definition (Stimulus preference assessment):

(Cooper, Heron, & Heward, 2007).

☐ Flashcard created   ☐ Learned to fluency

Definition (Advantages of using preference assessments):

(Green et al., 1988).

☐ Flashcard created   ☐ Learned to fluency

Example:
- Marvin is working to teach a student to make requests for preferred edibles using a picture exchange communication system. Unfortunately, the child is not demonstrating a preference and is equally likely to choose either of the two cards presented. He is equally likely to consume any edible that is associated with one of two cards. Marvin decides to do a preference assessment to see if he can identify an edible that the boy does *not* like. He conducts a paired stimulus preference assessment with eight items he thinks the student will potentially not prefer. He notices that initially the boy chooses the black licorice but then spits it out. Over several presentations the child's selection avoids this item. It is not consumed on any of the presentations scoring it as 0% or "not preferred."
- The Zippadeedooda Perfume Company is testing a new line of products. They hire ten women to rate their new line of fragrances. They ask the ladies to smell each of the 8 samples provided and use a Likert type scale to have them rate each of the fragrances; *really like, somewhat like, neutral, somewhat dislike, and really dislike.* Those that score the overall lowest ratings according to the test group are not marketed, as it is unlikely that their client base will find them appealing either.

Non-Example:
- Marvin's student has worked hard on his schoolwork and has earned a choice of an edible. Marvin takes a box of candies out of his desk containing eight different types of sweets and tells his student that he can pick one. The boy chooses a chocolate candy over all the other options and eats it. He cannot assume that the child dislikes the rest of the candies because he did not observe the boy eating any of the others.

Write another example:

Questions to ask your supervisor:

Relevant Literature:

Cooper J.O, Heron T.E, Heward W.L. (2007). *Applied behavior analysis* (2nd ed.) Upper Saddle River, NJ: Pearson

Green, C.W., Reid, D. H., White, L. K., Halford, R. C., Brittain, D. P., & Gardner, S. M. (1988). Identifying reinforcers for persons with profound handicaps: Staff opinion versus systematic assessment of preferences. *Journal of Applied Behavior Analysis, 21,* 31-43.

Hagopian, L. P., Long, E. S., & Rush, K. S. (2004). Preference assessment procedures for individuals with developmental disabilities. *Behavior Modification, 28*(5), 668-677.

Related Lessons:
D-01-Use positive and negative reinforcement
I-07-Design and conduct preference assessments to identify putative reinforcers
J-04-Select intervention strategies based on client preferences
Notes:

J-04 SELECT INTERVENTION STRATEGIES BASED ON CLIENT PREFERENCES.

The importance and ethical necessity of basing intervention strategies on client preferences

- As behavior analysts, it is our ethical responsibility to continually put our client's needs first, and this includes, considering which type of intervention may be more preferred by the clients we serve. As Bailey and Burch (2011) state, one of our core ethical principles is treating others with care and compassion and this encompasses giving our clients choices (Bailey & Burch, 2011).

- Historically, consideration of client preferences is an area that within behavior analysis, perhaps has not been given as much attention as it deserves. In one area of study, Hanley, Piazza, Fisher, Contrucci & Maglieri (1997) reported that, "few if any studies have examined the social acceptability of or consumer preferences" for the relevant treatment options but had instead given more weight to the opinions of the caregivers as opposed to those of the client (Hanley *et al.*, 1997, p. 460). Another interesting train of thought has been that "choice making is often not taught" (Bannerman, Sheldon, Sherman, & Harchik, 1990, p. 81).

- Another reason for considering clients' preferences over treatment options is it may make the intervention more *successful*. Data from Miltenberger, Suda, Lennox and Lindeman (1991) indicated it was very important for successful treatment, to consider client preferences when selecting interventions. Findings from many other studies have also supported this premise (e.g., Berk, 1976; Hanley, Piazza, Fisher, & Maglieri, 2005; Mendonca & Brehm, 1983; Perlmuter & Montry, 1973).

Selecting interventions based on client preferences

- There are methods reported in the literature for determining which treatment method is more preferred by a client*. As such, once it has been established that an intervention is necessary to treat a behavior, it is imperative then to consider assessing a client's preference for one treatment option over others to assist with the behavior change program. In this way, treatment is more likely to be successful, will likely have more social validity (Schwartz & Baer, 1991) and will be meeting more of our ethical standards as behavior analysts.

Write another example:

Questions to ask your supervisor:

Bailey, J. & Burch, M. (2011). *Ethics for Behavior Analysts*, 2nd ed. New York, London: Routledge/Taylor & Francis Group.

Bannerman, D. J., Sheldon, J. B., Sherman, J. A., & Harchik, A. E. (1990). Balancing the right to habilitation with the right to personal liberties: The rights of people with developmental disabilities to eat too many doughnuts and take a nap. *Journal of Applied Behavior Analysis, 23*, 79–89.

Berk, R. A. (1976). Effects of choice of instructional methods on verbal learning tasks. *Psychological Reports, 38*, 867-870.

Hanley, G. P., Piazza, C. C., Fisher, W. W., Contrucci, S. A. & Maglieri, K. A. (1997). Evaluation of client preferences for function-based treatment packages. *Journal of Applied Behavior Analysis, 30*, 459-473.

Hanley, G. P., Piazza, C. C., Fisher, W. W. & Maglieri, K. A. (2005). On The Effectiveness of And Preference For Punishment And Extinction Components Of Function-Based Interventions. *Journal of Applied Behavior Analysis, 38*, 51-65.

Mendonca, P. J. & Brehm, S. S. (1983). Effects of choice on behavioral treatment of overweight children. *Journal of Social and Clinical Psychology, 1*, 343-358.

Miltenberger, R. G., Suda, K. T., Lennox, D. B. & Lindeman, D. P. (1991). Assessing the acceptability of behavioral treatments to persons with mental retardation. *American Journal on Mental Retardation, 96*, 291–298.

Perlmuter, L. C. & Montry, R. A. (1973). Effect of choice of stimulus on paired-associate learning. *Journal of Experimental Psychology, 99*, 120-123.

Related Lessons:

E-08: Use the matching law and recognize factors influencing choice

I-07: Design and conduct preference assessments to identify putative reinforcers

J-02: Identify potential interventions based on assessment results and the best available scientific evidence.

J-05: Select intervention strategies based on the client's current repertoire

J-06: Select intervention strategies based on supporting environments

J-07: Select intervention strategies based on environmental and resource constraints

J-08: Select intervention strategies based on the social validity of the intervention

Footnotes

*1 See Hanley, Piazza, Fisher, Contrucci & Maglieri (1997) and Miltenberger, Suda, Lennox & Lindeman (1991) for more information about how to test clients' preferences for different interventions.

Notes:

Segment 23 – Scorecard
Supervision I

☐ Presentation (2-5 minutes)

K 1
☐ Assessment
☐ SAFMED learned to fluency
☐ Workbook boxes completed

K 6
☐ Assessment
☐ SAFMED learned to fluency
☐ Workbook boxes completed

K 2
☐ Assessment
☐ SAFMED learned to fluency
☐ Workbook boxes completed

K 10
☐ Assessment
☐ SAFMED learned to fluency
☐ Workbook boxes completed

K 3
☐ Assessment
☐ SAFMED learned to fluency
☐ Workbook boxes completed

Segment 23 – Individual Supervision Agenda

Supervisor: _____ **Supervisee:** _____

Meeting Date: _____ **Time of meeting – From:**_____ **To:**_____

This document covers supervisory period from ____/____/____ to ____/____/____

1. Pass-in/Review Homework:

    Did the Supervisee satisfactorily complete this homework assignment?   Yes / No

- If not, what is needed to complete assignment? Describe below.

2. Task List items addressed (K 1-3, 6, 10)

3. Definitions/SAFMEDs learned

    ☐ Flashcard(s) created   Was supervisee fluent with definitions? Yes ☐ No ☐

4. Discussion topics or activities completed during this meeting:

Evaluation of Supervisee's Performance		
(Record: S- "Satisfactory"; NI- "Needs Improvement"; U- "Unsatisfactory"; or NA- "Not Applicable")		
Arrived on time for meeting	Gave examples as needed	
Completed Homework Assigned	Accepted supervisory feedback appropriately	
Referred to literature/readings	Answered all questions thoroughly	
Maintained professional communication during supervision meeting		
Overall evaluation of supervisee performance during this meeting *(Circle one—use code above)*		S NI U
If "NI" or "U", please list corrective steps needed to achieve a score of "S"		

5. Homework assigned for next meeting

6. Closing questions/feedback

Segment 23 – Group Supervision Meeting Agenda

- <u>Meeting Topic</u>: Supervision I

- <u>Task List Items Reviewed</u>:
o K-01: Provide for ongoing documentation of behavioral services.
o K-02: Identify the contingencies governing the behavior of those responsible for carrying out behavior change procedures and design interventions accordingly.
o K-03: Design and use competency based training for persons

who are responsible for carrying out behavioral assessment and behavior change procedures.
o K-06: Provide supervision for behavior change agents.
o K-10: Arrange for the orderly termination of services when they are no longer required.

1. Housekeeping
    - Upon entry to meeting have supervisees hand in the previous week's homework assignment and discuss several "Housekeeping Items" related to supervision.
    - Take attendance for the meeting.
    - State the duration of today's meeting (90 minutes).
    - Distribute BACB® experience forms to supervisees.
2. Task List Lesson and Discussion
    - Discuss task list K-01: Provide for ongoing documentation of behavioral services.
    - Discuss task list item K-02: Identify the contingencies governing the behavior of those responsible for carrying out behavior change procedures and design interventions accordingly.
    - Discuss task list item K-03: Design and use competency based training for persons who are responsible for carrying out behavioral assessment and behavior change procedures.
    - Discuss task list item K-06: Provide supervision for behavior change agents.
    - Discuss task list item K-10: Arrange for the orderly termination of services when they are no longer required.
3. Homework Review
    - Review homework that was assigned at the previous supervision meeting.
4. Questions
    - Answer any questions related to the homework or topics discussed.
5. Closing Notes
    - *Assign Homework (task list boxes, presentation) from today's segment, due at next group meeting*
    - Close the meeting by inviting supervisees to request topics to be covered in upcoming meetings.

K-01 PROVIDE FOR ONGOING DOCUMENTATION OF BEHAVIORAL SERVICES.

Behavior analysts follow guidelines related to documentation in 2.10 and 2.11 of the Behavior Analyst Certification Board professional and ethical compliance code for behavior analysts Boundaries of Competence:

2.10 Documenting Professional Work and Research.

(a) Behavior analysts appropriately document their professional work in order to facilitate provision of services later by them or by other professionals, to ensure accountability, and to meet other requirements of organizations or the law.
(b) Behavior analysts have a responsibility to create and maintain documentation in the kind of detail and quality that would be consistent with best practices and the law.

2.11 Records and Data.

(a) Behavior analysts create, maintain, disseminate, store, retain, and dispose of records and data relating to their research, practice, and other work in accordance with applicable laws, regulations, and policies; in a manner that permits compliance with the requirements of this Code; and in a manner that allows for appropriate transition of service oversight at any moment in time.
(b) Behavior analysts must retain records and data for at least seven (7) years and as otherwise required by law. (BACB, 2014, p.9)

Written documentation of work products (such as raw data sheets, reports and spreadsheets) must be kept be kept in secure locations in the event that this information may need to be transferred to other professionals that are also supporting the client. Ongoing documentation and record-keeping also ensures accountability for services rendered. Documentation should be thorough and well-maintained; should the behavioral analysts' professional services be involved in legal proceedings, documentation must be detailed and comprehensive enough to meet judicial scrutiny (Bailey & Burch, 2011).

Record disposal must sufficiently eliminate all confidential records that may reveal client's private health information. Electronic transfer of client's identifying information and records under any insecure medium (e.g. public areas, fax and email) are prohibited by the Health Insurance Portability and Accountability Act (Cooper, Heron, & Heward, 2007).

Write another example:

Questions to ask your supervisor:

Relevant Literature:

Bailey, J., & Burch, M. (2011). *Ethics for Behavior Analysts: 2nd Expanded Edition.* Taylor & Francis.

Behavior Analyst Certification Board (BACB) Behavior Analyst Certification Board professional and ethical compliance code for behavior analysts. 2014. Retrieved from www.bacb.com/Downloadfiles/BACB Compliance Code.pdf.

Cooper, J. O., Heron, T. E., & Heward, W. L. (2007). *Applied behavior analysis* (2nd ed.). Upper Saddle River, NJ: Prentice Hall.

Notes:

K-02 IDENTIFY THE CONTINGENCIES GOVERNING THE BEHAVIOR OF THOSE RESPONSIBLE FOR CARRYING OUT BEHAVIOR CHANGE PROCEDURES AND DESIGN INTERVENTIONS ACCORDINGLY.

Behavior is understood to be a product of the environment in which it occurs. This is the same for all organisms, including the client, the caretakers, the professionals working with the client, and ourselves. A well trained behavior analyst accounts for the environmental arrangement for all of the individuals involved in the behavior change process.

For instance, if a procedure is very effortful and will not produce an effect for several weeks, what will reinforce the behavior of the family member/teacher who will be implementing it? If a procedure produces lots of aggression or screaming, it should be considered that these are often aversive stimuli to the people implementing it.

"Treatment drift occurs when the application of the independent variable during later phases of an experiment differs from the way it was applied at the outset of the study." (Cooper et al., 2007, p. 235). This is often the result of a practitioner's behavior meeting competing contingencies after having followed the plan for a period of time.

High treatment integrity can be achieved by creating a thorough and precise definition for the independent variables, simplifying the treatment procedures, providing ample training and practice to all individuals responsible for treatment, and assessing the contingencies each person's behavior will meet while following through with these interventions.

Other factors that can help improve treatment integrity and regulate the behavior of those involved in the experiment include using less expensive and less intrusive procedures, seeking help and input from the participants family members and other people close to them, setting socially significant but easy-to-meet criterion for reinforcement, eliminating reinforcement gained outside of performing the target response, and contrive contingencies that will compete with natural contingencies.

Example:
Don has been asked to help deliver a new differential reinforcement program to decrease his student's self-injury. However, he has been short of staffing lately and cannot do this consistently throughout the day. This has caused the program to be run without integrity and the self-injury to remain at the same rates. Rick, the BCBA who designed the program, started observing the classroom to see why the program was not working. After noticing that Don was only delivering the reinforcers intermittently and missing opportunities for reinforcement, Rick decided to retrain Don and ask the principal for extra staff when someone calls out sick.

Non-example:
Roger is implementing a new response cost program to decrease verbal protesting for one of his students. However, even though the program has been run as designed for several weeks, there has been no effect on the verbal protesting of the student. The supervisor collected integrity data and found that the plan had been run as prescribed. The problem is likely related to the procedure itself and not its implementation.

Write another example:

Questions to ask your supervisor:

Relevant Literature:

Cooper, J.O., Heron, T.E. & Heward W.L. (2007). *Applied Behavior Analysis* (2nd Ed.), Upper Saddle River, NJ. Pearson Prentice Hall. 235-236, 603-604, 607-609, 652, 659-678.

Fryling, M.F., Wallace, M.D., & Yassine, J.N. (2012). Impact of treatment integrity on intervention effectiveness. *Journal of Applied Behavior Analysis*, 45, 2, 449-453.

DiGennaro-Reed, F.D, Reed, D.D, Baez, C.N, & Maguire, H. (2011) A parametric analysis of errors of commission during discrete-trial training. *Journal of Applied Behavior Analysis*, 44,611–615.

Wheeler, J.J, Baggett, B.A, Fox, J., & Blevins, L. (2006). Treatment integrity: A review of intervention studies conducted with children with autism. *Focus on Autism and Other Developmental Disabilities*, 21, 45–54.

Wilder, D.A, Atwell, J., & Wine, B. (2006). The effects of varying levels of treatment integrity on child compliance during treatment with a three-step prompting procedure. *Journal of Applied Behavior Analysis*, 39, 369–373.

McIntyre, L.L, Gresham, F.M, DiGennaro, F.D, & Reed, D.D. (2007). Treatment integrity of school-based interventions with children in the Journal of Applied Behavior Analysis 1991–2005. *Journal of Applied Behavior Analysis*, 40, 659–672.

Peterson, L, Homer, A.L, & Wonderlich, S.A.(1982). The integrity of independent variables in behavior analysis. *Journal of Applied Behavior Analysis*, 15, 477–492.

St. Peter Pipkin, C, Vollmer, T.R, & Sloman, K.N. (2010). Effects of treatment integrity failures during differential reinforcement of alternative behavior: A translational model. *Journal of Applied Behavior Analysis*, 43, 47–70.

Related Lessons:

J-01: State intervention goals in observable and measurable terms.

K-03: Design and use competency-based training for persons who are responsible for carrying out behavioral assessment and behavior-change procedures.

K-04: Design and use effective performance monitoring and reinforcement systems.

K-05: Design and use systems for monitoring procedural integrity.

K-06: Provide supervision for behavior-change agents.

K-08: Establish support for behavior-analytic services from direct and indirect consumers.

Notes:

K-03 DESIGN AND USE COMPETENCY BASED TRAINING FOR PERSONS WHO ARE RESPONSIBLE FOR CARRYING OUT BEHAVIORAL ASSESSMENT AND BEHAVIOR CHANGE PROCEDURES.

Write another example:

Rationale
In order for staff and family members to collect accurate data and to carry out a behavior intervention plan effectively and consistently, all staff must receive training. Inconsistent applications of procedures may lead to slow improvement or have effects that make behavior worse than before treatment.

Training models
Much research has studied competency based training for staff, teachers and parents. Parsons and Reed (1995) increased staff performance by using classroom-based instruction, observation, and feedback on the work site. Shore et al. (1995) provided training in data collection, calculation, and review of treatment procedure, followed by training in treatment implementation in-situ with feedback and assistance. A third phase of instructing supervisors how to train direct service providers was implemented. Sarokoff and Sturmey (2004) provided staff with a written definition of the plan, feedback regarding their baseline performance, rehearsal with reinforcement and corrective feedback, and in-situ modeling and rehearsal for 10 minutes. Miles and Wilder (2009) used Behavior Skills Training (BST) that involved providing a written description, reviewing baseline performance, rehearsal and feedback, and then repeating modeling and rehearsal until the staff completed three trials accurately.

BST has also been used to train individuals to conduct behavioral assessments such as functional analyses. For example, Iwata et al. (2000) and Lambert, Bloom, Clay, Kunnavatanna, and Collins (2014) trained participants to conduct functional analysis conditions with adequate fidelity.

Elements of competency-based training
- Clear instructions
- Modeling
- Rehearsal
- Feedback
- Repetition until skills mastered
- Treatment Integrity data monitored

Threats to accuracy and reliability
Poor staff training can lead to inaccurate baseline, functional assessment and treatment data. Systematic training of occurrence and nonoccurrence and other critical data collection information and providing booster training will help to minimize the following challenges:
- Observer drift
- Observer reactivity

Questions to ask your supervisor:

Relevant Literature:

Cooper, J. O., Heron, T. E., & Heward, W. L. (2007). Applied Behavior Analysis: 2nd Edition. Pearson Education, Inc..

Iwata, B. A., Wallace, M. D., Kahng, S., Lindberg, J. S., Roscoe, E. M., Conners, J., ... & Worsdell, A. S. (2000). Skill acquisition in the implementation of functional analysis methodology. *Journal of Applied Behavior Analysis, 33*(2), 181-194.

Lambert, J. M., Bloom, S. E., Clay, C. J., Kunnavatana, S. S., & Collins, S. D. (2014). Training residential staff and supervisors to conduct traditional functional analyses. *Research in developmental disabilities, 35*(7), 1757-1765.

Miles, N. I., & Wilder, D. A. (2009). The effects of behavioral skills training on caregiver implementation of guided compliance. *Journal of applied behavior analysis, 42*(2), 405-410.

Parsons, M. B., & Reid, D. H. (1995). Training residential supervisors to provide feedback for maintaining staff teaching skills with people who have severe disabilities. *Journal of Applied Behavior Analysis, 28*(3), 317-322.

Sarokoff, R. A., & Sturmey, P. (2004). The effects of behavioral skills training on staff implementation of discrete-trial teaching. *Journal of Applied Behavior Analysis, 37*(4), 535-538.

Shore, B. A., Iwata, B. A., Vollmer, T. R., Lerman, D. C., & Zarcone, J. R. (1995). Pyramidal staff training in the extension of treatment for severe behavior disorders. *Journal of Applied Behavior Analysis, 28*(3), 323-332.

Related Lessons:

D-04 Use modeling and imitation training
D-05 Use shaping
E-03 Use instructions and rules
F-03 Use direct instruction
K-02 Identify the contingencies governing the behavior of those responsible for carrying out behavior-change procedures and design interventions accordingly

Notes:

K-06 PROVIDE SUPERVISION FOR BEHAVIOR CHANGE AGENTS.

Smith, Parker, Taubman, and Lovaas (1992) found that knowledge transfer from a staff training workshop did not generalize to the group home. Research suggests that training is most effective if there is training and ongoing supervision in the environment where the behavior change program is occurring (Parsons & Reed, 1995; Sarokoff & Sturmey, 2004; Miles & Wilder, 2009)

Codding, Feinberg, Dunn and Pace (2004) found that treatment integrity increased following a one hour performance feedback session every other week. Social validity ratings provided favorable feedback for the frequent supervisions.

Cooper, Heron and Heward (2007) suggest that supervision of data takers and booster training is necessary to avoid observer drift.

Observing and graphing data will provide immediate feedback on the participant's performance. This can lead to quick decisions, modifications if necessary, or the termination of ineffective programs. This supervision is necessary to create the most effective interventions and troubleshoot areas for improvement. It is also important to observe the intervention in the natural environment in order to determine if the intervention is realistic and practical in the natural environment.

Summary of Rationale for Supervision of Behavior Change Agents
- Provides effective knowledge transfer for individuals implementing the intervention
- Increases motivation and treatment integrity
- Reduces error associated with data collection
- Allows for quick clinical decisions to modify or terminate programs which ensures the most effective treatment

Write another example:

Questions to ask your supervisor:

Relevant Literature:

Codding, R. S., Feinberg, A. B., Dunn, E. K., & Pace, G. M. (2005). Effects of immediate performance feedback on implementation of behavior support plans. *Journal of Applied Behavior Analysis, 38*(2), 205-219.

Cooper, J. O., Heron, T. E., & Heward, W. L. (2007). *Applied Behavior Analysis: 2nd Edition.* Pearson Education, Inc.

Miles, N. I., & Wilder, D. A. (2009). The effects of behavioral skills training on caregiver implementation of guided compliance. *Journal of Applied Behavior Analysis, 42*(2), 405-410.

Parsons, M. B., & Reid, D. H. (1995). Training residential supervisors to provide feedback for maintaining staff teaching skills with people who have severe disabilities. *Journal of Applied Behavior Analysis, 28*(3), 317-322.

Sarokoff, R. A., & Sturmey, P. (2004). The effects of behavioral skills training on staff implementation of discrete-trial teaching. *Journal of Applied Behavior Analysis, 37*(4), 535-538.

Smith, T., Parker, T., Taubman, M., & Ivar Lovaas, O. (1992). Transfer of staff training from workshops to group homes: A failure to generalize across settings. *Research in Developmental Disabilities, 13*(1), 57-71.

Related Lessons:
H-03 Select a schedule of observation and recording periods.
H-04 Select a data display that effectively communicates relevant qualitative relations
H-04 Evaluate changes in level, trend and variability.
K-02 Identify the contingencies governing the behavior of those responsible for carrying out behavior-change procedures and design interventions accordingly.
K-03 Design and use competency-based training for persons who are responsible for carrying out behavioral assessment and behavior-change procedures.
K-04 Design and use effective performance monitoring and reinforcement systems.
Notes:

K-10 ARRANGE FOR THE ORDERLY TERMINATION OF SERVICES WHEN THEY ARE NO LONGER REQUIRED.

Behavior analysts follow guidelines related to arranging for termination of services in 2.15 of the Behavior Analyst Certification Board professional and ethical compliance code for behavior analysts:

2.15 Interrupting or Discontinuing Services.

(d) Discontinuation only occurs after efforts to transition have been made. Behavior analysts discontinue a professional relationship in a timely manner when the client: (1) no longer needs the service, (2) is not benefiting from the service, (3) is being harmed by continued service, or (4) when the client requests discontinuation.

(e) Behavior analysts do not abandon clients. Prior to discontinuation, for whatever reason, behavior analysts: discuss the client's views and needs, provide appropriate pre-termination services, suggest alternative service providers as appropriate, and take other reasonable steps to facilitate timely transfer of responsibility to another provider if the client needs one immediately, upon client consent. (BACB, 2014, P. 10).

Before services are terminated, behavior analysts must discuss the client's needs with all pertinent parties (e.g. client's parents, legal guardians, school administrators). The client's welfare should be prioritized above all else and a transition plan should be put in place well before services are discontinued. Referrals to other professionals should be given if appropriate. (Bailey & Burch, 2005)

Write another example:

Questions to ask your supervisor:

Relevant Literature:

Bailey, J., & Burch, M. (2011). *Ethics for Behavior Analysts: 2nd Expanded Edition.* Taylor & Francis.

Behavior Analyst Certification Board (BACB) Behavior Analyst Certification Board professional and ethical compliance code for behavior analysts. 2014. Retrieved from http://www.bacb.com/Download-files/BACB_Compliance_Code.pdf.

Related Lessons:

G-07 Practice within one's limits of professional competence in applied behavior analysis and obtain consultation, supervision, and training, or make referrals as necessary.

K-09 Secure the support of others to maintain the client's behavioral repertoires in their natural environments.

Notes:

Segment 24 – Scorecard
Supervision II

☐ Presentation (2-5 minutes)

G 5
☐ Assessment
☐ SAFMED learned to fluency
☐ Workbook boxes completed

K 8
☐ Assessment
☐ SAFMED learned to fluency
☐ Workbook boxes completed

G 6
☐ Assessment
☐ SAFMED learned to fluency
☐ Workbook boxes completed

K 9
☐ Assessment
☐ SAFMED learned to fluency
☐ Workbook boxes completed

G 7
☐ Assessment
☐ SAFMED learned to fluency
☐ Workbook boxes completed

Segment 24 – Individual Supervision Agenda

Supervisor: _____ **Supervisee:** _____
Meeting Date: _____ **Time of meeting – From:**_____ **To:**_____
This document covers supervisory period from ____/____/____ to ____/____/____

1. Pass-in/Review Homework:

    Did the Supervisee satisfactorily complete this homework assignment?   Yes / No

- If not, what is needed to complete assignment? Describe below.

2. Task List items addressed (G 5-7; K 8-9)

3. Definitions/SAFMEDs learned

      ☐ Flashcard(s) created   Was supervisee fluent with definitions? Yes ☐ No ☐

4. Discussion topics or activities completed during this meeting:

Evaluation of Supervisee's Performance		
(Record: S- "Satisfactory"; NI- "Needs Improvement"; U- "Unsatisfactory"; or NA- "Not Applicable")		
Arrived on time for meeting		Gave examples as needed	
Completed Homework Assigned		Accepted supervisory feedback appropriately	
Referred to literature/readings		Answered all questions thoroughly	
Maintained professional communication during supervision meeting			
Overall evaluation of supervisee performance during this meeting *(Circle one—use code above)*		S	NI	U
If "NI" or "U", please list corrective steps needed to achieve a score of "S"			

5. Homework assigned for next meeting

6. Closing questions/feedback

Segment 24 – Group Supervision Meeting Agenda

- <u>Meeting Topic</u>: Supervision II

- <u>Task List Items Reviewed</u>:
- G-05: Describe and explain behavior, including private events, in behavior-analytic (non-mentalistic) terms.
- G-06: Provide behavior analytic services in collaboration with others who support and/or provide services to one's clients.
- G-07: Practice within one's of professional competence in applied behavior analysis, and obtain consultation, supervision, training, or make referrals as necessary.
- K-08: Establish support for behavior analytic services from direct and indirect consumers.
- K-09: Secure the support of others to maintain the client's behavioral repertoires in their natural environment.

1. Housekeeping
    - Upon entry to meeting have supervisees hand in the previous week's homework assignment and discuss several "Housekeeping Items" related to supervision.
    - Take attendance for the meeting.
    - State the duration of today's meeting (90 minutes).
    - Distribute BACB® experience forms to supervisees.
2. Task List Lesson and Discussion
    - Discuss task list item G-05: Describe and explain behavior, including private events, in behavior-analytic (non-mentalistic) terms
    - Discuss task list item G-06: Provide behavior analytic services in collaboration with others who support and/or provide services to one's clients.
    - Discuss task list item G-07: Practice within one's of professional competence in applied behavior analysis, and obtain consultation, supervision, training, or make referrals as necessary.
    - Discuss task list item K-08: Establish support for behavior analytic services from direct and indirect consumers.
    - Discuss task list item K-09: Secure the support of others to maintain the client's behavioral repertoires in their natural environment.
3. Homework Review
    - Review homework that was assigned at the previous supervision meeting.
4. Questions
    - Answer any questions related to the homework or topics discussed.
5. Closing Notes
    - *Assign Homework (task list boxes, presentation) from today's segment, due at next group meeting*
    - Close the meeting by inviting supervisees to request topics to be covered in upcoming meetings.

G-05 DESCRIBE AND EXPLAIN BEHAVIOR, IN-CLUDING PRIVATE EVENTS, IN BEHAVIOR-ANALYTIC (NON-MENTALISTIC) TERMS.

Behavior analysts must have a strong verbal repertoire when speaking about behavior analysis. This includes using behavior-analytic language when describing and explaining behavior, including private events.

Skinner's radical behaviorism rejected psychological models of behavior that relied on mentalistic explanations. Mentalistic approaches attributed the origination and cause of behavior to "inner" dimensions or mental entities (i.e., hypothetical constructs and explanatory fictions such as the unconscious or psyche). Mentalistic explanations of behavior often neglect the consideration and analysis of controlling variables in the environment and use circular reasoning to explain the cause and effect of behavior. Understanding the philosophy of radical behaviorism and the principles of behavior can assist behavior analysts in explaining behavior in behavior-analytic terms.

For example, you are conducting a functional behavior assessment in a school setting for a student who engages in high rates of aggression in the classroom. The teacher tells you that the student's aggression occurs because the student is frustrated and lives in an unpleasant environment at home. This is a mentalistic explanation. After several observations, you have determined that when academic demands are placed, the student engages in aggression and their aggression is reinforced by escape (i.e., academic demands are removed). This is a behavior-analytic explanation of behavior that accounts for behavior as it is a function of environmental variables.

Using behavior-analytic language to explain and describe behavior can be difficult as we are often exposed to mentalistic explanations (e.g., "wanting to" or "felt like it" as causes of behavior). Read Malott and Trojan-Suarez (2004) for a discussion about circular reasoning and talking about behavior.

Write another example:

Questions to ask your supervisor:

Relevant Literature:

Cooper, J. O., Heron, T. E., & Heward, W. L. (2007). Definition and characteristics of applied behavior analysis. *Applied Behavior Analysis* (pp. 1-23). Upper Saddle River, NJ: Pearson Prentice Hall.

Malott, R. W., & Trojan Suarez, E.A. (2004). Reinforcement. *Principles of Behavior* (pp. 28-35). Upper Saddle River, NJ: Pearson Prentice Hall.

Moore, J. (2008). *Conceptual Foundations of Radical Behaviorism.* Cornwall-on-Hudson, NY: Sloan Publishing.

Related Lessons:
FK-07 Environmental (as opposed to mentalistic) explanations of behavior
FK-08 Distinguish between radical and methodological behaviorism.
FK-31 Behavioral contingencies
FK-33 Functional relations
G-04 Explain behavioral concepts using nontechnical language.
I-01 Define behavior in observable and measurable terms.
I-02 Define environmental variables in observable and measurable terms.

Notes:

G-06 PROVIDE BEHAVIOR ANALYTIC SERVICES IN COLLABORATION WITH OTHERS WHO SUPPORT AND/OR PROVIDE SERVICES TO ONE'S CLIENTS.

Content area 2.03 (a) (Behavior Analysts' Responsibility to Clients) of the professional and ethical compliance code for behavior analysts states that, "When indicated and professionally appropriate, behavior analysts cooperate with other professionals, in a manner that is consistent with the philosophical assumptions and principles of behavior analysis, in order to effectively and appropriately serve their clients." In other words, it is our ethical responsibility to collaborate and communicate with all service providers and other individual stakeholders if it will best service our clients.

Example:
Mary has been exhibiting aggression during sessions with her occupational therapist whenever a novel task is presented. The BCBA has come up with a general behavior support plan for all staff working with Mary to decrease these behaviors. The plan involves multiple options that all are relevant to the addressing the function of the aggression. The BCBA sets up a training to discuss and explain the proper implementation of these intervention strategies, and get feedback from other service providers such as the occupational therapist to increase the social validity of the treatment and increase the likelihood of treatment fidelity.

Write another example:

Questions to ask your supervisor:

Relevant Literature:
Cooper, J.O., Heron, T.E. & Heward W.L. (2007). *Applied Behavior Analysis* (2nd Ed.), Upper Saddle River, NJ. Pearson Prentice Hall. 641-642, 675-676.
Kelly, A. & Tincani, M. (2013). Collaborative training and practice among applied behavior analysts who support individuals with autism spectrum disorder, *Education and Training in Autism and Developmental Disabilities*. 48, 1, 120-131.
Professional and Ethical Compliance Code for Behavior Analysts. Copyright © 2014 by the Behavior Analysis Certification Board®, Inc. ("BACB"), all rights reserved. (Content list items 2.02-2.03).

Related Lessons:
G-04: Explain behavioral concepts using nontechnical language.
G-07: Practice within one's limits of professional competence in applied behavior analysis, and obtain consultation, supervision, training, or make referrals as necessary.
G-08: Identify and make environmental changes that reduce the need for behavior analysis services.
I-06: Make recommendations regarding behaviors that must be established, maintained, increased, or decreased.
J-11: Program for stimulus and response generalization.
J-14: Arrange instructional procedures to promote generative learning (i.e., derived relations).
K-03: Design and use competency-based training for persons who are responsible for carrying out behavioral assessment and behavior-change procedures.
K-08: Establish support for behavior-analytic services from direct and indirect consumers.
K-09: Secure the support of others to maintain the client's behavioral repertoires in their natural environments.

Notes

G-07 PRACTICE WITHIN ONE'S LIMITS OF PROFESSIONAL COMPETENCE IN APPLIED BEHAVIOR ANALYSIS, AND OBTAIN CONSULTATION, SUPERVISION, AND TRAINING, OR MAKE REFERRALS AS NECESSARY.

Behavior analysts follow guidelines related to boundaries of competence in 1.02 of the Behavior Analyst Certification Board professional and ethical compliance code for behavior analysts:

1.02 Boundaries of Competence.

(a) All behavior analysts provide services, teach, and conduct research only within the boundaries of their competence, defined as being commensurate with their education, training, and supervised experience.

(b) Behavior analysts provide services, teach, or conduct research in new areas (e.g., populations, techniques, behaviors) only after first undertaking appropriate study, training, supervision, and/or consultation from persons who are competent in those areas... (BACB, 2014, p.4).

Practicing within your area of competence, training and experience

If, for example, a senior therapist working within an intensive behavior intervention program for preschoolers suddenly began working with adults with phobias then they would be in violation of this ethical guideline. Cooper, Heron, and Heward (2007) go on further to say that even within one's competence area, if a situation exceeds your training or experience then a referral to another behavior analyst should be made. If there is a gap in expertise, available then workshops and conferences may be accessed. Mentors, supervisors and colleagues can provide additional training.

Bailey and Burch (2011) relate this ethical boundary to the Hippocratic Oath, *"Do no harm"*. The guideline addresses the responsible conduct of behavior analysts, ensures the safety of clients, and protects the integrity of the field.

Write an example:

Questions to ask your supervisor:

Relevant Literature:

Bailey, J., & Burch, M. (2011). *Ethics for Behavior Analysts: 2nd Expanded Edition.* Taylor & Francis.

Behavior Analyst Certification Board (BACB) Behavior Analyst Certification Board professional and ethical compliance code for behavior analysts. 2014. Retrieved from www.bacb.com/Downloadfiles/BACB_Compliance_Code.pdf.

Cooper, J. O., Heron, T. E., & Heward, W. L. (2007). Applied behavior analysis: 2nd Edition. Pearson Education, Inc.

Houten, R., Axelrod, S., Bailey, J. S., Favell, J. E., Foxx, R. M., Iwata, B. A., & Lovaas, O. I. (1988). The right to effective behavioral treatment. *Journal of Applied Behavior Analysis, 21*(4), 381-384.

Related Lessons:
B-02: Review and interpret articles from the behavior analytic literature.
G-02: Consider biological/medical variables that may be affecting the client.
G-06: Provide behavior analytic services in collaboration with others who support and/or provide services to one's clients.
K-08: Establish support for behavior analytic services from direct and indirect consumers.
K-09: Secure the support of others to maintain the client's behavioral repertoires in their natural environment.

Notes:

K-08 ESTABLISH SUPPORT FOR THE BEHAVIOR ANALYTIC SERVICES FROM DIRECT AND INDIRECT CONSUMERS.

As a behavior analyst, it is important to conduct yourself with professionalism to your clients and their family and also to individuals from other disciplines that may support your client. You must enlist a circle of care around your client, which will help you to better understand your client through the lenses of another discipline. For example if you have a child who has feeding refusal, taking the time to enlist information from the nutritionist, speech pathologist, doctors and occupational therapists will help you to provide safe and effective treatment.

In addition, when providing treatment having help from people within the client's family, the community, and from the circle of care around your client will enable you to generalize skills to new environments, new people and new activities. These individuals can be a great asset in troubleshooting and providing additional data as well.

Additionally, when your goals are met, you will leave. In order for the continued support of your client and the maintenance of the goals, it is important to enlist individuals who will be with the client for a longer period.

Bailey and Burch (2010) provide a useful book on professional strategies. He provides several suggestions on how to establish a working relationship in the best interest of the client. Establishing yourself as a positive reinforcer for your colleagues by demonstrating integrity, basic meeting etiquette, providing a professional image, using nontechnical language, listening to others, and bringing their opinions into the assessment.

Write another example:

Questions to ask your supervisor:

Relevant Literature:

Bailey, J. S., & Burch, M. R. (2009). *25 Essential Skills & Strategies for the Professional Behavior Analyst: Expert Tips for Maximizing Consulting Effectiveness.* Taylor & Francis.

Bailey, J., & Burch, M. (2011). *Ethics for Behavior Analysts: 2nd Expanded Edition.* Taylor & Francis.

Behavior Analyst Certification Board (BACB) Behavior Analyst Certification Board professional and ethical compliance code for behavior analysts. 2014. Retrieved from http://www.bacb.com/Download-files/BACB_Compliance_Code.pdf.

Related Lessons:
G-07 Practice within one's limits of professional competence in applied behavior analysis, and obtain consultation, supervision, training, or make referrals as necessary.
K-09 Secure the support of others to maintain the client's behavioral repertoires in their natural environments.
K-10 Arrange for the orderly termination of services when they are no longer required.

Notes:

K-09 SECURE THE SUPPORT OF OTHERS TO MAINTAIN THE CLIENT'S BEHAVIORAL REPERTOIRES IN THEIR NATURAL ENVIRONMENTS.

Foxx (1996, p. 230) stated that in programming successful behavior change interventions, "10% is knowing what to do; 90% is getting people to do it…Many programs are unsuccessful because these percentages have been reversed." (Cooper et al., 2007, p. 652).

Being explicit yet simplistic in describing programs and protocols will help secure support from other individuals in a client's environment. If a behavior change procedure or program is too difficult, technical, or places unreasonable demands on the other individuals involved, they are less likely to implement these programs. In addition, adequate training of behavior procedures should be provided to ensure proper implementation by those interacting with the client in the natural environment. Specifically, training pertaining to the delivery of reinforcers, which maintain the individual's newly acquired behavioral repertoires.

Jarmolowicz et al. (2008) compared the effectiveness of conversational language instructions and technical language instructions when explaining how to implement a treatment to caregivers. They found that the caregivers that were given conversational language instruction implemented the treatment more accurately.

Example:
Richard is trying to generalize skills learned in the special education classroom for one of his students. He went to each teacher to explain how this will help the student in their class and answered any questions they may have about the programs. In addition, he conducted a training on the specific program and offered to consult with each teacher in order to make sure generalization was successful and the repertoire was maintained.

Write another example:

Questions to ask your supervisor:

Relevant Literature:
Cooper, J.O., Heron, T.E. & Heward W.L. (2007). *Applied Behavior Analysis* (2nd Ed.), Upper Saddle River, NJ. Pearson Prentice Hall. 641-642, 652.

David P. Jarmolowicz, SungWoo Kahng, Einar T. Ingvarsson, Richard Goysovich, Rebecca Heggemeyer, Meagan K. Gregory, and Steven J. Taylor (*2008*) Effects of Conversational Versus Technical Language on Treatment Preference and Integrity. Intellectual and Developmental Disabilities: June 2008, Vol. 46, No. 3, pp. 190-199.

Stokes, T.F., Baer, D.M., & Jackson, R.L. (1974). Programming the generalization of a greeting response in four retarded children. *Journal of Applied Behavior Analysis*, 7, 599-610.

Related Lessons:
H-01: Select a measurement system to obtain representative data given the dimensions of the behavior and the logistics of observing and recording.
J-01: State intervention goals in observable and measurable terms.
K-03: Design and use competency-based training for persons who are responsible for carrying out behavioral assessment and behavior-change procedures.
K-04: Design and use effective performance monitoring and reinforcement systems.
K-06: Provide supervision for behavior-change agents.
K-08: Establish support for behavior-analytic services from direct and indirect consumers.

Notes:

Segment 25 – Scorecard
Generalization

☐ Presentation (2-5 minutes)

J 11
☐ Assessment
☐ SAFMED learned to fluency
☐ Workbook boxes completed

J 12
☐ Assessment
☐ SAFMED learned to fluency
☐ Workbook boxes completed

J 14
☐ Assessment
☐ SAFMED learned to fluency
☐ Workbook boxes completed

FK 36
☐ Assessment
☐ SAFMED learned to fluency
☐ Workbook boxes completed

FK 37
☐ Assessment
☐ SAFMED learned to fluency
☐ Workbook boxes completed

Segment 25 – Individual Supervision Agenda

Supervisor: _____ **Supervisee:** _____
Meeting Date: _____ **Time of meeting – From:** _____ **To:** _____
This document covers supervisory period from ____/____/____ to ____/____/____

1. Pass-in/Review Homework:

    Did the Supervisee satisfactorily complete this homework assignment?   Yes / No

- If not, what is needed to complete assignment? Describe below.

2. Task List items addressed (J 11-12, 14; FK 36-37)

3. Definitions/SAFMEDs learned

    ☐ Flashcard(s) created   Was supervisee fluent with definitions? Yes ☐ No ☐

4. Discussion topics or activities completed during this meeting:

Evaluation of Supervisee's Performance				
(Record: S- "Satisfactory"; NI- "Needs Improvement"; U- "Unsatisfactory"; or NA- "Not Applicable")				
Arrived on time for meeting		Gave examples as needed		
Completed Homework Assigned		Accepted supervisory feedback appropriately		
Referred to literature/readings		Answered all questions thoroughly		
Maintained professional communication during supervision meeting				
Overall evaluation of supervisee performance during this meeting (*Circle one—use code above*)			S NI U	
If "NI" or "U", please list corrective steps needed to achieve a score of "S"				

5. Homework assigned for next meeting

6. Closing questions/feedback

Segment 25 – Group Supervision Meeting Agenda

- <u>Meeting Topic</u>: Generalization

- <u>Task List Items Reviewed</u>:
  - o J-11: Program for stimulus and response generalization.
  - o J-12: Program for maintenance.
  - o J-14: Arrange instructional procedures to promote generative learning (i.e., derived relations).
  - o FK-36: Response generalization.
  - o FK-37: Stimulus generalization.

2. Housekeeping
   - Upon entry to meeting have supervisees hand in the previous week's homework assignment and discuss several "Housekeeping Items" related to supervision.
   - Take attendance for the meeting.
   - State the duration of today's meeting (90 minutes).
   - Distribute BACB® experience forms to supervisees.

3. Task List Lesson and Discussion
   - Discuss task list J-11: Program for stimulus and response generalization.
   - Discuss task list item J-12: Program for maintenance.
   - Discuss task list item J-14: Arrange instructional procedures to promote generative learning (i.e., derived relations).
   - Discuss task list item FK-36: Response generalization.
   - Discuss task list item FK-37: Stimulus generalization.

4. Homework Review
   - Review homework that was assigned at the previous supervision meeting.

5. Questions
   - Answer any questions related to the homework or topics discussed.

6. Closing Notes
   - *Assign Homework (task list boxes, presentation) from today's segment, due at next group meeting*
   - Close the meeting by inviting supervisees to request topics to be covered in upcoming meetings.

J-11 PROGRAM FOR STIMULUS AND RESPONSE GENERALIZATION.

Behavior analysts teach socially significant skills to help clients function where they work or live. Program interventions for the client behavior to contact naturally occurring reinforcement contingencies in their typical environments using new skills. Generalization might result in a "a great deal of generalized behavior change; that is, after all components of an intervention have been terminated, the learner may emit the newly acquired target behavior, as well as several functionally related behaviors not observed previously in his repertoire, at every appropriate opportunity in all relevant settings, and he may do so indefinitely" (Cooper, Heron, & Heward, 2007, p. 621).

To increase stimulus generalization, the behavior analyst systematically varies where intervention is implemented, conditions under which it is implemented, and people who implement it in a gradual manner from acquisition through practicing stages. To develop a response class of functionally equivalent skills, the behavior analyst trains using a variety of responses that eventually may include incorrect responses and novel correct responses.

Relevant Literature:

Cooper, J.O., Heron, T. E., & Heward, W. L. (2007). *Applied behavior analysis.* Upper Saddle River, NJ: Pearson Education.

Stokes, T. F., & Baer, D. M. (1977). An implicit technology of generalization. *Journal of Applied Behavior Analysis, 10*(2), 349-367.

Related Lessons:

E-02 Use discrimination training procedures.

I-06 Make recommendations regarding behaviors that must be established, maintained, increased, or decreased.

J-02 Identify potential interventions based on assessment results and the best available scientific evidence.

J-12 Program for maintenance.

FK-11 environment, stimulus, stimulus class

FK-12 stimulus equivalence

FK-24 Stimulus control

FK-36 response generalization

Notes:

Example:

Stimulus generalization strategies Teach	Response generalization strategies Teach
• A range of appropriate situations and people to greet socially: Teacher; peer; parent; sibling; or stranger passing on sidewalk.	• A range of appropriate responses: "Hello"; "HI"; head nod; or "How are you?"
• A range of appropriate math addition sentences: Two plus two equals four; $$\begin{array}{r} 2 \\ +2 \\ \hline 4 \end{array} \quad 2+2=4$$	• A range of appropriate behaviors to show the math problem total: written number 4; saying "four;" or holding up four fingers.
• A range of ways for others to ask for a choice: "Tell me what you want"; "point to what you want"; "take one".	• A range of behaviors for appropriately making choices: point; take; sign; or tell.

Write another example:

Questions to ask your supervisor:

J-12 PROGRAM FOR MAINTENANCE

Response maintenance refers to "the extent to which a learner continues to perform the target behavior after a portion or all of the intervention responsible for the behavior's initial appearance in the learner's repertoire has been terminated" (Cooper, Heron & Heward, 2007, p. 703). Rusch and Kazdin (1981) note that withdrawing or gradually fading components of an individual's treatment package can support response maintenance.

Program for behavior learned in structured environments to be maintained with contingencies in the client's natural environment. Thin reinoforcement schedules so that the natural environment can support and continue to maintain similar rates in behavior (e.g. While learning to mand, a child may be given a chip every time she asks for a chip. However, as she becomes more adept with this goal, the schedule of reinforcement should move from a continuous schedule to an intermittent schedule because the child will not always be given a chip upon request in her natural environment.)

Response maintenance can often be confused with generalization across multiple exemplars. The key difference is that response maintenance is said to occur if the response can be maintained in settings and situations in which it was previously exhibited, *after* generalization to that setting and/or situation has already occurred at least once in the past. For instance, if an individual was taught how to purchase items at a store and did so successfully at some point at Starbucks, McDonald's and Target but did not exhibit this skill at Starbucks a month later, a lack of response maintenance is said to occur. If, however, the individual did not exhibit the skill at Macy's where the individual has never performed the skill, a lack of generalization is said to occur (Cooper, Heron, & Heward, 2007).

Questions to ask your supervisor:

Relevant Literature:

Cooper, J. O., Heron, T. E., & Heward, W. L. (2007). *Applied behavior analysis* (2nd ed.). Upper Saddle River, NJ: Prentice Hall.

Rusch, F. R. & Kazdin, A.E. (1981). Toward a methodology of withdrawal designs for the assessment of response maintenance. *Journal of Applied Behavioral Analysis, 14 (2),* 131-140.

Related Lessons:
J-06 Select intervention strategies based on supporting environments
J-07 Select intervention strategies based on environmental and resource constraints
J-08 Select intervention strategies based on social validity of intervention
J-11 Program for stimulus and response generalization

Write another example:

Notes:

J-14 ARRANGE INSTRUCTIONAL PROCEDURES TO PROMOTE GENERATIVE LEARNING (I.E., DERIVED RELATIONS).

Generative learning involves applying learning to novel contexts without being explicitly taught and is related to language and cognition. Deriving relations is based on the stimulus equivalence paradigm and procedures (Sidman, 1971). A small number of taught relations among stimuli may generate numerous derived relations (Wulfert & Hayes, 1988). Readers are encouraged to understand stimulus equivalence prior to arranging instructional procedures to promote generative learning. Experimental procedures often utilize matching-to-sample tasks or a computerized program called Implicit Relational Assessment Procedure (IRAP) to teach derived relations. It has been extensively studied in children with autism (Kilroe, Murphy, Barnes-Holmes, & Barnes-Holmes, 2014). The general instructional procedure involves providing explicit reinforcement for a series of conditional discriminations, after which untrained relations (i.e., derived relations) will emerge and can be subsequently reinforced.

Stimulus equivalence is one of several empirically supported examples of derived relations, as relations can be derived based on opposition, temporality, analogy, comparison, and distinction (Stewart, McElwee, & Ming, 2013). Relational Frame Theory (RFT) was developed as a behavior analytic account of human language and cognition (Hayes, Barnes-Holmes, & Roche, 2001) and addresses the need for a theoretical explanation for generative learning, Resources for learning RFT are included in the relevant literature section.

Example:
- A learner is taught that spoken word "apple" = picture of an apple = written word "apple" = picture of an apple. These two relations are directly taught. However, through this explicit training, the learner can derive that the spoken word "apple" = written word "apple." In this example, reinforcement should occur for successful matching of the two trained relations. Once the third relation is derived, the response should be reinforced.

Write another example:

Questions to ask your supervisor:

Relevant Literature:
Hayes, S. C., Barnes-Holmes, D., & Roche, B. (2001). *Relational frame theory: A post-skinnerian account of human language and cognition.* New York, NY: Plenum Press.
Sidman, M. (1994). Equivalence relations and behavior: A research story. Boston, MA: Author's Cooperative.
Stewart, I., McElwee, J., & Ming, S. (2013). Language generativity, response generalization, and derived relational responding. *Analysis of Verbal Behavior, 29,* 137-155.
Torneke, N. (2010). *Learning RFT: An introduction to relational frame theory and its clinical application.* Oakland, CA: Context Press.
Wulfert, E., & Hayes, S. C. (1988). Transfer of a conditional ordering response through conditional equivalence classes. *Journal of the Experimental Analysis of Behavior, 50,* 125-144.

Related Lessons:
E-06 Use stimulus equivalence procedures.
FK-11 environment, stimulus, stimulus class.
FK-24 stimulus control.
FK-34 conditional discriminations.

Notes:

FK-36 RESPONSE GENERALIZATION.

Definition (Response generalization):

(Cooper, Heron, & Heward, 2007).
☐ Flashcard created   ☐ Learned to fluency

Example:
- A young child learns to open a door at their house by turning a door knob. One day, while at a friend's house, they encounter a door that has a handle rather than a knob. The child is able to turn the handle and open the unfamiliar door. This is an example of response generalization because functional both responses are equal (they open result in the door being opened) but the response topographies are different.

Write another example:

Questions to ask your supervisor:

Relevant Literature:

Baer, D.M., Wolf, M.M., & Risley, T.R. (1968). Some current dimensions of applied behavior analysis. *Journal of Applied Behavior Analysis*, 1, 91-97.

Cooper, J.O., Heron, T.E. & Heward W.L. (2007). *Applied Behavior Analysis* (2nd Ed.), Upper Saddle River, NJ. Pearson Prentice Hall. 250-251, 620-622.

Fantuzzo, J.W., & Clement, P.W. (1981). Generalization of the effects of teacher and self-administered token reinforcers to nontreated students. *Journal of Applied Behavior Analysis*, 14, 435-447.

Goetz, E.M., & Baer, D.M. (1973). Social control of form diversity and the emergence of new forms in children's block building. *Journal of Applied Behavior Analysis*, 6, 209-217.

Sidman, M. (1994). *Equivalence relations and behavior: A research story*. Boston: Author's Cooperative.

Related Lessons:
B-01: Use the dimensions of applied behavior analysis (Baer, Wolf, & Risley, 1968) to evaluate whether interventions are behavior analytic in nature.
E-06: Use stimulus equivalence procedures.
E-11: Use pairing procedures to establish new conditioned reinforcers.
I-01: Define behavior in observable and measureable terms.
I-02: Define environmental variables in observable and measureable terms.
J-11: Program for stimulus and response generalization.
J-12: Program for maintenance.
J-14: Arrange instructional procedures to promote generative learning (i.e., derived relations).
K-09: Secure the support of others to maintain the client's behavioral repertoires in their natural environments.
FK-10: Behavior, response, response class.
FK-11: Environment, stimulus, stimulus class
FK-12: Stimulus equivalence
FK-37: Stimulus generalization.

Notes:

FK-37 STIMULUS GENERALIZATION.

Definition (Stimulus generalization):

(Cooper, Heron, & Heward, 2007).
☐ Flashcard created   ☐ Learned to fluency

Example:
A child says, "mommy" in the presence of her mother, but also says "mommy" when she sees her grandmother or daycare provider.

- Have supervisee identify the difference between response generalization and stimulus generalization.
- Have supervisee identify the difference between stimulus generalization and stimulus discrimination. Have him/her identify the qualities of each and give examples.
- Have supervisee give examples from their workplace of stimulus generalization.

Relevant Literature:
Baer, D.M., Wolf, M.M., & Risley, T.R. (1968). Some current dimensions of applied behavior analysis. *Journal of Applied Behavior Analysis*, 1, 91-97.

Cooper, J.O., Heron, T.E. & Heward W.L. (2007). *Applied Behavior Analysis* (2nd Ed.), Upper Saddle River, NJ. Pearson Prentice Hall. 394-396, Figure 17.1, 616, 632.

Cuvo, A.J. (2003). On stimulus generalization and stimulus classes. *Journal of Behavioral Education*, 12, 77-83.

Guttman, N., & Kalish, H. (1956). Discriminability and generalization. *Journal of Experimental Psychology*, 51, 79-88.

Johnston, J.M. (1979). On the relation between generalization and generality. *The Behavior Analyst*, 2, 1-6.

Stokes, T.F., & Baer, D.M. (1977). An implicit technology of generalization. *Journal of Applied Behavior Analysis*, 10, 349-367.

Related Lessons:
B-01: Use the dimensions of applied behavior analysis (Baer, Wolf, & Risley, 1968) to evaluate whether interventions are behavior analytic in nature.
E-06: Use stimulus equivalence procedures.
J-11: Program for stimulus and response generalization.
J-14: Arrange instructional procedures to promote generative learning (i.e., derived relations).
FK-10: Behavior, response, response class.
FK-11: Environment, stimulus, stimulus class
FK-12: Stimulus equivalence
FK-36: Response generalization.

Notes:

Write another example:

Questions to ask your supervisor:

SECTION THREE
Submitting the Application and Beyond

Chapter 4
Upon Completion of Supervision Hours

The technical guide is now complete. If the guide was effective, you should now have enough knowledge and system tools to do the following:

- Identify and reference the rules for providing supervised experience hours
- Identify and calculate the proper hours for supervising independent fieldwork in applied settings
- Assess supervisees as practitioners
- Assess supervisees Foundational Knowledge of ABA
- Structure Group Meetings using the Agenda for Group Meetings
- Use the 4th Edition Task List™ with your group
- Apply the 4th Edition Task List™ to improve, expand, and maintain supervisee's repertoire
- Balance individual and group supervision to improve and maintain the supervisee's behavior analytic repertoire
- Identify homework assignments
- Choose from a variety of possible presentation delivery modes for supervisees (i.e., calendar, assigned vs. requested topics)
- Connect with Trainaba.com for videos that can be played at group supervision for Weekly Behavior Analytic Lessons
- Incorporate Behavioral Skills Training into group supervision

We invite you to take an experimental approach to supervising experience hours. Please share your experience with this protocol with ben@trainaba.com. The data received from professionals will shape future versions of this document.

Thank you for using this book. If you like it, please tell a colleague or carry the discussion forward on LinkedIn. If you see a blind spot or something is unclear, please email ben@trainaba.com so we can fix the problem for everybody using the system.

TrainABA's goal is to develop a solid program for supervision through hard work and many trials with feedback. Eventually, we hope to deliver a practical supervision approach that serves the behavior analyst community. We hope you join us in making that dream a reality.

References

Agran, M. (Ed.). (1997). *Student-directed learning: teaching self-determination skills.* Pacific Grove, CA: Brooks/Cole Pub. Co.

Alberto, P., & Troutman, A. C. (2013). *Applied behavior analysis for teachers* (9th ed). Boston: Pearson.

Alessi, G. (1992). Models of proximate and ultimate causation in psychology. *American Psychologist, 47*(11), 1359.

Alexander, D. F. (1985). The Effect of Study Skill Training on Learning Disabled Students' Retelling of Expository Material. *Journal of Applied Behavior Analysis, 18*(3), 263–267. http://doi.org/10.1901/jaba.1985.18-263

Allen, K. D., & Evans, J. H. (2001). Exposure-based treatment to control excessive blood glucose monitoring. *Journal of Applied Behavior Analysis, 34*(4), 497–500. *Analogs to Reinforcement and Avoidance Part 1.* (n.d.).

Anderson, C. M., & Long, E. S. (2002). Use of a structured descriptive assessment methodology to identify variables affecting problem behavior. *Journal of Applied Behavior Analysis, 35*(2), 137.

Anderson, S. R., & Romanczyk, R. G. (1999). Early intervention for young children with autism: Continuum-based behavioral models. *Research and Practice for Persons with Severe Disabilities, 24*(3), 162–173.

Arco, L. (2008). Feedback for improving staff training and performance in behavioral treatment programs. *Behavioral Interventions, 23*(1), 39–64.

Athens, E. S., & Vollmer, T. R. (2010). An investigation of differential reinforcement of alternative behavior without extinction. *Journal of Applied Behavior Analysis, 43*(4), 569–589.

Austin, J., & Carr, J. (2000). *Handbook of applied behavior analysis.* New Harbinger Publications.

Axelrod, S. (1992). Disseminating an effective educational technology. *Journal of Applied Behavior Analysis, 25*(1), 31–35.

Ayllon, T., & Azrin, N. (1968). The token economy: A motivational system for therapy and rehabilitation. Retrieved from http://psycnet.apa.org/psycinfo/1969-15955-000

Azrin, N. H., & Holz, W. C. (1966). Punishment. *Operant Behavior: Areas of Research and Application,* 380–447.

Azrin, N. H., Vinas, V., & Ehle, C. T. (2007). Physical activity as reinforcement for classroom calmness of ADHD children: A preliminary study. *Child & Family Behavior Therapy, 29*(2), 1–8.

Baer, D. M. (1999). *How to plan for generalization.* Pro Ed.

Baer, D. M., Peterson, R. F., & Sherman, J. A. (1967). The development of imitation by reinforcing behavioral similarity to a model. *Journal of the Experimental Analysis of Behavior, 10*(5), 405.

Baer, D. M., & Schwartz, I. S. (1991). If reliance on epidemiology were to become epidemic, we would need to assess its social validity. *Journal of Applied Behavior Analysis, 24*(2), 231.

Baer, D. M., & Wolf, M. M. (1970). Recent examples of behavior modification in preschool settings. *Behavior Modification in Clinical Psychology,* 5–12.

Baer, D. M., Wolf, M. M., & Risley, T. R. (1968). Some current dimensions of applied behavior analysis1. *Journal of Applied Behavior Analysis, 1*(1), 91–97.

Baer, D. M., Wolf, M. M., & Risley, T. R. (1987). Some still-current dimensions of applied behavior analysis. *Journal of Applied Behavior Analysis, 20*(4), 313.

Bailey, J., Bailey, J. S., & Burch, M. R. (2010). *25 essential skills & strategies for the professional behavior analyst: expert tips for maximizing consulting effectiveness.* Taylor & Francis.

Bailey, J., Burch, M. (2011). *Ethics for Behavior Analysts* (2nd Expanded Edition). Taylor & Francis.

Bailey, J., & Burch, M. (2013). *Ethics for Behavior Analysts: 2nd Expanded Edition.* Taylor & Francis.

Bailey, J. S. (1991). Marketing behavior analysis requires different talk. *Journal of Applied Behavior Analysis, 24*(3), 445–448.

Balsam, P. D., & Bondy, A. S. (1983). The negative side effects of reward. *Journal of Applied Behavior Analysis, 16*(3), 283.

Bancroft, S. L., Weiss, J. S., Libby, M. E., & Ahearn, W. H. (2011). A comparison of procedural variations in teaching behavior chains: manual guidance, trainer completion, and no completion of untrained steps. *Journal of Applied Behavior Analysis, 44*(3), 559–569.

Bannerman, D. J., Sheldon, J. B., Sherman, J. A., & Harchik, A. E. (1990). Balancing the right to habilitation with the right to personal liberties: The rights of people with developmental disabilities to eat too many doughnuts and take a nap. *Journal of Applied Behavior Analysis, 23*(1), 79–89.

Barbetta, P. M., Heron, T. E., & Heward, W. L. (1993). Effects of active student response during error correction on the acquisition, maintenance, and generalization of sight words by students with developmental disabilities. *Journal of Applied Behavior Analysis, 26*(1), 111.

Barger-Anderson, R., Domaracki, J. W., Kearney-Vakulick, N., & Kubina Jr, R. M. (2004). Multiple baseline designs: The use of a single-case experimental design in literacy research. *Reading Improvement, 41*(4), 217.

Barlow, D. H., & Hayes, S. C. (1979). Alternating treatments design: One strategy for comparing the effects of two treatments in a single subject. *Journal of Applied Behavior Analysis, 12*(2), 199–210.

Baum, W. M. (1974a). Choice in free-ranging wild pigeons. *Science, 185*(4145), 78–79.

Baum, W. M. (1974b). On two types of deviation from the matching law: Bias and undermatching. *Journal of the Experimental Analysis of Behavior, 22*(1), 231.

Baum, W. M. (1979). Matching, undermatching, and overmatching in studies of choice. *Journal of the Experimental Analysis of Behavior, 32*(2), 269.

Baum, W. M. (1994). *Understanding behaviorism: science, behavior, and culture.* New York, NY: HarperCollins College Publishers.

Baum, W. M. (1995). Radical behaviorism and the concept of agency. *Behaviorology, 3*, 93–106.

Baum, W. M. (2011). What is radical behaviorism? A review of Jay Moore's Conceptual Foundations of Radical Behaviorism. *Journal of the Experimental Analysis of Behavior, 95*(1), 119–126.

Behavior Analyst Certification Board professional and ethical compliance code for behavior analysts. (2014). Behavior Analyst Certification Board (BACB). Retrieved from http://www.bacb.com/Download-files/BACB_Compliance_Code.pdf

Berk, R. A. (1976). Effects of choice of instructional methods on verbal learning tasks. *Psychological Reports, 38*(3), 867–870.

Bijou, S. W., & Baer, D. M. (1961). Child development, Vol 1: A systematic and empirical theory.

Birnbrauer, J. S. (1999, August). How to Evaluate Intervention Programs. Cambridge Center for Behavioral Studies, Inc. Retrieved from www.behavior.org/resources/552.pdf

Blough, D. S. (1963). Interresponse time as a function of continuous variabes: a new method and some data. *Journal of the Experimental Analysis of Behavior, 6*(2), 237–246.

Borrero, J. C., & Vollmer, T. R. (2002). An application of the matching law to severe problem behavior. *Journal of Applied Behavior Analysis, 35*(1), 13–27.

Bosch, S., & Fuqua, R. W. (2001). Behavioral cusps: a model for selecting target behaviors. *Journal of Applied Behavior Analysis, 34*(1), 123.

Boyce, T. E., Carter, N., & Neboschick, H. (2000). An Evaluation of Intraobserver Reliability versus Interobserver Agreement. *European Journal of Behavior Analysis, 1*(2), 107–114.

Brandon, P. K., & Houlihan, D. (1997). Applying behavioral theory to practice: An examination of the behavioral momentum metaphor. *Behavioral Interventions, 12*(3), 113–131.

Buehner, M. J. (2005). Contiguity and covariation in human causal inference. *Learning & Behavior, 33*(2), 230–238.

Bullock, C. E., & Hackenberg, T. D. (2015). The several roles of stimuli in token reinforcement. *Journal of the Experimental Analysis of Behavior, 103*(2), 269–287. http://doi.org/10.1002/jeab.117

Bush, K. M., Sidman, M., & De Rose, T. (1989). Contextual control of emergent equivalence relations. *Journal of the Experimental Analysis of Behavior, 51*(1), 29.

Buskist, W., Cush, D., & DeGrandpre, R. J. (1991). The life and times of PSI. *Journal of Behavioral Education, 1*(2), 215–234.

Callahan, K., Shukla-Mehta, S., Magee, S., & Wie, M. (2010). ABA versus TEACCH: the case for defining and validating comprehensive treatment models in autism. *Journal of Autism and Developmental Disorders, 40*(1), 74–88.

Call, N. A., & Lomas Mevers, J. E. (2014). The relative influence of motivating operations for positive and negative reinforcement on problem behavior during demands. *Behavioral Interventions, 29*(1), 4–20.

Carbone, V. J., Morgenstern, B., Zecchin-Tirri, G., & Kolberg, L. (2007). The role of the reflexive conditioned motivating operation (CMO-R) during discrete trial instruction of children with autism. *Journal of Early and Intensive Behavior Intervention, 4*(4), 658.

Carr, E. G. (1993). Behavior analysis is not ultimately about behavior. *The Behavior Analyst, 16*(1), 47.

Carr, E. G., & Durand, V. M. (1985). Reducing behavior problems through functional communication training. *Journal of Applied Behavior Analysis, 18*(2), 111–126.

Carr, E. G., & Smith, C. E. (1995). Biological setting events for self-injury. *Mental Retardation and Developmental Disabilities Research Reviews, 1*(2), 94–98.

Carr, E. G., Smith, C. E., Giacin, T. A., Whelan, B. M., & Pancari, J. (2003). Menstrual discomfort as a biological setting event for severe problem behavior: Assessment and intervention. *Journal Information, 108*(2).

Carrigan, P. F., & Sidman, M. (1992). Conditional discrimination and equivalence relations: A theoretical analysis of control by negative stimuli. *Journal of the Experimental Analysis of Behavior, 58*(1), 183–204.

Carr, J. E. (2005). Recommendations for reporting multiple-baseline designs across participants. *Behavioral Interventions, 20*(3), 219–224.

Catania, A. C. (1993). Coming to terms with establishing operations. *The Behavior Analyst, 16*(2), 219.

Catania, A. C. (2012). Discussion: The flight from experimental analysis. *European Journal of Behavior Analysis, 13*, 165–176.

Catania, A. C. (2013). *Learning* (5th ed). Cornwall-on-Hudson, NY: Sloan Pub.

Catania, A. C., & Overmier, J. B. (1971). Discriminative stimulus functions of drugs: Interpretations. In *Stimulus properties of drugs* (pp. 149–160). Springer.

Cautela, J. R. (1984). General level of reinforcement. *Journal of Behavior Therapy and Experimental Psychiatry, 15*(2), 109–114.

Charlop-Christy, M. H., Carpenter, M., Le, L., LeBlanc, L. A., & Kellet, K. (2002). Using the picture exchange communication system (PECS) with children with autism: Assessment of PECS acquisition, speech, social-communicative behavior, and problem behavior. *Journal of Applied Behavior Analysis, 35*(3), 213–231.

Cheney, C. D., & Pierce, W. D. (Eds.). (2013). *Behavior analysis and learning* (5th ed). New York, NY: Psychology Press.

Codding, R. S., Feinberg, A. B., Dunn, E. K., & Pace, G. M. (2005). Effects of immediate performance feedback on implementation of behavior support plans. *Journal of Applied Behavior Analysis, 38*(2), 205–219.

Colón, C. L., Ahearn, W. H., Clark, K. M., & Masalsky, J. (2012). The effects of verbal operant training and response interruption and redirection on appropriate and inappropriate vocalizations. *Journal of Applied Behavior Analysis, 45*(1), 107–120.

Conger, R., & Killeen, P. (1974). Use of concurrent operants in small group research: A demonstration. *Pacific Sociological Review*, 399–416.

Cooper, J. O. (2000). Tutoring Joe: winning with the Precision Teaching team. *Exceptional Children: An Introduction to Exceptional Children*, 268–270.

Cooper, J. O., Heron, T. E., & Heward, W. L. (2007). *Applied behavior analysis* (2nd ed). Upper Saddle River, N.J: Pearson/Merrill-Prentice Hall.

Cowdery, G. E., Iwata, B. A., & Pace, G. M. (1990). Effects and side effects of DRO as treatment for self-injurious behavior. *Journal of Applied Behavior Analysis, 23*(4), 497.

Cumming, W., & Berryman, R. (1965). The complex discriminated operant: Studies of matching-to-sample and related problems. *Stimulus Generalization*, 284–330.

Cuvo, A. J. (2003). On stimulus generalization and stimulus classes. *Journal of Behavioral Education, 12*(1), 77–83.

Dattilo, J., & Camarata, S. (1991). Facilitating conversation through self-initiated augmentative communication treatment. *Journal of Applied Behavior Analysis, 24*(2), 369–378.

Davis, H., & Hurwitz, H. M. B. (Eds.). (1977). *Operant-Pavlovian interactions*. Hillsdale, N.J.: New York: L. Erlbaum Associates ; distributed by the Halsted Press Division of J. Wiley.

Deitz, D. E., & Repp, A. C. (1983). Reducing Behavior through Reinforcement. *Exceptional Education Quarterly, 3*(4), 34–46.

Deitz, S. M. (1977). An analysis of programming DRL schedules in educational settings. *Behaviour Research and Therapy, 15*(1), 103–111.

DeLeon, I. G., & Iwata, B. A. (1996). Evaluation of a multiple-stimulus presentation format for assessing reinforcer preferences. *Journal of Applied Behavior Analysis, 29*(4), 519–533.

DeLeon, I. G., Iwata, B. A., Conners, J., & Wallace, M. D. (1999). Examination of ambiguous stimulus preferences with duration-based measures. *Journal of Applied Behavior Analysis, 32*(1), 111–114.

Delprato, D. J., & Midgley, B. D. (1992). Some fundamentals of BF Skinner's behaviorism. *American Psychologist, 47*(11), 1507.

Drash, P. W., High, R. L., & Tudor, R. M. (1999). Using mand training to establish an echoic repertoire in young children with autism. *The Analysis of Verbal Behavior, 16*, 29.

Durand, V. M. (1999). Functional communication training using assistive devices: recruiting natural communities of reinforcement. *Journal of Applied Behavior Analysis, 32*(3), 247.

Durand, V. M., & Carr, E. G. (1992). An analysis of maintenance following functional communication training. *Journal of Applied Behavior Analysis, 25*(4), 777–794.

Endicott, K., & Higbee, T. S. (2007). Contriving motivating operations to evoke mands for information in preschoolers with autism. *Research in Autism Spectrum Disorders, 1*(3), 210–217.

Engelmann, S. (1975). *Your child can succeed: how to get the most out of school for your child*. Simon and Schuster.

Epling, W. F., & Pierce, W. D. (1983). Applied behavior analysis: New directions from the laboratory. *The Behavior Analyst, 6*(1), 27.

Epstein, R. (1997). Skinner as self-manager. *Journal of Applied Behavior Analysis, 30*(3), 545–568.

Etzel, B. C., & LeBlanc, J. M. (1979). The simplest treatment alternative: The law of parsimony applied to choosing appropriate instructional control and errorless-learning procedures for the difficult-to-teach child. *Journal of Autism and Developmental Disorders, 9*(4), 361–382.

Fabrizio, M.S. (2001). *A Brief Overview of Fluency-Based Instruction for Learners with Autism*. Seattle, Washington: Fabrizio/Moors Consulting.

Fagen, J. W. (1978). Behavioral contrast in infants.

Fahmie, T. A., & Hanley, G. P. (2008). Progressing toward data intimacy: A review of within-session data analysis. *Journal of Applied Behavior Analysis, 41*(3), 319.

Falcomata, T. S., Roane, H. S., Hovanetz, A. N., Kettering, T. L., & Keeney, K. M. (2004). An evaluation of response cost in the treatment of inappropriate vocalizations maintained by automatic reinforcement. *Journal of Applied Behavior Analysis, 37*(1), 83.

Fantuzzo, J. W., & Clement, P. W. (1981). Generalization of the effects of teacher-and self-administered token reinforcers to nontreated students. *Journal of Applied Behavior Analysis, 14*(4), 435.

Favell, J. E., McGimsey, J. F., & Jones, M. L. (1980). Rapid Eating in the Retarded Reduction by Nonaversive Procedures. *Behavior Modification, 4*(4), 481–492.

Fawcett, S. B. (1991). Social validity: a note on methodology. *Journal of Applied Behavior Analysis, 24*(2), 235.

Ferster, C.B., Skinner, B.F. (1957). *Schedules of Reinforcement*. New York, Appleton-Century-Crofts, Inc.

Fields, L., Garruto, M., & Watanabe, M. (2011). Varieties of Stimulus Control in Matching-to-Sample: A Kernal Analysis. *The Psychological Record, 60*(1), 1.

Fillingham, J. K., Hodgson, C., Sage, K., & Lambon Ralph, M. A. (2003). The application of errorless learning to aphasic disorders: A review of theory and practice. *Neuropsychological Rehabilitation, 13*(3), 337–363.

Fisher, W., Piazza, C., Cataldo, M., Harrell, R., Jefferson, G., & Conner, R. (1993). Functional communication training with and without extinction and punishment. *Journal of Applied Behavior Analysis, 26*(1), 23–36.

Fisher, W., Piazza, C. C., Bowman, L. G., Hagopian, L. P., Owens, J. C., & Slevin, I. (1992). A comparison of two approaches for identifying reinforcers for persons with severe and profound disabilities. *Journal of Applied Behavior Analysis, 25*(2), 491.

Fisher, W. W., Kuhn, D. E., & Thompson, R. H. (1998). Establishing discriminative control of responding using functional and alternative reinforcers during functional communication training. *Journal of Applied Behavior Analysis, 31*(4), 543–560.

Fisher, W. W., Piazza, C. C., BowMAN, L. G., Kurtz, P. F., Sherer, M. R., & Lachman, S. R. (1994). A preliminary evaluation of empirically derived consequences for the treatment of pica. *Journal of Applied Behavior Analysis, 27*(3), 447–457.

Fisher, W. W., Piazza, C. C., & Roane, H. S. (2014). *Handbook of applied behavior analysis*. New York: Guilford Press.

Flora, S. R. (2004). *The power of reinforcement*. SUNY Press.

Foxx, R. M. (1982). *Decreasing behaviors of severely retarded and autistic persons*. Research Press.

Foxx, R. M. (1998). A comprehensive treatment program for inpatient adolescents. *Behavioral Interventions, 13*(1), 67–77.

Fryling, M. J., Wallace, M. D., & Yassine, J. N. (2012). Impact of treatment integrity on intervention effectiveness. *Journal of Applied Behavior Analysis, 45*(2), 449–453.

Gardenier, N. C., MacDonald, R., & Green, G. (2004). Comparison of direct observational methods for measuring stereotypic behavior in children with autism spectrum disorders. *Research in Developmental Disabilities, 25*(2), 99–118.

Gast, D. L., & Ledford, J. R. (2009). *Single subject research methodology in behavioral sciences*. Routledge.

Gersten, R., & Keating, T. (1987). Long-term benefits from direct instruction. *Educational Leadership, 44*(6), 28–31.

Gersten, R., Keating, T., & Becker, W. (1988). The continued impact of the Direct Instruction model: Longitudinal studies of Follow Through students. *Education and Treatment of Children*, 318–327.

Gersten, R., Woodward, J., & Darch, C. (1986). Direct instruction: A research-based approach to curriculum design and teaching. *Exceptional Children, 53*(1), 17–31.

Gewirtz, J. L., & Pelaez-Nogueras, M. (2000). Infant emotions under the positivereinforcer control of caregiver attention and touch. *Issues in Experimental and Applied Analyses of Human Behavior*, 271–291.

Glenn, S. S., Ellis, J., & Greenspoon, J. (1992). On the revolutionary nature of the operant as a unit of behavioral selection. *American Psychologist, 47*(11), 1329.

Goetz, E. M., & Baer, D. M. (1973). Social control of form diversity and the emergence of new forms in children's blockbuilding. *Journal of Applied Behavior Analysis, 6*(2), 209–217.

Graves, A. W. (1986). Effects of direct instruction and metacomprehension training on finding main ideas. *Learning Disabilities Research*.

Green, C. W., Reid, D. H., White, L. K., Halford, R. C., Brittain, D. P., & Gardner, S. M. (1988). Identifying reinforcers for persons with profound handicaps: Staff opinion versus systematic assessment of preferences. *Journal of Applied Behavior Analysis, 21*(1), 31–43.

Green, G. (2001). Behavior analytic instruction for learners with autism advances in stimulus control technology. *Focus on Autism and Other Developmental Disabilities, 16*(2), 72–85.

Gresham, F. M., Watson, T. S., & Skinner, C. H. (2001). Functional Behavioral Assessment: Principles, Procedures, and Future Directions. *School Psychology Review, 30*(2), 156–172.

Gross, A. M., & Drabman, R. S. (1981). Behavioral contrast and behavior therapy. *Behavior Therapy, 12*(2), 231–246.

Gunter, P. L., Venn, M. L., Patrick, J., Miller, K. A., & Kelly, L. (2003). Efficacy of using momentary time samples to determine on-task behavior of students with emotional/behavioral disorders. *Education and Treatment of Children*, 400–412.

Guttman, N., & Kalish, H. I. (1956). Discriminability and stimulus generalization. *Journal of Experimental Psychology*, *51*(1), 79.

Hackenberg, T. D. (2009). Token reinforcement: A review and analysis. *Journal of the Experimental Analysis of Behavior*, *91*(2), 257.

Hagopian, L. P., & Fisher, W. W. (1994). Schedule effects of noncontingent reinforcement on attention-maintained destructive behavior in identical quadruplets. *Journal of Applied Behavior Analysis*, *27*(2), 317–325.

Hagopian, L. P., Fisher, W. W., Sullivan, M. T., Acquisto, J., & LeBlanc, L. A. (1998). Effectiveness of functional communication training with and without extinction and punishment: A summary of 21 inpatient cases. *Journal of Applied Behavior Analysis*, *31*(2), 211–235.

Hagopian, L. P., Long, E. S., & Rush, K. S. (2004). Preference assessment procedures for individuals with developmental disabilities. *Behavior Modification*, *28*(5), 668–677.

Hagopian, L. P., Rush, K. S., Lewin, A. B., & Long, E. S. (2001). Evaluating the predictive validity of a single stimulus engagement preference assessment. *Journal of Applied Behavior Analysis*, *34*(4), 475–485.

Hains, A. H. (1991). Multi-Element Designs for Early Intervention Research Some Considerations. *Journal of Early Intervention*, *15*(2), 185–192.

Hake, D. F., & Azrin, N. H. (1965). Conditioned punishment. *Journal of the Experimental Analysis of Behavior*, *8*(5), 279.

Hall, R. V., & Fox, R. G. (1977). Changing criterion designs: An alternative applied behavior analysis procedure. *New Developments in Behavioral Research: Theory, Method, and Application*, 151–66.

Hall, R. V., Lund, D., & Jackson, D. (1968). Effects of teacher attention on study behavior. *Journal of Applied Behavior Analysis*, *1*(1), 1.

Hanley, G. P., Iwata, B. A., & Lindberg, J. S. (1999). Analysis of activity preferences as a function of differential consequences. *Journal of Applied Behavior Analysis*, *32*(4), 419–435.

Hanley, G. P., Iwata, B. A., Lindberg, J. S., & Conners, J. (2003). Response-restriction analysis: I. Assessment of activity preferences. *Journal of Applied Behavior Analysis*, *36*(1), 47–58.

Hanley, G. P., Iwata, B. A., & McCord, B. E. (2003). Functional analysis of problem behavior: A review. *Journal of Applied Behavior Analysis*, *36*(2), 147–185.

Hanley, G. P., Iwata, B. A., & Thompson, R. H. (2001). Reinforcement schedule thinning following treatment with functional communication training. *Journal of Applied Behavior Analysis*, *34*(1), 17–38.

Hanley, G. P., Piazza, C. C., Fisher, W. W., Contrucci, S. A., & Maglieri, K. A. (1997). Evaluation of client preference for function-based treatment packages. *Journal of Applied Behavior Analysis*, *30*(3), 459.

Hanley, G. P., Piazza, C. C., Fisher, W. W., & Maglieri, K. A. (2005). On the effectiveness of and preference for punishment and extinction components of function-based interventions. *Journal of Applied Behavior Analysis*, *38*(1), 51–65.

Hantula, D. A., & Crowell, C. R. (1994). Behavioral contrast in a two-option analogue task of financial decision making. *Journal of Applied Behavior Analysis*, *27*(4), 607–617.

Hardesty, S. L., Hagopian, L. P., McIvor, M. M., Wagner, L. L., Sigurdsson, S. O., & Bowman, L. G. (2014). Effects of Specified Performance Criterion and Performance Feedback on Staff Behavior A Component Analysis. *Behavior Modification*, 0145445514538280.

Harris, F. N., & Jenson, W. R. (1985). Comparisons of multiple-baseline across persons designs and AB designs with replication: Issues and confusions.

Hart, B. M., Reynolds, N. J., Baer, D. M., Brawley, E. R., & Harris, F. R. (1968). Effect of contingent and non-contingent social reinforcement on the cooperative play of a pre-school. *Journal of Applied Behavior Analysis*, *1*(1), 73–76.

Hart, B., & Risley, T. R. (1975). Incidental teaching of language in the preschool. *Journal of Applied Behavior Analysis*, *8*(4), 411.

Hartmann, D. P., Gottman, J. M., Jones, R. R., Gardner, W., Kazdin, A. E., & Vaught, R. S. (1980). Interrupted time-series analysis and its application to behavioral data. *Journal of Applied Behavior Analysis*, *13*(4), 543–559.

Hartmann, D. P., & Hall, R. V. (1976). The changing criterion design. *Journal of Applied Behavior Analysis*, *9*(4), 527–532.

Harvey, M. T., May, M. E., & Kennedy, C. H. (2004). Nonconcurrent multiple baseline designs and the evaluation of educational systems. *Journal of Behavioral Education*, *13*(4), 267–276.

Hawkins, R. P. (1979). The functions of assessment: Implications for selection and development of devices for assessing repertoires in clinical, educational, and other settings. *Journal of Applied Behavior Analysis*, *12*(4), 501–516.

Hawkins, R. P. (1984). What is "meaningful" behavior change in a severely/profoundly retarded learner: The view of a behavior analytic parent. *Focus on Behavior Analysis in Education*, 282–286.

Hawkins, R. P. (1986). Selection of target behaviors. *Conceptual Foundations of Behavioral Assessment*, 331–385.

Hawkins, R. P., & Dobes, R. W. (1977). Behavioral definitions in applied behavior analysis: Explicit or implicit. *New Developments in Behavioral Research: Theory, Method, and Application*, 167–188.

Hayes, S. C., Barnes-Holmes, D., & Roche, B. (2001). *Relational frame theory: A post-Skinnerian account of human language and cognition*. Springer Science & Business Media.

Hayes, S. C., Brownstein, A. J., Zettle, R. D., Rosenfarb, I., & Korn, Z. (1986). Rule-governed behavior and sensitivity to changing consequences of responding. *Journal of the Experimental Analysis of Behavior*, 45(3), 237–256.

Herman, R. L., & Azrin, N. H. (1964). Punishment by noise in an alternative response situation. *Journal of the Experimental Analysis of Behavior*, 7(2), 185–188.

Herrnstein, R. J. (1961). Relative and absolute strength of response as a function of frequency of reinforcement. *Journal of the Experimental Analysis of Behavior*, 4(3), 267.

Hesse, B. E. (1993). The establishing operation revisited. *The Behavior Analyst*, 16(2), 215.

Heward, W. L. (2005). Reasons applied behavior analysis is good for education and why those reasons have been insufficient. *Focus on Behavior Analysis in Education: Achievements, Challenges, and Opportunities*, 316–348.

Heward, W. L., Heron, T. E., Neef, N. A., Peterson, S. M., Sainato, D. M., Cartledge, G., … Dardig, J. C. (2005). *Focus on behavior analysis in education: Achievements, challenges, and opportunities*. Pearson/Merrill/Prentice Hall.

Higgins, J. W., Williams, R. L., & McLaughlin, T. F. (2001). The effects of a token economy employing instructional consequences for a third-grade student with learning disabilities: A data-based case study. *Education and Treatment of Children*, 99–106.

Holz, W. C., Azrin, N. H., & Ayllon, T. (1963). Elimination of behavior of mental patients by response-produced extinction. *Journal of the Experimental Analysis of Behavior*, 6(3), 407.

Honig, W. K. (1966). Operant behavior: areas of research and application. Retrieved from http://psycnet.apa.org/psycinfo/1966-35017-000

Horner, R. D., & Baer, D. M. (1978). Multiple-probe technique: A variation of the multiple baseline. *Journal of Applied Behavior Analysis*, 11(1), 189–196.

Horner, R. H., Carr, E. G., Halle, J., McGee, G., Odom, S., & Wolery, M. (2005). The use of single-subject research to identify evidence-based practice in special education. *Exceptional Children*, 71(2), 165–179.

Houten, R., Axelrod, S., Bailey, J. S., Favell, J. E., Foxx, R. M., Iwata, B. A., & Lovaas, O. I. (1988). The right to effective behavioral treatment. *Journal of Applied Behavior Analysis*, 21(4), 381–384.

Houten, R. V. (1979). Social validation: The evolution of standards of competency for target behaviors. *Journal of Applied Behavior Analysis*, 12(4), 581–591.

Hughes, J. C., Beverley, M., & Whitehead, J. (2007). Using precision teaching to increase the fluency of word reading with problem readers. *European Journal of Behavior Analysis*, 8(2), 221.

Ingvarsson, E. T., Kahng, S., & Hausman, N. L. (2008). Some effects of noncontingent positive reinforcement on multiply controlled problem behavior and compliance in a demand context. *Journal of Applied Behavior Analysis*, 41(3), 435.

Iwata, B. A. (1988). The development and adoption of controversial default technologies. *The Behavior Analyst*, 11(2), 149.

Iwata, B. A., Bailey, J. S., Brown, K. M., Foshee, T. J., & Alpern, M. (1976). A performance-based lottery to improve residential care and training by institutional staff. *Journal of Applied Behavior Analysis*, 9(4), 417.

Iwata, B. A., Dorsey, M. F., Slifer, K. J., Bauman, K. E., & Richman, G. S. (1994). Toward a functional analysis of self-injury. *Journal of Applied Behavior Analysis*, 27(2), 197.

Iwata, B. A., Pace, G. M., Dorsey, M. F., Zarcone, J. R., Vollmer, T. R., Smith, R. G., … others. (1994). The functions of self-injurious behavior: An experimental-epidemiological analysis. *Journal of Applied Behavior Analysis*, 27(2), 215.

Iwata, B. A., Smith, R. G., & Michael, J. (2000). Current research on the influence of establishing operations on behavior in applied settings. *Journal of Applied Behavior Analysis*, 33(4), 411–418.

Iwata, B. A., Wallace, M. D., Kahng, S., Lindberg, J. S., Roscoe, E. M., Conners, J., Worsdell, A. S. (2000). Skill acquisition in the implementation of functional analysis methodology. *Journal of Applied Behavior Analysis*, 33(2), 181–194.

Jacobson, J. W., Mulick, J. A., & Schwartz, A. A. (1995). A history of facilitated communication: Science, pseudoscience, and antiscience science working group on facilitated communication. *American Psychologist*, 50(9), 750.

Jarmolowicz, D. P., Kahng, S., Ingvarsson, E. T., Goysovich, R., Heggemeyer, R., & Gregory, M. K. (2008). Effects of conversational versus technical language on treatment preference and integrity. *Journal Information*, 46(3).

Jerome, J., Frantino, E. P., & Sturmey, P. (2007). The effects of errorless learning and backward chaining on the acquisition of internet skills in adults with developmental disabilities. *Journal of Applied Behavior Analysis*, *40*(1), 185.

Johnson, C., & Sidman, M. (1993). Conditional discrimination and equivalence relations: Control by negative stimuli. *Journal of the Experimental Analysis of Behavior*, *59*(2), 333–347.

Johnston, J. M. (1979). On the relation between generalization and generality. *The Behavior Analyst*, *2*(2), 1.

Johnston, J. M. (2013). *Radical behaviorism for ABA practitioners* (1 Edition). Cornwall on Hudson, NY: Sloan Publishing.

Johnston, J.M., Pennypacker, H.S. (1993). *Strategies and Tactics for Human Behavioral Research* (2nd ed.). Hillside, New Jersey: Erlbaum.

Johnston, J. M., & Pennypacker, H. S. (2009). *Strategies and Tactics of Behavioral Research* (3rd ed). New York: Routledge.

Kahng, S., Abt, K. A., & Schonbachler, H. E. (2001). Assessment and treatment of low-rate high-intensity problem behavior. *Journal of Applied Behavior Analysis*, *34*(2), 225–228.

Kamps, D., Wills, H. P., Heitzman-Powell, L., Laylin, J., Szoke, C., Petrillo, T., & Culey, A. (2011). Class-wide function-related intervention teams: Effects of group contingency programs in urban classrooms. *Journal of Positive Behavior Interventions*, 1098300711398935.

Kayser, J. E., Billingsley, F. F., & Neel, R. S. (1986). A comparison of in-context and traditional instructional approaches: Total task, single trial versus backward chaining, multiple trials. *Journal of the Association for Persons with Severe Handicaps*.

Kazdin, A. E. (1982). The token economy: A decade later. *Journal of Applied Behavior Analysis*, *15*(3), 431–445.

Kazdin, A. E. (2012). *Behavior modification in applied settings*. Waveland Press.

Kazdin, A. E., & Bootzin, R. R. (1972). The token economy: An evaluative review. *Journal of Applied Behavior Analysis*, *5*(3), 343.

Keller, F. S. (1968). Good-bye, teacher... *Journal of Applied Behavior Analysis*, *1*(1), 79.

Keller, F. S. (1994). The Fred S. Keller School: CABAS at work. *The Current Repertoire*, *10*, 3–4.

Keller, F. S., & Sherman, J. G. (1982). *The PSI handbook: Essays on personalized instruction*. TRI Publications.

Kelly, A., & Tincani, M. (2013). Collaborative training and practice among applied behavior analysts who support individuals with autism spectrum disorder. *Education and Training in Autism and Developmental Disabilities*, *48*(1), 120–131.

Kelly, M. B. (1977). A review of the observational data-collection and reliability procedures reported in the Journal of Applied Behavior Analysis. *Journal of Applied Behavior Analysis*, *10*(1), 97.

Kennedy, C. H., & Meyer, K. A. (1996). Sleep deprivation, allergy symptoms, and negatively reinforced problem behavior. *Journal of Applied Behavior Analysis*, *29*(1), 133–135.

Keohane, D.-D., & Greer, R. D. (2005). Teachers' use of a verbally governed algorithm and student learning. *International Journal of Behavioral Consultation and Therapy*, *1*(3), 252.

Kerr, K., Smyth, P., & Mcdowell, C. (2003). Precision teaching children with autism: Helping design effective programmes. *Early Child Development and Care*, *173*(4), 399–410.

Killeen, P. R. (2015). The logistics of choice. *Journal of the Experimental Analysis of Behavior*.

Kodak, T., Clements, A., & Ninness, C. (2009). Acquisition of mands and tacts with concurrent echoic training. *Journal of Applied Behavior Analysis*, *42*(4), 839–843.

Kodak, T., Lerman, D. C., Volkert, V. M., & Trosclair, N. (2007). Further examination of factors that influence preference for positive versus negative reinforcement. *Journal of Applied Behavior Analysis*, *40*(1), 25–44.

Koegel, R. L., Egel, A. L., & Williams, J. A. (1980). Behavioral contrast and generalization across settings in the treatment of autistic children. *Journal of Experimental Child Psychology*, *30*(3), 422–437.

Kratochwill, T. R. (1979). New Developments in Behavioral Research/Etzel, LeBlanc, Baer (Eds.). *Journal of Learning Disabilities*, *12*(3), 209–210. http://doi.org/10.1177/002221947901200321

Krause, T. R., Seymour, K. J., & Sloat, K. C. M. (1999). Long-term evaluation of a behavior-based method for improving safety performance: a meta-analysis of 73 interrupted time-series replications. *Safety Science*, *32*(1), 1–18.

Kubina, R. M. (2012). *Precision teaching book*. [S.l.]: Greatness Achieved Pub Co.

Kubina, R. M., Morrison, R., & Lee, D. L. (2002). Benefits of adding precision teaching to behavioral interventions for students with autism. *Behavioral Interventions*, *17*(4), 233–246.

Lahey, B. B., & Drabman, R. S. (1974). Facilitation of the acquisition of sight-word vocabulary through token reinforcement. *Journal of Applied Behavior Analysis*, *7*(2), 307–312.

Lalli, J. S., Casey, S., & Kates, K. (1995). Reducing escape behavior and increasing task completion with functional communication training, extinction, and response chaining. *Journal of Applied Behavior Analysis*, *28*(3), 261.

Lambert, J. M., Bloom, S. E., Clay, C. J., Kunnavatana, S. S., & Collins, S. D. (2014). Training residential staff and supervisors to conduct traditional functional analyses. *Research in Developmental Disabilities*, *35*(7), 1757–1765.

Laraway, S., Snycerski, S., Michael, J., & Poling, A. (2002). The abative effect: A new term to describe the action of antecedents that reduce operant responding. *The Analysis of Verbal Behavior, 18*, 101.

Laraway, S., Snycerski, S., Michael, J., & Poling, A. (2003). Motivating operations and terms to describe them: Some further refinements. *Journal of Applied Behavior Analysis, 36*(3), 407–414.

LaRue, R. H., Lenard, K., Weiss, M. J., Bamond, M., Palmieri, M., & Kelley, M. E. (2010). Comparison of traditional and trial-based methodologies for conducting functional analyses. *Research in Developmental Disabilities, 31*(2), 480–487.

Leaf, R., & McEachin, J. (1999). *A work in progress: Behavior management strategies and a curriculum for intensive behavioral treatment of autism.* Drl Books.

Ledford, J. R., Lane, J. D., Elam, K. L., & Wolery, M. (2012). Using response-prompting procedures during small-group direct instruction: Outcomes and procedural variations. *American Journal on Intellectual and Developmental Disabilities, 117*(5), 413–434.

Lerman, D. C., & Iwata, B. A. (1995). Prevalence of the extinction burst and its attenuation during treatment. *Journal of Applied Behavior Analysis, 28*(1), 93–94.

Lerman, D. C., & Iwata, B. A. (1996). A methodology for distinguishing between extinction and punishment effects associated with response blocking. *Journal of Applied Behavior Analysis, 29*(2), 231–233.

Lerman, D. C., Iwata, B. A., Smith, R. G., Zarcone, J. R., & Vollmer, T. R. (1994). Transfer of behavioral function as a contributing factor in treatment relapse. *Journal of Applied Behavior Analysis, 27*(2), 357.

Lerman, D. C., Iwata, B. A., & Wallace, M. D. (1999). Side effects of extinction: Prevalence of bursting and aggression during the treatment of self-injurious behavior. *Journal of Applied Behavior Analysis, 32*(1), 1–8.

Lerman, D. C., Kelley, M. E., Vorndran, C. M., Kuhn, S. A., & LaRue Jr, R. H. (2002). Reinforcement magnitude and responding during treatment with differential reinforcement. *Journal of Applied Behavior Analysis, 35*(1), 29.

Lerman, D. C., & Vorndran, C. M. (2002). On the status of knowledge for using punishment: Implications for treating behavior disorders. *Journal of Applied Behavior Analysis, 35*(4), 431–464.

Libby, M. E., Weiss, J. S., Bancroft, S., & Ahearn, W. H. (2008). A comparison of most-to-least and least-to-most prompting on the acquisition of solitary play skills. *Behavior Analysis in Practice, 1*(1), 37.

Lindberg, J. S., Iwata, B. A., Kahng, S., & DeLeon, I. G. (1999). DRO contingencies: An analysis of variable-momentary schedules. *Journal of Applied Behavior Analysis, 32*(2), 123–136.

Lindsley, O. R. (1985). *Quantified trends in the results of behavior analysis.* Presented at the Presidential address at the Eleventh Annual Convention of the Association for Behavior Analysis, Colombus, OH.

Lindsley, O. R. (1991). From technical jargon to plain English for application. *Journal of Applied Behavior Analysis, 24*(3), 449–458.

Linehan, M. M. (1977). Issues in behavioral interviewing. *Behavioral Assessment: New Directions in Clinical Psychology*, 30–51.

Litow, L., & Pumroy, D. K. (1975). A brief review of classroom group-oriented contingencies. *Journal of Applied Behavior Analysis, 8*(3), 341–347.

Lotfizadeh, A. D., Edwards, T. L., Redner, R., & Poling, A. (2012). Motivating operations affect stimulus control: A largely overlooked phenomenon in discrimination learning. *The Behavior Analyst, 35*(1), 89.

Lovaas, O. I. (2003). *Teaching Individuals with Developmental Delays: Basic Intervention Techniques.* ERIC. Retrieved from http://eric.ed.gov/?id=ED473063

Lovass, O.I. (1977). *The Autistic Child: Language Development through Behavior Modificiation.* New York: Irvington Press.

Luiselli, J. K. (2008). *Effective practices for children with autism: Educational and behavior support interventions that work.* Oxford University Press.

Mace, F. C. (1996). In pursuit of general behavioral relations. *Journal of Applied Behavior Analysis, 29*(4), 557–563.

Mace, F. C., & Belfiore, P. (1990). Behavioral momentum in the treatment of escape-motivated stereotypy. *Journal of Applied Behavior Analysis, 23*(4), 507.

Mace, F. C., Neef, N. A., Shade, D., & Mauro, B. C. (1994). Limited matching on concurrent-schedule reinforcement of academic behavior. *Journal of Applied Behavior Analysis, 27*(4), 585.

Magee, S. K., & Ellis, J. (2000). Extinction effects during the assessment of multiple problem behaviors. *Journal of Applied Behavior Analysis, 33*(3), 313–316.

Malott, R. (2012). *Issues in the Analysis of Behavior.* Behaviordelia.

Malott, R., & Garcia, M. (1991). The role of private events in rule-governed behavior. In P. Chase & L. P. Hayes (Eds.), *Dialogues on verbal behavior* (pp. 237–254). Reno, NV: Context Press.

Malott, R. W. (1988). Rule-governed behavior and behavioral anthropology. *The Behavior Analyst, 11*(2), 181.

Malott, R. W. (1992). Should we train applied behavior analysts to be researchers? *Journal of Applied Behavior Analysis, 25*(1), 83–88.

Malott, R.W., Tojan, E.A. (2003). *Principles of Behavior* (5th ed.). Upper Saddle River, New Jersey: Pearson Prentice Hall.

Malott, R. W., & Trojan, E. A. (2008). *Principles of behavior.* Pearson Prentice Hall Upper Saddle River.

Martens, B. K., Lochner, D. G., & Kelly, S. Q. (1992). The effects of variable-interval reinforcement on academic engagement: A demonstration of matching theory. *Journal of Applied Behavior Analysis, 25*(1), 143–151.

Matson, J. L. (Ed.). (2009). *Applied behavior analysis for children with autism spectrum disorders.* New York: Springer.

Matson, J. L. (Ed.). (2010). *Applied Behavior Analysis for Children with Autism Spectrum Disorders* (2009 edition). New York: Springer.

Matson, J. L., & Boisjoli, J. A. (2009). The token economy for children with intellectual disability and/or autism: A review. *Research in Developmental Disabilities, 30*(2), 240–248.

Matthews, L. R., & Temple, W. (1979). Concurrent schedule assessment of food preference in cows. *Journal of the Experimental Analysis of Behavior, 32*(2), 245–254.

Maurice, C. E., Green, G. E., & Luce, S. C. (1996). *Behavioral intervention for young children with autism: A manual for parents and professionals.* Pro-ed.

May Jr, J. G., & Risley, T.R., Twardosz, S., Friedman, P., Bijous, S., Wexler, D. (1975). Guidelines for the Use of Behavioral Procedures in State Programs for Retarded Persons. Retrieved from http://eric.ed.gov/?id=ED181619

Mazaleski, J. L., Iwata, B. A., Vollmer, T. R., Zarcone, J. R., & Smith, R. G. (1993). Analysis of the reinforcement and extinction components in DRO contingencies with self-injury. *Journal of Applied Behavior Analysis, 26*(2), 143–156.

Mazur, J. E. (1975). The matching law and quantifications related to Premack's principle. *Journal of Experimental Psychology: Animal Behavior Processes, 1*(4), 374.

Mazur, J.E. (2002). *Learning and Behavior.* Upper Saddle River, New Jersey: Pearson Prentice Hall.

McAllister, L. W., Stachowiak, J. G., Baer, D. M., & Conderman, L. (1969). The application of operant conditioning techniques in a secondary school classroom. *Journal of Applied Behavior Analysis, 2*(4), 277–285.

McCain, L. J., & McCleary, R. (1979). The statistical analysis of the simple interrupted time-series quasi-experiment. *Quasi-Experimentation: Design & Analysis Issues for Field Settings. Chicago: Rand McNally.*

McDougall, D. (2005). The range-bound changing criterion design. *Behavioral Interventions, 20*(2), 129–137.

McGee, G. G., & Daly, T. (2007). Incidental teaching of age-appropriate social phrases to children with autism. *Research and Practice for Persons with Severe Disabilities, 32*(2), 112–123.

McGee, G. G., Morrier, M. J., & Daly, T. (1999). An incidental teaching approach to early intervention for toddlers with autism. *Research and Practice for Persons with Severe Disabilities, 24*(3), 133–146.

McGee, G. G., Krantz, P. J., Mason, D., & McClannahan, L. E. (1983). A modified incidental-teaching procedure for autistic youth: acquisition and generalization of receptive object labels. *Journal of Applied Behavior Analysis, 16*(3), 329–338.

McGill, P. (1999). Establishing operations: Implications for the assessment, treatment, and prevention of problem behavior. *Journal of Applied Behavior Analysis, 32*(3), 393–418.

McIntyre, L. L., Gresham, F. M., DiGennaro, F. D., & Reed, D. D. (2007). Treatment integrity of school-based interventions with children in the journal of applied behavior analysis 1991–2005. *Journal of Applied Behavior Analysis, 40*(4), 659–672.

McLaughlin, T. F. (1983). An Examination and Evaluation of Single Subject Designs Used in Behavior Analysis Research in School Settings. *Educational Research Quarterly, 7*(4), 35–42.

McSweeney, F., & Weatherly, J. (1998). Habituation to the reinforcer may contribute to multiple-schedule behavioral contrast. *Journal of the Experimental Analysis of Behavior, 69*(2), 199.

McWilliams, R., Nietupski, J., & Hamre-Nietupski, S. (1990). Teaching complex activities to students with moderate handicaps through the forward chaining of shorter total cycle response sequences. *Education and Training in Mental Retardation,* 292–298.

Meany-Daboul, M. G., Roscoe, E. M., Bourret, J. C., & Ahearn, W. H. (2007). A comparison of momentary time sampling and partial-interval recording for evaluating functional relations. *Journal of Applied Behavior Analysis, 40*(3), 501–514.

Mendonca, P. J., & Brehm, S. S. (1983). Effects of choice on behavioral treatment of overweight children. *Journal of Social and Clinical Psychology, 1*(4), 343–358.

Michael, J. (1975). Positive and negative reinforcement, a distinction that is no longer necessary; or a better way to talk about bad things. *Behaviorism,* 33–44.

Michael, J. (1982). Distinguishing between discriminative and motivational functions of stimuli. *Journal of the Experimental Analysis of Behavior, 37*(1), 149–155.

Michael, J. (1988). Establishing operations and the mand. *The Analysis of Verbal Behavior, 6*, 3.

Michael, J. (1993). Establishing operations. *The Behavior Analyst, 16*(2), 191.

Michael, J. (2000). Implications and refinements of the establishing operation concept. *Journal of Applied Behavior Analysis, 33*(4), 401–410.

Michael, J. L. (2004). *Concepts and principles of behavior analysis.* Western Michigan University, Association for Behavior Analysis International.

Miles, N. I., & Wilder, D. A. (2009). The effects of behavioral skills training on caregiver implementation of guided compliance. *Journal of Applied Behavior Analysis, 42*(2), 405–410.

Millenson, J. R., & Leslie, J. C. (1967). *Principles of behavioral analysis.* Macmillan New York.

Miller, D. L., & Kelley, M. L. (1994). The use of goal setting and contingency contracting for improving children's homework performance. *Journal of Applied Behavior Analysis, 27*(1), 73–84.

Miltenberger, R. G. (2008). *Behavior modification: principles and procedures* (4th ed). Belmont, CA: Thomson Wadsworth.

Miltenberger, R. G., Suda, K. T., Lennox, D. B., & Lindeman, D. P. (1991). Assessing the acceptability of behavioral treatments to persons with mental retardation. *American Journal on Mental Retardation.* Retrieved from http://psycnet.apa.org/psycinfo/1992-13762-001

Mineka, S. (1975). Some new perspectives on conditioned hunger. *Journal of Experimental Psychology: Animal Behavior Processes, 1*(2), 134.

Moore, J. (2008). Conceptual foundations of radical behaviorism. Retrieved from http://phil-papers.org/rec/MOOCFO

Moore, J. (2009). Why the radical behaviorist conception of private events is interesting, relevant, and important. *Behavior and Philosophy*, 21–37.

Moore, J. (2011). A review of Baum's review of Conceptual Foundations of Radical Behaviorism. *Journal of the Experimental Analysis of Behavior, 95*(1), 127–140.

Moore, J., & Cooper, J. O. (2003). Some proposed relations among the domains of behavior analysis. *The Behavior Analyst, 26*(1), 69.

Moran, D. J., & Malott, R. W. (2004). *Evidence-based educational methods.* Academic Press.

Morse, W. H., & Kelleher, R. T. (1977). Determinants of reinforcement and punishment. *Handbook of Operant Behavior*, 174–200.

Moxley, R.A. (2004). Pragmatic selectionism: The philosophy of behavior analysis. *The Behavior Analyst Today*, 5, 108-125.

Mueller, M. M., Palkovic, C. M., & Maynard, C. S. (2007). Errorless learning: Review and practical application for teaching children with pervasive developmental disorders. *Psychology in the Schools, 44*(7), 691–700.

Nevin, A., Johnson, D. W., & Johnson, R. (1982). Effects of group and individual contingencies on academic performance and social relations of special needs students. *The Journal of Social Psychology, 116*(1), 41–59.

Nevin, J. A. (1974). Response strength in multiple schedules. *Journal of the Experimental Analysis of Behavior, 21*(3), 389.

Nevin, J. A. (1992a). An integrative model for the study of behavioral momentum. *Journal of the Experimental Analysis of Behavior, 57*(3), 301.

Nevin, J. A. (1992b). Behavioral contrast and behavioral momentum. *Journal of Experimental Psychology: Animal Behavior Processes, 18*(2), 126.

Nevin, J. A. (1996). The Momentum of Compliance. *Journal of Applied Behavior Analysis, 29*(4), 535–547. http://doi.org/10.1901/jaba.1996.29-535

Nevin, J. A., Mandell, C., & Atak, J. R. (1983). The analysis of behavioral momentum. *Journal of the Experimental Analysis of Behavior, 39*(1), 49.

Newcomer, P. L., & Hammill, D. D. (2008). Test of Language Development: Primary (TOLD-P: 4). *Austin, TX.* Retrieved from http://www.asha.org/SLP/assessment/Test-of-Language-Development-Primary,-Fourth-Edition-(TOLD-P-4).htm

Newman, B., Reinecke, D., & Ramos, M. (2009). Is a reasonable attempt reasonable? Shaping versus reinforcing verbal attempts of preschoolers with autism. *The Analysis of Verbal Behavior, 25*(1), 67.

Noell, G. H., Call, N. A., & Ardoin, S. P. (2011). Building complex repertoires from discrete behaviors by establishing stimulus control, behavioral chains, and strategic behavior. *Handbook of Applied Behavior Analysis*, 250.

O'Neill, R. E., Horner, R. H., Albin, R. W., Sprague, J. R., Storey, K., & Newton, J. S. (1997). *Functional assessment and program development for problem behavior. Pacific Grove, CA: Brooks.* Cole Publishing Company.

O'Reilly, M. F. (1997). Functional analysis of episodic self-injury correlated with recurrent otitis media. *Journal of Applied Behavior Analysis, 30*(1), 165–167.

Otto, J. (n.d.). *Discrete trial procedures vs. free-operant procedures.* Retrieved from http://old.dickmalott.com/students/under-gradprogram/psy3600/discrete_vs_free.html

Pace, G. M., Ivancic, M. T., Edwards, G. L., Iwata, B. A., & Page, T. J. (1985). Assessment of stimulus preference and reinforcer value with profoundly retarded individuals. *Journal of Applied Behavior Analysis, 18*(3), 249–255.

Parsons, M. B., & Reid, D. H. (1995). Training residential supervisors to provide feedback for maintaining staff teaching skills with people who have severe disabilities. *Journal of Applied Behavior Analysis*, *28*(3), 317–322.

Parsonson, B. S., & Baer, D. M. (1978). The analysis and presentation of graphic data. *Single-Subject Research: Strategies for Evaluating Change*, 105–165.

Partington, J. W., & Bailey, J. S. (1993). Teaching intraverbal behavior to preschool children. *The Analysis of Verbal Behavior*, *11*, 9.

Partington, J. W., & Sundberg, M. L. (1998). *The Assessment of Basic Language and Learning Skills (the ABLLS): Scoring Instructions and IEP Development Guide: the ABLLS Guide*. Behavior Analysts.

Pavlov, I. P., & Gantt, W. (1928). Lectures on conditioned reflexes: Twenty-five years of objective study of the higher nervous activity (behaviour) of animals.

Pavlov, P. I. (2010). Conditioned reflexes: An investigation of the physiological activity of the cerebral cortex. *Annals of Neurosciences*, *17*(3), 136.

Payne, S. W., Dozier, C. L., Neidert, P. L., Jowet, E. S., & Newquist, M. H. (2014). Using Additional Analyses to Clarify the Functions of Problem Behavior: An Analysis of Two Cases. *Education and Treatment of Children*, *37*(2), 249–275.

Pelios, L. V., & Sucharzewski, A. (2004). Teaching receptive language to children with autism: A selective overview. *The Behavior Analyst Today*, *4*(4), 378.

Pence, S. T., Roscoe, E. M., Bourret, J. C., & Ahearn, W. H. (2009). Relative contributions of three descriptive methods: Implications for behavioral assessment. *Journal of Applied Behavior Analysis*, *42*(2), 425.

Pennypacker, H. S. (1992). Is behavior analysis undergoing selection by consequences? *American Psychologist*, *47*(11), 1491.

Perlmuter, L. C., & Monty, R. A. (1973). Effect of choice of stimulus on paired-associate learning. *Journal of Experimental Psychology*, *99*(1), 120.

Peterson, L., Homer, A. L., & Wonderlich, S. A. (1982). The integrity of independent variables in behavior analysis. *Journal of Applied Behavior Analysis*, *15*(4), 477–492.

Petscher, E. S., Rey, C., & Bailey, J. S. (2009). A review of empirical support for differential reinforcement of alternative behavior. *Research in Developmental Disabilities*, *30*(3), 409–425.

Piazza, C. C., Patel, M. R., Gulotta, C. S., Sevin, B. M., & Layer, S. A. (2003). On the relative contributions of positive reinforcement and escape extinction in the treatment of food refusal. *Journal of Applied Behavior Analysis*, *36*(3), 309.

Pipkin, C. S. P., Vollmer, T. R., & Sloman, K. N. (2010). Effects of treatment integrity failures during differential reinforcement of alternative behavior: A

translational model. *Journal of Applied Behavior Analysis*, *43*(1), 47–70.

Poling, A. (1978). Performance of rats under concurrent variable-interval schedules of negative reinforcement. *Journal of the Experimental Analysis of Behavior*, *30*(1), 31–36.

Poling, A., Braatz, D., Johnson, C. M., Redmon, W. K., & Mawhinney, T. C. (2001). Principles of learning: Respondent and operant conditioning and human behavior. *Handbook of Organizational Performance: Behavior Analysis and Management*, 23–49.

Potts, L., Eshleman, J. W., & Cooper, J. O. (1993). Ogden R. Lindsley and the historical development of precision teaching. *The Behavior Analyst*, *16*(2), 177.

Powell, J., Martindale, A., & Kulp, S. (1975). An evaluation of time-sample measures of behavior. *Journal of Applied Behavior Analysis*, *8*(4), 463–469.

Pryor, K., & others. (1999). *Dont shoot the dog*. Bantam.

Rachlin, H. (1971). On the tautology of the matching law. *Journal of the Experimental Analysis of Behavior*, *15*(2), 249–251.

Reed, F. D. D., Reed, D. D., Baez, C. N., & Maguire, H. (2011). A parametric analysis of errors of commission during discrete-trial training. *Journal of Applied Behavior Analysis*, *44*(3), 611–615.

Rehfeldt, R. A., & Chambers, M. R. (2003). Functional analysis and treatment of verbal perseverations displayed by an adult with autism. *Journal of Applied Behavior Analysis*, *36*(2), 259–261.

Reimers, T. M., & Wacker, D. P. (1988). Parents' ratings of the acceptability of behavioral treatment recommendations made in an outpatient clinic: A preliminary analysis of the influence of treatment effectiveness. *Behavioral Disorders*, 7–15.

Resnick, L. B., Wang, M. C., & Kaplan, J. (1973). Task analysis in curriculum design: A hierarchically sequenced introductory mathematics curriculum. *Journal of Applied Behavior Analysis*, *6*(4), 679–709.

Reynolds, G. S. (1961). Behavioral contrast. *Journal of the Experimental Analysis of Behavior*, *4*(1), 57.

Reynolds, G. S. (1963). Some limitations on behavioral contrast and induction during successive discrimination. *Journal of the Experimental Analysis of Behavior*, *6*(1), 131–139.

Reynolds, G. S. (1975). A primer of operant conditioning.(Rev ed). Retrieved from http://psycnet.apa.org/psycinfo/1975-20047-000

Ricciardi, J. N., Luiselli, J. K., & Camare, M. (2006). Shaping approach responses as intervention for specific phobia in a child with autism. *Journal of Applied Behavior Analysis*, *39*(4), 445–448.

Richman, G. S., Riordan, M. R., Reiss, M. L., Pyles, D. A., & Bailey, J. S. (1988). The effects of self-mon-

itoring and supervisor feedback on staff performance in a residential setting. *Journal of Applied Behavior Analysis, 21*(4), 401.

Riordan, M. M., Iwata, B. A., Wohl, M. K., & Finney,
J. W. (1980). Behavioral treatment of food refusal
and selectivity in developmentally disabled children. *Applied Research in Mental Retardation, 1*(1),
95–112.

Roane, H. S., Lerman, D. C., Kelley, M. E., & Van
Camp, C. M. (1999). Within-session patterns of
responding during functional analyses: The role
of establishing operations in clarifying behavioral
function. *Research in Developmental Disabilities,
20*(1), 73–89.

Roane, H. S., Vollmer, T. R., Ringdahl, J. E., & Marcus,
B. A. (1998). Evaluation of a brief stimulus preference assessment. *Journal of Applied Behavior Analysis, 31*(4), 605.

Rosales, R., & Rehfeldt, R. A. (2007). Contriving transitive conditioned establishing operations to establish derived manding skills in adults with severe developmental disabilities. *Journal of Applied
Behavior Analysis, 40*(1), 105.

Rosales-Ruiz, J., & Baer, D. M. (1997). Behavioral
cusps: A developmental and pragmatic concept
for behavior analysis. *Journal of Applied Behavior
Analysis, 30*(3), 533–544.

Rusch, F. R., & Kazdin, A. E. (1981). Toward a methodology of withdrawal designs for the assessment
of response maintenance. *Journal of Applied Behavior Analysis, 14*(2), 131–140.

Sailor, W., Guess, D., Rutherford, G., & Baer, D. M.
(1968). Control of tantrum behavior by operant
techniques during experimental verbal training.
Journal of Applied Behavior Analysis, 1(3), 237–243.

Sarokoff, R. A., & Sturmey, P. (2004). The effects of
behavioral skills training on staff implementation
of discrete-trial teaching. *Journal of Applied Behavior
Analysis, 37*(4), 535–538.

Sasso, G. M., Reimers, T. M., Cooper, L. J., Wacker, D.,
Berg, W., Steege, M., … Allaire, A. (1992). Use of
descriptive and experimental analyses to identify
the functional properties of aberrant behavior in
school settings. *Journal of Applied Behavior Analysis,
25*(4), 809–821.

Schlinger, H., & Blakely, E. (1987). Function-altering
effects of contingency-specifying stimuli. *The Behavior Analyst, 10*(1), 41.

Schlinger, H. D. (2008). Listening is behaving verbally.
The Behavior Analyst, 31(2), 145.

Schlinger Jr, H. D. (1990). A reply to behavior analysts
writing about rules and rule-governed behavior.
The Analysis of Verbal Behavior, 8, 77.

Schmidt, F. L. (1992). What do data really mean? Research findings, meta-analysis, and cumulative
knowledge in psychology. *American Psychologist,
47*(10), 1173.

Semel, E. Wiig, E.H., Secord, W.A. (2003). *Clinical Evaluation of Language Fundamentals* (4th ed.). Toronto,
Canada: The Psychological Corporation/A Harcourt Assessment Company.

Seys, D. M., & Duker, P. C. (1978). Improving residential care for the retarded by differential reinforcement of high rates of ward-staff behaviour. *Behavioural Analysis and Modification, 2*, 203–210.

Shanks, D. R., Pearson, S. M., & Dickinson, A. (1989).
Temporal contiguity and the judgement of cau-
sality by human subjects. *The Quarterly Journal of
Experimental Psychology, 41*(2), 139–159.

Shapiro, E. S. (2011). *Academic skills problems: Direct assessment and intervention.* Guilford Press.

Shore, B. A., Iwata, B. A., Vollmer, T. R., Lerman, D.
C., & Zarcone, J. R. (1995). Pyramidal staff training in the extension of treatment for severe behavior disorders. *Journal of Applied Behavior Analysis, 28*(3), 323.

Sidman, M. (1971). Reading and auditory-visual equivalences. *Journal of Speech, Language, and Hearing Research, 14*(1), 5–13.

Sidman, M. (1994). *Equivalence relations and behavior: A
research story.* Authors Cooperative. Retrieved
from   http://psycnet.apa.org/psycinfo/1994-
98777-000

Sidman, M. (1997). Equivalence relations. *Journal of the
Experimental Analysis of Behavior, 68*(2), 258.

Sidman, M. (2009). Equivalence relations and behavior:
An introductory tutorial. *The Analysis of Verbal Behavior, 25*(1), 5.

Sidman, M., & Tailby, W. (1982). Conditional discrimination vs. matching to sample: An expansion of
the testing paradigm. *Journal of the Experimental
Analysis of Behavior, 37*(1), 5–22.

Sidman, M., Willson-Morris, M., & Kirk, B. (1986).
Matching-to-sample procedures and the development of equivalence relations: The role of naming. *Analysis and Intervention in Developmental Disabilities, 6*(1), 1–19.

Sigafoos, J. (2005). From Premack to PECS: 25 years
of progress in communication intervention for
individuals with developmental disabilities. *Educational Psychology, 25*(6), 601–607.

Singh, J., & Singh, N. N. (1985). Comparison of word-
supply and word-analysis error-correction procedures on oral reading by mentally retarded children. *American Journal of Mental Deficiency.* Retrieved   from
http://psycnet.apa.org/psycinfo/1985-31100-
001

Skinner, B.F. (1938). *The Behavior Of Organisms.* New
York: Appleton-Century.

Skinner, B. F. (1938). The behavior of organisms: An
experimental   analysis.   Retrieved   from
http://psycnet.apa.org/psycinfo/1939-00056-
000

Skinner, B. F. (1953). *Science and human behavior.* Simon and Schuster.

Skinner, B.F. (1957). *Verbal Behavior.* New York: Appleton-Century.

Skinner, B.F. (1979). *The Shaping of a Behaviorist: Part two of an autobiography.* New York, NY: University Press.

Skinner, B. F. (1981). Selection by consequences. *Science, 213*(4507), 501–504.

Skinner, B. F. (1984). The evolution of behavior. *Journal of the Experimental Analysis of Behavior, 41*(2), 217–221.

Skinner, B. F. (1989). *Recent issues in the analysis of behavior.* Prentice Hall.

Skinner, B. F. (2014). *Contingencies of reinforcement: A theoretical analysis* (Vol. 3). BF Skinner Foundation.

Slocum, S. K., & Tiger, J. H. (2011). An assessment of the efficiency of and child preference for forward and backward chaining. *Journal of Applied Behavior Analysis, 44*(4), 793–805.

Smith, R. G., & Iwata, B. A. (1997). Antecedent influences on behavior disorders. *Journal of Applied Behavior Analysis, 30*(2), 343–375.

Smith, R. G., Iwata, B. A., & Shore, B. A. (1995). Effects of subject versus experimenter-selected reinforcers on the behavior of individuals with profound developmental disabilities. *Journal of Applied Behavior Analysis, 28*(1), 61–71.

Smith, T., Parker, T., Taubman, M., & Lovaas, O. I. (1992). Transfer of staff training from workshops to group homes: A failure to generalize across settings. *Research in Developmental Disabilities, 13*(1), 57–71.

Snell, M.E., Brown, F. (2006). *Instruction of Students with Severe Disabilities* (6th ed.). Upper Saddle River, New Jersey: Merrill/Prentice Hall.

Spooner, F. (1984). Comparisons of backward chaining and total task presentation in training severely handicapped persons. *Education and Training of the Mentally Retarded,* 15–22.

Sprague, J., Sugai, G., & Walker, H. (1998). Antisocial behavior in schools. In *Handbook of child behavior therapy* (pp. 451–474). Springer.

Spriggs, A.D., Gast, D.L. (2010). *Visual Representation of Data* (D. L. Gast (Ed.). New York, NY: Routlege.

Stewart, I., McElwee, J., & Ming, S. (2013). Language generativity, response generalization, and derived relational responding. *The Analysis of Verbal Behavior, 29*(1), 137.

Stock, R. A., Schulze, K. A., & Mirenda, P. (2008). A comparison of stimulus-stimulus pairing, standard echoic training, and control procedures on the vocal behavior of children with autism. *The Analysis of Verbal Behavior, 24*(1), 123.

Stokes, T. F., & Baer, D. M. (1977). An implicit technology of generalization. *Journal of Applied Behavior Analysis, 10*(2), 349.

Stokes, T. F., Baer, D. M., & Jackson, R. L. (1974). Programming the generalization of a greeting response in four retarded children. *Journal of Applied Behavior Analysis, 7*(4), 599–610.

Stokes, T. F., & Osnes, P. G. (1989). An operant pursuit of generalization. *Behavior Therapy, 20*(3), 337–355.

Striefel, S., Bryan, K. S., & Aikins, D. A. (1974). Transfer of stimulus control from motor to verbal stimuli. *Journal of Applied Behavior Analysis, 7*(1), 123–135.

Suen, H. K., Ary, D., & Covalt, W. (1991). Reappraisal of momentary time sampling and partial-interval recording. *Journal of Applied Behavior Analysis, 24*(4), 803.

Sundberg, M. L. (2008a). *VB-MAPP Verbal Behavior Milestones Assessment and Placement Program: a language and social skills assessment program for children with autism or other developmental disabilities: guide.* Concord, CA: AVB Press.

Sundberg, M. L. (2008b). Verbal behavior milestones assessment and placement program: The VB-MAPP. *Concord, CA: AVBPress.*

Sundberg, M. L., Loeb, M., Hale, L., & Eigenheer, P. (2002). Contriving establishing operations to teach mands for information. *The Analysis of Verbal Behavior, 18,* 15.

Sundberg, M. L., & Michael, J. (2001). The benefits of Skinner's analysis of verbal behavior for children with autism. *Behavior Modification, 25*(5), 698–724.

Sundberg, M. L., & Partington, J. W. (1998). Teaching language to children with autism and other developmental disabilities. *Pleasant Hill, CA: Behavior Analysts Inc.*

Sweeney-Kerwin, E. J., Carbone, V. J., O'Brien, L., Zecchin, G., & Janecky, M. N. (2007). Transferring control of the mand to the motivating operation in children with autism. *The Analysis of Verbal Behavior, 23*(1), 89.

Sweeney, M. M., & Shahan, T. A. (2013). Effects of high, low, and thinning rates of alternative reinforcement on response elimination and resurgence. *Journal of the Experimental Analysis of Behavior, 100*(1), 102–116.

Tarbox, J., & Hayes, L. P. (2005). Verbal behavior and behavioral contrast in human subjects. *The Psychological Record, 55*(3), 419.

Tarbox, R. S., Ghezzi, P. M., & Wilson, G. (2006). The effects of token reinforcement on attending in a young child with autism. *Behavioral Interventions, 21*(3), 155–164.

Taylor-Santa, C., Sidener, T. M., Carr, J. E., & Reeve, K. F. (2014). A discrimination training procedure to establish conditioned reinforcers for children with autism. *Behavioral Interventions, 29*(2), 157–176.

Terrace, H. S. (1963). Discrimination learning with and without "errors". *Journal of the Experimental Analysis of Behavior, 6*(1), 1–27.

Test, D. W., Spooner, F., Keul, P. K., & Grossi, T. (1990). Teaching adolescents with severe disabilities to use the public telephone. *Behavior Modification, 14*(2), 157–171.

Theodore, L. A., Bray, M. A., Kehle, T. J., & Jenson, W. R. (2001). Randomization of group contingencies and reinforcers to reduce classroom disruptive behavior. *Journal of School Psychology, 39*(3), 267–277.

Thomas, D. R., Becker, W. C., & Armstrong, M. (1968). Production and elimination of disruptive classroom behavior by systematically varying teacher's behavior. *Journal of Applied Behavior Analysis, 1*(1), 35–45.

Thomason-Sassi, J. L., Iwata, B. A., Neidert, P. L., & Roscoe, E. M. (2011). Response latency as an index of response strength during functional analyses of problem behavior. *Journal of Applied Behavior Analysis, 44*(1), 51–67.

Thompson, R. H., Iwata, B. A., Conners, J., & Roscoe, E. M. (1999). Effects of reinforcement for alternative behavior during punishment of self-injury. *Journal of Applied Behavior Analysis, 32*(3), 317–328.

Thompson, T. J., Braam, S. J., & Fugua, R. W. (1982). Training and generalization of laundry skills: a multiple probe evaluation with handicapped persons. *Journal of Applied Behavior Analysis, 15*(1), 177.

Thoresen, C. E., & Mahoney, M. J. (1974). *Behavioral self-control.* Holt McDougal.

Torneke, N. (2010). *Learning RFT: An introduction to relational frame theory and its clinical application.* New Harbinger Publications

Tryon, W. W. (1982). A simplified time-series analysis for evaluating treatment interventions. *Journal of Applied Behavior Analysis, 15*(3), 423–429.

Twyman, J. S. (1998). The Fred S. Keller School. *Journal of Applied Behavior Analysis, 31*(4), 695–701.

Ulman, J. D., & Sulzer-Azaroff, B. (1975). Multielement baseline design in educational research. *Behavior Analysis: Areas of Research and Application,* 377–391.

Ulrich, R. E., & Azrin, N. H. (1962). Reflexive fighting in response to aversive stimulation. *Journal of the Experimental Analysis of Behavior, 5*(4), 511.

Vanselow, N. R., & Bourret, J. C. (2012). Online interactive tutorials for creating graphs with Excel 2007 or 2010. *Behavior Analysis in Practice, 5*(1), 40.

Vedora, J., Meunier, L., & Mackay, H. (2009). Teaching intraverbal behavior to children with autism: A comparison of textual and echoic prompts. *The Analysis of Verbal Behavior, 25*(1), 79.

Vollmer, T. R. (1994). The concept of automatic reinforcement: Implications for behavioral research in developmental disabilities. *Research in Developmental Disabilities, 15*(3), 187–207.

Vollmer, T. R., Borrero, J. C., Wright, C. S., Van Camp, C., & Lalli, J. S. (2001). Identifying possible contingencies during descriptive analyses of severe behavior disorders. *Journal of Applied Behavior Analysis, 34*(3), 269.

Vollmer, T. R., & Iwata, B. A. (1992). Differential reinforcement as treatment for behavior disorders: Procedural and functional variations. *Research in Developmental Disabilities, 13*(4), 393–417.

Vollmer, T. R., Iwata, B. A., Zarcone, J. R., Smith, R. G., & Mazaleski, J. L. (1993). Within-session patterns of self-injury as indicators of behavioral function. *Research in Developmental Disabilities, 14*(6), 479–492.

Vollmer, T. R., Marcus, B. A., Ringdahl, J. E., & Roane, H. S. (1995). Progressing from brief assessments to extended experimental analyses in the evaluation of aberrant behavior. *Journal of Applied Behavior Analysis, 28*(4), 561.

Vollmer, T., Roane, H., Ringdahl, J., & Marcus, B. (1999). Evaluating treatment challenges with differential reinforcement of alternative behavior. *Journal of Applied Behavior Analysis, 32*(1), 9.

Vorndran, C. M., & Lerman, D. C. (2006). Establishing and maintaining treatment effects with less intrusive consequences via a pairing procedure. *Journal of Applied Behavior Analysis, 39*(1), 35–48.

Walker, G. (2008). Constant and progressive time delay procedures for teaching children with autism: A literature review. *Journal of Autism and Developmental Disorders, 38*(2), 261–275.

Ward-Horner, J., & Sturmey, P. (2010). Component analyses using single-subject experimental designs: A review. *Journal of Applied Behavior Analysis, 43*(4), 685–704.

Ward-Horner, J., & Sturmey, P. (2012). Component analysis of behavior skills training in functional analysis. *Behavioral Interventions, 27*(2), 75–92.

Watkins, M. W., & Pacheco, M. (2000). Interobserver agreement in behavioral research: Importance and calculation. *Journal of Behavioral Education, 10*(4), 205–212.

Watson, D., & Tharp, R. (2013). *Self-directed behavior: Self-modification for personal adjustment.* Cengage Learning.

Watson, P. J., & Workman, E. A. (1981). The non-concurrent multiple baseline across-individuals design: An extension of the traditional multiple baseline design. *Journal of Behavior Therapy and Experimental Psychiatry, 12*(3), 257–259.

Weatherly, J. N., King, B. M., & Arthur, E. I. (2002). Rats' lever pressing for 1% sucrose and food-pellet reinforcement: In search of negative behavioral contrast. *The Psychological Record, 52*(4), 507.

Weatherly, J. N., Melville, C. L., & McSweeney, F. K. (1996). Picking, pecking, and pressing: A cross-species demonstration of behavioral contrast. *The Psychological Record*, *46*(2), 351.

Welsh, D. H., Bernstein, D. J., & Luthans, F. (1993). Application of the Premack principle of reinforcement to the quality performance of service employees. *Journal of Organizational Behavior Management*, *13*(1), 9–32.

Wheeler, J. J., Baggett, B. A., Fox, J., & Blevins, L. (2006). Treatment Integrity A Review of Intervention Studies Conducted With Children With Autism. *Focus on Autism and Other Developmental Disabilities*, *21*(1), 45–54. http://doi.org/10.1177/10883576060210010601

White, O.R., Haring, N.G. (1980). *Exceptional Teaching* (2nd edition). Colombus, OH: Charles E. Merrill.

White, O. R., Sugai, G., & Horner, R. (2005). Trend lines. *Encyclopedia of Behavior Modification and Cognitive Behavior Therapy*, *3*, 1589–1593.

Wilder, D. A., Atwell, J., & Wine, B. (2006). The effects of varying levels of treatment integrity on child compliance during treatment with a three-step prompting procedures. *Journal of Applied Behavior Analysis*, *39*(3), 369–373.

Wilder, D. A., Normand, M., & Atwell, J. (2005). Noncontingent reinforcement as treatment for food refusal and associated self-injury. *Journal of Applied Behavior Analysis*, *38*(4), 549–553.

Williams, B. A., & Fantino, E. (1978). Effects on choice of reinforcement delay and conditioned reinforcement. *Journal of the Experimental Analysis of Behavior*, *29*(1), 77–86.

Windsor, J., Piché, L. M., & Locke, P. A. (1994). Preference testing: A comparison of two presentation methods. *Research in Developmental Disabilities*, *15*(6), 439–455.

Witt, J. C., Daly, E. M., & Noell, G. (2000). *Functional assessments: A step-by-step guide to solving academic and behavior problems*. Sopris West.

Wolery, M. (1994). Procedural fidelity: A reminder of its functions. *Journal of Behavioral Education*, *4*(4), 381–386.

Wolf, M. M. (1978). Social validity: The case for subjective measurement or how applied behavior analysis is finding its heart. *Journal of Applied Behavior Analysis*, *11*(2), 203.

Worsdell, A. S., Iwata, B. A., & Wallace, M. D. (2002). Duration-based measures of preference for vocational tasks. *Journal of Applied Behavior Analysis*, *35*(3), 287.

Wulfert, E., & Hayes, S. C. (1988). Transfer of a conditional ordering response through conditional equivalence classes. *Journal of the Experimental Analysis of Behavior*, *50*(2), 125.

Zhan, S., & Ottenbacher, K. J. (2001). Single subject research designs for disability research. *Disability and Rehabilitation*, *23*(1), 1–8.

47070317R00210

Made in the USA
Middletown, DE
16 August 2017